# Soweto Blues

# SOWETO BLUES:

## Jazz, Polular Music, and Politics in South Africa

*Gwen Ansell*

continuum
NEW YORK • LONDON

2004

The Continuum International Publishing Group Inc
15 East 26 Street, New York, NY 10010

The Continuum International Publishing Group Ltd
The Tower Building, 11 York Road, London SE1 7NX

*www.continuumbooks.com*

Printed in the United States of America

Library of Congress Cataloging-in-Publication Data

Ansell, Gwen.
    Soweto blues : jazz and politics in South Africa / Gwen Ansell.
      p.   cm.
    Includes bibliographical references (p.   ) and index.
    ISBN 0-8264-1662-4 (hardcover : alk. paper)
    1. Jazz—South Africa—History and criticism.   2. Music—Political aspects—
South Africa.   I. Title.
    ML3509.S6A57   2004
    781.65'0968—dc22                                          2004011875

# Contents

# Introduction

In 2000, the Ford Foundation made a grant to the independent radio training and production house ABC Ulwazi to create a radio series on the relationship between South African and American jazz. I was the series writer and producer and, together with colleagues, interviewed close to sixty musicians, young and old, and others on the scene. The result was the eight-part series *Ubuyile/Jazz Coming Home*, which was broadcast on South Africa's one hundred-plus community radio stations over the following year.

The series was popular. On some stations, like Alexandra Township's Alex-FM, listeners rang in to request repeats and share their own stories of the music. This popularity (and the constraints of eight, twenty-minute programmes, which allowed us to use only a fraction of the fascinating testimony we had collected) emphasised the need for a book. As we recorded and broadcast, virtually each week brought news that another veteran musician had died. Some, we had interviewed; others, we had not. Each time a musician died, a library of music and social history burned to ashes. Many societies undervalue the insight of their musicians. Apartheid South Africa buried the identity, work, and knowledge of black and progressive players, so our loss was doubly great. The book thus became increasingly necessary, as did adding to the archive of recorded interviews. A second round of interviewing was begun in 2001, looking at the history of South African jazz in exile, and while funding has not yet materialised for a second radio series, I have been able to use some of that testimony here too.

My thanks go to the Ford Foundation and Professor John van Zyl of ABC Ulwazi for the initiation of the project and the maintenance of the Living History Archive of interview recordings. Also at ABC Ulwazi, Dominique Luycks-Mabaso steered the radio programmes, Peter Makurube and Phumzile Mlungwana shared the mammoth task of interviewing, Agnes Tlaka set up appointments and smoothed ruffled feathers, and Gideon Joubert and Colin October sound engineered with precision and flair. Everybody else in the organisation offered encouragement and listening ears—thanks for that too. And Xoli Norman composed and Paul Hanmer and McCoy Mrubata played a wonderful signature tune that, sadly, readers won't get to hear.

It was jazz critic Alyn Shipton who heard the series and agreed that there was a book in it, and both my editors at Continuum, Janet Joyce and currently David

Barker, provided encouragement and prompt responses to e-mails full of writer's neuroses. Gabriella Page-Fort conceived and Tosh Thomas Hall created a great cover, based on Sam Nhlengethwa's 'Midnight Blue'. Judy Seidman drew the maps, but also gave invaluable critical feedback, particularly when my obsession with musical detail lost me the big picture—trust an artist for that. Lesego Rampolokeng and Keorapetse Kgositsile engaged in e-mail dialogue on the text. Music scholar Brett Pyper reminded me of all the thorny musical questions that needed answering, and Helena Barnard provided Afrikaans translations. A number of photographers made beautiful pictures and were unstinting with their time around discussion and selection. And my research assistant, Darryl Rule, did the transcriptions as well as myriad boring tasks, swiftly and without complaint. I am in the debt of everyone on this list.

But the biggest thanks go to the musicians—for their memories, for their generosity in sharing those memories with the original project (and with me personally as a music writer), and for their music. I hope this book goes a little way towards ensuring that their indomitable spirit is never forgotten.

Oh, and for the late ZDM: 'I Thought About You'.

*Chapter One*

# Where It All Started

We're calling my father's spirit back. We need his wisdom.

—Duke Ngcukana

In March 2003, a community gathered to unveil a tombstone in the black township of Langa, in Cape Town, for a local jazz hero.

Baritone saxophonist and bandleader Christopher Ngcukana, known respectfully as 'Mra' and colloquially as 'Chris Columbus', lived from 1927 to 1993. He had been as great an explorer of modern music as his namesake had been of oceans. He started his career with a close-harmony group of vaudeville singers, the Bantu Young Ideas, in 1943, and by the end of the decade he was leading the first of many innovative ensembles. According to his son, Duke, a trumpeter: 'When Third Stream music came along through Ornette Coleman and such people, my father knew that. He was only playing that sort of music . . . and now few people could play with him, because he was interpreting all that old music differently'.[1]

The ceremonies preceding the unveiling of the stone took place in a flapping blue-and-white tent covering the front garden of a modest township home. Old and young, relatives and neighbours, gathered for ritual and remembering. For a week before, ceremonial grain beer, *umqombothi*, had been brewing. The night before, an ox was slaughtered. Most of the meat was shared with guests, but one shoulder was reserved for the family to consume to close the ceremonies. People were in suits, Madiba shirts, modern street clothes, and the traditional wrapped cloths of white or the deep ochre that won the Xhosa people their colonial descriptor as 'red blanket people', decorated with distinctive borders of black beading and braid. Another son, singer Fitzroy, had a cell phone tucked into the waist of his wrap, earning wry comments about how those who now live in Johannesburg couldn't stay away from the little contraptions. The air was thick

1

**Ceremonies preceding the unveiling of the tombstone of Chris Columbus Ngcukana.**
*Credit: Tomas Films; thanks to the Ngcukana family*

with dust from the township's unpaved roads and smoky from the meat roasting in the backyard.

Chants, libations, and dialogue with the spirits of ancestors all reminded the family of the precepts and traditions of their clan. The family had also arranged a live concert at a club, to which all the musicians of Cape Town had been invited, to remind the community of Ngcukana's musical legacy. For son Ezra, another reed player, the day involved an additional gig, at the international North Sea Jazz Festival, being staged for its fourth year in Cape Town city centre. 'When we buried my father ten years ago', said Duke, 'we sent his spirit to travel. Now, when we unveil the tombstone and do all this, we're calling him back so we can benefit from the wisdom he gained'.[2]

Columbus's father had come to Cape Town in the 1920s with his second wife. Preparations for the unveiling turned up a relative from his first marriage, previously unknown to the family: a sinewy, majestic old farmer from the remote rural foothills of the Eastern Cape with a close knowledge of the traditions. Behind closed doors, it was this man who mentored the sons—Fitzroy the singer, Ezra the saxophonist, and Duke the trumpeter, schooled and sophisticated jazz musicians all—in the intricate, syncopated rhythms of the rite's Xhosa songs with their woven voices, hand claps, and foot stomps. The roots of Chris Columbus's sound are also here, long before Ornette, and even long before the aspiring Bantu Young Ideas singer heard American dance band records from a windup gramophone in his family's home.

This book tells of the journeys—in both directions—between village and city, between saxophone and cell phone, between Langa and Cape Town, between America and Africa that, over the past century, have created the unique sound dubbed 'South African jazz'.

The term itself is contentious. As in America, some politically aware South African players dislike the term for its social connotations. 'The term jazz was used to describe the music of brothels. It was simply another way of denigrating the creativity of African musicians', says percussionist and composer Ndikho Xaba.[3] And, as in the rest of the world, many musical explorers resent the constraints of an externally defined musical box.

Black South Africans themselves constantly debated the music's relation with American and African roots—and still do. But apartheid overlaid the word *jazz* with other, more sinister connotations. In some critical and ethnomusicological contexts, the music was evaluated initially by the old, highly romanticised categories of 'primitive' and 'authentic'. Then, under apartheid, the white authorities found it unacceptable that black musicians should be acknowledged as capable of playing such 'sophisticated' music. And so symbolic annihilation became part of the hegemonic staging and broadcasting of jazz. Playing behind a screen at Cape Town City Hall while a white musician mimed his notes, reedman Winston Mankunku Ngozi was billed as Winston Mann. In radio broadcasts, pianist Tony Schilder heard himself rechristened Peter Evans, and trumpeter Johnny Mekoa became Johnny Keen. In the late twentieth century, the tables turned: the critics' yardstick was now the degree of musical 'Americanness', and the South African jazz was denigrated as falling short of the standard when it employed African idioms in composition or playing. Never was it allowed to stand on its own terms.

For all these global and local reasons, many South African players prefer other labels, mostly no label at all. Yet when, in 2000, Johannesburg production house ABC Ulwazi put together a broadcast series, *Ubuyile/Jazz Coming Home*, on the history of South African jazz, all fifty-six of the singers, players, and a few listeners interviewed agreed that their music could be placed in some relationship with the category the world calls jazz. Some embraced the term wholeheartedly; others added reservations like those listed above.

The testimony of those musicians is the primary source for Chapters 3 to 8 of this book, although the first chapters sketch in historical background beyond the living memory of even the oldest interviewee. It is primarily the story of how it felt to make music in the times to which South African jazz was the sound-

## Political and language groups in South Africa around 1800

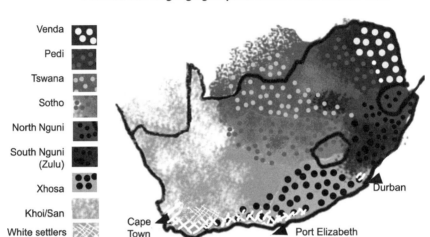

Venda
Pedi
Tswana
Sotho
North Nguni
South Nguni (Zulu)
Xhosa
Khoi/San
White settlers

Cape Town
Port Elizabeth
Durban

Unlike the later blueprints of apartheid (see p. 214), political, residential, linguistic, and cultural boundaries never neatly coincided, with considerable movement and shifting allegiances among peoples. *Credit: Judy Seidman*

track.[4] The interviews reflect myths, dreams, partial memories, and impressions, as well as hard information; the best popular music gains its power as the vehicle of visions and passions, particularly when created under the kind of cultural repression apartheid imposed. The stories of these men and women—some, like Hugh Masekela, Sibongile Khumalo, and Abdullah Ibrahim, also stars on the world stage; others, like Chris Columbus, loved and known best in their own communities—shed a powerful light on the history they lived and the music they made.

Almost as soon as jazz went on record in America, in the early decades of the twentieth century, those wax impressions arrived in South Africa. They landed on fertile ground, for South Africans had a rich and dynamic musical culture of their own, into which they had already drawn aspects of earlier and parallel African-American musics.

Explorers, missionaries, and colonisers from the fifteenth century onwards had dubbed the traditional societies they found in southern Africa 'tribes' and had rapidly developed ethnographic practices founded on the belief that these groups—Zulu, Xhosa, Pedi, and others—were ethnically or even genetically distinct from one another. This reflected the racial ideologies prevalent in those eras, but it also served the colonial project well. It provided an ostensibly objective basis for divide-and-rule policies and served as an effective mask for the reality that many divisions reflected politics, not ethnicity: 'tribes' were in fact states, and the minor-sounding 'chiefs', actually princes and kings. Many late-twentieth-century historians worked to set this picture right and described the relationship between the active construction of tribal identity and the mainte-nance of colonial rule:

> [After the Anglo-Boer War,] [t]he first aim of [the British] native admin-istration was to ensure a regular labour supply to mines and white farms. . . . The army even compiled a History of the Native Tribes of the Transvaal from oral traditions in an attempt to understand and control the relations between chiefdoms.[5]

The revised picture shows, across a long period of African history, a far greater permeability of cultural borders than those early ethnographers ever al-lowed, between what apartheid legislation after 1948 further downgraded from separate 'tribes' to forcibly separated 'groups'.

Colonial and apartheid musicologists also applied the dominant framework of difference to their studies, using it to underpin definitions of musical styles placed on an evolutionary scale from most 'primitive' (the so-called Bushmen or San peoples) to the most 'advanced' (Europeans, with Indonesians and Indians only slightly behind). Thus Percival Kirby, author of what, six decades later, remains the most detailed taxonomy of the country's African musical instru-ments, asserted that in South Africa it was possible to study 'the musical practices of three different epochs in human history as represented by our Bushmen, Hot-tentots and Bantu [by observing] the evolution of musical instruments'.[6]

On this reading, more 'advanced' instruments were invariably seen as 'bor-rowed' from more 'advanced' groups, while more 'primitive' instruments (such as single-note flutes) in groups defined as 'advanced' were invariably called 'sur-vivals'. Such views were to prove very potent in shaping how the authorities treated modern, hybrid urban forms such as jazz.

> By representing African politics as rigidly banded, stationary socio-cultural units, social anthropology created an artificial universe of tribes that would serve as an ethnographic basis for apartheid. [Later] cultural inventions, mothered but not determined by harsh historical necessity, were deplored as expressions of deracination and analysed as symptoms of social disintegration rather than as new vehicles of self-construction.[7]

Such views contrast sharply with those of modern musicians. South African bass player Ernest Motlhe tells of a conversation with Dizzy Gillespie in London, where the trumpeter told him: 'I hear you are from the Pedi people in South Africa. Man! Those people have the most advanced skill of time, rhythmically. You can't play a single piece of rubber pipe and still keep time, because those things wobble—but your people can do it!'[8]

But what were the musical practices of these early kingdoms? As elsewhere in Africa, there was great diversity in indigenous styles and instruments: blown, struck, and bowed instruments, rattles, and shakers, as well as exclusively vocal music. Early European travellers recorded in their journals a picture of a complex system of music. Vasco da Gama, landing at Cape Saint Blaise near Mossel Bay in 1497, was greeted, as his journal noted, by a band of 'Cape Hottentots who performed on four or five flutes of reed at once; [S]ome of them played high and others played low, harmonising together very well'.[9] What these travellers observed was music linked to spiritual and medical practices, where certain materials of instrument-making and categories of player were associated with particular ceremonies and passages of community life. It also was the music of status, pleasure, and recreation, including court music designed to dignify the compounds of the kings, and musical occasions for social commentary, criticism, and debate (the so-called praise songs).

Chris Columbus's ancestors, the Xhosa-speaking Nguni peoples of the Eastern Cape, for example, had a rich and intricate style of music, in which mouth bows were prominent, and which also featured split-tone (overtone) singing. David Dargie, a musicologist who has studied the style intensively, describes 'the basic rule of Xhosa music':

> 'Xhosa people', said [Amelia No-Silence Matiso,] . . . 'like to put salt into their songs'. They "put salt" . . . by always doing more than one would expect to the song. They are never content just to sing it straight. They add more and more parts to the songs—overlapping polyphonic parts, harmony parts. They add salt to the rhythm—it is never enough just to perform one rhythm at a time, the melody must have its rhythm and the body movement/clap must have another which fits against it, even though quite different. It is not enough for some people just to play one melody on the *umrhube* mouth bow; using the overtones, they play the melodies of the leading singer and then at the same time they whistle the melodies of answering singers. Some people are not content to sing one melody at a time—using the techniques of *umngqokolo* overtone singing, [some] can sing more than one note at the same time.[10]

From the earliest period of contact with seamen, soldiers, traders, and churchmen, European instruments were added to the mix and incorporated into musical life. Lutes and later guitars had arrived early with the Portuguese on the East African coast and travelled south and west as trade goods, gifts, and models to be copied by ingenious local instrument makers. The *ramkie* of the Cape (a hollow-bodied, long-necked, strummed string instrument) is thought to have taken its name from the Portuguese *rebequinha*. Other portable instruments, such as the harmonica, concertina, and accordion, were also traded. The guitar was particularly important as a vehicle of syncretism all across Africa because of

**A traditional healer divines with bones, while his assistant plays a mouth bow, Johannesburg, 1930s.** *Credit: Historical papers, University of Witwatersrand Library*

the ease with which it could reproduce (but also, through the idiomatic requirements of its playing, subtly transform) any music, traditional or modern, that took its player's fancy.

The tunes of military bands, church choirs, and farm and mining town entertainers were sometimes appropriated and adapted. Colonial wars introduced brass-band instruments. Kirby, whose original research was conducted in the 1930s, noted that the keys of the Chopi *mbila* (xylophone) were 'cut from . . . wood taken from the blockhouses built in the days of the old wars'.[11] He also describes Zulu drums modelled on the marching-band bass drum,[12] end-blown trumpets with detachable mouthpieces,[13] and pipes carved to resemble colonial police whistles.[14] Two major waves of wars were fought in what is now South Africa before the best known, the Anglo-Boer War of 1899–1902, with countless skirmishes—to suppress rebellious princes or intervene in wars between them—in between. The Cape wars of the late eighteenth and early nineteenth centuries ran parallel to widespread early missionary activity. The Zulu Wars of the 1860s saw large numbers of British regiments with their characteristic red-coated brass bands marching the length and breadth of Natal. Even allowing for Kirby's tendency to ascribe imitation rather than origination to African craftsmen, such creative borrowing is hardly surprising.

Alongside the gun came the Bible. Again, it was the British-ruled Eastern Cape (later dubbed by apartheid Transkei and Ciskei) that was the focus for the development of church choral music, especially after the building by the first eleven converts of the Presbyterian Mission School with its formally constituted choir at Lovedale in 1821. The missionaries saw their role as one of 'civilising' native peoples, and this involved expunging community traditions—often involving drink, dance, and song—they considered 'barbaric' and 'immoral'. Lovedale and other mission stations provided formal training in music to African converts, impelled by the goal of creating hymnody in local languages to provide a substitute for native song. The mission teachers used sol-fa notation, a practice that has stayed with African choirs up to the present day, but one that tended to restrict students to vocal rather than instrumental music. Those who wanted to learn harmonium, organ, or piano had to seek tutors in staff notation. The focus on song fitted in with former traditional patterns of worship, as did the use of hymns involving part singing; the focus of those hymns on the monotheistic Christian God, did not. The kinds of part songs and the relationship between words and music were also very different. Composer Mzilikazi Khumalo sees one of the strengths of traditional composition as 'the relationship between the way the [African] words sound and the way the music sounds. To me, that's the great marriage'.[15] Veteran chorister Deborah Matthews, a descendant of one of the greatest nineteenth-century hymn writers, John Knox Bokwe, noticed the shift when she first learned choral singing as a girl: 'The English songs had a completely different balance'.[16] Often, the new hymns bent and distorted African-language words to fit Scottish Presbyterian tunes.

The missionaries' conversion campaign had received a great boost when Ntsikana, a Xhosa prince, became a Christian in 1816. He was a nationalist who believed this modern faith and the powerful patronage it seemed to offer would help his people to survive. Alongside the new religion, he encouraged his people to give up body painting and traditional dancing and learn to read. He was also a mystic and an accomplished composer: his beautiful Great Hymn, 'Ulo Thixo Mkulu' ('Thou, Great God'), combined African and Western musical features. It was not published until 1876, more than fifty years after Ntsikana's death, but it is still sung today.

The church, too, was responsible for the flowering of brass-band music, particularly in the area of the old South African Republic (later the Transvaal) in the late nineteenth century. Pedi- and Tswana-speaking peoples there had long played in large ensembles of reed flutes and drums and used a large, strident war horn, the *phalaphala*. Modern brass-band instruments played louder and more reliably and were provided free to faithful congregants. German Lutherans and the British Salvation Army were most active in 'saving' the urban youth through band training—the contribution of the Salvation Army brass bands to training jazz players has been a constant until today. Drummer Lulu Gontsana grew up in the Eastern Cape in the 1970s. Rhythm had always attracted him, 'but my family couldn't afford a kit. So I did what everybody else did who wanted to be a musician but with a poor family. I went to the Salvation Army—we used to joke and call it the Starvation Army!—just to learn very fast to read music. They had a drummer, though, so they gave me the trumpet'.[17]

Mission education initially seemed to promise both the favour of the imperial power and the promotion to elite status. By the late nineteenth century, however, it became clear to many African Christians that the most elite role they could hope for was a modest place as teacher, pastor, or clerk, still subject to regulation and denied rights because of their colour. In return for this, they had given up precious elements of their heritage, including music. It began to look like a poor bargain. The same aspirational nationalism that had drawn their parents and grandparents to Christianity in the first place, now led composers like Bokwe and Tiyo Soga, both of whom had been ordained after theological training in Scotland, to return to tradition. Soga collected and documented old praise songs and lore. Bokwe explored ways of composing that could employ Xhosa verse without distortion. Another composer, Benjamin Tyamzashe, held 'tea meetings' (*itimitin*: the prevalent Christian answer to traditional beer parties), where he played traditional Xhosa songs for guests on his harmonium.[18] Yet others deserted the mission stations and set up breakaway African Christian communities that restored many elements of tradition to their services and songs.

Nevertheless, the musical skills the missionaries taught had a broad reach. By 1885, 15,568 African scholars were enrolled in mission schools across South Africa, a fivefold growth over the previous twenty years.[19] In the 1900s, mission school children in Durban, given new shoes by their charitable teachers, were tapping the hard soles on the ground and slapping the stiff leather as they performed traditional dances. The style, *is'cathulo*, found its way to the docks, where dockworkers slapped their rubber boots. It travelled to Johannesburg, acquiring a guitar accompaniment on the road, and became the 'gumboot dance' now associated with city labourers and miners.

The musical fluency of the Eastern Cape's converts fed into many later enterprises. The comfortable country town of Queenstown in the 1860s was a place that drew many Africans from the surrounding rural areas to work connected with carting, the wool industry, the new railways, and various small enterprises. The bustling economy allowed African farmers to expand from subsistence practices and develop their land, and their families were prominent and enthusiastic converts to Christianity. Seventy years later, Queenstown bore the soubriquet 'Little Jazz City' because of the number and sophistication of its vaudeville companies and ragtime bands. Pianist Pat Matshikiza, himself the son of one of those early bandleaders, Meekley 'Fingertips' Matshikiza (who led the Big Four and the Blue Rhythm Syncopators), attributes this vibrant scene to the legacy of choral singing:

> We had more singers. And it seems as if we excelled because when that art is common, everybody wants to sing and they don't want to give another person a chance from another town. And they are highly com-

Choral composer Tiyo Soga.

petitive to improve. You want a good tenor? There's three. You want a soprano? There's five. Almost every house had a piano. And somebody in a choir, almost every family.[20]

Farther West, around the seaport at the Cape of Good Hope, communities of urban workers with their own distinctive musical culture had begun more than two hundred years earlier.

Slavery had begun in the Cape in 1652, with the arrival of the Dutch East India Company, and by the time it was formally ended in 1834 (although slaves were bound to serve another four years' 'apprenticeship' before really being freed), their numbers stood at just over 36,000. A quarter were brought from Africa, mainly what is now Mozambique, another quarter from Madagascar, and the rest from South Asia, India, and Indonesia (then, the Dutch East Indies). After the abolition of the slave trade in 1808, whenever the British Royal Navy seized a ship with African human cargo bound for America, the captives were released—again into 'apprenticeship', this time for fourteen years—in Cape Town. But from the 1770s onward, the community of slaves born in the Cape had begun to outnumber new arrivals.[21] Before this date, historians have argued, mortality rates were so high and the slave population so volatile that 'the transmission of a cultural heritage was extremely difficult even among people originating in the same place'.[22]

From the earliest years, however, slavery in Cape Town itself seems not to have been the isolated confinement of an Alabama plantation. 'Slaves had access to the money economy of the Cape'[23] and at night socialised with soldiers, sailors, company labourers, and servants, as well as other nonelite citizens across boundaries of race and language, so much so, that in 1686, the Dutch East India Company promulgated a common curfew for all these groups.[24] Life for slaves in the rural areas was, of course, more dependent on the whim of their farmer-owners.

In the city, there was also a small community of what the ordinances called 'free blacks' (freed or escaped slaves or convicts) and travellers from elsewhere in the world, such as former sailors, who were restricted to earning a living from petty trading and occupations such as fishing. Some originated in South Asia rather than Africa and, like the descendants of the Indonesian slaves, were Muslim. Malayu was the first language of many of these people, who rapidly came to be referred to, without distinction, as 'Malays'. In both city and countryside lived the Khoikhoi, the original inhabitants of the area. Colonisation and the Cape Wars had massively disrupted Khoikhoi society, and even after limited rights of land ownership and free movement were restored to them in 1828, many worked for farmers or city masters under conditions legally distinct from, but little better than, slavery. After emancipation, all these groups and the most impoverished European labourers lived, for a long period, side by side.

Throughout the period, music was an important feature of Cape life. The first 'Batavian' (Indonesian) prisoners and slaves in the colony were rebels against the

Dutch, often spiritual leaders adhering to a form of Islam that was Sufic in inspiration and embraced music as a part of worship. They came from a region with
a sophisticated classical tradition of court music (known today in the West
through gamelan orchestras). Once freed from bondage, this community was
able to build religious, cultural, and commercial links with other Muslim communities from Zanzibar to the Ottoman Empire. One well-documented musical
expression of their tradition was the *khalifa*, a whirling religious dance inspiring
a trance state during which participants could slash or pierce themselves with
swords and skewers without bleeding or apparent pain. By the late nineteenth
century, a form of *khalifa* was being presented as a public entertainment: 'mystic
revels, erratic gambols and a monotonous lay',[25] commented the English-run
*Cape Argus* sourly in 1888. Contemporary observers also described a distinctive
canon of song performed at the 'Javanese' New Year and at weddings.

An indication of the cultural scene is provided by the column *Life at the
Cape: By a Lady*, which appeared in the *Cape Monthly Magazine* (1860s–1870s).
Writing about the early 1860s in the Cape, the anonymous 'lady' noted:

> Any fresh arrival with a little singing talent is soon regarded as a great
> acquisition, for although the colonial-born ladies are capital horsewomen
> and especially good in the dancing line, they are not given to the drudgery
> that good music demands . . . musical parties are thus an especial treat.
> All simple ballad music is deservedly honoured, and the clever natives
> soon pick up the most complicated operatic overtures, and after one
> hearing at a concert will whistle the score, in capital time, of nearly every
> piece that has taken their fancy. They are admirable mimics and especially
> clever with the accordion and the violin, playing entirely by ear. It is quite
> a treat to hear them whistling in roving quartette bands on fine moonlit
> evenings. . . . Their accuracy is surprising![26]

The Khoikhoi, as da Gama had observed, were gifted players with an established musical culture. Slaves with musical talent commanded a high price, and
the seventeenth-century governor of the Cape kept a slave orchestra. Because of
the paucity of respectable entertainment outside their estates, both Dutch and
English landowners liked to maintain, at the very least, a team of servants who
could, when ordered, change 'the curry-comb for the violin and [put] the spade
aside to play the violincello'.[27]

Slaves, servants, and free blacks also created music for their own recreation,
on the streets and sandy strands on Sundays, when they were freed from work,
and in the taverns and bars that clustered below the fort and around the harbour.

> The result of this multi-ethnic, non-racial integration was the develop-
> ment of an urban sub-culture, marginal if contrasted to the norms of
> the dominant classes, and cosmopolitan when the variety of people who

participated in its assemblage is considered . . . the embryonic form of the urban working-class culture that developed in the nineteenth and twentieth centuries.[28]

The Cape's 1853 Constitution gave the vote to all citizens. Despite the huge economic inequalities and social prejudices that riddled society, in Cape Town itself, poor and working-class people of all races lived together for more than three decades, before residential zoning began to be introduced.

> Records of the Cape Supreme Court mention a painter from Scotland married to a coloured woman, a Zulu man living with a woman from St Helena, an Alice McPherson married 'by Malay rites' to an Afghan mattress-maker, an American labourer [and] a cowboy from Mexico. . . . Music was very much part of the popular culture. . . . When theatres opened a show in Cape Town, coloured musicians often backed the performance. . . . Every new tune brought to Cape Town on the waves of European fashions and fads was soon learned and broadcast by these musicians.[29]

The most significant of these fashionable imported musics for the development of South African jazz was the minstrel music of America. South African jazz pianist and educator Hotep Galeta describes what Cape Town popular history remembers as the first contact with 'Coon music':

> [During the American Civil War] the Confederate warship, the *Alabama*, came into the port of Cape Town to replenish its supplies. . . . A mixed crew of British mercenaries and Southern whites manned the ship. On board there was also a small contingent of African-American slaves who served as cleaners and mess stewards and provided some musical entertainment for the crew. . . . The local population flocked to the waterfront to look at her. It was then that the African-Americans gave their impromptu musical recitals at the dockside where the *Alabama* was moored. When the inhabitants of Cape Town enquired from the white crew who the black entertainers were, the reply was: 'These are just our Coons' ([o]r, more succinctly put: 'Our Niggers!').[30]

This was in July 1863, more than twenty-five years before the first formal visit by an African-American performance group. The event is also recorded in the musical archives in a famous Cape minstrel song—still sung—'Daar Kom die Alabama' ('Here Comes the Alabama'), which performers assert is a relic of the black seamen's performance. Some music historians would modify this account of a direct transfer between the Confederate warship and the Cape Town dockside,[31] but the *Alabama* incident, the song, and the way both are remembered in oral tradition are all very revealing. They show the open and eager interest with which the Cape musicians looked on music from elsewhere. The song itself, which juxtaposes lyrics about the arrival of the ship with a possibly much older indigenous verse about sleeping on 'a bed of reeds', illustrates with what accomplishment imported musical inspirations could be transformed into original Cape Town music. Most importantly, the whole narrative is an early marker of the coded significance of a particular discourse around African-American music—as the music of African slaves taken to America who successfully won their freedom—for South Africans of colour struggling under their own form of bondage.

When black South Africans are asked to tell the story of American jazz, they invariably begin as veteran trumpeter Banzi Bangani and trombonist Jonas Gwangwa did:

> Now, going back to the history of the black Americans, who were called negroes in those days, it was when they wanted a bit of liberation from slavery. Those guys, they would organise their meetings in a sort of music. Let's say, for example, songs like Saints Go Marching In. They would sing anything describing the place where they are supposed to meet, plus the time when they are supposed to meet. In a song form . . . plus comforting one another; praising the Lord for comfort from the hardship they were in as slaves.[32]

> The music was like underground music. It was used to pass messages and you'd hear a song with them talking about what they called the Freedom Train—that is, people escaping into Canada. You hear people singing about 'Early in the morning when the sun goes down'—there was a message in the song.[33]

White American 'coon' shows, with their grotesque blackface and racist images of idyllic (for some) Southern plantations staffed by happy and rhythmically gifted, if intellectually challenged, 'darkies', had enchanted the white South Africans who saw Joe Brown's Band of Brothers in the Cape Colony in 1848—when Cape slavery was well within living memory—or the Harvey Christy Minstrels in 1862. It was the minstrel show stereotype of 'Jim Crow' that inspired white bosses 'eventually . . . to call their African labourers and servants Jim'.[34] Sheet music of minstrel songs came in by sea, and white and coloured entertainers in the Cape and elsewhere incorporated these into their repertoires. Africans also knew about these shows: 'In 1880, at least one black minstrel troupe, the Kafir Christy Minstrels, was operating in Durban'.[35] Percival Kirby, ever eager to document Africans learning from whites (and far less keen to explore where Christy first got the idea from) reported that the well-known 'bones' which were a feature of the Christy Minstrel performance of former days [remain.] . . . I have not been able to determine whether the Zulu got the idea of using this instrument from the European or not. The Chwana almost certainly did; the Rev. A. Sandilands who has been for years a missionary in Bechuanaland, assured me that the fact is admitted by the Chwana themselves.[36]

For white audiences, the minstrel show was merely another imported theatrical fashion, which by 1890, as city facilities and tastes became more sophisticated, had given way to light opera and travelling repertory drama companies direct from London. But with emancipation after the U.S. Civil War, American minstrelsy had evolved into an African-American performance form that was to impress South Africans of colour far more strongly. This new minstrel show retained some of the old stereotypes in its comic segments, but it also revived authentic elements of African-American culture that had survived in slave communities and combined all this with acting, singing, and playing of a highly polished, concert hall standard, including arias from Verdi operas. For South Africa, it was Hampton graduate Orpheus McAdoo and his American (later Virginia) Jubilee Singers, who first visited Cape Town in 1887 and toured as far as Kimberley and Johannesburg four times during the 1890s, that made the biggest and most long-lasting impact.

In Cape Town, thousands of working-class coloured men formed performance clubs in the wake of McAdoo's visits.[37] These clubs, along with the already established 'Malay choirs', were the genesis of the 'Cape Coon' (that is what they called themselves), marching troupes whose street performances and contests are now an established tradition of Cape Town's New Year celebrations. Some of McAdoo's artists experienced the usual wage-related falling-outs with their director, quit the troupe, and settled permanently in the country as concert promoters and music teachers, such as Will P. Thompson, who worked in both Cape Town and Kimberley.[38] In the mission schools, African and coloured students started to form their own close-harmony quartets and string bands to perform at concerts.

McAdoo's performers brought with them both political and musical ideas. The politics were ambivalent. Many in his troupes embraced their certificated status as 'honorary white' American visitors who did not need a pass to move around the country and socialised happily with imperialist-minded Britons. They patronisingly described the African workers they saw behind barbed wire in the mine compounds as 'a very good and generous kind of creature'.[39]

Yet McAdoo himself experienced harassment and wrote home that '[t]he native today is treated as badly as ever the slave was treated in Georgia'.[40] One of the jokes told in a comic section of his show went as follows:

One of the corner men asked a brother where he would like to be buried when he dies. The brother replied that he would like a resting-place in a nice quiet Methodist cemetery, and then asked where his questioner would like to be laid. The latter answered: In a Dutch cemetery. 'Why?' asked the brother. The answer was: 'Because a Dutch cemetery is the last place the Devil would go to look for a black man'.[41]

McAdoo addressed gatherings and told newspaper reporters in glowing terms about the educational opportunities and routes to advancement for people of colour in America. With variable success, he also arranged scholarships for promising young Africans who approached him and inspired others to seek the same.

New musical ideas came not only from the Jubilee Singers' performances, but from the impact of these efforts. One example was Kimberley-based soprano and teacher Charlotte Manye (later Maxexe), who, inspired by the Jubilee Singers, joined a disaster-fraught overseas tour with a South African group modelled on them. Stranded in the United States, Manye was rescued by the African Methodist Episcopal (AME) Church, studied at Wilberforce University, and returned to found Wilberforce College outside Johannesburg and to become a social worker and a vigorous campaigner for the African National Congress (ANC). The AME sought to innovate and Africanise African-American church traditions and, through its visiting missionaries, collaborated and shared ideas on politics and hymnody with the 'Ethiopian' (nationalist) churches in South Africa. A later head of music at Wilberforce would be Wilfred Sentso, leader of the Synco Fans vaudeville troupe, which, in the 1930s, performed music in Johannesburg that would far more explicitly foreshadow jazz.[42] The hymnody of the AME also helped to shape the musical thinking of another, later jazzman, pianist Abdullah Ibrahim:

> My grandmother was a founding member of the AME Church in Kensington, which is a suburb of Cape Town. She played the piano. That's where I first learned the spirituals and the hymns and the gospel songs— the African-American experience. When I was a very young child. That church was started in protest against racism among American Christians in Philadelphia, so you can understand why it was a strong social force for us too and why the music impressed us so much.[43]

In Cape Town, 'Jubilee' styles and repertoire reached beyond the working men's clubs. They were heard by singers in the Malay choirs. They were taken up by the players of violins and guitars (along with bones and banjos) performing at social occasions where the *vastrap*, with its rhythms borrowed from Dutch farmers' folk tunes, and the fast-paced *tickey draai*—whose translated title literally exhorted dancers to 'spin on a three-penny piece'—were danced.

These were the musical skills that people of colour from the Cape took with them when they responded to their own need for better prospects, as well as the growing hunger of industrialisation for their labour. As they travelled, others picked up the ideas from them—or brought along their own riffs on what McAdoo had seeded. A description of Xhosa surface workers in Johannesburg forty years later recalls: 'When they came to the mines, they came with this coon thing . . . coming together in a crowd like the coons do, marching up and down'.[44] Farther north, 'by the 1920s, minstrelsy performance had [extended] deep into remote parts of the countryside. These shows particularly impressed Zulu migrant workers from the Kwazulu Natal regions who combined stylistic elements of minstrelsy performance with *ingoma* dance (characterised by high-kicking footwork) and *izingoma zomtshado* (wedding songs). . . .'[45]

Peripatetic musicians and skilled workmen and clerks who also had musical skills went where the mine camps and canteens were. Their first stop was Kimberley, in the years after the discovery of diamonds in 1867. Kimberley 'boasted a thriving community of middle-class Africans. . . . Music-making provided one of the main bonds of interest and association for members of this community'.[46]

The pressures of colonial rule had intensified mobility within the country's diverse musical landscape. Forcible removals, wars, and later taxation were used to secure African labour for farms, diamond diggings, and, after 1886, the gold reef of the Witwatersrand around Johannesburg. During the last forty years of the nineteenth century, South Africa was beginning its industrial revolution, and 'the decade between 1890 and 1900 saw some of the most dramatic changes in the history of the subcontinent, and the rise of an industrial giant which increasingly welded the societies of the area into a single political economy serving the interests of a handful of mine magnates'.[47]

It was impossible to pay a hut or poll tax without cash income, so African subsistence farmers had perforce to become wage labourers. The need for manufactured goods—including the guns some chiefs tried to accumulate to resist colonisation—also pushed (predominantly) men into waged contract work. Large, bleak, rigidly disciplined labour compounds housing male workers from all over the southern African region and equally mixed but more homely informal settlements (where women and children could live too) began to sprawl around the mines, ports, and early cities. Thomas Packenham, a historian of the Anglo-Boer War, drew on contemporary accounts to discuss one such, the 'other Johannesburg',

a city in itself—the African location where the 'mine boys' lived. The mines had an unquenchable appetite for cheap labour; eighty-eight thousand Africans were employed on the Rand in that year of 1898. This other Johannesburg was, by all accounts, an appalling place: full of typhoid, pneumonia and, what was nearly as bad, illegal Johannesburg-brewed liquor.[48]

The unskilled mineworkers were often Zulu speakers 'imported in large gangs from Natal, walking all the way and often not paid until they had walked home again. Increasing numbers of Shangane (Tsonga or Chopi) workers came from Portuguese East Africa as the gold mines in the Eastern Transvaal, which had previously employed them, declined.'[49] Other experienced and more skilled miners, often Sotho-speakers or Afrikaans-speaking coloured men from the Cape, came from the Kimberley diamond fields. Many Zulu men loathed underground work, but they discovered they could use their traditional training as adjutants to officers in their own royal army to leave the compounds and secure somewhat better paid work as domestic servants in the city itself. By the early 1920s, there were more than 200,000 migrant mineworkers in the city and perhaps another 100,000 male domestic workers, labourers, laundrymen, and others. (Women and children did not officially exist and so were not counted.) For all, the harshest living conditions prevailed, and even if working men had partners and children in the location, laws denying their right to be in town at all kept their wives out of formal economic activity.[50] The 'illegal, Johannesburg-brewed liquor' Packenham describes was not invariably 'bad'—brewing it was, however, the only 'respectable' way (sanctioned by traditional custom if not colonial law) for these women to secure an income.

> Nearby, in more comfortable circumstances, lived the mixed-race community, the Cape coloured people. . . . They were the carpenters and tram-drivers, the carters and craftsmen; their wives worked as servants or washerwomen. Finally, there were a couple of hundred Indians from Natal. They ran cheap shops and stalls in the market and the poor whites depended on them.[51]

Later, after the Anglo-Boer War, indentured Chinese mine labourers were imported under conditions of near-slavery. From its earliest days, then, Johannesburg was a place full of Africans speaking many languages and carrying with them many cultural traditions—and working with and for an equally mixed bunch of European migrants: Portuguese, English, Italian, Irish, and East Europeans, many of them Jews fleeing czarist pogroms. Other industrial and commercial centres saw similarly mixed communities developing. But because Johannesburg grew so large, so fast, on the basis of the mining boom, local Tswana-speaking people found their labour in demand on surrounding farms to feed the hungry city and did not seek work in town. The scale and impact of migration on Johannesburg was probably the most dramatic in the region.

The African shantytowns around the city and the racially mixed slums within it must have been terrifyingly crowded, foul, and noisy for those coming in from relatively thinly populated rural areas with free-running streams and clean air. William Plomer, who schooled in Johannesburg—but far from industrial noise—in the twentieth century's first decade, describes even his genteel streets in his autobiography as 'orchestrated with the clanging, hissing and whining sounds of trams, with the clop-clop of horses' hooves and occasionally the crack of a forty-foot wagon whip'.[52]

One sound in particular made an impression: the sound of the steam train. It was the steam train that brought many of the migrant workers to Johannesburg: as Hugh Masekela sings it, to the 'filthy, funky hostels'.[53] It was the steam train that had made large-scale extractive industry economically viable in a place like Johannesburg, far from the sea, and created tough navvying jobs in its construction. It had been the need for rail lines that had provided the occasion for land grabs and conflict between imperial powers in South Africa before the Anglo-Boer War, and rail lines that had determined some new military tactics during it.

City noise and the steam trains opened the ears of new urbanites to new sounds: louder, more urgent, more strident. 'The train', wrote David Coplan in his analysis of SeSotho migrant poetry, 'is of particular importance as a kind of master metaphor for the multidimensional, unending life process of migrant labour'.[54] But the train is also a mechanical polyrhythm: wheels bumping over rattling rails, pistons clattering, chimneys hissing steam, whistles punctuating breaks. That, at any rate, was its musical resonance for Jasper Cook, a trombonist who grew up in Natal as a white child fascinated by both railways and the early sounds of South African jazz:

> I've always loved trains. And marabi music for me always seemed to have that same quality as the sound of a train: it just goes on and on, but as it goes on it always changes and you know it's going somewhere.[55]

However dirty and noisy, these urban settlements also provided a space where, in the last years of the nineteenth century and the first years of the twentieth, a new sense of community could be forged, and indignation over conditions expressed and shared. African and coloured alike were ruled by pass regulations that restricted their movement and prevented them from buying property. They had neither the means nor the social acceptance to attend the entertainments of whites (although white music-hall songs were certainly known and played), so they created their own:

> Tuning their favourite instrument, the guitar, to their traditional five- or six-note scales, African domestic workers often played at location entertainments or performed in the streets. . . . As in Kimberley, miners played trade store instruments as they strolled. . . . Their music became an important resource for developing inter-ethnic urban African styles.[56]

These entertainments inevitably also included alcohol. Brewing had been a customary part of rural life: a normal domestic activity for women and a vital part of ceremonies and the exchange economy of the countryside. The traditional brew was low in alcohol and nutritious. But the colonisers saw time spent on non-Christian religion or social bonding as 'idleness' and realised that African farmers who grew enough grain to brew the surplus were unlikely to spend much time working for them. These attitudes hardened as industrialisation demanded an even stricter kind of work discipline. The 1880s and 1890s saw growing moves to regulate and tax 'native' beer out of existence everywhere.

In the Cape, farmworkers were forbidden to brew or buy alcohol, but their white employers could pay them via the *dop* (tot) system where a portion of the wage was paid in liquor. This created a convenient dependence on the employer and probably blurred the edges of intolerable working conditions. In the Transvaal, the Afrikaner government sold a profitable concession to one A. H. Nellmapius to brew spirits at the People's Hope Distillery in Hatherley, near Pretoria. While local beer was forbidden to compound-dwelling miners (ineffectively, as Packenham saw), more than 500 white-run 'canteens' sold highly adulterated 'Kaffir whisky' to them at the rate, in 1897, of 1,000 gallons a day. The previous year, mine officials had estimated that at any one time a quarter of all miners were incapacitated by drink. Many died from it.[57] So, in that same year, prohibition was introduced. Africans were forbidden to buy, sell, or drink any kind of liquor on the Witwatersrand.

Until the British victory in the Anglo-Boer War in 1902, bootlegging—to which the authorities winked a large eye in the interests of tax revenue—confined this legislation largely to paper as far as the Hatherley distillery was concerned. Raids on 'native' women brewers continued vigorously, but the bootleggers—often poor East European Jews excluded from white high society under the disparaging epithet 'Peruvians'—ran covert, barricaded liquor 'forts' linked by tunnels to legitimate bottle stores. After the war, the British administration and the mine owners smashed the 'forts' and the liquor gangs that ran them.

But these were not the only kinds of gangs. In the 1890s, the Zulu-speaking 'Ninevites' began as a self-protection brotherhood, handing out beatings to white employers who cheated or mistreated their domestic servants. By 1912, they had become an extensive and feared criminal network controlling burglary, brewing, and prostitution. They dressed flamboyantly and played mouth organs as they marched through the streets.[58] Among other groups who adopted the Ninevite model of organisation were the gangs of young men, the Amalaita, who banded together to resist and evade the pass laws, but who were also associated with housebreaking and mugging.

A racist moral panic about the supposed rape threat posed by adult African 'houseboys' had hit the Transvaal around 1908, and employers began replacing their male servants with young women and teenage boys, mostly Tswana- and Pedi-speaking. These young people came from communities with a tradition of pipe-playing and marching in age regiments, and the Amalaita fused these customs with what they saw of the Scottish military bands playing on bandstands in

the city parks: '[P]ennywhistle and drum music . . . accompanied their parades
. . . [and] short, accordion-pleated tartan skirts called 'Scots rokkies' [were] worn
by female members'.[59] At least one distinguished jazz musician took his first
musical inspiration from the heirs of these first Amalaita, later called AmaSkotish
from their kilts. Alto saxophonist Ntemi Piliso was born in Alexandra Township
in 1925:

> My first impression about jazz music as a young boy was when a group
> of chaps in Alexandra were playing the penny-whistle, and they were
> imitating Scottish people with the dressing up, but in an African version.
> So I was so excited with this music that I managed to obtain one of these
> instruments. But these chaps did a different job at night, because they
> were thugs at night, so I was not allowed to mix with them. But because
> I loved music, naturally I started hiding myself and learning the musical
> points from these people, even though I did not associate with them
> when they were doing other things.[60]

If the cities were tough for black workers before 1913, the pressures of overcrowding and low wages increased after the passage of the Native Land Act in
1913. ('We cannot afford a wage to make it possible for [a black miner] to live
in an urban area' said the Witwatersrand Chamber of Mines in 1907.)[61] Ninety-
three percent of the land of the Union of South Africa was designated for white
development. In the 7 percent of 'scheduled tribal areas', Africans could no
longer own land as individuals. Prosperous black farmers were redefined as
'peasant squatters' and expelled from their lands. On white-designated land, Africans could remain only if they gave labour to the farmer for a portion of each
year. The reserves rapidly became overcrowded, and land and grazing were
eroded and exhausted, but these reserves were the basis of an important ideological construct: that no African, wherever born or resident, was entitled to a permanent home anywhere else. Through the 1920s and 1930s, more and more
people left the reserves, particularly from the Eastern Cape and Basutoland (now
Lesotho), to seek work on big white-owned farming estates, on the mines, and
in the cities.

There was anger at the impact of these rules throughout black society. It was
expressed most explicitly in the song 'iLand Act', composed by R. T. Caluza and
the first anthem of the South African Native National Congress (founded in
1912, the NNC was the forerunner of today's African National Congress): *We
cry for our land / Zulu, Xhosa and Sotho / Unite! / We are mad over the Land Act /
A terrible law that allows sojourners / To deny us our land.*[62]

In 1921, a city inspector observed similar indignation at the other end of the
black social scale:

> A kaffir playing a sort of one-string banjo made of a piece of hollowed
> wood and what looked like a paraffin tin. In excellent English, he went

through a scene depicting a "boy's" arrest for not having a pass, the plea
being that he was an African in his own country and did not need one.[63]

Caluza, who composed and performed hymns, traditional music, songs of
social commentary, dance tunes, and even ragtime, represents the kind of erudite
musician that the mission-led black education system was producing. He taught
at the Ohlange Institute in Natal, originally founded by the Reverend John Dube
on the model of Tuskegee, where he had studied—another instance of the impression made by African-American models of self-reliant development. Caluza
turned the Institute Choir into a profitable touring group, then branched out
into other kinds of performance, playing for rowdy location dances as well as the
stylish and refined clerks and domestic servants who frequented Johannesburg's
Inchcape Hall.

The cities were home not only to poor labourers crushed together in compounds and slumyards. There were also teachers, clergymen, clerks, and others
aspiring to equality with whites on the basis of their very real social and economic achievements. For this group, the visit of the Virginia Jubilee singers had
been a key moment, offering as it did a model of progressive civilisation. 'Jubilee
music' fit well into a society that already had a strong choral tradition, musical
literacy, and even outlets for composition and music publishing through the
'Lovedale Series' imprint. Songs like 'iLand Act' gave voice to both the identity
and the aspirations of this group. They were part of a repertoire known as *makwaya* music, whose early development is strongly associated with graduates of
the missions in Natal and the Eastern Cape. *Makwaya* music included European
or American-derived hymns, African-composed pentatonic hymns, suitably
adapted traditional songs, and ragtime, spirituals, and more recent vaudeville
pieces. Some of these were choreographed 'action songs', designed consciously
as an alternative to 'pagan' dances in Natal, a part of South Africa where traditional religion remained very strong. School concerts, the *eistedfodds* organised
in the 1920s by the South African Bantu Board of Music, and the Johannesburg
versions of tea meetings became a platform for performance, alongside literary
and political discussion—and political organisation.

The first 'official' African location, the Malay Location, had been established
next to Vrededorp in 1892. A new 'temporary' settlement was recognised near
the Klipspruit sewage dump in 1904. Others followed. But the black middle
classes preferred to live in places like the new suburb of Sophiatown, west of
Johannesburg. Initially established in 1897 as a speculative building venture
aimed at poor whites, the area proved unpopular with them—it was far from
the city centre and close to another sewage works—and lots were sold indiscrimi-
nately, increasingly to freehold buyers of colour. By the 1920s, so great was their
demand for freehold land in a serviced suburb—as opposed to the unserviced
locations the authorities were beginning to build west of the city—that Sophiatown land prices rose far higher than those in neighbouring white areas. New-

clare and Alexandra were other, relatively new freehold townships where people of colour could buy both plots and houses. As well as concerts, these city sophisticates saw the silent movies at the 'bioscope', and were impressed by the show dancing they saw and its soundtracked successor, tap dancing.

Although the black population of Johannesburg was growing—pushed by the effects of the Land Act and pulled by the demands of industry, especially during World War I—its permanence was precarious. Black miners worked on fixed-term contracts. Other urban workers stayed only by virtue of documents issued by their employer, without which they could not remain overnight in the city. This law, the 1923 Urban Areas Act, did not drive black workers away, but it rendered their need for facilities and resources and their entitlement to human rights invisible. Other laws passed during the 1920s further restricted black urban workers' land ownership, residence, opportunity to acquire skills or do skilled work, and capacity to bargain for wages. The 1927 Native Administration Act reduced all blacks to 'tribesmen' under the authority of a government-designated chief. Everywhere except the Cape (where some freeholders of colour still had the vote) this removed Africans from direct engagement with parliamentary politics. The laws were not consistently enforced—it was not until 1936 that the freeholders of Sophiatown received their first warnings—but invoked whenever it suited the authorities.

Those authorities also began to concern themselves with the policing of black leisure time. In the mine compounds, they began providing spaces for weekend recreation, particularly encouraging the practice of 'tribal' dancing, over which their patronage would dramatically expand in the following decades. In the city, in 1924, a curious coalition of black campaigner and writer Sol Plaatje, the American-educated, early Ghanaian nationalist Dr. Aggrey, white American missionaries like the Reverend Ray Phillips, and some more liberal mine magnates, led, in 1924, to the foundation of the Bantu Men's Social Centre. Initially, this building was envisaged primarily as a reading room. Its aim was to '[play] an active part in shaping Native leisure-time activities, moulding Native character and enlarging Native outlook'.[64] Educational films were shown there, and lectures and ballroom dancing classes were held. It was the base for the Bantu Board of Music. Within a decade, it would become a key rehearsal and performance space for the new popular musical styles.

Urban discontent created the earliest black trade unions, most famously the Industrial and Commercial Workers Union (ICU), and to a series of strikes and boycotts, which in their turn were met with more repressive legislation. In 1923, the Native National Congress changed its name to the African National Congress and adopted the colours (green, black, and gold) and the anthem ('Nkosi Sikelele I'Afrika') that it still uses today.

In the same year, a fifteen-year-old boy travelled from Rhodesia (Zimbabwe) to find work in Johannesburg:

He came on a bicycle. All the way. He worked as a cleaner, and then his boss taught him how to cook and made him a chef. Then his boss bought a milling company and employed him there. Meanwhile, he had a wife, and my mother now was running a shebeen in Doornfontein. . . . All non-whites were thrown into the same pot, living together. The Bantu Men's Social Centre [BMSC] was for everybody; boxing was for everybody; dancing was for everybody.[65]

The speaker is the young Zimbabwean's son, Lucky Michaels, who carried forward his father's heritage as a restaurateur by opening Johannesburg's most famous jazz club, the Pelican, in Orlando Township in 1972. And it is the experience of families like the Michaels in the 1930s and 1940s—dancing at the BMSC and Inchcape Hall, running a shebeen in slumyard Doornfontein and later a restaurant in the city—that illuminates the direct prehistory of South African jazz in those decades: the era of vaudeville, *marabi*, and finally something called jazz.

# Notes

1. Interview for *Ubuyile*, April 2000.
2. Conversation with the author, Langa, 29 March 2003.
3. Interview for *Ubuyile*, May 2000.
4. Excellent detailed historical accounts and musicological analyses exist that cover the same period from these more technical viewpoints. See, for example, works by Christopher Ballantine and David Coplan cited in the bibliography.
5. N. Parsons, *A New History of Southern Africa*, 2nd ed. (London: Macmillan 1993), 202.
6. P. Kirby, *The Musical Instruments of the Native Races of South Africa*, 2nd ed. (Johannesburg: Witwatersrand University Press, 1968), xii.
7. D. Coplan, *In the Time of the Cannibals* (Johannesburg: Witwatersrand University Press, 1994), 26.
8. Interview with the author, July 2001.
9. Kirby, op. cit., 135.
10. D. Dargie, *Nguwe Lo! A Listeners' Guide to a Selection of Xhosa Music* (Munich: self-published, 1994), 2.
11. Kirby, op. cit., 57.
12. Ibid., 45.
13. Ibid., 81.
14. Ibid., 131.
15. Interview for ABC Ulwazi radio series *Let the People Sing*, Johannesburg, 2002.
16. Ibid.
17. Interview with the author for arts supplement *The Good Weekend*, 1999.
18. D. Coplan, *In Township Tonight* (Johannesburg: Ravan Press, 1985), 28–38, passim.

19. 'The thing that is not round: the untold story of black rugby', in *Beyond the Tryline: Rugby and South African Society*, ed. A. Odendaal et al. (Johannesburg Ravan Press, 1995.

20. Interview with the author, 1999.

21. Figures from D. Constant-Martin, *Coon Carnival* (Cape Town: David Phillip, 1999) 49–51, passim.

22. Ibid., 51.

23. W. Dooling, 'The castle in the history of Cape Town', in *Studies in the History of Cape Town, vol. 7*, ed. E. Van Heynigen (Cape Town: UCT Press, 1994), 19.

24. Ibid.

25. Quoted in Constant-Martin, op. cit., 70.

26. Ibid., 58.

27. 'A Lady', *Life at the Cape over a Hundred Years Ago* (Cape Town: Struik, 1998), 37.

28. Quoted in Constant-Martin, op. cit., 59.

29. Ibid., 54.

30. Ibid., 66–67.

31. H. Idris Galeta, 'The development of jazz in South Africa' (Cape Town: Zethebi Music, 2000).

32. Constant-Martin, op. cit., 84.

33. Banzi Bangani, interview for *Ubuyile*, June 2000.

34. Jonas Gwangwa, interview for *Ubuyile*, June 2000.

35. V. Erlmann, 'A feeling of prejudice: Orpheus M McAdoo and the Virginia Jubilee Singers in South Africa 1890–1898', in *Regions and Repertoires: Topics in South African Politics and Culture*, South African Studies, vol. 7, ed. S. Clingman (Johannesburg: Ravan Press, 1991), 8.

36. Ibid.

37. Kirby, op. cit., 231.

38. Coplan, *In Township Tonight*, 39.

39. Ibid., 40.

40. Jubilee Singer Mamie Smith, quoted in Erlmann, op. cit., 13.

41. Quoted in Constant-Martin, op. cit., 86.

42. Erlmann, op. cit., 12.

43. C. Ballantine, *Marabi Nights: Early South African Jazz and Vaudeville* (Johannesburg: Ravan Press, 1993), 36.

44. Abdullah Ibrahim, interview with the author for *The Star Tonight*, 2000.

45. Dan Twala, quoted in Coplan, *In Township Tonight*, 95.

46. A. Impey, 'Refashioning identity in post-apartheid South African music: a case for isicathamiya music in Kwazulu Natal', in *Culture in the New South Africa, vol. 2*, ed. R. Kriger and A. Zegeye (Cape Town: Kwela Books, 2001), 231.

47. Erlmann, op. cit., 13.

48. Coplan, *In Township Tonight*, 46.

49. T. Packenham *The Anglo-Boer War* (Johannesburg: Jonathan Ball, 1982), quoted in *Reef of Time: Johannesburg in Writing*, ed. D. Ricci (Johannesburg: A. D. Donker, 1986), 56.

50. Parsons, op. cit., 172.

51. Packenham, in Ricci, op. cit., 56.

52. W. Plomer, Autobiography, in Ricci, op. cit., 90.

53. Lyrics by Hugh Masekela, copyright to Chisa Music.

54. Coplan, *In the Time of the Cannibals*, 125.

55. Interview for *Ubuyile*, August 2000.

56. Coplan, *In Township Tonight*, 49.

57. P. La Hausse, *Brewers, Beerhalls and Boycotts* (Johannesburg: History Workshop/Ravan Press, 1988), 16.

58. Coplan, *In Township Tonight*, 49.

59. Ibid., 62.

60. Interview for *Ubuyile*, May 2000.

61. Quoted in Parsons, op. cit., 238.

62. Quoted in Coplan, *In Township Tonight*, 73.

63. Quoted in ibid., 64.

64. BMSC Annual Report, 1926, quoted in Ballantine, op. cit., 20.

65. Interview for *Ubuyile*, May 2000.

## Chapter Two

# New Sounds of the Cities

Sack tents. Marabi: all-night sessions. Yes, those were the nice days!

—General Duze, guitarist[1]

E llis Park in Doornfontein is today one of Johannesburg's prestige sports stadiums. Situated beside a red-brick technical college, its other neighbours are featureless wholesale outlets, office blocks, and pubs. Regularly, on weekend afternoons, the streets through this nondescript scenery clog with cars full of hooting, flag-waving rugby football fans—predominantly white—here to support local teams like the Cats and the Blue Bulls in grunting, sweating, bone-crunching contests.

The crowds that thronged the Doornfontein streets seventy years ago were very different. Since the turn of the century, the city had been filling with large numbers of people from the country's rural areas. Both the republic government and the City Council had fought a losing battle to segregate these groups from one another, locate their ostensibly 'temporary' residences as far as possible from polite society and commerce, and regulate their lives as tightly as those of the contract mineworkers in the compounds.

City workers preferred homes near their jobs without long and expensive commutes. Besides, the alternatives for those who could not afford to buy freehold property in suburbs like Sophiatown were not attractive. The historic Klipspruit location, for example, was bounded on three sides by a sewage plant. It was mainly composed of V-shaped corrugated iron shelters placed directly on bare ground. Annual infant mortality was close to 400 per 1,000.[2] In addition, many of those flocking to the cities were job seekers, as yet lacking the income to pay any rent.

Employers saw that they could extract more overtime from workers who lived close to the workplace, and they sought special licences to house in town

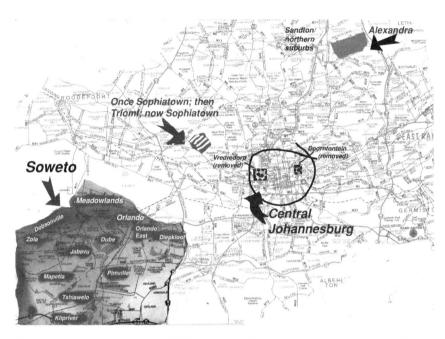

**Black settlements in and around Johannesburg. Doornfontein was the centre of marabi culture in the racially mixed city centre of the 1930s. Over the first half of the twentieth century, residential patterns polarised, with rich whites moving to the greenfield northern suburbs like Sandton, and blacks moved forcibly southwest to Soweto.** *Credit: Judy Seidman*

those of their workers not already accommodated in suburbs, locations, compounds, or rented city space. Warehouses and factories put up additional housing compounds in their yards. Other workers and migrants into the city often sublet from people with access to these spaces, and family members moved in. Abandoned industrial and commercial premises on the city margins were partitioned off into rooms, and cheap rooming houses were established. Doornfontein had begun its life as a rich suburb of 'bluegum and cypress lined streets where every house had its stable and coach-house.'[3] In the 1890s, the rich had begun a steady migration to the northern suburbs, and Doornfontein properties and plots began to be divided up for increasingly poor and finally black tenants. The resulting warren of rented rooms and yards carries the label of the birthplace of Johannesburg's city music, but other settlements, such as the now long-disappeared Prospect Township, also nurtured it. According to Phil Bonner and Lauren Segal, 'The [black, urban] population continued to rise during most of the 1920s, when every imaginable space was filled by people desperate for accommodation. Landlords grew rich by renting out rooms. By 1927, over 40,000 people lived in the unregulated, unhygienic and boisterous world of the slums.'[4]

Urbanisation continued apace throughout the whole country o\
two decades. Official census figures estimated the population at 50 percent pᴇᴀ.
ant in 1921, and at 10 percent peasant in 1951 (although women, increasingly
left to manage the lands as men became migrant workers, were not counted in
this later figure). By the same year, the population of Cape Town was 630,000
(half coloured, a tenth black); the population of Durban was 500,000 (one-third
Asian, one-third black), and Pretoria's was 285,000 (more than half white).[5]

It was this whole urban world—the 'slumyards'—that gave birth to one of the
grandparents of modern South African jazz: marabi. Historians argue about the
origin of the term. It may come from the SeSotho language, where *ho raba raba*
is a verb meaning 'to fly about'—very appropriate for the freestyle dance that
accompanied the sounds. Pianist Abdullah Ibrahim asserts the term 'came from
Marabastad, an old, old, Pretoria location where they first made this music'.[6]

Trombonist Jonas Gwangwa defines the style: 'marabi—an African music
translated to Western instruments at the stokvels and the parties.'[7] There were
polyrhythmic and interlocked elements, drawn from tradition, and these were
fitted around the three-chord structure of modern songs and played with whatever instruments were at hand. The modern songs could be anything: the melodic line of a composed hymn or the chorus of an American pop tune; 'any
tune that crosses my mind . . . I play it', recalled marabi pianist of the 1920s
Edward Sililo, who had worked Ma Jeremiah's shebeen in Doornfontein.[8] It was
an intimate music, suited to small domestic spaces, converted kitchens, and sack-
roofed backyards where the sound of piano or organ needed no amplification.
However, marabi was not simply a music but a whole lifestyle, created during
the 1920s—and extinct by the end of the 1940s. Workers recently arrived from
the rural areas of southern Africa fought to find ways, appropriate to their new
circumstances, of keeping alive valued aspects of their identity and humanity.
Says music historian Christopher Ballantine, marabi's 'cyclical nature betrays
roots deep in indigenous African musics'.[9]

It was the marabi gene that endowed the new city music with its cyclical
chord structure and its archive of musical references from many communities,
which continues to allow South African jazz to rediscover and reshape historic
elements to refresh jaded modern sounds. But South African jazz was, in many
senses, the child of a mixed marriage. As in the smoky Dickensian towns of
Britain's industrial revolution a century earlier, South African cities were home
to a 'respectable' class, as well as marabi's 'rough' working class. From its other
grandparent, the vaudeville and choral music of skilled artisans, teachers, ministers, and clerks, the country's jazz drew its international frame of reference and
its brass-heavy band format.

Many musicians (like R. T. Caluza), performances, and audiences crossed
between the two. Yet much as these two discourses lived in symbiosis, in an era
of growing African nationalism, the 1930s and 1940s were equally the site of

contestation between them, to define the 'authentic' sound of modern black society. But the playing field was never level. In Dickens's cities, a few at least of the poor from London rookeries and cotton town slums had been able to rise, to find new, broader spaces for economic and cultural expression. In South Africa, the relentless process of racially structured underdevelopment that had already, in the 1900s, reduced prosperous black farmers to squatters and sharecroppers, was also at work in the towns. The era saw the progressive squeezing of the urban space—social, cultural, political, and physical—in which black urbanites could become or be middle class.

Even the oldest musicians alive at the end of the twentieth century could only recall marabi society and its music through impressions formed and tales told during childhood:

> We didn't call it jazz at the time. We called it marabi. We were not using horns. Marabi music was composed of a vocalist, self-made drums and an organ. So this one chap would sing the whole night on three chords. But it was not monotonous to the ear, because they varied it. . . . There was this fellow called Zuluboy Cele. I heard of him, but I had never associated with him; I was a bit young at the time. Now, marabi music was composed of a chord progression of, say, I–IV–V. Zuluboy took that progression and instrumentalised it. But before him, one person that I remember hearing of very well was called Ntebetjane. One [of the] most popular song[s] that he sang was called 'Ntebetjane uFana Nemfene' (Ntebetjane looks like a baboon). It was the basis of African jazz: it had those chords. Even today, we base our music mostly on I–IV–V. You can always recognise African jazz from that chord progression.[10]

Saxophonist Ntemi Piliso, interviewed in 2000—one year before his death at age seventy-four—described what was, by the 1930s, a formed and recognised style. (Some older musicians still dub jazz tunes of later decades 'marabi' as a way of describing their structure.) The Ntebetjane of legend had played its earliest version. Ntebetjane had been one of the peripatetic musicians who first found work in urban drinking dens. Like a wandering bluesman asserting with defiant irony that he 'may be black and ugly', Ntebetjane immortalised himself through that lyric—but no one remembers what he really looked like. His peers had names like Toto, Highbricks, and Nine Fingers, and had come from Transkei, the Cape, Kimberley, Natal, and other rural areas over preceding decades. They were sometimes semiprofessional, weekend musicians alongside their other trades and sometimes full-timers who found in the canteens and rent parties of the slumyards a place to grow their music and give it visibility. Each added something to the Johannesburg sound.

Cape musicians had brought their country dances, like the *tickey draai*. Xhosa-speaking workers had their *tula n'divile*, the name of a popular folk song used to attract patrons into shebeens, and later of any music used in this way. It was also a nickname given to Western Native Township, where it was heard. According to broadcaster, Dan Twala, 'it meant "You keep quiet; you haven't heard what I've heard. I'll tell you!" Everybody was trying to be original and come with his own little style [at] their sort of *timitin* there, and I say all right, I can sing a song, and I put half a crown on the table and ask you to come and sing . . . to augment the funds of the people holding the party'.[11] Saxophonist Wilson 'Kingforce' Silgee asserted that 'marabi is *tickey draai* plus *tula n'divile'*.[12]

Miners from Basutoland (now Lesotho) brought *famo* music, played on homemade percussion instruments and concertinas, or sometimes a pedal organ. Both the shop-bought and homemade instruments could impressively mimic the drone that underpinned traditional Sotho vocal music. *Famo* had been a term for the hip-thrusting, skirt-twitching women's steps of a traditional courting dance. In the disordered and impoverished circumstances of the city, the formal, community-linked social rituals of courtship were difficult (families lived far away), expensive (marriage-price conventions were based on rural resources like cattle), and illegal (wives were not supposed to settle with their husbands in the cities). So *famo* dances became the venues for more desperate and temporary, alcohol-fuelled courtships—an instance of both the dislocating impact of labour migrancy and the way communities strove to hold this dislocation within a re-cognisable cultural frame.

Zulu-speakers, using a term reflecting their pessimistic view of the filthy, all-consuming city, dubbed their shebeen music *nduduma*; ('mine dumps'). In venues where they predominated, the music was the evolved folk style *ingom'ebusuku* ('night music'), based on a blend of hymns, vaudeville, and village songs that grew from after-hours dance and song contests in their hostels (and a precursor of the *isicathamiya* style now made internationally famous by Ladysmith Black Mambazo). Competitive dances to develop and demonstrate fighting fitness and athleticism had been a historic feature of regimental activity in the Zulu royal army; now they wore an urban jacket. Durban saxophonist Dalton Khanyile claimed marabi from those roots: 'marabi is *nduduma*, Caluzafied'.[13] Guitarist General Duze, also from Natal, agreed, but he was careful to emphasise the down-market image of marabi, as opposed to its more sophisticated child, jazz:

Marabi came from Natal. Mkhumbane and places like that is where it originated, from what I know. We enjoyed playing their stuff, but we changed it because of the orchestration thing. To them, it was just that line of melody and improvisation thereafter. But it did add something to jazz, because many of the elderly people had started with . . . [and] enjoyed marabi. So they could pick the music up from there, and then we played the instrumental version of the same thing. . . . But as jazzmen, we were the cream of the young guys. A musician was somebody big. You had to dress up properly: look like a schoolteacher, not a marabi player![14]

So, marabi was *'tickey draai* plus *tula n'divile'* (Cape folk dance plus Xhosa tavern song) or *'nduduma*, Caluzafied' (Zulu migrant song with a vaudeville treatment). Everybody, it seems, was keen to trace it back to their own home region. Yet the drinking places of the urban settlements were not as tightly ethnically exclusive as all this might imply. There were places where specific communities of 'homeboys' gathered to reminisce, meet up with new arrivals who might have news, and help those new arrivals find their footing. There, the music too reflected home. There were many more places where everyone gathered. In the slums, 'the most distinct feature was its racial mix . . . Africans, Indians, coloureds, Chinese and whites of many diverse origins (British, Lebanese, East European Jews) lived side-by-side and borrowed many elements from one another's social lives . . . the slumyard dialect of *flaaitaal* [clever speech] combined elements of Afrikaans, English and African languages'.[15] Marabi can be claimed by musicians from different regions because a little piece of each of those regions and more went into its making. Veteran singer and music teacher Sophie Mngcina describes how she hears the traces of different roots:

> Our music is jazz—I mean, what's this rhythm? It's also ragtime. We did sing those things. When you start delving into the music . . . you hear the rhythms you heard as a young girl. For me, the Sothos were rappers, and more on the bluesy side. The Zulus, the music they were playing, maskandi, they were playing ballads with acoustic guitar, and they had a special way of strumming—which I think most of the modern musicians don't really care for. And you could hear the rhythms of the Bacas—they used their voices towards a string bass; they used tins with car tyres inside—you should hear this rhythm! The Xhosas have a syncopated sort of rhythm which is also like—I mean it is jazz![16]

Essentially, it was a national sound. And however the traditional element is labelled, the result of the fusions can be defined in Piliso's words:

> [After Zuluboy Cele] what you have is an original African form, modern instruments, and that call-and-response pattern which Fletcher Henderson drew out of ragtime and which was around in jazz until bebop made a decisive break.[17]

The social arena within which marabi was shaped, the shebeen, took its title from the Irish term meaning 'little shop' and its forms of organisation from the sisterhoods and savings clubs, secular (*simpato/stokvel*) and religious (*manyano*) of Tswana-speaking women, which had themselves originated in the organisations of rural society. Tswana towns had been divided into wards, and 'regiments' organised cooperative work parties on this basis. So *stokvel* parties were organised on a circuit, rather than simultaneously; women cooperated to brew beer, look after children, and pay liquor fines for one another. Marching bands accompanied the religious *manyano* parades; now they also advertised *stokvel* parties and were one source from which, a few years later, brass instruments were at hand to modernise marabi. In 1941, the newspaper *Bantu World* described 'the noises of brass bands turning hymns into jazz tunes . . . in tents, rooms and under sacking all over the location'.[18] According to journalist Andrew K. Lukhele,

> No history of stokvels is complete without mention of the impact they had on the development of shebeens, and vice versa. These shebeens were usually operated by women . . . [and] black women began to use the stokvels as a means of protection against police harassment. . . . [S]tokvels became more than just organisations for the circulation of money and evolved into comprehensive systems for members in times of hardship. . . . Some shebeens allow stokvel members (for a fee) to host their parties at their venues. Stokvels have also been used to finance shebeeners. . . .[19]

None of this gives the real flavour of the music, or the atmosphere. To do that, you had to be there. The late Godfrey Moloi, occasional musician, raconteur, reformed gangster, and liquor king, in his youth frequented the shebeens of Mkhumbane, a township outside Durban, where the port's prewar predilection for string music had persisted:

> You could hear Tin Pan Alley on a piano high up on the hills of Tin Town, and the sound of *igeja*, a weeding hoe hung on a string and hit with a piece of iron as a drum cymbal to keep rhythm. Every household that lived a little above the average had a piano, and sold *jwejwe*, a greenish concocted home brew at one shilling per milk bottle pint. So on weekends you paid two and six (25c) admission to the dance party. The landlord who engaged the best pianist would always get a good house, especially if he got a violinist too. The best violinist was Mareyiza. He was a real draw-card.[20]

This was in the early 1940s, when marabi society was mostly broken down by removals, and the music was mutating, but the elements are all there: home-brewed beer and music that blended the instruments of the rural heartlands and the parlour. Singer Thandi Klaasen was a child in the suburb of Sophiatown in the 1930s, slightly wealthier but only marginally less overcrowded than Doorn-fontein, with the same recreations and tactics for fundraising. For her, marabi conjures a magical world of adult sophistication, glowing in the candlelight:

> Ha! Marabi! Our mothers used to have these tents, but during the day our fathers used to build these tents from sacks and they would go and buy about 4–5 packets of candles or these lighted paraffin stoves. And

Rooiyard, a Johannesburg slumyard. The tin drums were used for washing—or for brewing beer. *Credit: Historical papers, University of Witwatersrand Library*

they'd have an accordion, yeah, and they will have a tin, with this long rope, and that's our bass. And our mothers are dressed up in style. And the floor, it's just a floor *ka mhlaba* (earth). And there was *iTeacher* (a doorman/supervisor) at the door, and we'd look after the younger children; we were not allowed to go in there. And they would play 'Tamatie Sous' and you must see how they would sway, our mothers, to marabi! But then, my dear, there are those who are looking out for the police when they come. Because if the police come they must blow off those candles and things, and hide because of the beer. Our beer, yes! How could we drink the white people's beer? That was for the white people.[21]

The core of the marabi economy was beer. Before the 1930s, employment opportunities for black women in the cities were minimal. Despite Johannesburg's *swart gevaar* ('black peril') panic of the 1900s, most domestic servants were still men. Influx control regulations barred male contract workers from bringing in or establishing families and deliberately pitched wages too low to support urban dependents. But women came—and stayed, and fought to keep families together. The ratio of men to women in the towns changed from 12:1 in 1900 to 6:1 in 1927, to 3:1 by 1939 (equalizing only in the late 1960s).[22] Some women followed brothers, husbands, or sweethearts, though many never found those they sought. Some found the notion of urban independence, and the chance to earn, more attractive than a life lived out on barren reserve lands, where customary patriarchal restrictions persisted long after the agricultural resources that had made them workable were exhausted. According to Lukhele,

[W]hen they were forced to find ways to generate extra income, it was only natural that many of them turned to an old skill—the African women's traditional skill of brewing beer. This was easy for them because in the rural areas it was the task of every woman to brew for her husband. In some ways the first shebeens were like the Christian 'tea parties' except that they served liquor. They were popularly known as *itimiti*. Members and guests at an *itimiti* paid an entrance fee and bought food and drinks inside. The women took turns to organise these parties in such a way that members in turns received money from all the other members of the group. . . . One of the special attractions of these marabi parties was the different brews which the women prepared.[23]

Town life, though, did not have either the freedom to brew or the ordered regularity of a Tswana village. Voluntarism gave way to commercialisation as the economic screws tightened. The skilled labour bar—the regulation dividing 'white' from 'black' work (blacks were only allowed to be 'unskilled')—was lowered to create opportunities for white immigrants to the cities, so black male wages fell. Competition for jobs intensified. Through beer sales, women could access the revenues of migrancy—and a few men could afford to live with their families. Law and labour contracts made many of these unions unstable; female-headed households were numerous. As in all poor communities, prostitution also lurked as an economic last resort for women in and around the brewing business. Some commentators have chosen to dwell on images of tawdry glamour: the shebeen queen, generous with her ample charms. But predominantly, selling beer was a strategy for prosaic domestic survival.

The enticements of the *tula n'divile* songs denoted music as a way to win more customers, creating a lively environment despite squalid surroundings. It justified admission charges and put cash into the pockets of the players themselves that also circulated around the slumyard economy. While never sealed off from other segments of black society, peasant or petit bourgeois, marabi was the culture of a nontribal working class in formation. Low wages and rising city rents made it increasingly difficult for men to send money home to their rural relatives,[24] and their relationship with families elsewhere stretched and sometimes snapped. As shebeen patrons began to see themselves differently—city residents, not temporary sojourners—the more modern-sounding, syncretic music of the shebeens helped to shape and reinforce that new identity, even as it was also shaped by it.

Through the 1930s, the authorities took steps to clear the racially mixed slums of the city. The pretext was fear of the disease bred by overcrowding, but while conditions were indeed dangerously insanitary, an equally powerful motive was that a booming economy was turning run down areas on the fringes of cities into prime real estate. In the prelude to World War II (and more so during the war itself), manufacturers were eager to replace male domestics with women, so the men could be dragooned into heavy industry and arms manufacture. Six thousand Africans had been ordered out of the city in the mid-1920s, and by 1933, all but three areas of Johannesburg had been proclaimed white. Parts of the Doornfontein slums remained as isolated, vulnerable islands. The council laid out Orlando Township for a limited number of black families. (Council statements described Orlando as a 'paradise for natives'. The reality diverged so far from the propaganda that many black families took one look and refused to stay.) By then, the dynamic female entrepreneurs of the liquor trade—'shebeen queens' or 'aunties'—and the informal economy and autonomous culture they helped build, had established survival mechanisms that would twist, but not break, under new enforced living patterns. During and after the war, the need for labour led to a short-term relaxation of influx control rules, but little additional house building. So the overcrowded, unsanitary conditions of city slums were replicated in Orlando and the other outlying areas designated for people of colour. These economic drivers extended and gave greater permanence to black city residence all over the country.

Over the same period, the onslaught against the shebeens was intensified. The scene was set for a protracted guerrilla struggle over drink and recreation. Women and their families needed the revenues from beer. Black communities—policed everywhere else within an inch of their lives—needed the solidarity, affirmation, and independence of unregulated meeting spots. The authorities feared these bases of social and economic self-reliance. Furthermore, if they were to finance more township construction and policing without eating into funds earmarked for enhancing white amenities, they needed to get their hands on that revenue. Their model was the beerhalls that had been established in Natal in 1908. These gave councils a monopoly on the production and sale of sorghum beer, with the proceeds used to regulate black housing, work discipline, and leisure through the funding of single-sex hostel construction and police force wages. The passage of the 1937 Native Laws Amendment Act allowed this model of municipal monopoly to spread throughout South Africa. For the councils, sorghum beer was 'pink gold'.

The Natal-model municipal beerhalls provided spartan models:

> The building is divided by a high wire fence and one portion is set aside for the sale of native beer [through] the purchase of a ticket. . . . [The native] passes through a turnstile and presents the ticket to the barman.

The native is supplied with the beer in a tin which he takes to the sitting accommodation. He then leaves the building through a turnstile.[25]

In times and at places where it was the only option, this 'drinking in a cage', as it was called, effectively drained money from men's pockets that would otherwise move through the family and community economy. Because the single-sex beerhalls, unlike shebeens, with their women, conversation, and music, were structured with a single-minded focus on drinking, they contributed to a culture of cheerless alcoholism among many male workers.

This grim new environment, not just the removals, killed marabi. Novelist Modikwe Dikobe observed that 'Marabi parties could not take place in Orlando because the community spirit was lost'.[26] So were the customers, since the new township was miles from the workplaces that had provided them. Spartan community halls lacked the intimacy (and acoustics) that made a pianist and a can of stones an ample sound. The illegal sale of home brew could never go undetected, and fun, too, was regulated:

[A]ll night entertainments are not allowed in private houses—that is, entertainments that are conducted for money—by reason of disorder, rowdiness and being a nuisance to neighbours. (Orlando Advisory Board regulation, 1933)[27]

In Natal in the late 1920s, the beerhall system had been fought with boycotts, and the Women's Auxiliary of the ICU had smashed up the beerhalls. Protesters had been teargassed, and the Natal movement was crushed only after the police shot dead four workers' leaders in 1930. But similar protests against beerhalls and liquor raids flared up sporadically around the country during the 1930s and early 1940s, along with strikes by various groups of black workers, riots, bus boycotts, and land invasions to claim new settlement space. By 1942, strikes had become so numerous that war emergency regulations were created to outlaw them; but they persisted, and the regulations had to be reintroduced annually for the next eleven years.[28] However, during the 1930s, the ICU was in decline, and political parties like the ANC were paralysed by protracted policy debates (including argument over their relationship with the Communist Party). This highly militant but scattered activity thus did not coalesce into national campaigns of action for some years.

Nevertheless, the climate of resistance found its way into the music, as Ntemi Piliso recounted:

I composed a song called 'Sip and Fly'. You see, the aunties used to get on top of the hill and brew skokiaan. And then you go up as a customer. And the cops are downstairs. Their cars can't go up. So they had to foot

it and negotiate that steep hill. Meanwhile, you are getting down the
other side. So you sip—and you fly![29]

On the one hand, marabi was an environment that provided comfort and
helped its community make sense of brutal and bewildering new circumstances.
On the other, it existed within a social and legal discourse where simply to survive was defiance. The music reflects both those conditions of its creation.

Brewing at the top of a steep slope was one option. Another was to bury the
containers underground. But the pressures of raids and concealment encouraged
the switch from weak, nourishing traditional beer to new, chemically boosted
brews that required neither the sunlight nor the generous fermentation time of
village recipes. Sometimes sugar, fruit, potatoes, and bread were added to the
fermenting grain, but the fastest, most deadly kick came from cheap brandy,
methylated spirits, or even battery acid. *Skokiaan* was the generic term for this
stagger-inducing stuff (and for a classic 1947 African jazz composition by August
Musarurgwa, later recorded by Louis Armstrong under the unwittingly ironic
title 'Happy in Africa'). Other names were 'pineapple', 'Barberton', and the prophetic *isikilimikwiki* ('kill-me-quick').

> Marabi: that was the environment. . . . You get there, you pay your ten
> cents, you get your share of whatever concoction is there and you dance
> . . . from Friday night right through to Sunday evening. You get tired,
> you go home, sleep, come back again; bob a time each time you get in. It
> got itself infiltrated in me.[30]

But alcohol was not the only aspect of the campaign to police black leisure
time. Race-mixing and the 'detribalisation' of natives frightened the authorities;
both threatened their vision of the tribal reserves as the 'true home' of African
men, from which labour could be siphoned into mines and cities when needed—
then poured back and tightly stoppered.

Cultural identity, and thus music, was central to this project. From the earliest days, the new urban musics had been associated with Africans who were
neither traditionalists nor white-collar Christians: *abaphakathi* ('middle people'),
rural Zulu-speakers had called them; *sebono morao* ('those who have turned their
backside to their homeland') said the Basotho in the city. Ethnomusicologist
Percival Kirby noted in disapproving tones the marabi structure of these 'middle'
people's music in the early 1930s:

> The kraal native who buys one of these [cheap European guitars] never
> performs European music on it; further, since instruments of this kind
> are popular with pagan tribesmen, Christian natives are seldom seen with
> them. . . . The native generally contents himself with a rhythmical strum-
> ming of two or perhaps three of the primary chords.[31]

These modernisers created their own flamboyant style, in dress as well as music, which trumpeter Hugh Masekela saw during his youth in the townships:

All across [c]entral, southern and East Africa, box guitars were available, along with gramophones and records by cowboys [like Gene Autry and Tex Ritter] at [the] concession stores that were always adjacent to mining hostels and barracks. Migrant labourers would purchase boots, cowboy hats, box guitars, buckle belts and khaki pants and shirts that they would adorn with multi-coloured patches and beads.[32]

Their impact could be dramatic. Tony McGregor, the brother of pianist and bandleader Chris McGregor, grew up on a remote mission station in the Eastern Cape. His childhood memory is of the return of contract mineworkers (*amajoini*: those indentured to the mine recruitment agency) to their village in the 1940s, not only graduates of wage labour, but cultural brokers too:

Most of the people living in the area where we lived didn't have radios or record players or anything like that. But there was one source of influence especially from the Johannesburg area. *Amajoini* would come home, and bring with them radios and pennywhistles. So that was starting to infiltrate back into the remote areas of the Transkei. They'd walk along the road, and I used to find them, you know—Wow! They'd have these little silver bells sewn into the legs of their trousers to make a rhythm as they walked, and they'd be playing the pennywhistles. Magical sounds![33]

For the authorities, the answer to the problem of these outlaws was retribalisation, a project that began in a piecemeal and only partly conscious fashion in the 1940s, but which was honed and fine-tuned obsessively by the policies introduced under Grand Apartheid in the 1950s and thereafter. In the mines, employers sought to defuse and redirect the potentially dangerous energies of large groups of exploited workers penned in single-sex compounds by fostering competitive tribal dancing, initially as an internal pastime and later as something that could be put on display to predominantly white audiences. These displays demonstrated to visitors that miners were apparently healthy and happy (though health statistics and labour protests told a different story) and also spotlighted their 'cultural otherness/difference'[34]—from whites and from each other.

The dances also played a role in designing that difference and in creating a cultural wedge between the two categories of black city residents: settled families and male migrants who commuted on contract between prisonlike hostel residence and neglected rural reserves. Ethnomusicologist Hugh Tracey was instrumental in setting up the first arena for the public display of mine-dancing, at the Consolidated Main Reef Mine in Johannesburg in 1943. In his foreword to a 1952 book of photographs of the dances, Tracey pays tribute to compound man-

**Mine-dancing in the company arena.** *Credit: Historical papers, University of Wit-watersrand Library*

ager Lewis G. Hallett, 'who encouraged the use of, and indeed improvised, many of the dance costumes now associated with the different tribes'.[35]

Tracey gave lectures on African music at the BMSC and advised on recording policy for the Gallo record label. Alan Silinga, composer of one of the best-known songs in South Africa's jazz canon, 'Ntyilo Ntyilo', felt Tracey's influence on his own vocal group, the Gay Darkies, in the 1940s:

> When the group decided, in 1947, that they wanted to make a record, their [broad] repertoire caused problems. Hugh Tracey had recently been put in charge of Gallo's Black recording activities. . . . Tracey's antipathy towards any Black music that was not strictly indigenous was well-estab-lished, and he turned down the Gay Darkies after they refused to record something 'traditional'. Silinga had crossed swords with Tracey the previous year when he had stood up during a lecture at the BMSC to challenge Tracey's assertion that Black music utilised a different scale from Western music.[36]

Something similar was being engineered in Cape Town, with attempts to bring the Coon troupes of the coloured (mixed heritage) community wholly under white control and shift their language of performance from English to

A school band in the 1930s showing minstrel influence. *Credit: Historical papers, University of Witwatersrand Library*

Afrikaans. The political identity of the Coon troupes had been another contested site during the early twentieth century. American and West Indian radicals had been among those settling in Cape Town, and some troupes from District 6, the city's most diverse working-class area, had given explicit support to the African People's Organisation, a party with similar politics to the ANC's precursor, the Native National Congress. Many troupes without any declared party allegiance had been involved in economic struggles in the 1920s to resist the exploitation of their displays by white promoters. By the late 1930s, however, radical and aspirant middle-class members of Cape Town's coloured community were denouncing the New Year Coon Carnival for sowing the seeds of hooliganism, playing into white stereotypes, or accepting segregated audiences.[37] While the home language of most troupes was Afrikaans, the language of the parades and songs was English and the repertoire and references jazzy and international, particularly American. This did not accord with a hardening official position that the coloured community was an 'appendage to the Whites'—which meant culturally Afrikaans. In 1939, the academic and poet I. D. du Plessis, 'seconded by musicologist Percival Kirby, was . . . the one to insist that Coons should abandon "imported songs" and "get back to the melodies of the country and its people."'[38] By the late 1940s, on the eve of apartheid, du Plessis had become a regular adjudicator at carnival song contests, and Afrikaans songs were shouldering their way into the repertoire.

If it was the modernism of black city workers that alarmed the white authorities, it was the 'backwardness' of their lifestyle that distressed their more genteel peers. Black newspapers like *Bantu World* and *Umteteli wa Bantu* began to fill with letters and editorials condemning the marabi menace: '[I]f, as one letter-writer in the *Bantu World* put it in 1937, "we are making headway" towards "civilisation", then the danger of marabi was that it would "retard our steady progress" precisely because of its "backwardness" and "paganism" '.[39]

Residence restrictions meant the urban black elite often lived close to marabi culture, but these clerks, teachers, and pastors saw the lifestyle as tempting the youth with the most backward elements of rural recreation combined with the lowest kind of Western culture. Ragtime and the new jazz, infiltrating via radio, records, and the cinema, were often castigated similarly for their moral dangers.

The music was indeed dangerously seductive: Kingforce Silgee and several other early jazz performers were the children of pastors and teachers. Jazz and gospel trumpeter Banzi Bangani, who grew up in the East Rand mining town of Springs in the 1930s, tells a typical story:

> My father was not in good health, and he was an *umfundisi* (a priest). Now when I would take the trumpet home, my father would scold me. He'd say: 'Go away with that thing. You're making noise, and I am sick. I don't want to see you with it—those are the Devil's things!' Then I would just leave home with a sad heart, and go to the mine dumps where it was very quiet, attempting songs. The first song I attempted was 'Tuxedo Junction', and the next was 'In the Mood', which I liked, because it had a bit of complicated fingering.[40]

These respectable parents had very different musical models. Mission-run schools had offered opportunities to acquire a high level of music education, as pianist Pat Mashikiza from Queenstown describes:

> I grew up in a piano home, [and when] I was sent to St Matthews College, there was nobody playing the church organ; the British lady who was in charge had gone home. So the chaps said: 'You must play organ'. I said no, I only know piano. They said: 'Shut up, we know you read music— Hey! Here's an organist!' So on Sunday morning we were standing in line with the other pupils and the master came to me: 'Can you please play?' I was committed, and I told myself I mustn't make any mistakes. As organist, I was privileged, exempted from doing manual (workshop) so I could practice. And even when the lady teacher came back, she was impressed and said: 'No, you're doing fine. Carry on.'[41]

Some of this social group had studied overseas, on scholarships at American or British seminaries and colleges. Many were involved in temperance movements—seeing alcohol abuse as a cause, rather than a symptom, of the dislocation of black community life—or were leaders of youth movements like the Pathfinders (Black Christian Boy Scouts). All saw the achievements of 'Africans in America' as a key model of 'what black people could achieve in a white-dominated world'.[42] They admired 'Jubilee' choral and classical music and colleges like Booker T. Washington's Tuskegee with its message of self-reliant self-improvement.

School and church halls provided venues for concerts and recitals, an extension of the old 'tea meetings' where funds were raised by competitive bidding for a soloist or a song. The repertoire—building on the tradition of songs like Caluza's 'iLand Act'—sometimes had a political dimension, particularly at events organised by the Teachers' Union. Hymns and other composed works—including, for example, sections of Handel's *Messiah*—dominated the *eisteddfod* choir contests for a floating trophy organised by the South African Bantu Board of Music, based at the BMSC (and replaced, in 1947, by the Johannesburg Bantu Music Festival Committee).

But the black middle classes needed space for relaxation as well as edification, and this musically literate community also patronised vaudeville performances with music, comedy, and genre scenes reminiscent of the old minstrel shows. Out of and alongside these (and often featuring the same performers) grew what music historian Christopher Ballantine describes as 'the crucible in which black jazz developed in South Africa'[43]: the institution of so-called concert and dance.

Curfews, pass laws, and the difficulty of transport between township and town also helped shape 'concert and dance', an all-night performance typically running between 8:00 P.M. and 4:00 A.M. As the name suggests, the first half was a seated vaudeville concert; then the chairs were cleared to the sides of the hall, and the second half was a dance. Concert and dance employed large ensembles, modeled on American swing bands, whose sound, unlike marabi, was big enough to fill the communal halls newly built in the townships. Established city venues like the BMSC and Inchcape Hall in Johannesburg were well patronised by better-paid workers, and male domestic workers from the neighbouring British colonies of Rhodesia and Nyasaland (Zimbabwe, Zambia, and Malawi) gained a particular reputation for their ballroom dancing skills. As the 1940s advanced, however, the waltzes of the 'dance' segment were crowded by something far hotter, faster, and jazzier.

The archetypal concert and dance entertainers were the Motsieloas, Griffiths and Emily, who led a number of variety troupes, most notably the Pitch Black Follies. Both were teachers. Griffiths had begun his working life in Kimberley, studied elocution in London, and returned to work as an actor, voice coach, and impresario. He used to recite nursery rhymes in English as part of his stage performance, to demonstrate his command of both the language and the accent. Griffiths was an ardent advocate of black education and had been the patron of Z. K. Matthews, the first African graduate from a South African university (who later went on to become an ANC activist, treason trialist, and Botswana diplomat).[44] Guitarist General Duze remembered the Motsieloas' troupe as the place where he learned to dance: 'That's where I met Langkop, in their cast. He taught me tap-dancing. That got me far on the stage. He was the one who did the Fred

Astaire/Ginger Rogers thing with one of the ladies in the cast'.[45] Griffiths returned to London to record, and later became the first black talent scout for a
South African record company, Gallo, almost until his death in 1945. Emily was
a respected pianist and arranger, who played for the couple's various bands for
more than twenty years and with the Merry Blackbirds, as well as singing for a
time with her own female quartet in Cape Town, the Dangerous Blues Girls. She
started a piano school in Alexandra Township and was a fierce disciplinarian, as
Blackbirds vocalist Marjorie Pretorius remembered: 'Emily Motsieloa was a no-
nonsense workaholic and a perfectionist. We rehearsed at the BMSC in the evenings, four times a week. It was no child's play. I was cooked as a musician in
that tradition of discipline'.[46]

The various popular music styles overlaid and penetrated one another, so
that it is hard to set a definite date at which one style was 'in' and its predecessor
'out'. In the 1930s, the popular dance that succeeded marabi was *tsaba-tsaba*,
tracing a rhythmic pattern of advance and retreat between partners, with the
dancers separated by a cry of *'Tsaba!'* ('Get away!') when they drew too close.
*Tsaba-tsaba* did not start its life as an elite dance; it was far too obviously traditional in inspiration, but like many pop styles everywhere, it soon found its way
into vogueish up-market dance halls and on to the sharpest modern recordings.
In 1939, the Motsieloas recorded 'Tsaba-Tsaba No 1': the melody, with its stops
and starts, mirrors that dance. However, the metre is regular and the singing
relentlessly jolly, very far from a cue for dance hall closeness. By the mid-1940s,
Godfrey Moloi's sharp eye for style reveals how Americanised dancing and costume were becoming (*tsotsi* being a version of the term *zoot suit*):

It was the end of World War II and the tsotsi came in. This narrow-
bottomed style of trouser was named the tsotsi because of the shape and
parents never liked it. I remember some parents, teachers and cops used
to ask you to take them off without taking your shoes off; this was quite
a problem! But all in all the boys looked good in their black tsotsis, white
shirt out, black and white shoes and straw hat: the Panama. The girls
looked good too in their white wedge-heeled shoes, red or blue German-
print dresses with white stripes around the hem and neck, white berets
or Mexican straw hats. That was the time of the Jim-Jam jive and the
Jitterbug, which was named from a movie where a young scientist broke
a canned fruit bottle full of bugs in the middle of a dance floor and the
bugs spread, biting everybody on their legs. Then the dance step changed,
the band tempo changed and it was the beginning of the jumping, kicking
and swaying: the Jumpin' Jive.[47]

It was at concert and dance that many youngsters of the 1930s and 1940s,
like Thandi Klaasen, first heard something they later identified as jazz:

The Jazz Maniacs. *Credit: Historical papers, University of Witwatersrand Library*

I didn't know what is or was jazz then. I could only hear this beautiful sound and listening to a singer like Emily Kwenane, and she would [scat] and I would say to myself: *Thixo!* (Lord!) what is this woman doing with this song? I would run to the Communal Hall to hear this wonderful woman singing and my foot is beating all the time.[48]

The most popular bands of the era in Johannesburg were probably the Merry Blackbirds and the Jazz Maniacs. The very first professional band had been Japanese Express, which started in 1929; basing its instrumentation on earlier coloured bands that featured a violinist, the Japanese Express played the larger marabi parties and some more refined socials. By the 1940s, the Blackbirds and the Maniacs were only two from a list of more than two dozen in Johannesburg. Across the country, the list multiplies: the No-Name Swingsters in Springs; the African Quavers in Kimberley; the Chisa Ramblers in Germiston; the New Synfonators in Bloemfontein; Dalton Khanyile and the Chromatic Swing Band in Durban; William 'Sax-O-Wills' Mbali and his Blue Rhythm Syncopators in Queenstown; Chris Columbus and the Bantu Young Ideas in the Cape. At this time, pianist Abdullah Ibrahim was working in another Cape Town group called the Tuxedo Swingsters. Hugh Masekela adds more on bands, musical literacy, venues, and audiences:

The Merrymakers were a big band from Springs, but they couldn't read.
They played everything by ear. The Harlem Swingsters out of Alexandra,
the Jazz Maniacs, some of them read, like a lot of bands out of the Eastern
Cape, like the Modernaires. It was also a matter of accessibility of reading—to read music, you had to be taught, and a lot of the music teachers
were here in Johannesburg, in Sophiatown. But Griffiths Motsieloa who
was very schooled came from . . . the vaudeville revues, and they made
[music] like Dixieland. There was an elite coming out of the townships.
There were different types of audiences for the Harlem Swingsters and
the Jazz Maniacs and those people. The elite didn't go to the same dances
as the others. But every township had a municipal hall. The old townships
maybe had five to ten thousand people. Some were too small [to have
halls]. But Springs, Brakpan, Benoni, Germiston, Roodeport, Randfontein, Krugersdorp, Boksburg: all those places had municipal halls. And
that was the circuit of these groups. In every township on every weekend
there was a concert and dance Friday, Saturday, through Sunday.[49]

Where did the players find their music? Despite the suspicions with which
more elite patrons and players viewed marabi, input came from that source.
Some younger or sharper marabi players, working in the last years of its era,
acquired brass instruments and moved across into band work. Peter Rezant, the
immensely sophisticated bandleader who led the Blackbirds, described how the
tunes, too, migrated: 'You couldn't avoid it at that time. . . . They were little
ditties, you know, coming from the townships. . . . And somebody would be
suggesting, who'd been toying around with them, and ultimately we'd play
them'.[50]

Rezant's dazzling half-century career began in the late 1920s, and the Merry
Blackbirds (whose edge, everyone agreed, was that every member was a schooled
musician) played to audiences from mineworkers to white socialites in Johannesburg's northern suburbs. Journalist, musician, and Pat Matshikiza's uncle, Todd
Matshikiza wrote a retrospective in the 1950s, beginning with a visit to a dance:

The hall was chock-full of people. The hall was chock-full of music. It
was good music from Peter Rezant and his Merry Blackbirds. I said to
the fellow next to me, 'What do you think of this fellow, Peter Rezant?'
The fellow next to me said, 'Man, firs' class'. . . . [In 1936, at the Empire
Exhibition,] I saw the large, huge showboat on a big lake, 'Peter Rezant
and his famous Merry Blackbirds Orchestra appearing here daily and
nightly'. I went to the showboat every day. Judges, lawyers, policemen
and pimps. Ladies and gentlemen and thieves. They didn't come in ones.
They didn't come in twos. They came in tens to hear Peter Rezant and
his Merry Blackbirds. . . . My cousin Joe says he felt real small at your
last dance. You and your band turned out smart. Kitty bows, nugget

shines, toothbrush smiles, gold cufflinks. And there he was, waltzing, waltzing—in brown shoes and grey pants. Heavens! Thanks. Firs' class, firs' class, Peter Rezant.[51]

The repertoire also featured the more up-tempo 'ragtime' compositions of men like Caluza and later Wilfred Sentso. Sentso, who had headed the music department at Charlotte Manye's Wilberforce Institute, went on to found both the Synco Music Schools (with branches in several townships) and the vaudeville band the Synco Fans, to edit the first black music magazine, *African Sunrise*, and to publish sheet music of local compositions. American material came to dominate concert and dance programmes (particularly the 'dance' segment). Its main sources were the new electric media—gramophone records, movies, and radio—as trombonist Jonas Gwangwa describes:

> Our people were listening to American records and seeing from the movies what people were doing out there—the Cab Calloways, the Duke Ellingtons. All those movies came in. And our guys were reading music by then. The Merry Blackbirds, the Jazz Maniacs were some of those disciplined bands, reading music, costumed and all that like any other big band in the US at the time. . . . Some of that core of musicians were also people who'd played in the entertainment unit of the army in World War II. People like Gwigwi Mwrebi, you know, who was a sergeant in the army.[52]

Todd Matshikiza wrote: 'Africa was drunk with American and English works, and quite inevitably too . . . the missionaries had taught that the music of Africa was barbarian'.[53] The passionate affair with African-American culture probably reached its zenith in Sophiatown in the 1950s. The admiration had a range of motives, both political and cultural. Poet Don Mattera remembers listening to the South African Broadcasting Corporation jazz programme in Sophiatown in the 1940s and hearing a message as well as a sound:

> At 10-o-clock they would give us 15 minutes of jazz, and we would leave what we were doing every Saturday to switch on our little Pilot radios and stand and do our jiving there [in] this brief moment of generosity from our oppressors. . . . It's not just jazz music; it's coupled with the hopes and aspirations of the native people, of the African-American people.[54]

There had been short broadcasts from white municipal radio in South Africa since the 1920s; gradually, broadcast hours and footprints were extended, and a 'rediffusion' system of cable services, initially to the Natal hostels and by the 1950s into townships like Orlando, was created. Until the consolidation of the rigidly ethnically divided Radio Bantu in 1960, music policy was inconsistent, with some division of days and hours for different languages and traditional styles, but also time devoted to both American and South African jazz.

Listening on the East Rand, trumpeter Johnny Mekoa got the same political message:

> You had those 78 breakable records that came from the States. You had those needle gramophones that you had to wind to get the spring full. And you had records of the Count Basie Orchestra, Duke Ellington, you know. . . . People were listening to this music at home because we felt this is our music and these are our black heroes. The attraction to that kind of music was that the rhythms were more like our mbaqanga'. [*Mbaqanga* was another term for some types of South African jazz.][55]

The America that was loved was both illusory and real. The reality was that 'Africans in America' had achieved much formal emancipation from the kind of legal oppression that rendered life for all South Africans of colour intolerable— and that was to increase. That achievement had come through a struggle whose history was known to politically aware South Africans. In his autobiography, author Peter Abrahams writes of entering the BMSC in the mid-'30s in search of a job. The first voice he heard was that of Paul Robeson, played on a gramophone. He also discovered the writings of W. E. B. Du Bois: 'For all the thousands of miles, for all the ocean, between the land and people of whom he wrote, Du Bois might have been writing about my land and people . . . Countee Cullen . . . Langston Hughes . . . St[e]rling Brown . . . Claude McKay . . . Jean Toomer. . . . I became a nationalist, a colour nationalist, through the writings of men and women who lived a world away from me'.[56] African-American institutions of education and culture functioned and produced graduates of high calibre. The reality also included creative modern music, which, for many listeners besides Johnny Mekoa, had a flavour of 'our music' (and which, at that time, was attracting fans and imitators in many countries). America held out the promise that 'we can do it too' (a phrase used in black newspapers of the time and by many of the interviewees for this book). America also connoted a sophisticated modernism that stood in opposition to both the rural, tribal image the authorities were trying to foist on black urbanites and the close-minded Calvinism of those authorities themselves. After the 1936 British Empire Exhibition (when some white and foreign visitors refused to believe that the jazz bands providing entertainment were not African-American), the hope developed that following overseas models might lead to overseas success. However, the authorities frequently denied passports to black players even when they had firm offers of work abroad.

The persistent illusion was that those suave, tuxedo-clad players behind their music stands in the movies enjoyed complete equality, respect, and participation at every level of American society. South African exiles twenty years later rapidly discovered the truth behind that dream.

More people loved American music than knew the full story. Yet there was contact between black South Africans and their African-American peers beyond the rather sheltered experience of scholarship seminarians. Hugh Masekela talks of marriages between black South African women and African-American sailors:

> You know, if you go to Brooklyn, for instance, you'll find a lot of old grandmothers who married black merchant seamen in the early 1920s, 30s and 40s. And they used to come back and forth to South Africa [bringing] their records and telling people about Louis Armstrong and Count Basie. . . .[57]

Masekela also talks about the ports as a continuing source of recordings and information:

> That's why, when you heard [the musical] *Zonk*, for instance, those guys got all that from the negro jazz fans that they found when they travelled with the African revues. [The *Zonk* troupe had performed for other Allied soldiers during its wartime life.] Even when I travelled with the African Jazz and Varieties in 1956—Cape Town, Port Elizabeth, East London and Durban—as soon as we got there, Skip [Pahlane] and those guys, they knew all the hotels, the boarding houses where the negro seamen were staying. 'Cos we could also live in those hotels, like Mrs Phillips' [place] in Durban, for instance.[58]

The same had been true for one of the great players of the earlier era: guitarist Alpheus Nkosi, as his colleague General Duze recounted:

> Jazz in Durban in the 40s used to be very strong. If I remember well, there was a tenorman: Khanyile, Dalton Khanyile. Wow! Great tenorman. And a humble guy, very soft-spoken, no pride—a real Zulu gentleman. I don't remember the name of all his trio, but it had Alpheus Nkosi on guitar, a buddy of mine [w]ho wrote [the song] 'Lizzie, M'Thandwa Sam'. . . . We used to call Alpheus 'Yankee', because he spoke American English most of the time: 'I'll tell ya what! Dat other guy dere, blows bull, man! Don't play no jazz, nix!' . . . Alpheus became an American because he was always mixing with the sailors, being in Durban.[59]

Imported records were hugely important as a source of new approaches and tunes. In the late 1930s, Ntemi Piliso 'started listening to the music of Johnny Hodges, who was playing with the Duke Ellington Band at the time. I was so impressed with him that I started imitating him with the pennywhistle because I was not blowing an instrument then'.[60] Duze 'had a group of young people that I used to live with in George Goch [Eastern Native Township]. We used to queue at Polliacks [record shop] through the nights to get records from America. We'd spend Saturday night, and a bottle of brandy—yeah! The whole night till Sunday morning listening to jazz music. Everybody would bring his music and we'd sit and play.'[61] In Cape Town, pianist Henry February, who was already entertaining audiences with 'ragtime', was thunderstruck when he heard

> Teddy Wilson in the late 40s. That's the first time I heard jazz—well, I didn't even know such a term as jazz. Didn't know what it was. But when I heard that kind of piano playing, I was completely unconscious. As if I'd been hit. . . . Then, I couldn't play jazz. Wasn't a jazzman; I used to play syncopation—what was called ragtime. And I used to sit at home and think how the hell did these people do a thing like that? How can they be so clever as to be able to be improvising around? And I thought that I'll have to go to the best teachers in town, white teachers in studios in the centre of town. But that didn't do anything for me. Eventually, I thought the only thing for it is I'll have to get some music, and some records, and try to get it up here [in my head]. And I managed to get it.[62]

By the 1930s, local records were also being produced and sold. In 1926, the Gallo company had been founded, backed by the English Decca company, and in 1932 set up its first recording studio in Johannesburg. Before that date, South African artists (including Caluza, for the HMV label) had been taken to London to record. Companies saw the market potential in rural styles, particularly the Zulu close-harmony vocal music that they knew migrant mineworkers would buy. The most famous recording of that genre was 'Mbube', by Solomon Linda and His Original Evening Birds. 'Mbube' was picked up (as 'Wimoweh') around the world in the following four decades, by, among others, Pete Seeger (who later tried to find out how to pay royalties) and by Jimmy Dorsey, Yma Sumac, the Tokens, the Springfields, the Spinners, the Tremeloes, Glen Campbell and Karl Dallas, Robert John, Brian Eno, and countless movie scores and advertising jingles (who didn't). Had royalties been paid, the sum has been estimated at over $15 million.[63] Only in 2003 did the Gallo record company begin to make restitution to Linda's impoverished descendants.

Early marabi was not put on record, although some recorded vaudeville versions of marabi songs (including 'Ntebetjana uFana Nemfene') have survived to illustrate the chords, if not the feeling. David Coplan suggests that this was mainly due to 'the record companies' ignorance of the size, sophistication and commitment of urban African communities, rather than from any conscious desire to advance homeland identification among them'.[64] Ignorance there was, and it persisted. (In the early 1990s, record companies were still issuing much of their local black jazz catalogue on cassette at a time when township jazz *stokvels* were spending thousands on imported American jazz CDs at city-centre shops.) But there were other reasons for the companies' neglect of marabi, and one was ideology. Gallo's first A&R man was Griffiths Motsieloa, the sophisticated vaudevillian who scorned 'low-class' music. As South African jazz came to sound more sophisticated and international, he began to commission it. Within ten years he was made assistant to ethnomusicologist Hugh Tracey, who was passionate about preserving traditional sounds. Tracey's distaste for syncretic music brought him very close to the official view that black workers were only temporarily city dwellers and should stay true to the 'pure' tribal music of their official rural homelands.

Coplan also says marabi musicians feared that recording their music would allow other artists to steal it.[65] Many early players certainly feared the theft implicit in the recording deals they got, which usually included complete rights to the master, no royalties, and sometimes purchase outright of the name of the band, so that recordings by other musicians could be issued under it. Kingforce Silgee often told interviewers that the Jazz Maniacs held off recording for this reason. In 1941, Wilfred Sentso wrote an article in *Umteteli wa Bantu*, citing a flat fee of four guineas for all rights to both sides of a 78 rpm disc, and commenting: '[M]usic houses do a large turnover in Bantu recorded music while the artists themselves go starving. . . . After all, the songs are yours, the voices are yours, the work is yours. The firm only comes in to collect the profits. . . . Fats Waller gets four hundred pounds'.[66]

The first jazz recording, 'Izikhalo Zika Z-Boy', backed by 'Tsaba Tsaba No. 1', was made by the Jazz Maniacs in 1939. The title translates formally as 'Z-Boy's Lament', and the lyrics deal with 'a sense of wandering in the wilderness, abandonment and fear about the future'.[67] In fact, it would be better called 'Z-Boy's Blues': an African blues of harsh city life with short, repeated verses delivered in tones of weary resignation. Z-Boy was the band's leader, Solomon 'Zulu-boy' Cele, whom Ntemi Piliso remembered as the moderniser of marabi. Todd Matshikiza told Cele's story in *Drum* magazine in 1957:

Then there was a man, a transport driver in Johannesburg, whose ear for sound and mind for creativeness was driving him crazy. His name was 'Zulu Boy' Cele. He said that this big bold sound [of swing] was ideal for transporting the musical ideas he had in mind. He had been, for many years, a house pianist in the Marabi joints, and he always wanted to paint Marabi tones on broader canvases and bigger scales. He bought a saxophone and learned to play it. In his band were Wilson Silgee, who studied at the Adams School of Music; Jacob Moeketsi, who had studied classical music; guitarist Victor Hamilton; Palmer Mochumi and Isaac Nkosi. He said, Let's go and see the movies. *Pennies from Heaven* they heard there, and Z-Boy said to them, 'Listen carefully to that piece, we've got to play it tonight'. And they played it that night. . . . So much in demand were the Jazz Maniacs that in 1944 they were accepting double engagements because they did not wish to disappoint their patrons.[68]

These double engagements led to lawsuits, bankruptcy, and decline, and Cele was mysteriously murdered, his body found on a railway line in 1944.

In their heyday, the Maniacs were credited with playing covers of recordings 'exactly like the American bands were playing'.[69] Yet while many artists strove to reproduce faithfully what they heard on the discs, others did not, and as the 1940s progressed, this search for indigenous inspiration intensified. 'We used to listen to a lot of records—Louis Armstrong, Buck Clayton, Harry James, whatever. And then we'd try to imitate the guys, but also come out with what we have within. Not exactly tracing everything that they do, but now and then add up something in our solos and improvisation', recalled Banzi Bangani.[70]

The bands also wrote original tunes and played them in swing style, as Hugh Masekela explains:

Our people had the art of interpreting and picking up things from everywhere and making them their own. So you find the Harlem Swingsters and the Jazz Maniacs and the Savoys would play all the Duke Ellington and Count Basie favourites, like 'One-O-Clock Jump' and 'Take the A Train'. . . . They'd play all the hits. . . . But then they'd have things like 'Tamatie Sous' which were their own songs, and which were orchestrated in the same way.[71]

It was not just for recording that the rewards were small—although it was for recording that they were smallest. Sometimes, bands had a nonplaying 'owner' rather than a leader. Ntemi Piliso's first training came in a band owned by the mysterious and elegant 'Casablanca' who arrived in Alexandra Township, set up a band—and then disappeared into jail. '[The owner] made a certain price and out of that price he would divide 20–30% amongst the players. Then the rest goes to him. That's because the instruments were his', said Joseph Molifi, trombonist with the Sharpetown Swingsters.[72] Players could expect fees of around 15 shillings for a show at the start of their careers or in unknown bands. An established star could earn far more than that, out of the proceeds of what might be up to a guinea per head entrance fee at the best venues. While less successful bands in less well-resourced communities needed to maintain nonmusical day jobs in order to eat, the stars did so mainly to secure the pass for city residence. Blacks could not be registered as professional musicians; the classification they fell under was either 'day labourer' or 'vagrant'.

Building a music career was often a matter of opportunity: access to tuition, to instruments, to places where there was an audience. For those without music-reading skills, it was a matter of apprenticeship, as trumpeter Banzi Bangani describes. His hero was trumpeter David Mzimkulu, one of the stars of the tour-ing *Zonk* band:

> [When they were in town,] there was a certain house where they would put up and drink there. I'd steal money at home, and go to him in the morning, wake him up. 'Mzimkulu? Eh, Bra' Mzimkulu? I'm here. Please play your trumpet for me'. He says, no buti (*little brother*). And then I'd tell the auntie there, please give him a nip (*shot of brandy*). Then he'd take that nip and say: 'Right, now let's play something.' He was my first inspiration.[73]

The apprenticeship system was still going strong a decade later, when another East Rand trumpeter, Johnny Mekoa of Benoni, began playing. When he started with the No-Name Swingsters in Benoni, he was nicknamed 'Schoolboy':

> It was a great oral tradition. They would make the saxophone part by playing, and you had to listen to your part. First the saxophones, then the trombones, then the trumpet players and the rhythm section and then you hear the band cook, man! And then he points at you and says: 'Schoolboy! Solo!' And you know, there were no fake books at that time, you never knew about chord progressions and what-what—but it was [by] ear![74]

Sometimes, the chances came through pure serendipity. Banzi Bangani was the cousin of another trumpeter, Elijah Nkwanyana, hailed by journalists as the most exciting of his generation. In the early 1940s, Bangani played in a Springs band owned by Peter Ntsane, alongside a couple of his teachers. The younger Elijah wasn't yet playing in public, though the two used to practice together. Their break came when one teacher got delayed:

> Then I said to Peter Ntsane: 'Look, man, I can play this thing. And I am not the only one. Look up there at the guy who is peeping through the window'. (Because he had no money to come into the show) 'That is Elijah. My cousin'. . . . So I told Elijah we must rush home and put on our long clothes. He took his brother's trouser. He just folded that thing up with a big round lump at the bottom because it was so big. . . . The first song was 'Tuxedo Junction', and we went for it. We did it with something modern, you know. It was our thing that was within us. Man! The applause that went down there! . . . And the teachers went and told Peter Ntsane: 'We are not going to sit here and be outplayed by our own students. We are quitting'. And they left on the spot.[75]

If records were important in shaping the sound of the new jazz, the cinema played an equal role in shaping its image, and that of the fans who followed it.

By the 1930s, several commercial cinemas open to blacks had been established in Johannesburg, and these were augmented by free film showings, outdoors in the townships, and at centres like the BMSC. One famous 'bioscope'—as South Africans sometimes still call cinema—was the Odin, which also staged concerts and talent contests in the manner of the Apollo Theater in Harlem. Dolly Rathebe was a heroine of the new jazz scene, famed for her talent, her beauty, and her spirit—all of which are still apparent sixty years later. She recalls how she learned her first American songs:

> We'd ask the owner of the cinema—I remember it was the Reno Bioscope—to please, please bring us American films and we would pack that cinema. I remember *Cabin in the Sky,* where Lena Horne sang 'Salt Lake City Blues' . . . and then when we were going home we'd rehearse the song to get it right.[76]

Nonsinging fans, too, were rehearsing material from the movies—not always to the same constructive effect. George 'Kortboy' Mpalweni became one of the most notorious Sophiatown gangsters. The cinema was a big influence on his youth:

> In the 30s, [the Odin] was known as the Undermoon Hall, the spot where African jazz was born. The other cinema was the Balansky, a low-class rather degenerate movie house. There was always the danger at the Balansky of an empty bottle hitting you from behind, or of having someone urinate on you if you sat below the balcony. . . . In the busy streets [the youngsters] would gather around in a group, one relating a motion picture with simulated sound provided by the rest. Gangster films were the most popular.[77]

There were few strict social boundaries in black music and entertainment. As part of concert and dance sessions, singers and instrumentalists would perform in refined tones for the concert, and some would come back after the intermission to play hot for the dance portion. But some bands had a character that spoke more to one end of the social scale than the other, as Dolly Rathebe explains:

> The vocalist for the Jazz Maniacs, Emily Kwenane, she was a balladeer. Graceful, you know, where our parents used to go with their ball-gowns. The Merry Blackbirds were a sophisticated lot. Whenever they played, it would be an occasion. But if it was the Maniacs at the Odin Cinema, it would be house full. Oh, I was very good at the jitterbug. I used to dance very well. I was a springbok; a real tomboy. . . .[78]

In the same way, economic divisions among people of colour were flexible. The tendency of the laws, even before 1948, was to push black workers down and together: the teacher could never become a superintendent and might live beside the manual labourer, who might himself be an engineer 'classified out' of his trade by job reservation. But both (if they could afford it) could buy freehold property in some suburbs, and until those laws were tightened and codified after 1948, there was a little space to grow. At the end of Chapter 1, we left Lucky Michaels' mother running a bustling shebeen in Doornfontein.

> Off the proceeds of the shebeen, we bought a restaurant. My mother had been working all this time and she decided: look, this working thing is enough now. What we do is, let's open our own restaurant. My father being a cook, he left his boss and was the cook in his own restaurant, a few blocks from the shebeen: Michaels' Restaurant. [Nelson] Mandela and them used to eat there before he was arrested. This was in 1947. There were about five good restaurants for black people operating in the city at that time: Michaels' Restaurant, Blue Lagoon, Kapitan's, Vela Mabuza had a restaurant. . . . It just depended on the entrepreneurship of the person. Like my father, Felicia Mabuza's grandfather with his res-taurant, the Indian guy with Kapitan's. Those were the entrepreneurs of that period, and those entrepreneurs could buy property because there was no Group Areas Act yet. Obviously, with the restaurant my parents had, it could be a venue and that was how my father met up with General Duze and performers like that.[79]

The city gave a little of that role flexibility to women. One of the reasons for marabi's negative reputation had been that both music and beer-selling created a space to subvert women's conventional roles. In the reserves and the neigh-bouring British colonies, white administrators had adopted and codified a rigid interpretation of customary law, which accorded far better with Victorian patri-archy than tradition or village reality in its views of women, marriage, and mor-als. The overfarming of already poor ground since the Land Act, and a migrant labour system that regularly ripped families apart, made living within those rules increasingly impracticable. The women who came to the cities had the possibility of different lives, though the morality of city women was relentlessly dissected by male commentators, both black and white.

The format of vaudeville made women performers indispensable, and articu-late, educated young women with business skills—again, those musical daughters of preachers and teachers—could also earn a living from promotion and man-agement.

> The leading lights of the Pitch Black Follies were Lindi Makhanya, Elea-nor and Babsy Oliphant and Snowy Radebe. Although unusual, it was not unheard of for women to manage their own vaudeville troupes. One of Durban's most prominent companies from the mid-forties to the early

fifties was the Streamline Sisters ('brothers' were also included), which
was founded and directed by Paulina Phillips. Other troupes led by
women included the Madcaps from Mafeking founded by Mrs S M Mo-
lema; the Movietone Cabaret Girls led by Florence K Nthatisi of Bloemfontein; the Raven Girls of Pretoria managed by Mrs L Kgokong; Miss V
N Plaatje's Rhythm Girls of Kimberley; and the all-female Merry Makers
of Bloemfontein who were led and managed by Johanna Phahlane, also
an outspoken journalist and women's rights activist. [80]

Recordings and movies showed African-American women prominent as
singers with the swing big bands, and these role models also offered inspiration.
Marjorie Pretorius became a vocalist for the Merry Blackbirds in 1940. Before
that, her career had begun as a school chorister, winning prizes at BMSC *eistedd-
fods*. In Orlando Township, she recounts, 'I was discovered by Solomon "Zulu-
boy" Cele of the Jazz Maniacs. After recruiting me, Zuluboy formed a four-girl
group, the Harlem Babies. Our backing band was the Maniacs and our regular
venue was the BMSC'. Pretorius was the first vocalist to front a dance band in
the American style. She then worked with Sentso's Synco Fans before joining
Rezant. Pretorius named her biggest vocal influences as Emily Kwenane and Ella
Fitgerald,[81] the same pair of vocal stylists cited by many other musicians, including Dolly Rathebe and Thandi Klaasen.
     One of the attractions of concert and dance was the 'two-band stage', a de-
scendant of the competitive singing of *itimitin* and a parallel to American bands'
cutting contests. In the early 1950s, when close-harmony male groups came to
the fore, Klaasen saw a way to give the two-band stage a gender dimension:

> As time went by, I saw groups like the Manhattan Brothers, and realised
> that there were no groups of females. So I said to myself no, man, we
> have to challenge these men! [Klaasen then formed the Quad Sisters vocal
> quartet.] And I spoke to Dambudzo [Mdledle of the Manhattan Brothers]
> and he said 'Lord! We'll each take one side and challenge you!' Our first
> challenge to the Manhattan Brothers was at the Bantu Men's Social Cen-
> tre and the place was packed.[82]

When asked who won, she laughs uproariously and spreads her hands and
says: 'It wasn't really that kind of competition—but of course, my dear, the
women did!'
     Ideas of women's equality were not new among female performers. It had
been chorister and jubilee singer Charlotte Manye who had founded the Wom-
en's League of the Native National Congress, which, as early as 1920, had successfully challenged women's pass laws (and later became the Women's League
of the ANC). And it was Johanna Phahlane (as 'Giddy' Phahlane, leader of the
Merry Makers vaudevillians of Bloemfontein) who wrote a regular column in

**The Manhattan Brothers.**

*Bantu World* in the mid-1930s (under the nom de plume 'Lady Porcupine') advocating women's political rights:

> [M]odern woman refuses to spend her time dressing only for the captiva-
> tion of gentlemen, as some may think, but will struggle hard to earn
> her living in many ways as a nurse, teacher, singer, actress, dance, cook,
> dressmaker, housekeeper, laundress etc. and is very much anxious to
> make men comprehend that she can do without them. . . . [Modern
> woman] also has the right to struggle for freedom. Women of the race,
> we have to march—Forward![83]

It was in the 1940s that the various currents of South African resistance—of
women, of workers, of people of colour dictated to by whites, of Africans colonised by the West—began to be articulated more consistently as parts of a single
struggle. All of these tensions affected black musicians, personally and through
the general discourse of life in their communities. Many bandleaders of the time
denied they were 'political'—although this may have been because publicly declared politics were risky and could have been bad for business, especially for
bands that worked at white functions, as the Merry Blackbirds did. (Peter Rezant
said that staying away from politics 'was the success of the band'.[84]) Nevertheless,
many vaudeville troupes, and the Blackbirds and the Maniacs, played for functions of the ICU, the ANC, and the Communist Party.

Black musicians were also involved in their own labour struggles, as white players squeezed them out of lucrative engagements. Laws clearly forbidding black performers at white venues were not yet in place, although the patchily enforced 1934 Liquor Amendment Act did bar their presence except as menials in places where the sale of white liquor was licenced. But white audiences at spots like the Log Cabin nightclub enjoyed the playing of bands like the Blackbirds and the Maniacs. The whites-only Johannesburg (later Transvaal) Musicians Union waged an ultimately successful campaign to ensure that such gigs dried up. The union secretary's report for 1942–1943 smugly noted:

> Recently the committee has had to handle the question of the employment of Native bands in European places of entertainment. We have interviewed the authorities and with their assistance we have succeeded to date in preventing this form of competition from continuing.[85]

Black musicians lost work, income, the permit for city residence that came with such jobs and the chance to move from semipro to full-time professional status.

Two ANC presidents, Pixley ka Seme and his successor, Dr. A. B. Xuma, had considerable involvement with music. Seme managed a vaudeville company, Pixley's Midnite Follies; Xuma managed Wilfred Sentso's band, and his American-born wife, Mamie Hall, wrote, produced, and directed a grand fund-raising historical revue for the ANC in 1943 called 'The Progress of a Race', whose programme notes advertised: 'Come and see the slaves arrive from Africa. See them work on their master's plantation. Watch them develop and sing the Negro Spirituals. Hear them plan their freedom'. Its last two performances coincided with the ANC national conference.[86]

The mid-1940s were an important period for black politics. In 1944, the ANC Youth League was founded by Anton Lembede, with a membership that included Nelson Mandela and Oliver Tambo. The Youth League was to be a vital forum for the development of more radical policies: its founding declaration advocated 'a people's free society where racial oppression and persecution will be outlawed'.[87] The ANC saw itself as part of the pan-Africanist movement towards freedom for all people of African ancestry in Africa, America, and the Caribbean. Passports were denied to South African representatives hoping to attend the Pan-Africanist Congress held in London in 1945, where delegates included Kwame Nkrumah, Jomo Kenyatta, and W. E. B. Du Bois. In 1946, the African Mine Workers Union called its 75,000 supporters out on strike to demand the minimum wage recommended by a government commission; the strike was brutally crushed as miners were shot and driven back down the mines at gunpoint. This demonstrated the powerlessness of the government's 'Native Representative' structures and fostered increasing cooperation and organisational ties between

the ANC, trade unions, the organisations of South Afric
and the Communist Party.

The pan-Africanism of political movements had its c
ing of notions of excellence in black music. Already, t
commentators were asking: 'What is wrong with us? . . . \
who condemned the Negroes for trying to sing Brahms, I
disregarding their spirituals while Europeans singing the... ...... ....ssing great
fortunes?'[88] In the 'concert' segments of all-night entertainments, vaudevillians
began to seek original material composed by Africans and to aim for genre scenes
that were more authentic and less caricatured. In the 'dance' segments, original
songs were already in the repertoire, and had been since the days of Caluza's
ragtime. The *tsaba-tsaba* dance that succeeded marabi was, in critic Walter
Nhlapo's words, 'dusky South Africa's own creation art',[89] and in this more self-
aware political climate, that made it worthy of praise and emulation.

By the late 1940s, bands were consciously seeking to define and add African
elements to their work, just as black painters working at the newly founded Polly
Street Centre were analysing the visual elements of West and Central African art.
One term for what they were producing was *mbaqanga*. 'We called it African
stomp', said critic Doc Bikitsha, 'because there was this heavy beat . . . of the
Zulu traditional'.[90] *Mbaqanga* was the IsiZulu word for stiff porridge, homely
sustenance for players and audiences. Although in this early period it was used
interchangeably with other terms for the new African jazz, it came over the years
to be applied largely to neotraditional music with jazz-styled instrumentation—at which point, *mbaqanga* acquired less approving connotations, a lot
closer in meaning to 'fast food'.

'Round about the year 1948, the indigenous jazz idiom was born and we
looked around for a tag . . . a name which would describe this form of music
adequately and yet avoid the confusion of overseas influence. We called it African
Jazz', wrote Gideon Jay, music critic for the 1950s magazine *Zonk*.[91] Todd Matshikiza claimed to have been in at the birth, during a tour by the Harlem Swingsters, with whom he was pianist:

African Jazz was reborn. The original product—Marabi—had died when
American swing took over. [We] recaptured the wonderful mood over an
elevating early breakfast of corn bread and black tea in the open air after
a bout of heavy drinking the previous evening. Gray [Mbau] put the corn
bread aside and started blowing something on the five tone scale. We
dropped our corn bread and got stuck into Gray's mood. . . . We syncopated and displaced accents and gave endless variety to our 'native'
rhythms. We were longing for the days of Marabi piano, vital and live.
. . . It was [legendary Marabi musician] Tebejane's original material, but
treated freshly, with a dash of lime.[92]

Vaudevillian supreme R. T. Caluza.

This fresh, astringent music and its politics had only a short time to flower, for it was not the only thing born in 1948. With the victory of the Nationalist Party in that year's election, tough but piecemeal restrictions began to be consolidated and reconstructed into the total state policy of apartheid (separateness). Based on the firm declaration that South Africa was a white man's country, the next four years saw the passage of draconian laws. Mixed marriages, then all sexual contact between whites and nonwhites, were banned. Everyone had to be registered as a member of a specific race group, with, if an urban resident, the conditions of their 'temporary' residence even more tightly defined. The licences, passes, and permissions people of colour needed were consolidated into a single book that had to be carried at all times and produced on demand, with women now universally included. A commission of enquiry into black education eventually resulted in the banning of the curricula that had given the African jazz generation such cultural erudition, and the closing of the schools that taught them, for they were deemed useless to people fit only to be 'hewers of wood and drawers of water'. Any person, and any expressed opinion, could be defined as 'communist' (whatever they believed their own politics to be) and banned. The 1950s Group Areas Act gave the authorities the power to 'declare' any residential areas, anywhere, as the exclusive terrain of a specific race group. Lucky Michaels' father had come full circle:

Obviously, when the Group Areas Act came in, my father lost the restaurant [a]nd had to find a front for it. A white attorney called Smith. And my father became his employee.[93]

# Notes

1. Interview for *Ubuyile* 2000.
2. P. Bonner and L. Segal, *Soweto: A History* (Cape Town: Maskew Miller Longman, 1998, 13.
3. W. Botha and L. Husemeyer, *The City That Leaped to Life* (Johannesburg: private publication, n.d.), 46.
4. Bonner and Segal, op. cit., 14.
5. N. Parsons, *A New History of Southern Africa*, 2nd. ed. (London: Macmillan, 1993), 272.
6. Discussion with the author at North Sea Jazz Festival, 2001.
7. Interview for *Ubuyile*, 2000.
8. C. Ballantine, *Marabi Nights: Early South African Jazz and Vaudeville* (Johannesburg: Ravan Press, 1993), 26.
9. Ibid., 5.
10. Interview for *Ubuyile*, 2000.
11. Dan Twala, quoted in D. Coplan, *In Township Tonight* (Johannesburg: Ravan Press, 1985), 96.

12. Ibid., 97.

13. Ibid., 105.

14. Interview for *Ubuyile,* 2000.

15. Bonner and Segal, op. cit., 14.

16. Interview for *Ubuyile,* 2000.

17. Interview with the author for the *Mail and Guardian,* 1997.

18. *Bantu World,* 18 January 1941.

19. A. K. Lukhele, *Stokvels in South Africa* (Johannesburg: Amagagi Books, 1990), 7–9.

20. Godfrey Moloi, *My Life* (Johannesburg: Jonathan Ball, 1991), 15.

21. Interview for *Ubuyile,* 2000.

22. Bonner and Segal, op. cit., 19.

23. Lukhele, op. cit., 7–8.

24. Bonner and Segal, op. cit., 19.

25. P. La Hausse, *Brewers, Beerhalls and Boycotts* (Johannesburg: History Workshop/Ravan Press, 1988), 22.

26. Bonner and Segal, op. cit., 18.

27. Ballantine, op. cit., 66.

28. Parsons, op. cit., 276.

29. Interview for *Ubuyile,* 2000.

30. Quoted in Ballantine, op. cit., 29–30.

31. P. Kirby, *The Musical Instruments of the Native Races of South Africa,* 2nd ed. (Johannesburg: Witwatersrand University Press, 1968), 257.

32. (Johannesburg) *Two-Tone* 11, no. 2 (1995): 7.

33. Interview for *Ubuyile,* 2000.

34. J. Nauright, *Sport, Cultures and Identities in South Africa* (Cape Town: David Philip, 1997), 116.

35. Hugh Tracey, foreword, in Andrew Tracey, *Dances of the Witwatersrand Gold Mines* (Johannesburg: Johannesburg Music Society, 1952).

36. As told to Rob Allingham, Johannesburg *Two-Tone* 11, no. 11 (1995): 4.

37. D. Constant-Martin, *Coon Carnival* (Cape Town: David Phillip, 1999), 118–121, passim.

38. Ibid., 123.

39. Ballantine, op. cit., 75.

40. Interview for *Ubuyile,* 2000.

41. Ibid.

42. Ballantine, op. cit., 6.

43. Ibid., 12.

44. Interview for *Ubuyile,* 2000.

45. Frieda Matthews, *Remembrances* (Cape Town: Mayibuye Books, 1995), 13.

46. Z. B. Molefe and Mike Mzileni, *A Common Hunger to Sing* (Cape Town: Kwela Books, 1977), n.p.

47. Moloi, op. cit., 3.

48. Interview for *Ubuyile,* 2000.

49. Ibid.

50. Ballantine, op. cit., 29.

51. *Drum*, September 1954; reprinted in M. Nicol, *A Good-Looking Corpse* (London: Minerva, 1995).

52. Interview for *Ubuyile*, 2000.

53. *Drum*, July 1957; in Nicol, op. cit.

54. Interview for *Ubuyile*, 2000.

55. Ibid.

56. Peter Abrahams, *Tell Freedom* (London: Faber & Faber, 1954), 190–197, passim.

57. Interview for *Ubuyile*, 2000.

58. Ibid.

59. Ibid.

60. Ibid.

61. Ibid.

62. Ibid.

63. The full story has been told by Rian Malan in *Rolling Stone* magazine and is accessible on http://www.3rdearmusic.com/forum/mbube.

64. Coplan, op. cit., 137.

65. Ibid.

66. Quoted in Ballantine, op. cit., 46.

67. Ibid., 100.

68. *Drum*, July 1957; reprinted in Nicol, op. cit.

69. Ballantine, op. cit., 15.

70. Interview for *Ubuyile*, 2000.

71. Ibid.

72. Ian Jeffrey, *The Sharpetown Swingsters: Their Will to Survive*, DSG Dissertation Series (Johannesburg: University of the Witwatersrand, 1985), 47.

73. Interview for *Ubuyile*, 2000.

74. Interview for *Ubuyile*, 2000.

75. Ibid.

76. Ibid.

77. Derrick Thema, *Kortboy: A Sophiatown Legend* (Cape Town: Kwela Books, 1999), 18.

78. Interview for *Ubuyile*, 2000.

79. Ibid.

80. Molefe and Mzileni, op. cit., n.p., and Ballantine, op. cit., 47–50.

81. Ibid.

82. Interview for *Ubuyile*, 2000.

83. *Bantu World*, 30 May 1936, in Ballantine, op. cit., 50.

84. Ballantine, op. cit. 55.

85. Ibid., 71–72.

86. Ibid., 51–52.

87. Parsons, op. cit., 277–279.

88. *Bantu World*, 13 July 1935, in Ballantine, op. cit., 57.

89. *Bantu World*, 12 July 1941, in Ballantine, op. cit., 60.

90. Ballantine, op. cit., 61.

91. Gideon Jay, 'Pick of the disks off the record,' Johannesburg, *Zonk*, February 1955, p. 45, quoted in Jeffrey, op. cit.

94. *Drum*, August 1957, quoted in Ballantine, op. cit.

93. Interview for *Ubuyile*, 2000.

*Chapter Three*

# Athens on the Reef

Sophiatown was like a Mediterranean city—full of life and excitement; colonial Johannesburg was boring and dull . . . very much behind the times. You couldn't even get a decent cup of coffee in Johannesburg. Whereas Sophiatown Africans were modern people.

—Jurgen Schadeberg, *Drum* magazine photographer[1]

icture this: sharp-suited gangsters ride the streets in wallowing Cadillacs; gorgeous chorus girls swirl the yards of flowered fabric of their skirts; a saxophonist blows hot; an intense journalist pounds a typewriter, Chandleresque cigarette wreathing him in smoke; a boxer spars moodily on a rooftop, tall city tenements towering behind.

The boxer's face may look familiar, the cityscape less so. It is not New York, but Johannesburg, and he is Nelson Mandela, punching off the tensions of his day in the dock with the 156 other accused of the five-year (1956–1961) Treason Trials. Black-and-white photographs like these, from the pages of the illustrated magazine *Drum*,[2] have created a collective memory of a time and a place representing the most concentrated essence of South African black urban culture, at the precise time when apartheid was grinding it into the dust. Alongside the hard-news images of the corpses of schoolchildren, women marching, and soldiers with guns, they are probably the most widely seen pictures of the country before 1990. They have a quality of myth and movie, neither accidental. Since the authorities refused to acknowledge people of colour as actors in South Africa's discourse of urbanisation, it was from the American movies that city life, blown up to mythic proportions, was learned by the younger generation: New York's Hell's Kitchen, private eyes, crime, boxing, glamour—and jazz. Their grandparents or parents might have been recently arrived from the rural areas, or participants in another discourse altogether where black city dwellers had been freeholders (in a few places, even voters) and ambitious professionals, but the teenagers of the 1950s had been born in town, and that space, those aspirations—the black city—was being closed down.

Riffing on Charles Dickens, journalist Stan Motjuwadi, writing seven years before the end of apartheid, called the era 'the best of times, the worst of times . . . the 1950s begat the present—and perhaps the future'.[3] Another journalist, Arthur Maimane, acknowledges the myth and perhaps shows more of the appropriate private-eye cynicism (he wrote detective fiction for *Drum*): 'Sophiatown— everybody who did not know it has romantic memories of it'.[4] The power of those images, and the world they evoked, has been pervasive in South African music styles even up to today, partly because of how other, rural musics were manipulated by apartheid and therefore viewed by politically conscious musicians.

Sophiatown was not the only bastion of nontribal urbanity. Cape Town had District 6, and Durban, Pietermaritzburg, Port Elizabeth, and other cities all had what the authorities deploringly referred to as their 'black spots'. Sophiatown, however, is the best documented, and that can be attributed to the concentration of print media in Johannesburg, particularly to the magazine *Drum*. Founded as a monthly magazine in 1951, *Drum* began its life under former tank commander and Springbok cricketer Bob Crisp, who adopted a paternalistic, stereotyped, and backward-looking news focus on tribal customs and farming. After four issues, the magazine was losing its owner, Jim Bailey, £2,000 a month, a considerable sum in those days. Bailey fired Crisp and appointed a new editor, the Englishman Anthony Sampson, who investigated his readers and was told at the Bantu Men's Social Centre: 'Give us jazz and film stars, man! We want Duke, Satchmo and hot dames. Yes, brother, anything American. You can cut out this junk about kraals and folk-tales and Basutos in blankets—forget it! You just trying to keep us backward, that's what! Tell us what's happening right here on the Reef!'[5] In response, *Drum*, while continuing to have white editors, appointed a black advisory board and began recruiting a team of black journalists, including Henry Nxumalo, Arthur Maimane, Can Themba, Nat Nakasa, Bloke Modisane, and Casey Motsisi. On the advisory board sat Dr. A. B. Xuma, an ex-president of the ANC. One of the board's first recommendations was that the column 'Music for the Tribes' be dropped, and Todd Matshikiza—a journalist as well as a talented jazzman—began to contribute jazz record reviews interviews and features.

There were other magazines: the lightweight *Zonk!*, an entertainment and sports magazine had grown out of a wartime 'Native Corps' revue (and later a movie) of the same name, and by 1956 the government was covertly financing *Bona* to advance its own policies. But *Drum* became the market leader. Not only did it provide 'Satchmo and hot dames' and news of both African-American affairs and events in the rest of Africa, but it also offered a wry and literate look at contemporary South Africa through analysis, fiction, and solid, tough investigative reporting, and—on the model of overseas magazines such as *Picture*

*Post*, from which the next editor, Tom Hopkinson, was recruited—large, high-quality photographs. Photographer Jurgen Schadeberg joined the staff in 1951, a young and idealistic emigre from Germany, who worked with Henry Nxumalo on one of the magazine's earliest investigative stories. A year after it was founded, *Drum* published a shocking expose of conditions on the potato farms of the Transvaal:

> Henry was a most courageous journalist. Most journalists if they had to do a story about prison conditions would investigate from former prisoners. He wouldn't do that. He'd make sure to find a way of going to prison—commit a small crime: pass laws, drunken behaviour, something like that—and eventually he was arrested for pass laws and went to prison, to The Fort, for a couple of weeks and then wrote about it. He also signed up as a labourer and went to the potato farms at Bethel where there were conditions of near-slavery. And I would follow him around and go to different farms. Took pictures of the labour conditions and so on. Pretended to be a German tourist, which wasn't so difficult: my accent was still very heavy.[6]

Schadeberg was the trainer of a team of remarkable black photographers, including Peter Magubane, who remembers the *Drum* offices as

> [not] a world of separate toilets. It had a different, an international atmosphere. All the whites were foreigners: people eager to pass on their knowledge; a learning environment. There was no 'Yes boss', no 'boys'. We weren't dictated to, everyone worked together. Production was king; primary message: don't come back without a story! . . . The feeling was that of Fleet Street.[7]

Hindsight is not always 20/20 vision: salary disparities between black and white journalists on *Drum* were real and large, though no worse than the general industry standard. And, since Bailey was the son of a mine magnate, 'We were discouraged from writing about the mines', remembers Arthur Maimane. 'It was Bailey's children's inheritance'.[8] Nevertheless, it was *Drum*, above all publications, that portrayed the black city life of the 1950s. Its epitome was the historic freehold suburb of Sophiatown, now far more crowded and less neat than in the 1920s, as residents were crowded together by the legislative pressures on other areas of mixed housing. Poet Don Mattera grew up there and remembers the cultural diversity:

> There were great families like the Mabuza family—Felicia Mabuza—her grandfather, paternal grandfather, his brother was Early Mabuza, who was an amazing young jazz drummer. . . . And they were a very affluent

family and so was ours. And so were many Indian families and Chinese families. And they all played together. Lenny Lee was one of the great jazz trumpeters in Sophiatown—he was Chinese, very strongly Chinese, but he had broken away from the Buddhist Chinese cultural hold, so he mixed freely with other young players like Hugh Masekela. . . . There was another Chinese family—Ah Lun—who had all black women—his children today are still walking around, and his young brother Giap; they had two beautiful sisters and oh! they were just crazy Chinese women; but they didn't live a Chinese life—they lived with black people; they intermingled with so-called coloureds and Indians in Sophiatown. Then there was the Yung family; also Chinese—one of the handsomest families—they wore the best American clothes, they spoke *tsotsitaal*; they mixed with the people. Sophiatown was that kind of melting pot; it brought all cultures, all peoples together. It pulled strands of music together, all languages together—Italians, French, Dutch people living there, there were Boers living there. All mixing in this melting pot of great culture, of jazz. . . . So because Sophiatown represented the antithesis of what the Boers wanted—apartheid, Calvinistic music, a Calvinistic history, Calvinistic norms, Calvinistic values—and here comes this jazz by these niggers, and here comes the sound from Sophiatown by these darkies . . . this was too much for these people. They had to do away with it. But they thought that when they would destroy it they would destroy the music as well, they would destroy the cultures as well, they would destroy our memory—but you know, like I say in my book—memory is a weapon.[9]

Singer Thandi Klaasen also grew up in Sophiatown. For her, it is the sound of the streets that is most memorable:

My mother was a good singer in church and my father was a bible-thumper. My father sang very well, and their choir used to hit all the streets . . . and mothers and grannies and everybody used to follow them round. Preaching the name of the Lord! But you'd just get round the corner and *die ouens spiel* [people were playing] jazz, blues, rhythm n'blues. Not that I knew it was called rhythm n'blues then. But I could just listen to these bands playing and listen to these women from the record players and the radios coming out of the windows: Ella Fitzgerald, 'Body and Soul'. And I said to myself: I'm gonna sing this kind of music![10]

It wasn't just a sound, but a look, too; a fixation on brands. While the gangsters and successful musicians had the most money to spend in this way, all urban young people aspired to dress well; to be 'Jewished' (dressed from the predominantly Jewish-owned city-centre clothing stores) in 'can't-gets' (exclusive imports)—which was probably what attracted so much fashion advertising to *Drum*:

> All the fashions were American. We had a gang called the Americans. They used to move around with smart cars. Just as today it has to be a Benz or a BMW, then, it used to be the Buick, open coupe. And you have to wear that fashionable hat, and the double-breasted jacket and so forth, just to emulate the Americans.[11]

> [The Americans gang members] squandered money on expensive designer labels . . . Mayfair and Hagar slacks, Floren shirts, Pyramid handkerchiefs, Stetson and Wooldro hats, Haycock and Paris belts, cashmere jerseys. . . . [They] used to change twice a day and never wore a shirt twice. . . . The Americans looked stunning in their big fedoras cruising the dirty Sophiatown streets in a big white Cadillac.[12]

> The fashions! We knew what we were wearing. We'd never wear a skirt for five shillings. We were wearing labels—Florsheim, Pyramid![13]

> [By the end of the '50s] we were [starting to get out of the zoot suit and] into this whole Ivy League thing, you know. Because it was always American, American. You'd find one or two people who went into the English thing . . . and there were a few people who went into the Italian styles with those short jackets, . . . especially guys from Pimville, a few guys. . . . But we went into the American college thing, . . . where we had those striped shirts all buttoned up and high, narrow pants without pleats and no turn-ups and a little cap with a belt behind. Yes, the three-button jacket. . . .[14]

> The car was a Caddy, the place was Harlem, the movie was *Cabin in the Sky*—and we thought we were free![15]

Cape Town pianist Henry February sees this admiration for American style among jazz players and fans as merely a natural extension of love for the music, 'because when you heard what they were playing, they were like demigods. You idolised them. So automatically, now, you have this soft spot for the Yankees'.[16] Jurgen Schadeberg links it to the situation created by apartheid and points out that there was a broader awareness at play:

> During this period there was a dynamic cultural explosion [that] related to a number of things. [Because of the wall between them and white society,] people adopted more and more an association with American society. [We] saw Louis Armstrong, Charlie Parker, Lena Horne and so

*King Kong* cast walking down the streets of Sophiatown. *Credit:* Sony Records: *Sounds From Exile*

on as role models. But the other reason was political. You saw it in the north—Ghana, Tanzania and so on—the rejection of colonialism and the movement for the independence of Africa. So people felt very positive about the future. At that time, in the early '50s, they did not take the apartheid regime so seriously. It was so ridiculous, it couldn't last.[17]

Cape Town's District 6 provided a similar context. People of colour from a range of backgrounds lived together, in overcrowded and impoverished conditions, but with access to cinema, radio and recordings, places where concerts and dances could be held, and a lively street culture, including choirs, church-based bands, and Coon troupes.

Writer and educator Nomvula Ngcelwane grew up in District 6 and remembers 'the African Mills Brothers, deeply inspired by the Mills Brothers of the United States . . . they were real professionals [who] performed in black trousers, off-white jackets, white shirts and black bow ties. Sometimes they preferred white trousers and floral shirts or, if the occasion called for it, African traditional attire'. Ngcelwane recalls the African Mills Brothers performing at afternoon 'spends', a relative of concert and dance, where 'the first half was for vocal music by various groups . . . it was expected of the audience to keep still and listen. During the second half of the programme, dance and jive music was played by bands like the Merry Macs from Langa and sometimes bands from the Muslim community'. She also describes a wedding reception where 'one of District Six's *maskandas* (itinerant musicians) played the piano, some Coloured guys blew saxophones and a tall African man was the drummer'.[18] Out of this blend of traditions, Cape Town was creating a distinctive jazz style:

[M]usicians from all communities played together in an idiom they all knew, as listeners from all communities came to enjoy jazz sessions. Young musicians wanted to assert their distinctiveness both from other musical styles and from types of music that did not sound sufficiently African to their ears. A Cape Town subculture developed after World War Two as elements of African and Coloured music were introduced into American jazz. A 'coloured beat' became the creativity of Cape Town musicians. It included the *ghoema* beat of the *moppies* [upbeat Malay choir songs] and *ghoema* dances in the swing characteristic of jazz, while retaining something of the elasticity of *langaarm*, the dance music partic- ular to the Cape, derived from a mixture of *vastrap* [quickstep] square dance and ballroom dance.[19]

To earn a living, Cape jazzmen played in all these root contexts as well as in jazz, sometimes meeting kindred spirits in unexpected places, as pianist Tony Schilder remembers, discussing the night he met his favourite bass player:

You know, they had these *langaarm* bands: those terrible sax sounds, banjos and whatnot. I went to play a gig in a place called Horston, near Hermanus. There were 10 saxophone players. And the 10th player that came in was the most incredible player I'd ever heard. . . . So I said, what's your name? He said: Johnny Gertze. Now, Johnny later was a bass player [who] used to play with Abdullah Ibrahim in the Jazz Epistles. But at this time we were young, about the same age. When I heard this one beautiful sax sound coming out of all these terrible sax players that are blowing mad there, and the people stomping barefooted in the sand, I said, listen, come, just sit over here so we can jam. And the two of us were jamming while they were playing this terrible dance music, and the banjos going, and the drummer hitting away at his cymbals, while we played lovely cool jazz.[20]

Schilder and Gertze later teamed up in a quartet, which was the point at which Gertze traded his saxophone for a double bass. Because of the semiprofes- sional nature of the scene, a facility for multi-instrumentalism was vital.

In the late 1940s and early 1950s, then, in all of South Africa's cities, a music they themselves called jazz was linking progressive players. What did it sound like? It existed parallel to, and came out of, the big-band swing that had preceded

it, but it was often being played by smaller lineups and behii
Some of the purely instrumental groups were stretching the s¡
improvisation, on the model of their bebop counterparts in tł
and the modern jazz jam sessions that ran at Sophiatown's Odi
last years of the 1950s were the place where this interest flowered. The melodies
had the looping, repeated motifs of African traditional music, over a syncopated
beat perfect for jiving. Saxophonist Ntemi Piliso believed it was predominantly
the chord structure that transformed the music from merely a clone of swing to
something unique:

> African jazz, when we started, we emulated the Americans, the big bands,
> but we played African jazz because we took the chord progressions from
> marabi. . . . We categorise it as African jazz because when you say jazz,
> you tend to think of American jazz—and we were using that style as a
> big band. . . . Where the saxophone section plays a phrase and the brass
> section answers, that type of arrangement the Count Basies and so forth
> were using. But the melody—you can see, feel, it's African. . . . You can
> do whatever you like, put in American phrases, but you'll come back to
> that marabi trend. It's a cultural thing; it won't die.[21]

African-language lyrics were created for American standards. African traditional songs were simplified in structure and taken up-tempo—literally 'jazzed
up'. One such was 'Jikele'maweni', a traditional Xhosa song that, with new lyrics,
became a hit for the Manhattan Brothers in 1954.[22] Guitarist General Duze,
whose day job was for many years as librarian at the Gallo record company,
recalled 'Dambudzo [Mdledle, the Manhattans' leader] was the one who had
already thought to bring the Xhosa element into jazz, long before the
youngsters. . . .'[23] As the decade advanced, the more urgent, vamping, bluesy
style of boogie-woogie was applied to both songs and melodies, creating breaks
where the soloists had to improvise faster and hotter. (There was even a hit close-
harmony song called 'uBoogie-Woogie'.) Banzi Bangani's teacher, trumpeter
David Mzimkulu, typified the earlier African jazz style as he played with the
Havana Swingsters. In his time, he had been hailed as the finest of his generation.
What has survived of his playing shows he had clearly listened to Satchmo and
had good ideas of his own, too. But his solo on a tune like 'Emaxambeni', one
of the Havanas' few surviving recordings,[24] is stylish and measured, with none of
the fireworks that might disturb strict-tempo dancers. By the 1950s, Bangani was
listening to Louis Jordan and Dizzy Gillespie, and when his group played a two-
band stage with the Havanas, there was no doubt how younger audiences' tastes
were turning:

> The Havana Swingsters were playing. And after they played their first,
> second, third number, the youngsters there say no, man, we want the

Johannesburg All-Stars. (That's what we called ourselves, because Johannesburg is a great name—if it's known you are from Johannesburg, you are well-respected. You wouldn't say the Springs or Payneville All-Stars because nobody knows about that!) Anyway, they said no, we want the All-Stars. Get off, man, you're playing s**t! Get off! Because they used to play that old type of, you know, big-band . . . and this was when the small group, the boogie-woogie thing, was coming in. When we came on—Elijah [Nkwanyana] and me, Sydney Nthalo on piano, Willie Malan from the Jazz Maniacs on drums, General Duze on guitar—man! We smashed the place. . . . After, I went backstage to see [David] Mzimkulu, I could see he was sort of down and disappointed. I said, don't you remember me? I'm that young boy that used to buy you some nips some time. He shakes his head and says: Ah, sonny, now I see you. You've grown a bit. . . .[25]

Jazz provided a common language, allowing musicians to transcend the barriers apartheid was erecting. Tony Schilder was classified coloured, but he was sometimes able to work with musicians who were white. And it was in the black townships, like Langa outside Cape Town, over a jazz tune, that musicians from all three groups were able to establish common ground:

In those townships was the only place we could go to listen to jazz and to participate: Langa and Nyanga and Gugulethu. We were frustrated, because jazz was only appreciated in the townships really. . . . Some of the guys from the white areas used to come with me to Langa. I'd say: come and dig these guys; come, listen to the way they play, man! Some of them, they'd say, well, this is great. There were a few of us who decided there should be no apartheid in music. You can go anywhere in the world and play music. You don't have to speak the language, you can just say to the guy 'Green Dophin Street', and you're talking.[26]

Schilder's experience in Langa was not unique, but neither was it common, even in his own career:

[Playing with white guys,] I still had to go in round the back. And when I have a break, I can't go with the white guys. If I want a drink, I have to go round the back and go to the [c]oloured [b]ar. These were all the indignities that we suffered. Stumbling blocks were put in our path by the white musicians. They wanted all the gigs for themselves. They felt threatened. That's why they had a white musicians union. [So] they said, 'We must be very careful of him—he's a coloured: they drink like mad, pitch up late'. . . . So I had to be very careful of myself.[27]

Segregation and the enforcement of labour bars were deepening the trenches between blacks and whites at every level. Duze was another player who retained some white friends, but that did not lessen his dislike of the new laws:

I grew up next to whites, playing with white children. Hence my language. And I never felt the difference. The only time you'd feel the pinch was when you met a Dutch [Afrikaner] policeman—[then you'd ask yourself,] Ee! What's happening now? We are all people, *finish and klaar* [and that's that]. It didn't feel good when we started being treated differently. Some of the white musicians were still nice to me . . . and I still had friends on the other side of the apartheid line. But I felt it for those who could not express themselves.[28]

For the young trombonist Jonas Gwangwa, starting his career at the end of the decade, the restrictions and prejudice continued:

There were some white clubs that we'd steal in and play . . . there was one called Moopen's here in town and another one in Hillbrow. Of course, that was all illegal at the time. I remember when we were the group the Jazz Epistles and we went around the city clubs, so that we could play somewhere. We'd go into a restaurant; like there was a Hamburger Club here making food and everything; and . . . we negotiated with the owners. They said OK, you can bring a piano. And we really popularised the place. But of course we would get just £1.10s and a piece of steak and you eat that in the kitchen and stay there, you know. You couldn't mix with the audience, and we went to some other place to do our drinking.[29]

The steak would not have pleased pianist Henry February:

We weren't allowed to play in places where liquor was sold, but [only] in the places where people could bring their own liquor. I don't know why. It was almost as if we were savages or something. . . . So the whites had it easy because the white musicians—the worst musicians in the world, some of them—could walk in there and get a job. And you, as a musician that's quite competent, just because you're black, you're not allowed to play there. . . . Some [places] even say, no, man, we'll give you a plate of food. I tell them what the hell?! Do you think I'm going to play just for food? I'm a professional musician. I play for money![30]

The pass laws were a particular impediment, requiring blacks in the city to justify their presence on demand by producing a document signed by their employer or some other white authority. At night, an extra paper, the *nagpass* ('night pass'), was also needed—and musicians were mainly night workers. Ntemi Piliso remembered:

> We used to play in the locations most of the time. Because when you play in town like at the BMSC and you finish at midnight or 4 am, there are no buses to take you back to the township. . . . You had to play hide and seek from the hall to the station. . . . There was this *nagpass* and if you don't work for a white person—because they owned all the factories and things—you haven't got a *nagpass* and no-one to say you were working late and so forth. Most of us only had a daily labour pass, which means you are self-employed as a musician and some of the police did not know what that thing was all about. . . . The Manhattan Brothers were arrested once and then [the police started saying,] sing something to prove you are a musician. Then one suggested they sing 'Don't Fence Me In', and they said, no, we'll sing 'Don't *Lock* Me In'![31]

Banzi Bangani's memories were similar:

> I remember we were from a show at BMSC we'd done with Louisa Emmanuel and some other women singers. We took the last train. And Elijah [Nkwanyane] lost his ticket! . . . The ticket examiners at that time were white. Raw, terrible guys! [They made us play for them] and they started calling other ticket collectors to listen too. There was no other thing we could have done, so we played until our lips were swollen up and cracked and bleeding . . . until we got off. And they said, *"Jah! Jele spiel mooi, jele kaffirs"* (You niggers play well,) but they were also swearing at us, calling us black whatevers all the time. Eh well, so long as we were not going to jail![32]

The cruelty of the Boer police shook Jonas Gwangwa:

> Sometimes you were invited to come and play in the suburbs and the people have to apply to the police station—they give you a piece of paper to say that you have been performing. But sometimes those *boere* boys they just get so mean—they take it from you and say, 'Now you don't have it! *Waar vanaf kom jy*? (So where do you come from?)' Otherwise they would make you perform in the middle of the night. In the middle of the street, you'd be tap-dancing at 3 am![33]

Thandi Klaasen recalled one particular incident:

> They asked me, '*Kan jy Suikerbossie gesing?*' (Can you sing 'Sugar-bush'?—a traditional Afrikaans song which was an international hit for

Eve Boswell.) 'Oh yes,' and I start singing—I don't have my pass singing. I'll be arrested, so I'm singing. And they were smiling and ⎍aughing, and I'm singing—but inside me, I'm just swearing and crying, telling them what I think of them![34]

Dolly Rathebe recounted her treatment while filming *Jim Comes to Jo'burg*:

[When we were filming,] all the cast members were housed in Yeoville (a bohemian white suburb) because of problems with the police and passes. . . . One night I just walked across the street to go to sleep, there is a police van speeding round the corner. I was arrested, and when I tried to explain to them about the film and that I am Dolly Rathebe, they just said No! Fuck that! And took me to jail. The next morning the whole crew was looking for me, but I managed to alert them from jail. Later the newspaper had a headline: 'First Bantu Film Star Arrested for Night Pass'. By the way, I was a Bantu then.[35]

Rathebe was the top jazz and blues singer of her generation and considered so beautiful that a *flaaitaal* metaphor was coined for her. 'It's dolly' meant 'It's wonderful' and was an abbreviation of '*S'Dolly se boude!*' ('It's Dolly's thighs!') The 1949 movie *Jim Comes to Jo'burg* was one of a handful of South African films (including *The Magic Garden*, *Song of Africa*, and *Zonk!*, a film version of the World War II Native Corps revue) that was made for the black cinemas. Most told similar moralising tales of a young rural man, coming to and being corrupted by the big city and realising he would be better off back in his tribal reserve. The exception was Lionel Rogosin's *Come Back Africa* (an ANC slogan of the time, the translation of *Mayibuye I'Afrika!*). This was filmed in secret and showed some of the reality of township life. Despite their preaching, the films provided an effective showcase for many young musicians: Duze and Bangani also appeared with Rathebe. Bangani remembered: 'We played in *Jim Comes to Jo'burg*. At that point, the African Inkspots had no bassist, so I played bass and left Elijah [Nkwanyane] on trumpet . . . and after that, we really started pushing. We got into recordings where we met guys like Zakes Nkosi, Mackay Davashe, Kippie Moeketsi. . . . Playing at places like the Odin in Sophiatown, playing what we called progressive jazz'.[36]

*Jim Comes to Jo'burg* became a scornful metaphor among black intellectuals for all back-to-the-homelands literature. But there was still musical cross-fertilisation between urban and traditional styles. Rathebe scored an early hit with the song 'Sindi', a bluesed-up version of a neotraditional concertina tune, 'Good Street', dedicated to a Sophiatown thoroughfare. The record was taken back to the United States by Sidney Poitier and picked up by Johnny Hodges under the title 'Something to Put Your Foot To'.[37] Edward Ntsiki, a veteran of World War II

and an avid music-goer after his demobilisation, describes the mood of Rathebe's
shows:

> We used to run after this Dolly Rathebe. At the centre, the dancing centre,
> DOC—Donaldson Hall here in Orlando. We used to love it. When Dolly
> got [o]nto the stage there would be madness—madness! [For the song
> she sang,] 'Into Yam', . . . was [a] masterpiece![38]

The apartheid legal framework was creating a society where black existence
was inscribed, literally, at the margins. This cramping of the physical and creative
space comes across again and again in musicians' narratives. They formed their
groups at the margins: the Skylarks, Miriam Makeba's first successful vocal
group, 'was formed at the corner of Troye and President Street, where Gallo used
to be. There are some steps there. They used to sit there and compose . . . while
uBaas (the white recording director) isn't there until ten, but he has told you to
be there at eight. And when he arrives, he doesn't even apologise. It's just: are
you ready?'[39] They spent their breaks, not in the venue, but over 'a nip [tot of
spirits] in the passage'.[40] They rehearsed at the margins: 'Victor Hamilton was
working [as a driver] for a dress shop at Ansteys building and I was working at
Victoria Pharmacy. Lunchtime, we'd go to the garage where he parks the car, go
and learn a few chords every day'.[41] And, increasingly, they lived at the margins
as an intensified process of removals began to whitewash the remaining black
spots and move informal settlers farther from the city.

In response to both continuing accommodation shortage and black city settlement, legislation was passed to train Africans as cheap construction labour
(the jobs had formerly been designated whites-only), so long as they worked only
in African areas. Levies were raised from employers. House plans were developed
for a three- or four-room, 40-square-metre house on a small plot that also
housed a bucket latrine and had access to a communal water tap. There were no
streetlights or refuse collection services other than for night soil. These were the
infamous 'matchboxes'—officially the 51/6 plan house—that would have
cramped even a small family. If they were intended to counteract the unsanitary
overcrowding of informal settlements, they were doomed from the outset. One
man who was moved to Johannesburg's Naledi Township recalled, 'They built a
house that is not plastered inside. . . . They didn't care that this house is being
built for a human being. The houses were built for animals. Most of the things,
like plastering, have been done by people out of their own expenses'.[42] White
society presented these building efforts rather differently:

> To possess your own lavatory pail might not seem to be the ultimate in
> human ambition. Nevertheless, on yesterday's smiling, sunny Sunday, a
> pail and dustbin presented to each of 12 Bantu families by the superin-
> tendent at Jabavu Township represented a passport to a new life and a

new hope. Pail in hand, the Bantu clambered on to a lorry that held all their possessions and were taken to a stand. . . . Proudly, each family put the new pail into [their little house].⁴³

No allowance was made for larger or multigeneration families or different cultural living patterns—or even for the large furniture, such as a piano, that more affluent city dwellers might own. Rents were relatively high, particularly for those who had previously been squatting, and transport costs added more financial burdens. Apart from council-controlled communal halls or beer halls, there were few recreation facilities. Though presented as a 'city within a city' with opportunities for self-management and economic advancement, '[s]uffocating regulations stamped out virtually every sign of individual initiative and enterprise. . . . Licenses for shopkeepers were tightly restricted. . . . Herbalism and undertaking were the most profitable enterprises . . . making death and disease the largest industry'.⁴⁴ In Johannesburg, this growing cluster of bleak housing estates, containing more than half a million people to the southwest of the city, did not even have a name until 1963, when it was christened Soweto, a contraction of 'Southwestern Townships'.

Similar townships were being created throughout the country, and there was no choice about moving to them. The authorities created categories among urban blacks. There were 'tribal' migrants, needed by the mines and other heavy industry, who must stay in bachelor hostels and could settle permanently only after an almost impossibly long unbroken period of labour for the same employer. There were 'semitribal' immigrants, in the cities only at the sufferance of the authorities, to be discouraged, residentially segregated in their tribal categories, and their numbers reduced. And there were the 'detribalised' urban blacks, seen as dangerously emancipated and ambitious. (Farm-born blacks were outside this system, condemned to permanent servitude and never allowed to enter the cities as work-seekers, to ensure white farmers copious cheap labour.)

The removals were thus one method of not only dividing up the race groups, but also retribalising urban blacks. According to Lucky Michaels,

When apartheid came in, after '51 . . . the coloured was made to believe that he was the number two citizen in the country, and the Indian was the number three citizen and the black man was fourth in line. . . . And there was a step further, too. Among the black community, they started to separate out, for example, Shangaans—you had a Shangaan area in Meadowlands—and Sothos had a Sotho area, and Zulus had a Zulu area and those were the kinds of break-ups.⁴⁵

Tony Schilder remembers:

If you walked into a township, you had to clear yourself with the cops, first go to the police station. The police station was right on the corner, right at the entrance to the township. That's how they built them, so you can't go in or out anywhere else. You have to go through the front entrance. But I used to go through. You know, you're not even thinking. I used to drive right past the police station. Then the next minute the cops are there. Where are you going? What are you doing? To buy *dagga* [marijuana] or what? . . . It didn't matter to me, really. Because I'm not white. I am a black person. I live just down the road there. Just because I am a little bit fairer. . . .[46]

Don Mattera felt the divisiveness:

We saw that our names had been destroyed, that our families had been scattered to the four winds, our friends that grew up with us were now called by their tribal names—Shangaan, Pedi, Tswana, Zulu, Xhosa, Venda and so forth—we wondered why we were being left behind. And we were told: *nee, julle's boesmans*—you are coloureds, mixed bloods, but your turn will come. And some of us refused to be called mixed bloods . . . and threw in our lot with the oppressed.[47]

For both a work permit and access to residence, black citizens had to carry documents detailing their racial and tribal status. This was decided in the pass office (the Non-European Affairs Department) by a bureaucrat asking questions such as Who is your chief? and Which river do your people swim in?—to which many young urbanites knew only the haziest of answers—or by applying 'scientific' tests of race. One was the infamous 'pencil test'. A pencil was pushed into a person's hair: if it held, that person was definitely African; if it slid through, the person might get away with claiming coloured status. The street-smart shaved their heads. Another was to slap the applicant or hit his kneecap. If he expressed his pain as 'Eina!', he was coloured. If he yelled 'Eissh!', he was black. 'Then', wrote *Drum* journalist Can Themba, 'you pass into an inner room where you are curtly told to drop your trousers, all of you in a row. You may be a dignified businessman, a top-class lawyer, a wood-merchant, anybody. You will find yourself naked. Well, you wanted a permit to work in Johannesburg, didn't you?'[48] A byzantine matrix of classifications was created for the coloured community: Cape Coloured, Malay, Hottentot, concluding with the catch-all 'Other Coloured' for those the authorities deemed unclassifiable, but nevertheless nonwhite. As Jurgen Schadeberg had observed, it was so ridiculous that no one at the outset believed it could last.

Yet, inexorably, through the 1950s, the machinery of classification and relocation proceeded, all over the country. Again, Tony Schilder:

We were put out of our home because we were the wrong colour. And that was taken over by white people under the Group Areas Act. They

gave you, like, six months to get out. And the landlord couldn't accept
the rent because, legally, if they accepted the rent you'd still got the right
to stay there. And my mother was only too happy with that part of it,
because at least now she could buy food. For a family of ten. . . . The first
places to go were Dieprivier, Plumstead, Claremont, well before District 6
[was removed]. They were sent to the Cape Flats [which were] established
especially for coloured people. And then just beyond the Flats were the
black townships.[49]

Lucky Michaels:

They evicted the owners of property from Sophiatown with no proper
compensation. We were owners. We may not have had ninety-nine-year
leases and all that kind of thing, but we were the owners. My grandmother was paid £12 for her property in Tucker Street. I've got papers
for that.[50]

Don Mattera:

When you see the piles of debris, you see your father's house that gave
you warmth and support and food, you see the rubble of bricks, you
see your things lying where they are lying, and somebody says, 'Hey, die
Boere—hulle's sterk!' The Boers are strong! And you know they are only
strong when we make them strong . . . our strength makes them weak.[51]

Sophiatown, Mattera's suburb, was cleared in 1955. Residents tell tales of
pianos flung onto lorries, arriving irreparably broken and too large to fit into the
new house. On the rubble, the authorities built a white suburb they named Tri-
omf (Triumph). As Sophiatown died, a composer called Strike Vilakazi wrote
the popular anthem of the removals, the song 'Meadowlands', sung by Nancy
Jacobs and Her Sisters, with *Drum* journalist Todd Matshikiza at the piano. The
song is as rich in nuance as a traditional fable, with verses in three languages:
IsiZulu, SeSotho, and the language of the city streets, *tsotsitaal.* Over an infectious jive beat, the Zulu and Sotho verses could be read as sunnily positive (by
anyone with no sense of irony):

> Let's go, let's go, let's go to Meadowlands
> We'll work night and day, going straight to Meadowlands
> Have you heard what the white people say?
> Let's all go to Meadowlands . . .
> Our beloved place

Bureaucrats are not noted for their sense of irony; the head of the Peri-Urban
Health Board congratulated Vilakazi on the song, and, according to one source,
treated his applications for housing permits thereafter with instant approval.[52]

The *tsotsitaal* lines say something else entirely:

> Have you heard what the tsotsis all say?
> We're not leaving; we're staying right here
> Staying here, staying here,
> Staying here in our beloved place.

'*Ons daak nie, ons pola hie*' ('We're not leaving, we're staying right here') was the slogan painted on every wall before the lorries and bulldozers moved into Sophiatown. Interpretation depends entirely on how the listener reads that juxtaposition of the views of 'white people' and *tsotsis*, and the status accorded to the utterances of Zulu-speakers—whom Dolly Rathebe scornfully called 'turkeys'. I have not interviewed any musician of the era who saw the song as anything other than, in Don Mattera's words, 'protest, lamentation for what had become of us'.[53] Former Sophiatown resident Bra Luke, asked in a magazine interview about resistance to the removals, answered immediately, '*Toe sing ons daai song wat ou Strike ga-compose het*' ('We sang the song that Strike had composed').[54]

The ambivalence towards gangsters was pervasive. On the one hand, gangsterism in the black city was brutal and bitterly resented. *Tsotsis* had been named for the zoot suits they adopted just after World War II, but the name was also conveniently close to the Sotho verb *ho tsotsa*, meaning 'to behave thuggishly'. Word-play was a feature of African traditional verse, with its layered metaphors and multiple messages, and it was retained in song lyrics and the urban argot of *flaaitaal/tsotsitaal*, a useful subversive device, since the meaning drawn from a particular set of words was determined by the listener's cultural grounding as well as the words themselves.

But gangsterism also had a range of forms and social meanings. Many gangs had started out as genuine self-protection groupings for country boys prey to the wicked city, to exploitative employers, or to other groups who were traditional or economic rivals; to survive, they had to learn that wickedness themselves. Just as traditional home-brewing became commercialised, vigilantes began to demand protection money for what had been a voluntary community duty. From there, they progressed to trade in *dagga* and bootleg liquor and control of prostitution. Excluded from mainstream capitalism, gangsterism was also a genuine alternative way for them up the economic ladder.

Prohibition provided the ideal route. The cat-and-mouse games with the police were growing more sophisticated, with white vagrants hired to buy small quantities from legitimate outlets, and larger consignments stolen or home-brewed. As Modikwe Dikobe's poem 'Shebeen Queen' indicates, adulteration to stretch the consignment was common:

> Drink, my dear
> This is pure brandy

Brewed in Korea
Bottled in Malay Camp
Delivered by the flying squad

Don't cough, my dear
You'll scare the customers
The ingredients are excellent:
Methylated spirit, tobacco juice, yeast, marijuana
And of course a pint of vinegar
For colouring[55]

Gathering inspiration from movies about Al Capone, the drink was delivered to the shebeens disguised in florists' vans or undertakers' hearses. Shebeens could be sordid covert drinking dens for the poor, or high-class salons with extravagant decor and sophisticated music, lacking only legality. The bootleggers of the 1940s and '50s were sometimes the township mayors and councillors, or 'homeland' politicians of the 1960s and 1970s—apartheid's corrupt black machine politicians—although that was as far as the system could let them rise. There was also an element of political outlawry: gangsterism gave a defiant finger to white authority. A number of gangsters, including Don Mattera, matured into activists seeking other ways of overturning injustice. But the system was the bigger enemy, so 'if it's the police asking you which way did those *tsotsis* go', remembers Thandi Klaasen, 'and they went that way, you'd tell the police this way—the opposite direction!'[56]

Gangsters ranged from the elite to the lumpen. Many commentators have pointed out that in unequal and immobile societies, crime becomes the mirror image of the dominant economic structure (and sometimes works covertly with it). That was the motif of Bertolt Brecht's *Threepenny Opera*, and it has a resonance in the minute gradations of criminal class in Sophiatown, as described by Arthur Maimane:

You had the *klevahs* [hip people] and they were in three categories. At the top, were the *manne*: the quarter-million boys. Many of them were real masterminds and intellectuals: I had a maths teacher, a graduate, who realised he could do better planning payroll robberies. One of his protections was that the police never recognised him. To them, all black people looked alike because they never looked at us as real human beings. Below them were the *manne vat notch* [stolen goods guys]: they were robbers, but they robbed in the city and we benefited, because we bought the goods cheaply. Around them moved the sophisticates: journalists, musicians, political figures—respected for their intellectual achievements. The cattle, the law-abiding people, were not *klevahs*. They were 'situations': they had steady jobs, preferred to speak English and kept their heads down. Right at the bottom were the *moegoes* (ignoramuses), some who had recently come to town—including those *tsotsis* who were stupid and disloyal enough to prey on black people in our own community. As a writer for *Drum*, I walked a razor's edge between the lawbreakers, the law-abiding and the oppressors.[57]

For musicians, the *tsotsis* were both fans and a major nuisance. According to Jonas Gwangwa,

The gangsters were people who were seeing things in the movies. . . . [They] used to terrorise us, especially the ladies. They loved the singing and they'd say: I'm taking that one tonight. . . . All the beautiful ladies: Miriam Makeba, Dolly Rathebe. They were going through that whole thing of the moll, the gangsters' moll. . . . You had to have a gangster boyfriend so that you could be protected; but that could also lead to gang wars, and for us guys, it was just rough. . . . Like the very first show we had with the Huddleston band in Daveyton Social Centre, quite a lot of people died because [gangsters] went there and said, 'Sophiatown one side; East Rand [other] side', and they had a knife-to-knife fight. And they just wanted us to play, because to them it was that movie thing—and we were playing the soundtrack!'[58]

Tony Schilder:

There was a place called the Sun Valley Hall in Langa. And we're playing there, having a wonderful time, and the first thing that happens is a gang comes in. And if they don't like your music, you've got a problem. But if they like your music, they leave you alone. . . . I used to change it into a beat they can dance to, because they come in to dance. . . . But we had our real problems with the police, not the gangsters—the gangsters were jazz lovers. The only thing, if they couldn't afford to pay, they used to break their way into the hall. You'd tell them everyone else paid, and they'd say: 'Well, we're not paying!' But they were coming in to listen, you know?[59]

That some groups of gangsters were also patrons of the music is illustrated by a story from Ntemi Piliso. His township, Alexandra, was notorious for the activities of its *tsotsis*, particularly the Spoilers and Msomi gangs. On a Friday night, they expected to be able to see their favourite bands perform. It paid to have allies:

The gangsters used to like us musicians, but they were fighting each other wherever we would go. . . . When we come in now for the dance at about midnight, that is when the riots started. The gangsters are already hot:

they have already taken some drink. Then they start fighting. Even though they were not attacking us, it would affect us, because in the confusion we would have to run. . . . I don't remember a show where I didn't have to run a bit! . . . I failed a show once and I was fetched [by the gangsters] at home to give a reason. But fortunately I was so popular that when they got to Alexandra, they met up with some other gangster who knew me and honoured me a lot . . . an individual who was involved with the Spoilers in Alexandra . . . so they ganged up together and eventually we had a party . . . they did not punish me.[60]

However, the attitude to women performers—as to women generally in a deeply patriarchal society—was far less respectful, as singer Dolly Rathebe recalls:

We used to have it very tough in those days. . . . Sophiatown was like New Orleans—it had the jazz, the fashion, everything! We had competition with Orlando—we used to call them turkeys because they spoke too much of the native languages like Zulu. To us, it sounded like gobble, gobble. We were proud of our Afrikaans and English. Those from Alexandra were real raw and uncouth and used to go and raid other townships, starting fights and kidnapping women. They came for me once, said: After the show, you're coming with us! I had to go with them. What choice did I have? Oh yes, it was tough. . . . The police didn't care about it, because later I reported that this guy had taken me against my will, but nothing happened. We were just *kaffir meids* [black girls], Bantus, so they didn't care. We found ways to survive. The Americans were the best-dressed gangsters in town and eventually I settled with one of them. He looked after me. It was just that kind of life, and we'd grown up with it.[61]

A younger star of the times (and today), Abigail Khubeka, when asked about the same pressures, says wryly:

Thank God, I don't remember! I was young, and naive, and wearing blinkers, and I was stunning. The gangsters were rough, and you had to be a gangster's moll to survive, but I was determined to be what I am today and somehow, one went through it all without being scarred.[62]

Not all gangsters were jazz fans. Among the lumpen *moegoes* so despised by sophisticated criminals were the 'Russians', an organisation that dominated the off-duty activities of many Basotho migrant miners and industrial workers. Originally self-protection vigilantes, the Sotho gangs were instantly recognisable by their sticks, hats, and all-enveloping blankets, whose colours denoted regional affiliations back home in Lesotho. They had for a time dubbed themselves 'Berliners' and 'Japanese' as well as Russians. But in World War II, it had been the

Russians 'who had been the powerful people who stopped the Germans',[63] and that name came to dominate. The Russians fought against the young *tsotsi* gangs who stole from all workers, without any regard for group loyalty—but also against the sophisticated Sophiatown Americans, which may give another resonance to their title during the cold war era. Russians dominated the Soweto suburb of Naledi, and in the late 1950s, at the peak of their activity, their sticks began to be exchanged for guns, and their role was often to support conservatism and the township authorities, by becoming township policemen or by more informal methods:

> It was during the days of *azikhwelwa* [the township bus boycotts]. Now whilst we were playing, these [Russian] people came into the hall and confronted us as if this was an entertainment for these *azikkhwelwa* people, because they were against this *azikhwelwa* affair. . . . [T]hey came in and started assaulting everybody inside the hall, so everybody had to flee for safety.[64]

The music of the Russians was *famo*, played on the organ or accordion and often used to stir up grim, reckless courage for a gang fight. Like *famo*, other traditional (and neotraditional) musics could potentially invoke the memory of a rural identity to reinforce conservatism. Fostering these musics became a far more conscious part of the apartheid project in the 1950s. The late Govan Mbeki, a historian and ANC leader, described how Zulu music and culture were subverted:

> Tribal ceremony, especially the Zulu wardance, that beautiful body-building exercise, receives special attention from the Native Affairs Department in the hope that its fervour will somehow reproduce the past, when Zulus were united in unquestioning allegiance to tribal authority. But now authority is centred elsewhere. Thus Cyprian Bekhuzulu, dressed in Victorian-style chief's uniform . . . [presides] over Zulu dancing and this, it is hoped, will make the Zulus believe they are reliving their prowess in the days of Shaka, Dingane, Cetewayo and Dinizulu. But behind the House of Zulu and controlling it, are the field agents of the Government Native Commission.[65]

The obverse of the coin of acknowledging some black urban residence, but confining it within the townships, was the development of the 'homelands'. The Tomlinson Commission, which reported in 1955, pointed out that 'native reserves' were inadequate to support the black population, and recommended forms of economic development that took the areas far too close to autonomy for the liking of the South African government. But the government acknowledged the reality of Tomlinson's findings and began to explore ways of creating self-governing 'Bantustans': nominally self-governed, rural labour dormitories for white-controlled industries on their borders. The culmination of these plans was the 1959 Promotion of Bantu Self-Government Act, which made every black person living in South Africa—wherever they had been born—a citizen of one of these fake states, and removed the last shreds of black representation in the white parliament. By 1962, the tight, immutable tribal nature of townships in reserves was confirmed in an administrative regulation:

> Ethnic character of population of township: Whenever any township is situated within the area of jurisdiction of any chief or headman, no person other than a member of the tribe of that chief or of the community over which that headman has been appointed or who has joined such tribe or community shall, save with the approval of the Bantu Affairs Commissioner, be permitted to become an occupier of such township.[66]

In the years before, the administration of the reserves had been tightened and bureaucratised, and sharecropping and free grazing were restricted. These measures removed the reserves' minimal remaining autonomy and 'turned chiefs into junior civil servants who had to carry out government policies efficiently or be dismissed'.[67]

In reaction, the 1950s saw a series of peasant revolts, all put down with instant severity. In 1950, fourteen peasants among a community tearing down antigrazing fences were shot by police at Witziehoek in the Drakensberg Mountains. In 1956, the peasant community at Mmamathola rose up against grazing restrictions, and their chief was deposed and replaced. In 1957, rural women protested against being forced to carry passes in Lichtenburg; four men were shot when they tried to protect the women against police beatings, and in the nearby Hurutshe reserve another chief was deposed for supporting the women's protests. Also in 1957, a four-year, military-scale revolt began in Pondoland in the Eastern Transkei, growing from a revolt against interference in the chieftaincy to a general rebellion against apartheid laws. In 1958, in Sekhukhuniland, riots were violently suppressed when the government imposed its own chieftainship candidate. In 1960, the government bombed Ngquza Hill, where the rebels had their stronghold, killing more than a dozen men. While not all the idealistic folklorists whose support was drawn in saw the direct connection, the government had very good reasons for fostering conservative, neotraditional sounds—for rural and urban listeners—during this decade.

Neotraditional sounds survived in the cities, in hostels (where they received a fresh transfusion with every new batch of migrant workers), and in some residential communities. A particular tradition was the competitive vocal performance of Zulu *isicathamiya*, for which an outside judge was often recruited. *Drum* photographer Jurgen Schadeberg found himself gently press-ganged by one such performance:

One day in Johannesburg, around 1952 or so, I was driving around in
my little car. I was lost; it was evening, getting dark. I was lost in the
southern parts of Jo'burg, where there were sort of mines around, factories. . . . I couldn't find my way until I came to a small building which was
a hall. And I found—well, I heard noises, music, singing and I decided
to ask my way. There must have been 80 or 100 people in this hall. There
was a stage, and on this stage there were people singing. Small choirs. I
watched, and then people clapped and threw pennies on the stage. So
they sang again, the same group. I got involved in this, so I said: I must
take pictures. I got back to the car, got my camera out. . . . There was a
little band who played. Everybody loved them and they walked off. Nobody threw pennies. Then another group came up, and they threw pennies again. And people sort of welcomed me and shook my hand and
said how nice of me to come and so on. About half an hour later, they
asked me if I could judge the competition. This was Friday night, and
there was beer and drinks, which was illegal in those days. And they gave
me a long pencil and sat me in a corner. I had to judge those groups of
choirs, those bands and so on. . . . I spent the whole night shooting
pictures. I went home at 5 or 6—they were going to carry on till Sunday
evening. I went back another Saturday and there they were, doing the
same thing over again. There was this fascination about singing and
music and choirs . . . [among] people who lived and worked in the
neighbourhood. . . .[68]

Only the Pondoland rebellion was fully and successfully linked with urban
political solidarity, but the 1950s also saw large-scale urban protest and a shift in
the policies of the African National Congress towards mass mobilisation that
could actively confront the government. In a period of visible economic boom—
strengthened by South Africa's very successful export of uranium (a by-product
of gold mining) as atomic fuel to Britain and America—black workers' wages
were kept down, and their conditions worsened.

At the start of the decade, a May Day stay-away attracted the support of 70
percent of all black workers. In 1952, the ANC embarked on the Defiance Campaign, a phased plan for the mass breaking of pass and other restrictions by
volunteers trained in passive resistance methods. In the next two years, more
than 8,000 volunteers were arrested, and ANC membership rose fourteenfold.
By 1953, the police were using live rounds on crowds of defiers in the cities of
the Eastern Cape, and the state was extending its emergency powers. The ANC
ended the campaign and worked on developing an alliance with radical white
and coloured political groups (the Congress Alliance). It founded a nonracial
trade union federation (South African Confederation of Trade Unions, or
SACTU) and women's league (Federation of South African Women, or
FEDSAW). In June 1955, the Kliptown Congress of the People was attended by

almost 3,000 delegates from all these groups. Chaired by a white man of Afrikaner descent (the only Congress Alliance leader not restricted by the police), it adopted the Freedom Charter—based on the United Nations' Declaration of Human Rights—as its blueprint for the future. The Freedom Charter made an unequivocal commitment on culture: 'The doors of learning and culture shall be opened!'

In 1956, 20,000 members of FEDSAW marched on Pretoria to protest the universal imposition of passes for women and chanted: '*Watint'Abafazi, Watint'Imbokodo*' ('When you strike the women, you have struck a rock!'). This and other intensifications of the struggle against apartheid led to the arrest of 156 Congress Alliance leaders and militants, including Z. K. Matthews and Nelson Mandela, for fomenting communist revolution against the state. A former South African Nazi, Oswald Pirow, led a fanatical but incompetent prosecution, which used the concept of communism much as Senator Joseph McCarthy was using it in the United States. 'Even words like "people", "oppression" and "democracy", [the prosecution] described as "communist-orientated" . . . [They] seem to have the word "communist" on the brain!' wrote Z. K. Matthews in a letter from detention.[69] It took until early 1961 for the last accused to be acquitted, though most had won bail during the trial's final years. The year 1957 saw national boycotts of the overpriced buses that transported township dwellers to their city work (*'Azikhwelwa'*—'We will not ride!'—was the slogan) and attacks on forced removals and the government-monopoly beerhalls in the Durban settlement of Mkumbane. In 1959, a breakaway group from the ANC founded the Pan-African Congress (PAC), under the leadership of Robert Sobukwe and with a gold star on its flag for the new nation of Ghana. The PAC argued that the ANC had weakened too much its emphasis on African control of the struggle and future control of the land. It was successful in recruiting 25,000 members, many of them migrant workers. The trial, the protests, the fierce debates on African identity sparked by the PAC–ANC split, and white paranoia over *swaart* and *rooi gevaar* (black and red perils) formed the backdrop to everything that happened in the later years of the decade.

The government soon grasped that radio was an important aspect of social control. Although the 1950s continued the practice of setting aside hours for Africans in the general programming from the South African Broadcasting Corporation (SABC), through the decade, these began to be divided along linguistic lines, with special programmes for Zulus, Xhosas, Sotho-speakers, and so on. There was a one-hour jazz programme, *This Is African Jazz*, hosted by 'uMgibe', pianist Gideon Nxumalo. He was the broadcaster who popularised the term *mbaqanga* for the new music, although some black social critics were now using the dismissive term *msakazo* (broadcast music), and attacking the separate development propaganda that intruded on the sounds. General Duze was closely involved with those early days of African broadcasting, creating continuity music:

> Gideon Nxumalo—uMgibe—was a great guy. From Bloemfontein. He could play Mozart on the piano and then switch to jazz somewhere in the middle. Beautiful stuff! I worked in his trio later. But I can say I helped him get the job with the SABC, because the main presenter, Mr. Hlubi, wanted some young man to help him, and Gideon could type. That's how we got him the job there. . . . There would be a jazz programme, broadcasting from the SABC in Commissioner Street. It was local recordings—I used to listen a lot to [white South African bandleader] Roy Martin—and American records. Macrae Taylor was the boss, and he enjoyed his jazz; [he] used to come in and listen to us playing and applaud. Later, they used to have sports features. Dan Twala used to come in and read the Bantu sports features and then we'd come in and finish the programme off with music. It was the radio that helped me get attached to Ella Fitzgerald. When she was working with Chick Webb . . . 'A Tisket, A Tasket'. That was when I first heard Ella scatting. She'd sing the song and then go to town on it. Wow! She did things to that tune: a different version every time she sang the melody. . . .[70]

In 1952, the cable Rediffusion radio service was extended to Orlando Township, although many residents might have preferred streetlights and paved roads. Trombonist Jonas Gwangwa was an avid listener who learned a lot, but he also noticed the potential for censorship on a piped service, and how anything resembling political commentary was gradually squeezed out after 1960:

> I had listened to a whole lot of music actually from Rediffusion, because I'm from Orlando and that's how I got into the *mbaqanga* and knew all the bands from the sounds—I could tell you this is the Cool Six, this is the African Swingsters—just listening to them. Because after some time you just got into the sounds. . . . [It cut] us off from the rest of the music, but . . . we were fortunate to be exposed because one was too young to be going to the dance-halls and things like that. . . . [On Rediffusion] we had a programme of black bands and singers and storytellers—we had a whole lot of sketches, radio plays, you know. I mean, that culture was kind of rich at the time. We were supposed to be part of the whole apartheid structure, but it opened up some doors for us, otherwise we wouldn't have been able to hear the music. And then the South African government realised that we're bringing these people together and they're beginning to appreciate themselves now—stop! Besides, the Gideon Nxumalos . . . started talking and playing relevant songs, and especially after Sharpeville, the massacre, you see. And they were fired.[71]

**General Duze (left) in performance. Bass player unknown.** *Credit: Historical papers, University of Witwatersrand Library*

The SABC played a proactive role in the sound of the music and the way it was presented: 'Producers like the SABC's Michael Kittermaster insisted on making their own artistic judgements over the protests of African performers. Most often, temporary ensembles were created at Broadcasting House for specific programmes'.[72] It was becoming important for the apartheid project that the music of different groups be located within separate discourses, a process that musicians like Tony Schilder found wounding and absurd:

I got involved politically because, for instance, when I used to play for the SABC—and it was on radio, so no one could see me—they still changed my name. They didn't want people to think it was a coloured guy playing, so they changed my name to Peter Evans, because somebody there thought I played a bit like Bill Evans. . . . I had a hell of a row with them . . . listen, what difference does it make what my name is? Either you play my music or you don't! But because I had to make a living, I took all that crap from them. They used to give the coloured people Sunday morning, 7 o-clock. So now most of the white people were in church; they couldn't listen. And then they used to change your name also. But the mere fact that it was on 7–8 on a Sunday morning, you knew that whoever's playing on that programme was a coloured. That's what we had to contend with. . . .[73]

Political songs were actively censored. The SABC banned a song about the bus boycotts, the revolutionary hymn 'Vukani Mawethu!' ('People, Awake!'), and many others. The SABC made its own recordings, often trading on the naivete of young broadcasters, such as Thandi Klaasen, and their thirst for the novel fame of this new mass medium:

They didn't pay us. We were being used—used! But we didn't care at that time, as long as they can tell us: you will be on the radio at nine o'clock. . . . That was our wages . . . going recording at the SABC, at the back [door]. We never used to use the front. . . . You'll go in and just sing, sing, sing. And you don't have to say you need water or whatever—you'll just go out the same way you went in. Outside again, this guy will talk to you, on the pavement: goodbye, it was nice, you must listen tomorrow morning. No pay, nothing. When we walk in the street [we're saying] you must listen tomorrow, we're singing at the radio. Because we didn't know that we were supposed to be paid. Nobody tipped us off.[74]

The growing importance of broadcasting as a medium for exposing and marketing music created the potential for a profitable commercial relationship with the record companies—so long as the product was right. A new generation of producers and a new system, that of the studio 'stable', was developing. The stable system meant that artists were signed to a label, but they recorded under a range of group names (sometimes bought outright from their originators for a single payment), as Banzi Bangani explains:

I was scared of signing contracts, because I didn't go so much [to] school. Now Elijah [Nkwanyane], he was very much better than me, because he went up as far as secondary school. So we used to share in composing, but Elijah used to take care of contracts, so his name would come up more on recordings. We had some band at the studio: Zakes Nkosi, Boycie Gwele, and so on. But now, if a recording is about you, you'll come up with your name for the band. And yet it's still us. If it's Ntemi [Piliso], it will be the Alexandra All-Star Band. If it's Elijah, it will be called Elijah's Jazz Band. Whatever. But it's always us.[75]

Producers were not always musically knowledgeable, expecting that the players would invent relevant parts when required, particularly with a less familiar instrument, like Jonas Gwangwa's trombone:

[T]he music that we played was *mbaqanga*—we played a few of those *mbaqanga* records; Troubadour label, various artists, with Michael Xaba and Bra Ntemi. . . . And we'd get into the studio, you know, and they'd be rehearsing the saxophone part, and I['d] wait on the side and say no, I'm waiting for my part. They'd say, 'Do what trombones do—do something!'[76]

These producers were men like Cuthbert Matumba (whose recordings of predominantly *msakazo* sounds gave his label, Troubadour, the lion's share of the 1950s black record market) and Rupert Bopape of EMI. They had a brilliant sense of what would sell, but little patience with articulate and argumentative modern jazzmen, or with the complex modern jazz that was becoming harder to market as the SABC, the main showcase, indicated its preference for less defiantly urban styles. So they used their studio sidemen to back more compliant rural or neotraditional musicians, or wide-eyed novices. One style that emerged under Bopape's tutelage was *simanje-manje*. The imperative Zulu phrase means 'Now-now!' and the style turned the smooth, stylish female close harmonies of the Quad Sisters and the Skylarks into rapid-fire, repeated phrases for four female voices, backed by saxophones and a modern rhythm section and accompanied on stage by neotraditional dancing that emphasised the singers' shaking hips.

The jazz musicians who remained were capable of musical and lyrical subversion. Singer Mary Thobei believes that Troubadour's runaway success was partly owed to its tolerance for songs with contemporary references, so long as they maintained a commercial formula:

We had our own 'Special Branch', a sort of bush telegraph, and as a result we knew what would happen in our communities, be it social or political. . . . Take, for instance, the big Azikhwelwa bus boycott in Alexandra Township and the death of ANC leader and Nobel prizewinner Chief Albert Luthuli. We cut best-selling records based on these incidents. You would hear or see something in your community, and the following day you would be in the studio recording it. . . . Cuthbert [Matumba] would say he had heard over the radio that something was going to happen and 'I want everybody now because by tonight [at] five o'clock it must be out and I'm going to advertise it. . . . We at Troubadour were ahead of the opposition with this type of thing because the other studios didn't think like this.[77]

Young musicians were the most pliable in producers' hands, and an ideal format for the new recordings was what came to be known as 'pennywhistle jazz', or *kwela*. Flutes and whistles of various kinds had long been a feature of rural music, and in many communities they were the particular province of the young boys tasked with herding cattle or goats. The tradition was visible in towns through the activities of *Amalaita* gangs and AmaSkotish marching bands and a cheap (around 7 shilling), factory-made six-hole whistle was often the first instrument a young, aspiring musician could afford, and a vehicle for trying out what was heard on records. Young pennywhistlers found work in established bands, too. Saxophonist Barney Rachabane hit his early teens at the end of the 1950s. He found his first work in the townships with Ntemi Piliso and with revered bandleader Zakes Nkosi, who was drawing strains of the Swazi music of his family into big-band compositions for the African Swingsters:

> I was playing in Bra Zakes' band and the wedding band with Bra Ntemi in Alexandra. That's where I grew up with those guys, playing at weddings in the townships while I was still at school, so I could only use the weekends. I used to play in the streets, pennywhistles. But I wanted to play like Zakes and Kippie [Moeketsi], so I picked up the sax. In the townships, music was the life. You found the older guys saying the only way to play was to join up with the old guys and play alongside them to learn more.[78]

The pennywhistle was ideal to attempt clarinet solos like those played by Benny Goodman, and some popular American boogie-woogie records used a flute to weave an obligato line around vocals in a way that also provided musical ideas. The style was played at *stokvel* parties and by young buskers on the streets, as poet Keorapetse Kgositsile describes:

> At a very early age, African boys have to live by their wits. At nine, when pretty often all they have to go home to for dinner is a few slices of bread and jam, they have to hustle for a few pennies to buy fish crumbs from some fish and chip shop which would, anywhere else in the world, throw them away. So in South African cities like Johannesburg one finds boys ranging from about nine to early teens pennywhistling and dancing in white suburb sidewalks and entrances to train stations to catch a few pennies from whites enthralled by the agility of 'pickaninnies'. So we get together, we buy, steal or borrow some pennywhistles, we get a wooden box that is not too heavy for us to carry around, we make a small hole in the box and insert a string through the hole and we have a pennywhistle and a self-made, one-string bass. No matter what your turn of mind, the lyricism and sometimes bluesy anguished happiness of this seemingly casual music touches your sensibility. The music, sometimes robust, at times whirling, always brutally moving and demanding, has all the ingredients of township life. Traditional tribal rhythms mingle freely with

township beats, West African highlife, Afro-American jazz and rhythm n' blues to produce a distinctly South African sound.[79]

*Kwela* is the Zulu term for 'Climb up!' or 'Get on!' and police vans were nicknamed *kwela-kwela* for the way the police roughly jostled suspects in—and the urgent need to make a quick exit from the scene. *Kwela!* was also a shout of encouragement during the popular *pata-pata* (touch-touch) dance, where couples patted one another's bodies up and down—a dance to which most white commentators ascribe a purely sexual connotation. But percussionist and composer Ndikho Xaba points out that *pata-pata* carried layers of significance:

> They do it with us as they did with America. Just as jazz was taken only as the music of the brothels, so our music is always associated in the same way. The *pata-pata*, for example. It is a social dance and people are certainly enjoying themselves—but I wonder if those who give it a particular meaning have ever seen a white policeman patting someone down?[80]

It may have been white listeners who christened the music, from the satirical spoken introduction to an early recording: the 1956 'Tom Hark' by Elias Lerole and his Zig-Zag Flutes. The introduction enacts street gamblers switching swiftly to busking as the police van arrives, with a cry of 'Here comes the *kwela-kwela*'— and that last word of *tsotsitaal* may have been the only one white listeners' ears could catch. 'Tom Hark' was a huge international success, recorded by the Ted Heath Orchestra in Britain. Lerole, Lemmy 'Special' Mabaso, and Spokes Mashiane were the teenage heroes of the genre, although none got rich. It was Rupert Bopape who copyrighted 'Tom Hark', and Lerole was paid a flat fee of £8.

Over a somewhat leaden guitar and drums, Kippie Moeketsi moved with the times to record 'Clarinet Kwela'. He used every ounce of his jazzman's brain to make it more than a hop, skip, and jump jive. Where a pennywhistle would have filled in with fast, florid embroideries, Kippie pulled back, leaving air between the classic marabi chords. This was swing, rather than boogie-woogie style, cheekily ornamented with a soaring trill that out-Goodmans Benny Goodman.[81]

The result of this kind of 'underground' jazz playing was that, while the most progressive experimental modern jazz remained a minority taste, familiarity with the conventions of jazz and an ear for a good solo penetrated all sectors of black society, making the broader church of jazz an enduringly popular music. 'Even today', notes Pops Mohamed, a multi-instrumentalist and club music producer, 'young people's music is *kwaito* [South African hip-hop], but they still also love their good old jazz'.[82]

All over the country, instrumental music was a young man's game. Particularly in the Cape, young men often socialised as the group of age-mates who had undergone traditional manhood initiation together, and these groups could form the nuclei of bands or sports teams, as Chris Columbus' son, the trumpeter and educator Duke Ngcukana, describes:

During that time, people would come together. Normally, they would be initiates: a group of fourteen or fifteen would go to the bush and so forth. And when they came out they would decide what to do with their lives, and invariably they would pick sport or music. If they played music, they bought instruments. Each guy would come in with a different instrument that they couldn't play yet. And then my father would teach them: four or five trumpets; five or six saxophones; four or five trombones—perhaps the brightest of them all would play piano. But normally, you always look for the first trumpet and then teach the first alto saxophone—those two are the most important voices.[83]

Banzi Bangani, stranded after a failed band tour to Cape Town, found himself pulled into the same kind of project. There, he started the band training of the man who was to become the most revered saxophonist of the late 1960s and 1970s, Winston Mankunku Ngozi:

When I was in Cape Town, I was approached by guys from a well-known rugby club, the Buffaloes. They said, Bra Banzi, we want you to teach us to play instruments. Some of them guys never played an instrument before. I said, Gentlemen, I do not know. Let's meet and see. And I looked at them, at the height of some of them. . . . You see, I liked the shorter guys on trumpets and altos and the taller guys to play tenor. There was one really hefty guy: I started him on baritone. I started with these guys in February. In November, at the closing of the schools, they were on stage. And after, that's where Mankunku comes from.[84]

Mankunku himself chuckles nostalgically when reminded of this incident:

'Bra' Banzi? Hey, yes, he was my teacher. . . . A lot of musicians also played rugby and the club was their place, so they also rehearsed there, kept instruments there. I joined their band when I was a kid. I always loved music. My father was a preacher, so there was always music around the house: religious music, hymns. But also my uncles were musicians. They played for parties and things, and they belonged to the rugby club in Retreat. They had a lot of records. . . . I used to listen to all the old big bands: Glenn Miller, things like that. I can't describe it, but there was something in the music that just pulled me. . . . I wanted to play piano, and by then there was no piano in the house, so the following day I went to the club and pulled out a trumpet. Banzi was there, teaching the band.[85]

Music and sport both offered a route out of poverty and shared a working-class fan base, so their close connection is not surprising. In 1953, sportsman turned singer Jake Ntuli, the newly crowned Empire flyweight boxing champion, guested with the Manhattan Brothers on the boogie-woogie song 'Organ Grinder Swing'. As well as a spoken outro, Ntuli gets a whole verse to himself:

> I'm Jake Ntuli, flyweight king
> With me boxing is the thing
> Round or short or fat or tall
> Hit them once—and down they fall!

Ntuli has a reedy tenor voice, and his sense of pitch is rather less accurate than his lethal right hook.

In Johannesburg, pressures were reducing the opportunities for performances. White musicians' union rules, liquor restrictions, and pass requirements made city venues and late hours hard to manage for both players and audiences—and racially mixed venues almost impossible. Anyone out on the streets at night was fair game for both the *tsotsis* and the police, and where black victims were concerned, the behaviour of the two was not always distinguishable. One of the most famous dance halls, Inchcape Hall, burned down in 1951. The nonracial modern jazz sessions at the Odin Cinema in Sophiatown, run by Pinocchio Mokaleng ('He knew nothing but jazz and the blues', recalls Thandi Klaasen. 'Studying those people was his life'[86]), were ended by the clearance of the suburb itself.

The BMSC, however, remained, and new ventures and enterprises were developing. Musicians endured entertainment taxes and pass regulations to tour, in South Africa and beyond:

> I had to travel to Klerksdorp, Potchefstroom, places I'd never seen before. . . . The band was all drinking and smoking *dagga*, but I never drank, I just looked on. And I needed my sleep also. I remember once in Klerksdorp they were all sitting up and drinking, and I asked [the bandleader] Mackay Davashe where can I sleep. And he looked at me sternly and said: 'We sleep in the truck when we go to the next place. We are playing music here, and we have no time for sissies!'[87]

> Dolly [Rathebe] joined us as a guest with the Harlem Swingsters. We went to Lourenco Marques in 1951, which is called Maputo now. So we practiced some Portuguese songs, but when we got there, they wanted swing! We were trying to satisfy their tastes, but they just began to shout, 'Ve vant swing! Ve vant swing!' So we just played swing as if we were in South Africa.[88]

In 1952, promoter Alfred Herbert created the African Jazz and Varieties Show for white audiences, with the patronisingly titled 'Sheila's Night'—a segregated early-evening Thursday matinee—for their domestic servants. Herbert was the son of Sarah Sylvia ('Madam' Sarah, she preferred to be called), who had toured South Africa, leading a Yiddish theatre company in the 1940s. She taught Yiddish songs to both Thandi Klaasen and Dolly Rathebe (whose popularity won her the opening spot) for her son's show. Herbert was a feckless entrepreneur with a taste for gambling, who created a programme somewhere between concert and dance and burlesque. He gave his artists regular work, including tours (he was able to secure passports for most performers), and promised wages of £35 a week. This meant that he attracted many top acts to his programmes, despite his penchant for pushing the staging towards the sensational and stereotyped. 'We had to have bodyguards, because we dressed in short African attire and it was very sexy', remembers Dolly Rathebe.[89] Economic reality with Herbert did not always live up to the promise. Thandi Klaasen was a regular with the show, and she recalls his failings, but with affection:

> I used to sing even Jewish songs. Sarah Sylvia, Alfred Herbert's mother, taught me. She used to make me sing it in the classic style, *Rosjinkes mit Mandlen*, and that was one of the songs that made my name, especially with the Jewish people in Cape Town. Dolly Rathebe was in the shows, Dorothy Masuka, Sonny Pillay, Ben 'Satch' Masinga, The Woody Wood-peckers. . . . Oh, the singers! What was nice with Alfred Herbert was he used to let us tour from one place to another and he would pay us. But sometimes one week he doesn't pay us. He would tell us: the money's been eaten by the horses, so I don't have [it]. But I owe you. . . . He will pay us, though. He never robbed us. Whether he was under-paying us, we didn't care. At least we always had something to take home to our families. . . .[90]

Another patron of the music—and far better-loved than Herbert—was the Reverend Trevor Huddleston, a tireless British Anglican missionary, educator, and campaigner, who formed the Huddleston Boys' Band in which Hugh Masek-ela, Jonas Gwangwa, and many others got their first break. Huddleston's ener-getic publicity for the plight of young South Africans overseas won Hugh Masekela the gift of a trumpet from Louis Armstrong and other donations of instruments. Jonas Gwangwa remembers asking to play 'the big thing' and being handed a trombone, which was not what he had in mind. No one could show him how to play it, but once more, the movies came to his aid:

> I started playing in 1954. . . . I was given the instrument by Father Trevor Huddleston at Saint Peter's School. I'm a self-taught musician even in just holding the instrument. I saw from a Glenn Miller picture how to

hold it; it was a new instrument and it was a time when Glenn Miller was hot. . . . [T]he very first people that picked me up was a singing group, the Boston Brothers. Sam, the bandleader, got me to go and do their background because Manhattans had a saxophone—Kippie Moeketsi . . . Inks [the African Inkspots] had a trumpet, so I'm going to look for different sounds on the trombone for the Bostons.[91]

Apartheid restrictions eventually made Huddleston's work and vigorous campaigning impossible, and the Anglican Church recalled him. His 1954 farewell concert at the BMSC drew unpaid performances from almost every black player of note in Johannesburg and was a major fundraiser for its sponsor, the recently formed Union of South African Artists (usually called Union Artists).

Union Artists had been formed by garment workers' union organiser Guy Routh, who, during the 1930s and 1940s, had worked with radical black companies such as the Bantu People's Theatre (later the African National Theatre), writing his own plays and showcasing the work of black playwrights.[92] He was joined by liberal entrepreneur Ian Bernhardt, who had staged an all-black production of Shakespeare's *Comedy of Errors* the previous year. Union Artists tried—and in a well-publicised minority of cases, succeeded—in securing better contracts for black recording artists and campaigned for the international boycott of shows before segregated audiences. When apartheid forced Routh, too, out of the country, Bernhardt, with the collaboration of other liberals, like producer Leon Gluckman, put his major efforts into organising shows. ('The audience potential is cut to ribbons [by segregation]', Gluckman told the press. 'If it were not so tragic, it would be ludicrous'.)[93]

From the proceeds of the Huddleston farewell concert, Union Artists bought Dorkay House, a block or two away from the BMSC. Intended as a training venue and administrative centre for Union Artists, Dorkay House still survives, although today it is crippled by lack of funding. In the late 1950s, it ran talent contests and small shows, leading eventually to various series of touring concerts, Township Jazz and Dorkay Jazz among them. Artists welcomed the chance to work and their relative artistic freedom, but there were aspects of Union Artists they liked less: the segregated audiences; Bernhardt's sometimes haphazard, anxiety-inducing financial management ('We called him Ian Heartburn,' says Jonas Gwangwa[94]), the patronising trappings of talent contests. 'It was our labour that had bought that place', argued trumpeter Dennis Mpale, 'but it was Heartburn and his boys who picked the winners'.[95]

However, they loved Dorkay House, with its opportunities to meet and share ideas with a wide range of fellow musicians. Concert singer Sibongile Khumalo is the daughter of the late Professor Khabi Mngoma, at various times a classical music teacher at Dorkay. By the 1960s, she was visiting the place herself as a fascinated young girl, but she also remembers her father's accounts of the earlier decade:

It was just interesting, that whole mix, you know—[a drama group] on the first floor; music education on the third floor. There was a sense of respect for each other. . . . In those days, the jazz musicians were the crème de la crème of performing artists; the guys to look up to. . . . People would meet on the fire escapes when they were on breaks, or go upstairs to get some kind of music literacy: just the basic five lines and four spaces of music. . . . There was a respect and a sharing of creativity.[96]

Dorkay House rapidly became the first port of call for a new musician in town. When Pat Matshikiza arrived in Johannesburg in 1962, he went in search of a long-lost aunt in the townships:

The lady says can I help you; and when I gave her my name she says, Ooh! You are my nephew! How's your mother? Do you remember your cousin Vivian? . . . No, you must stay with us! When Vivian arrived home, he said, who's this? Okay, tomorrow we'll wake up early. I'll set the alarm. I'm taking you to Dorkay House; we're playing with Letta Mbulu, all the jazz musicians. You've got a job.[97]

Sibongile Khumalo's father was teaching for the African Music and Dance Association, working alongside jazzmen like Kingforce Silgee and with informal input from writers like Ezekiel Mphahlele, with whom he also collaborated in the Syndicate of African Artists, a broader cultural development body whose magazine, *Voice of Africa*, got itself banned in 1952. Other visiting teachers, such as American jazz professor John Mehegan, used the place as a contact point:

[T]his American jazz pianist came to South Africa on a lecture tour . . . he was actually promoting his book on jazz improvisation, so he would have clinics, you know, jazz workshops, and he took Kippie [Mocketsi], myself and Hugh [Masekela] and put us on scholarship and we used to do all these sessions with him. And he toured the country. While he was in Durban touring, he had to do this concert and he had met a good bass player, Claude Shange, and some white musicians. But when he performed, he couldn't take Claude Shange onto the stage because black and white couldn't perform together. And while he was still playing on stage he had a bass behind—Claude got on stage and played behind the curtains. It really upset him, but he said, well, you can't stop the music; you don't see the man, but you can't, you know. . . . That was one of the sad things about it. We got to do an LP with him; actually, it was the first LP made by black people in South Africa, 'cos all we black people could record before was 78s. . . .[98]

The albums that emerged, two volumes called *Jazz in Africa*,[99] provide the first public statement of the music that was superseding boogie-woogie jive among serious jazzmen. The first bebop albums had arrived in South Africa shortly after their release in the United States, by the personal and dockside routes described in Chapter 2. They soon also appeared in specialty shops. Charlie Parker made a particular impression:

When I first heard Bird and those guys, the music was very exciting—it hit me like a thunderbolt—but I couldn't work out exactly what they were doing. I just shut myself away with the thing, and played it over and over. I think I didn't come out for a day or two! And by that time I'd got it. Other guys were doing the same thing, and we talked about it and tried it out.[100]

One of those others was Ntemi Piliso:

We were all into swing . . . then all of a sudden there was this bebop sound. That left us puzzled. We all found Charlie Parker's tunes like 'Moose the Mooch' very difficult to do, maybe because of our deep-rooted swing influence. But not Kippie. He refused to be beaten until he got the tune right.

Another altoist, Peter Mokonotela, recalls, 'Kippie rifled through all the keys of the alto. He played the ballad "Blue Moon" using difficult notes. He would take our altos and show us.'[101]

At the Odin sessions, and later on the back fire escape at Dorkay House, this 'progressive' music was honed. So what Mehegan was able to get recorded was music at the cusp, with elements of the old swing training and discipline, plus the risk-taking and speed of bebop and a conscious African awareness, on original and standard compositions. 'Body and Soul' is there, and 'Yardbird Suite', plus a nod to the times in the form of some novelty pennywhistle swing. Two compositions from Mackay Davashe are featured: the African blues 'Twelve by Twelve' and the powerfully Xhosa-inflected 'Mabomvana (Little Red)'. Mehegan is an accomplished, although sometimes relentlessly busy, pianist, whose jauntiness asserts itself on a second version of 'Mabomvana', retitled 'Johnny's Idea', where, with timing and pace regularised, closed up, and quickened, only the chords still identify the song as African jazz. A very young Jonas Gwangwa on trombone and Hugh Masekela on trumpet have a hatful of risky ideas that sometimes outrun their fingers, and lots of licks borrowed from jump jive, bebop, and the blues. You can hear them fizzing with the music that was developing inside them. The three horns trade phrases, tight as they must have been on a live bandstand, but it is saxophonist Kippie Moeketsi who is the revelation. Intricate ascending scalar runs and harsh blues shouts create a unique, sometimes surprising voice that also knows when to employ space and restraint, and, on 'Body and Soul', a pathos that speaks across nearly fifty years to the listener. The album prefigures the considerably more challenging *Jazz Epistles Volume 1*, with which these hornmen, plus Dollar Brand on piano, Johnny Gertze on bass, and a boxing champion called Makhaya Ntshoko on drums, were to greet the next decade. The Syndicate of African Artists commissioned serious black composition and writing, and one of its beneficiaries was Todd Matshikiza, a talented polymath—teacher, pianist, composer, radical, and *Drum* journalist—whose range of interests and ideas typifies the intellectual leaders of the decade. Matshikiza was a Dorkay House regular.

Born in Queenstown in the Eastern Cape, Todd was the brother of the vaudevillian Meekley 'Fingertips' Matshikiza (and the uncle of Pat). He wrote various works for the choir at Lovedale College, where he both qualified and taught. He moved to Johannesburg and set up a private music school, but he also worked in a bookshop and as a razor-blade salesman while he established himself in jazz (with the Manhattan Brothers and the Harlem Swingsters) and, in 1952, in journalism at *Drum*, where colleagues like Jurgen Schadeberg had huge admiration for his skill with both words and music:

> Todd Matshikiza was a great guy—a very talented person. He had two music hits on Broadway later on. He wrote the music for the jazz opera *King Kong*. He was composing, but he also wrote wonderful articles. And his style was called Matshikeze because he invented new forms of expressing himself with words. It was outstanding; a special language that he wrote. He was wonderful to go out with . . . with a wonderful laugh. I can still hear him laughing now. . . . We often went together and did many stories. I used to live in a suburb called Kensington and my parents, who also immigrated to South Africa, lived near there. I rented a couple of rooms in a small apartment house. On a Sunday, Todd, Kippie [Moeketsi] and his bass player used to come to my place. I had an old piano and off we'd go, the whole weekend, bashing away. I had a guitar— I'm no good at it, hopeless! But still I also banged away. We had a few gallons of wine. . . . The neighbours weren't very keen on these black people making these noises in a white suburb. But it was great fun.[102]

In 1953, Matshikiza wrote *Makhaliphile*, a choral overture dedicated to Huddleston, for a concert to raise funds for a swimming pool in Orlando. It also opened the 1954 farewell concert. In 1956, the Syndicate of African Artists commissioned his *Uxolo*, a work on a massive scale for choir and brass band. 'Todd wrote in a specific way', says Sibongile Khumalo. 'He wrote great choral works, using a brass band because it was impossible for him at that time to get access to a full orchestra. We don't need to go into the politics of all that, it's obvious. But he wrote in that certain way because this was a man who interacted with jazz musicians, understood what [both] genres were all about. . . . I think that only happened because there was that kind of contact [that was happening at Dorkay House].'[103]

Out of Dorkay House, too, came the musical team that was to create South Africa's most famous musical play: *King Kong*. The play was based on the rise and fall of boxing champion Ezekiel Dlamini. Percy Tucker, the architect of South Africa's first ticket booking agency, describes in his autobiography how its white liberal patrons saw the creation of the show:

> In 1958, lawyer and writer Harry Bloom accompanied Ian Bernhardt one evening to listen to some new black singing groups. . . . [He] was en-thralled by these young performers. Like Bernhardt, he felt the time was ripe to develop black potential in vehicles more substantial than concerts. He conceived the idea of developing a jazz opera and set about looking for a suitable story that would embody the unique flavour of township life. . . . When he read reports of the death of Ezekiel Dlamini, he knew he had found his subject. . . . Watching [the directors at work], Arnold [Dover] had worked on a film with Africans and was prepared for their improvisatory spontaneity. Leon [Gluckman] instinctively knew how to control his ebullient and sometimes unruly company, making demands on them without resorting to any of the trappings of authority which attached to his status and his skin.[104]

Todd Matshikiza wrote the music and some lyrics. In his autobiography, he describes how the process felt from his perspective:

> I think *King Kong* will make a marvellous excuse for a theatrical produc-tion. Your people are so much alive, especially for this sort of thing. . . . I will put some of the language down as spoken in the township, can you give me a few phrases; for instance, what do you say when a policeman approaches, what is the lingo? More and more white people came around black people telling us to never mind the regulations, let's get to Rupert's place and put down as much African lingo as we can, although Rupert's place is in the heart of the White kingdom and blacks are shot at sight after nine, 'specially if you're talking some lingo. . . . Every night I dreamed I was surrounded by pale-skinned, blue-veined people who changed at random from humans to gargoyles. I dreamed I lay at the bottom of a bottomless pit. They stood above me, all around, with long sharpened steel straws that they put to your head and the brain matter seeped up the straws like lemonade up a playful child's thirsty picnic straw. . . . [After rehearsal] I am on the brink of a nervous collapse be-cause I have been listening to my music and watch it go from black to white, and now purple.[105]

Looking back on a shared Sophiatown past: the two divas Tandi Klaasen and Dolly
Rathebe. *Credit: Cedric Nunn*

Jonas Gwangwa was a member of the orchestra. His memories catch both the excitement and the problems of the production:

I had been to *Pyjama Game*, which came to perform at Wits [the University of the Witwatersrand], and I saw something I had never seen before, you know: a live musical—I had always seen musicals in the movies. But I was so taken up and when I heard Ian Bernhardt say we are gonna have a musical, I said, are you gonna have anything like *Pyjama Game*? He said, 'Yes, that's what we're gonna have'. I says, 'I'm in it!' . . . I was in the team with Hugh [Masekela]; we were in the team that was arranging—actually we were the copyists. Everything was new about this thing—there had never been copyists before, and Spike Glasser, who was the musical director, was working alongside Kippie Moeketsi, Mackay Davashe, [and] Sol Klaaste doing the orchestration and arranging. The music, of course, was by Todd Matshikiza, and a big band was put together and we rehearsed . . . Miriam Makeba, the Manhattan Brothers. The story was *King Kong*. *King Kong* was about a boxer, a heavyweight, who was quite popular and who had been arrested when it was alleged that he killed his girlfriend. And the whole drama was about his life and his love life, and of course he died in prison. . . . *King Kong* was a very popular guy who used to do his road work right in town here, you know, greeting people as he goes, and quite a figure. . . . [*King Kong*] was the first black South African jazz opera and it was well done. The problems that arose were . . . you cannot really tell the truth, you know? It was alleged that [Ezekiel Dlamini] committed suicide, but we believed that he was killed in prison and thrown into a dam which was being built. That was one of the biggest problems. And there were some people who were political activists here at home, like Dan Poho, who belonged to the garment workers union, a devout ANC activist at the time, who they refused a passport. Gideon Nxumalo suffered that; he couldn't go abroad. A few people couldn't be taken abroad when *King Kong* was leaving because they were politically active. But the main thing was the real story of Dlamini, you know, *King Kong*. That was just the whole apartheid South Africa . . . that couldn't allow people to tell the real story.[106]

Dambudza Mdledle of the Manhattan Brothers played the title role, and Miriam Makeba, the female lead, the shebeen queen, Joyce, who presides over the legendary Back O'the Moon drinking den. A fourteen-piece orchestra backed the sixty-three-member cast, the cream of the era's modern jazz players. Among them was reed player Kippie Moeketsi, whose contribution to modern jazz led to comparisons with Charlie Parker. Moeketsi's full story belongs in the 1960s, the pivotal decade for the silencing of progressive black culture and, for a time, his own horn.

The show opened on 2 February 1959 at the Wits University Great Hall and was an immediate success: the white *Star* newspaper called it 'the greatest thrill in 20 years of South African theatre-going'.[107] In South Africa, it repeated packed runs over the next two years before securing a London booking for early 1961. It played in many cities, but not in the administrative capital, Pretoria, where the council refused permission. 'By the time the company left for London, 200,000 South Africans had seen *King Kong*. Two-thirds of them were white'.[108]

*King Kong* contains every stereotype: the overphysicalised boxer; the oversexualised shebeen queen; the knife fight; the cute boys playing *kwela* pennywhistle; the Runyonesque gangsters—and, again, the bad end of a city black man. For liberal white audiences, it must have been immensely comforting, allowing them to admire the talent of the black cast (for there was genuine resentment of the absurdity of segregation) while not really challenging the cartoon of township life that conventional wisdom drew. Radical activist Marius Schoon argued that *King Kong* had an even stronger impact:

> It was not only white liberals who filled the halls and bought the LP. . . . [T]he most popular record in any shebeen was *King Kong*. . . . [P]rogressive (which did not of necessity mean liberal) whites regarded it as a step towards our dynamic culture of the future. It was not only the show itself that came like a breath of mountain air in the stodgy South Africa of 1959, but also the stimulation of contact between young people of different colours that took place in a series of parties surrounding *King Kong*. I have heard it said that if it had not been for *King Kong*, the African Resistance Movement ([ARM], one of the small, white, direct-action groups that emerged after Sharpeville) may well never have been formed.[109]

Veterans of the ARM say this is nonsense, and that the play and the socialising around it were simply part of the backdrop to a far more focused growth of radical white political conscience.[110] Yet despite its political flabbiness, the tight production and the brilliant interpretation of the score by a supremely talented cast transcended every stereotype and still do.

By the end of the 1950s, many creative black South Africans had despaired of peaceful change. They planned to leave or increased the pace of a reckless lifestyle that might offer other exits. They broadened their vision of political struggle to meet their oppressors' violence with a people's war. Jazz society had been dispersed and relocated; its context changed so dramatically that much old music seemed sterile, and the time was ripe for something new. Just how dramatic the changes were was about to be viciously demonstrated outside a location called Sharpeville.

The overture to *King Kong* is played by Moeketsi on clarinet (his first instrument). The mood is not light, comic, or cute. Rather, it is the mood of the Berlin of Kurt Weill or Hannes Eisler: dark, haunted, and foreboding. In a conversation with raucous horns, Moeketsi utters slow, minor-key phrases, note-perfect and frighteningly contained: the descant of a dying nightingale.

# Notes

1. Interview for *Ubuyile*, 2000.
2. These photographs have subsequently been published in a number of collections, including J. Schadeberg *Softown Blues: Images from the Black '50s* (Johannesburg: Nedbank, 1994).
3. Stan Motjuwadi, 'Lest We Forget,' in *The Fifties People of South Africa*, ed. J. Schadeberg (Johannesburg: Bailey's African Photo Archives, 1987), 5–6.
4. A. Maimane, 'Sophiatown', lecture at the Grahamstown Arts Festival, 1 July 2002.
5. A. Sampson, *Drum: A Venture into the New Africa* (London: Collins, 1956), 20.
6. Jurgen Schadeberg, interview for *Ubuyile*, 2000.
7. Quoted in M. Alfred, *Johannesburg Portraits* (Johannesburg: Jacana Books, 2003), 85.
8. Quoted in M. Nicol, *A Good-Looking Corpse* (London: Minerva, 1995).
9. Don Mattera, interview for *Ubuyile*, 2000.
10. Thandi Klaasen, interview for *Ubuyile*, 2000.
11. Ntemi Piliso interview for *Ubuyile*, 2000.
12. Derrick Thema, *Kortboy: A Sophiatown Legend* (Cape Town: Kwela Books, 1999), 32.
13. Thandi Klaasen, interview for *Ubuyile*, 2000.
14. Jonas Gwangwa, interview for *Ubuyile*, 2000.
15. Maimane, op. cit.
16. Interview for *Ubuyile*, 2000.
17. Ibid.
18. N. Ngcelwane, *Sala Kahle District Six* (Cape Town: Kwela Books, 1998), 89–99, passim.
19. D. Constant-Martin, *Coon Carnival* (Cape Town: David Phillip, 1999), 133.
20. Interview for *Ubuyile*, 2000.
21. Ibid.
22. The Manhattan Brothers' version of this song can be heard on the compilation *From Marabi to Disco* (CDZAC61, Gallo, 1994).
23. Interview for *Ubuyile*, 2000.
24. On *African Jazz n'Jive* (CDZAC75, Gallo, 2000).
25. Interview for *Ubuyile*, 2000.
26. Ibid.
27. Ibid.
28. Ibid.
29. Ibid.
30. Ibid.
31. Ibid.
32. Ibid.

33. Ibid.
34. Ibid.
35. Ibid.
36. Ibid.
37. Z.B. Molefe & M. Mzileni *A Common Hunger to Sing* (Cape Town: Kwela Books, 1997).
38. Interview for *Ubuyile*, 2000.
39. Thandi Klaasen, interview for *Ubuyile*, 2000.
40. General Duze, interview for *Ubuyile*, 2000.
41. Ibid.
42. Letsatsi Radebe, quoted in P. Bonner and L. Segal, *Soweto: A History* (Cape Town: Maskew Miller Longman, 1998), 30.
43. Star, 18 July 1955, quoted in ibid., 29.
44. Ibid., 34.
45. Interview for *Ubuyile*, 2000.
46. Ibid.
47. Ibid.
48. Quoted in Nicol, op. cit., 369.
49. Interview for *Ubuyile*, 2000.
50. Ibid.
51. Ibid.
52. Rob Allingham, sleeve notes, *From Marabi to Disco*, op. cit.
53. Interview for *Ubuyile*, 2000.
54. Bra Luke interviewed by Miriam Tlali in *Staffrider* 4 no. 4 (1982): 2.
55. M. Dikobe, *Dispossessed* (Johannesburg: Ravan Press, 1983), 32.
56. Interview for *Ubuyile*, 2000.
57. Maimane, op. cit.
58. Interview for *Ubuyile*, 2000.
59. Ibid.
60. Ibid.
61. Ibid.
62. Ibid.
63. Letsatsi Radebe in Bonner and Segal, op. cit., 36.
64. Joseph Molifi of the Sharpetown Swingsters, quoted in Ian Jeffrey, *The Sharpetown Swingsters: Their Will to Survive*, DSG Dissertation Series, no. 6 (Johannesburg: University of the Witwatersrand, 1985), 69.
65. G. Mbeki, *The Peasants Revolt* (London: IDAF, 1984), 32.
66. Proclamation No. R293 of 1962, quoted in ibid., 149.
67. N. Parsons, *A New History of Southern Africa*, 2nd ed. (London: Macmillan, 1993), 296.
68. Interview for *Ubuyile*, 2000.
69. Frieda Matthews, *Remembrances* (Cape Town: Mayibuye Books, 1995), 141.
70. Interview for *Ubuyile*, 2000.
71. Ibid.
72. D. Coplan, *In the Time of the Cannibals* (Johannesburg: Witwatersrand University Press, 1994), 177.

73. Ibid.

74. Ibid.

75. Ibid.

76. Ibid.

77. Compiled from interviews in Mzileni and Molefe, op. cit. n.p., *Two-Tone* 1, no. 12 (December 1992/January 1993), and (Johannesburg) *Vrye Weekblad*, p. 13.

78. Interview for *Ubuyile*, 2000.

79. *Whistling for Pennies*, quoted in *Two-Tone* 1, no. 12 (December 1992/January 1993).

80. Interview for *Ubuyile*, 2000.

81. On *African Jazz n'Jive*, op. cit.

82. Interview for *Ubuyile*, 2000.

83. Ibid.

84. Ibid.

85. Conversation with the author, 29 March 2003.

86. Ibid.

87. Pat Matshikiza, interview with the author for *Star Tonight*.

88. Ntemi Piliso, interview for *Ubuyile*, 2000.

89. Ibid.

90. Ibid.

91. Ibid.

92. P. Tucker, *Just the Ticket* (Johannesburg: Jonathan Ball, 1997), 15.

93. Ibid., 127.

94. Conversation with the author, Botswana, 1988.

95. Conversation with the author, Johannesburg, 1997.

96. Interview for *Ubuyile*, 2000.

97. Interview with the author for *Star Tonight*.

98. Jonas Gwangwa, interview for *Ubuyile*, 2000.

99. Some tracks from the two albums have been re-released on *Jazz in Africa* Vol. 1 (CDN1004, Camden, 1998), although they are poorly labeled and confused on the sleeve notes with material from the later *Jazz Epistles* album.

100. Dennis Mpale, conversation with the author, Johannesburg, 1997.

101. *Two-Tone* 1, no. 3, (Johannesburg) *Vrye Weekblad*, 1992, p. 9.

102. Interview for *Ubuyile*, 2000.

103. Ibid.

104. Tucker, op. cit., 128–129.

105. T. Matshikiza, *Chocolates for My Wife* (Cape Town: David Phillip, 1985), 121–125, passim.

106. Interview for *Ubuyile*, 2000.

107. Quoted in Tucker, op. cit., 131.

108. Ibid., 133.

109. Marius Schoon, in *Medu Art Ensemble Newsletter* 4, No. 1 (1982): 44.

110. E-mail correspondence with Hugh Lewin, December 2003.

*Chapter Four*

# The Land Is Dead

The cry came from the women. '*Izwe Lethu*' (Our land) . . . hands went up. People gave the Africa salute. Toc-toc-toc-toc, I heard the guns. People started running. They were running towards me, but I couldn't run. Women, children, men. Running, leaping, laughing. But I couldn't run and they knocked me down. I could see people falling everywhere. Toc-toc-toc-toc, I heard the guns. There were men on the Saracens. One man I could see with his Sten gun, with the gun at the hip, swaying gently as he shot the people. He moved so slowly, like a man in a dream. . . . When the guns stopped there was silence. I have never heard that silence again. It is the silence when nothing lives. Only slowly does the living come back into that silence. But for a long time it was very quiet.

—Humphrey Tyler, in *Drum*[1]

On Monday, 21 March 1960, 69 people were killed and 186 wounded in the township of Sharpeville outside Johannesburg, when police opened fire on an unarmed crowd of Pan-African Congress demonstrators against the pass laws. Five more were killed in Langa Township outside Cape Town. The African National Congress declared a period of national mourning. A month later, the first, unsuccessful, attempt to assassinate South African prime minister Hendrik Vervoerd was made by a white farmer at an agricultural show. The decade that followed saw the steady stifling of all cultural expressions that opposed (or even mildly questioned) apartheid. A booming South African economy geared itself up for internal and external war. Many cultural historians call it the Silent Time—but it was far from silent. Like a climbing vine through concrete, music that was deliberately and defiantly assertive pushed through and hung on, as singer Sibongile Khumalo describes:

The burst of music creation in the '60s was very much a part of the process that resulted in the black-is-beautiful that eventually emerged in the '70s. The assertion of blackness, of African-ness, to my mind was a negation of the perception of the African as vagrant—that the African is unsophisticated, rural, dirty, backwards—however you choose to describe the African. It was: we can do it like you—if not better![2]

The state's attempted silencing took four main forms: the closing down of the last spaces for expression; the attempt to replace urban and politically aware discourses with synthetic, conservative, tribal substitutes; the creation of distractions; and—as a result of all the pressures on progressive cultural life—the driving of increasing numbers of artists into exile.

Many of these measures came from the blueprints of soldiers, bureaucrats, and former Nazis ensconced in the apartheid apparatus. In the field of culture, they also drew in the enthusiastic support of puritans who detested contemporary forms for their perceived immorality and naive folklorists anxious to preserve dying rural traditions. The brainchild of this coalition was an externally imposed definition of African culture as tribal, unchanging, and—although sometimes beautiful—irredeemably other.

Between 1960 and 1962, the South African Broadcasting Corporation replaced the piecemeal broadcasting of generic or language-specific African programmes in mainstream broadcasting hours with the creation of English and Afrikaans stations with a whites-only menu and Radio Bantu. Eventually thirteen separate stations for what were defined as the most important 'tribes'. White 'commercial' stations, also controlled by the SABC (which occasionally played African-American, but never black South African, music), later joined the broadcasting bouquet. Ethnomusicologist and university lecturer Dr. Yvonne Huskisson became the SABC's overseer of 'Bantu/Indigenous Music'. Her master's thesis on 'Bantu' music education, published in 1955, lays out many of the foundations of the policy she later directed.

Much of her writing is directed against the damaging, detribalising, and acculturising effects of Anglican missionary activity. This reflects the other cultural campaign raging at the time—in which the SABC was a key front—to assert the supremacy of Afrikaans over English culture. Africans and their politics are categorised: 'A generally-accepted theory is that, due to climatic conditions, Africans are emotionally inclined and greatly affected by music. This fact is demonstrated by the tremendous emotional pitch that is reached in African tribal dances.[3] . . . [T]he basic unit of Bantu social organisation is the family, concerning which there are definite behaviour patterns, wide recognition of kinship and a hierarchy of authority.[4] . . . In many respects, the tribe is an extension of the family, with the chief as the ruler of his people'.[5] Patriarchy is thus entrenched in this thesis as an essential and desirable feature of African life (despite the existence of groups within South Africa, including the BaLobedu, with their Rain

Queen, who are female-ruled), along with the authority of puppet homeland chiefs, inserted into and naturalised within this tradition.

It is vital that the integrity of tribal culture be preserved, Huskisson argues: 'A tributary cut off from the main stream is bound to alter its character entirely, either by degenerating into a basin of water or drying up entirely'.[6] Jazz, a 'popular, sex-stimulating music',[7] is a particularly dirty basin of water, since 'among all less developed people, groups or races . . . the form of expression that stimulates the baser impulses penetrate[s] the soul quicker than more advanced forms'.[8] Citing approvingly ethnomusicologist Percival Kirby's injunction to 'fight the machine with the machine',[9] a design for future educational (and broadcasting) policy is then sketched (the educational measures never materialised; formal music education was simply cut from the black curriculum):

The greatest jazz impact has been in the Transvaal. The most thorough measures should thus be devised to combat its influence on the musical outlook of the African child. This can only be effectively done by providing a strong alternative, as attractive, impelling and similar in its characteristics to jazz as possible. The answer lies in African indigenous music, whose rhythmic elements were the initial cause of the wholesale African acceptance of jazz. . . . If the African child was taught music which he felt was satisfying and was allowed to express the natural African rhythmic stimulus to accompany his school music with movement, the synthetic attractions of jazz would gradually assume ever-decreasing importance.[10]

The educational reforms were already in place. The 1953 Bantu Education Act had all but eliminated mission-supported schools, and Vervoerd, then education minister, had reformed the system 'so that natives will be taught from childhood to realise that equality with Europeans is not for them'.[11] Syllabuses were transformed, the use of English was drastically reduced, and, in 1957, segregated 'tribal' universities were created. The mission system had already been under strain, as increasing numbers of black parents tried to place their children in the relatively few schools offering what poet Oswald Mtshali called 'an amulet against / "*Slegs vir blankes* / For Whites Only'.[12] That amulet had been smashed. The broad music education that had nurtured not only European-influenced choral composers but exciting jazz experimenters and nationalist innovators, was gone.

Now the state had in radio, too, a powerful instrument for controlling musical innovation and, through the incentive of airplay-based sales, shaping the output of record companies. The new demographics of the townships—massive, male-only hostels full of workers officially just passing through from the reserves; sprawling townships lacking space or legal sanction for communal music-making—seemed eminently fertile ground for commodified music and for structuring anomic relationships between individual consumers and their radios or gramophones. It appeared an ideal laboratory for the creation of neotribal music. The strategy worked—but only to a point. Many of the artists whose recording careers benefited from the opportunities offered by Radio Bantu obediently decked themselves in beads, fur, and feathers and sang of the joys of tribal life or the virtues of acceptance, or even in praise of specific puppet leaders. They obeyed the requirements of producers like Rupert Bopape, who were increasingly being used by the record companies as their *indunas* (headmen)—the title given by the mine companies to the 'boss-boys' who conveyed their orders to hostel dormitory groups and work teams. Often, the musicians did not even see themselves as purveying state ideology: it was just a gig. Many consumers bought the products. Some of it was good music, for performers like the gravel-voiced singer Mahlatini had talent and imagination, and the backing bands were very often made up of jazz instrumentalists hanging round at the gates like labourers, waiting to be called for the 'piece job' that would justify their daily labour pass.

Broadcasting became the arbiter, taking what might have been fragments of diverse and changing styles and fixing them in stone as the complete definition of a tradition; but it took most of the decade for these definitions to harden, opening small temporary corners of creative space. In the process, the heritage the ideologues claimed to value so much, was changed and distorted. In his study of Sotho music, David Coplan notes that 1980s television broadcasts of Sotho music featured men performing in what had traditionally been women's styles[13] (but by virtue of their brevity and swing were far more broadcast-friendly) and that some traditional singers claimed to have learned their style from broadcasts.[14] Angela Impey, writing about Zulu *isicathamiya*, argues that it often outwardly satisfied the SABC while really carrying multiple messages:

[The performers] relied on their relative seclusion and apparent submissive stance to circumvent and even subvert the pervasive restrictions of the government. While claiming to be apolitical, therefore, *isicathamiya* song and dance provided a metaphor for social action. In the words of one of its main spokespeople, Paulus Msimango, '*isicathamiya* was our way of attacking with song'.[15]

Precisely because of the poverty and overcrowding that apartheid imposed, music was never only a commodity consumed by individuals. Making and hearing music took place within a context of social and political networks, harder to sustain in the townships, but still effective: ANC branches, trade unions, sports clubs, *stokvels*. People were makers of music as well as consumers, and could create songs to serve as 'nuggets of experience, ciphers of resistance, coping mechanisms and celebrations of extraordinary feats'.[16] One gramophone or radio was heard by many, and with the advent of cassette technology at the end of the decade, even officially censored works could be copied and circulated. 'One

would hear the sweet melodies by Miriam Makeba, Hugh Masekela, Bob Marley
and others on those mountains of Mahlabatini.[17] . . . An outsider would be
surprised to find that under those asbestos roofs there was a lot of political
debate . . . interrupted only by the sight of a stranger'.[18]

Nor could the planned tribal segregation of the townships completely over-
write previous experience. Often, illegal informal settlements persisted. Multi-
instrumentalist Pops Mohamed's family was moved to the East Rand, near the
old township of Kalamazoo, which, before it was demolished, made its mark on
his formative years:

> That was when the Group Areas Act came—1964 we went to Riegert
> Park, which was known as Stertonville then. There again, I used to wit-
> ness migrant workers going to the East Rand Property mines, coming
> with traditional instruments to the shebeens and playing their *mbiras* and
> their mouth bows. And all sorts of hand-made instruments. And then at
> the same time you would have jazz musicians playing Count Basie stuff,
> and there's an old out-of-tune piano in the shebeen. Someone would
> batter his way through. These traditional guys, you know, would be join-
> ing in on their traditional instruments, jamming, and unfortunately these
> sounds were not recorded—but they are in the back of my mind. This
> was in Kalamazoo where I grew up.[19]

Many black city people who had previously been sophisticated consumers of
jazz or classical music simply did not relate to the sounds now being foisted on
them. 'In another way, we fell into their trap', says Sibongile Khumalo. 'We
tended to look down at people [who] practised traditional music, as tribalists.
And that also negates our identity. The whole idea was to negate our identity'.[20]

Repression was designed to render these flaws in apartheid's cultural blueprint invisible. In 1960, the first of the decade's many states of emergency was
imposed. The powers of the police Special Branch (SB) were strengthened, and
training secured for it from the French colonial police, already notorious for
their skill as torturers in Algeria. By 1968, the SB had given birth to BOSS, the
Bureau of State Security, a full-blown, autonomous, secret police force. In 1963,
the Publications and Entertainments Act created a nine-member censorship
board to determine the 'desirability' of any local or international publication,
performance, or work of art. Novelist Nadine Gordimer predicted:

> The Bill will destroy the arts in this country, cripple intellect and prolong
> indefinitely the cultural inferiority of a frontier society from which we
> have just begun to emerge. . . . Such a society, by the inexorable law of
> returns, will get exactly what it has provided for: hack writing, hack paint-
> ing, hack theatre. The life of the mind in our country will die of safe-
> guards cynically imposed to stop people thinking.[21]

The results of all this were tragic, sometimes inexplicable, and often farcical. Ticket impresario Percy Tucker describes a production of the American musical *Show Boat*. Its American composer, Oscar Hammerstein had insisted that the South African show have a mixed cast. The authorities ruled that

> the black chorus would be permitted to grace the stage of the Civic [Theatre] provided they were kept on a different level, physically separate from the white cast. Anthony Farmer, contracted to both direct and design, met this request with minimal difficulty. Since in any event the 'black' sequences were largely self-contained, the almost naturally differentiated levels of boat and jetty, plus an ingeniously slightly raised ramp, met the letter of the law. . . . Since it was impossible physically to separate Queenie, the black family retainer, from the white characters, she was played by a blacked-up [white actress].[22]

The SABC censors later scratched a performance of Thelonious Monk's *Crepuscule with Nellie* from a studio recording by Abdullah Ibrahim. No reason was given; Ibrahim's discographer suspects the censor thought *crepuscule* was a sexual term.[23] Countless other instances, such as the banning of the children's novel *Black Beauty*, have been well documented. A jazz player, like saxophonist Barney Rachabane, well understood that 'if you were more on the American side, they couldn't play that music'.[24] Contralto Patty Nokwe's singing at music contests had gained her the reputation of 'the Marian Anderson of South Africa. . . . Patty recounts that tapes of her music were sent to . . . Radio Bantu. But they were turned down by . . . Yvonne Huskisson, who declared that "she sang too much like white people"'.[25]

The West Bantu Administration Board ruled that there were to be no local government-supported black cultural activities in the Johannesburg city centre. Like old or infirm black workers who had to be sent back to the reserves when they could no longer labour, the arts were being 'endorsed out'. In 1964, following repeated press-conference denunciations of apartheid by touring British pop singer Dusty Springfield, a Separate Amenities and Community Development Act was gazetted as part of Group Areas legislation: there were to be no further performances of any type before mixed audiences without special permission. By now, South Africa was out of the Commonwealth, and both the British actors' union, Equity, and British playwrights had imposed bans on performance before segregated audiences. A Copyright Bill steered through the South African parliament sought to shield the South African theatre from the impact of these bans by legalising the pirating of foreign works. The opportunities for public performance by black artists were cut further, as Abigail Khubeka recalls:

> We still used to go to the clubs and perform there, but I'm telling you, it wasn't easy. Once you were on stage, somebody, the bouncer, had to look

out for the police, and the minute the police came, you would run inside and alert the owner that the police were outside. And I would run to the kitchen and pretend I was washing dishes—in a cocktail dress and rubber gloves! Ja, until the police were out.

Johnny Mekoa:

Black musicians were smuggled into clubs. They would change your name. . . . Mine was—what? Johnny Keen.

Duke Ngcukana:

By the end in Cape Town there was only one club that would accommodate us as audience as well as musicians. And I remember in one place[26] Winston Mankunku had to change his name to Winston Mann because as a black man they wouldn't allow him. You had to change your name and be somebody else. It was very sad.

Tony McGregor:

On a lighter note, there's a wonderful story of a white lady jazz singer playing with the Indian jazz pianist Lionel Pillay. And the police came into the hall where they were performing and at that stage the act prevented performers from different races from performing on the same stage, and the police came in and wanted to stop the concert because it was an Indian pianist with a white singer, and the white singer said: 'no problem, I'll put my microphone down here on the floor in the audience and I'll carry on singing here, and then we're *not* singing on the same stage!'[27]

If the arts were being squeezed, more overt resistance was being hammered. Following Sharpeville, both the ANC and the PAC had established military wings, Umkhonto we Sizwe (Spear of the Nation/MK) and POQO (with a very similar resonance to the Irish nationalist Sinn Fein: Ourselves Alone), respectively. In 1962, Nelson Mandela was the last of a number of ANC leaders and activists arrested following a raid on a house in Rivonia. The accused were all found guilty of treason and sentenced to life imprisonment in the harsh, isolated stone-quarry prison of Robben Island. Provisions that effectively suspended habeas corpus, instituted indefinite solitary confinement, and provided for people to be 'banned' (forbidden to communicate with or be in the company of others) followed. By the late 1960s, more militants were receiving death sentences, and there were also many unexplained deaths in detention that were clearly either extrajudicial executions or deaths under torture.

Musicians were among those who showed their solidarity, with benefit shows to raise funds for defence all across the country. General Duze recalled being one of many musicians playing a solidarity benefit for the ANC Rivonia accused, who had formerly been enthusiastic fans of his music:

Spokes Mashiane, his guitarist and myself went to Kimberley for three nights of shows to fight the Rivonia Trial; spent three very nice nights there with the members who had organised the shows. But then [Nelson] Mandela had always been a fan of mine. Rohilahla liked his jazz and when we'd play in Newclare, he'd jive most of the night. . . . Even now, when he does the Madiba jive on TV, he reminds me of Western Native Township where he used to jive until 4 o'clock in the morning. . . .[28]

It was not only musicians playing jazz who felt the need to offer solidarity and join resistance. The 1960s saw a flowering of choral music with both implicit and explicit messages of defiance. 'For apartheid', says Sibongile Khumalo, '[organised choral singing] was a way of keeping the natives in check. But the natives . . . made it their own. . . . The one major contributor to the growth of choral music then was apartheid'.[29] Khumalo's father, the late professor Khabi Mngoma, was a pioneer of both the reclamation of indigenous music and the creation of new sounds.

Mngoma's father, David Mngoma, had been a traditional *maskandi* musician who played accordion. His son studied music and education at Adams College in KwaZulu Natal, then taught music and physical education, including boxing, at a school in Orlando:

He was one of the first to resign when Bantu Education came in, started his own school, the AmaAfrika School in Orlando East, got squashed there . . . did community work . . . all the time continuing to be involved with choral training and [what eventually became] the Soweto Teachers' Choir. . . . He decided to start a choir of his own, the Ionian Male Choir in the late 50s and then the Ionian Female Choir, both becoming the Ionian Music Society. . . . He then started to work for Reckitt & Colman, selling proprietary medicines; that was a way to get back into the schools, finding innovative ways to start health projects with music and drama linked to the products.[30]

For men like Mngoma, choral music remained a way of providing authentic forms of expression and development to African students. He saw no contradiction between conducting Handel's *Messiah*, working on original, nationally conscious modern music, and explaining Zulu lyric forms to fellow enthusiast Hugh Tracey.

Choral song was a channel of conscientisation, solidarity, mourning, and celebration; singing remained an integral part of communal events. While Radio Bantu featured choral music and its composers, it banned songs of struggle. After DJ Stan Nkosi began playing the hymn 'Vukani Mawethu' ('People, Awake!') following Sharpeville, it was banned, ostensibly because he was airing it too often. Composer Mzilikazi Khumalo tried to evade the censors by retitling a song 'Till When (Will We Be Free)?' as 'The Cry of the Israelites in Egypt', but it was still banned. 'U Ea Kae' ('Where Are You Going?'), originally a Sotho stick-fighting song, was seen as political because of the challenges to combat contained in its couplets, and banned. 'We are fighting a battle in our [own] way', said KwaZulu conductor Dr. James Hadebe.[31]

But the 1960s also saw, in the words of ANC activist Dr. Pallo Jordan, 'a change. The words move way from biblical codes and become much more direct. A hymn like 'Somlandela uJesus' ('We Will Follow Jesus') is changed to 'Somlandela Luthuli'. A song about a train [that helps us to move] becomes a song about Mandela'. Water Affairs Minister Ronnie Kasrils, another struggle veteran, adds that many songs also became 'more rhythmical and repetitive—they were essentially becoming marching songs'.[32]

When the *King Kong* cast left for London in 1961, 'in the silence that followed [the announcement of their flight], the whole cast spontaneously sang 'Nkosi Sikelele I'Afrika',[33] the anthem of the African National Congress.' That song, a venerable nationalist hymn written by Enoch Sontonga in 1897, posed particular problems for the SABC censors because of its widespread currency. Huskisson attempted to downplay its significance, in an essay on its composer: 'An abortive attempt was made by the African National Congress, using *Nkosi Sikelele i'Afrika* to close their meetings, to insinuate that the ordinary Bantu singing this anthem were doing so in support of their organisation, its aims and policies'.[34]

Other composers were writing directly revolutionary songs. Born in 1920, Vuyisile Mini was a trade union organiser working among dockworkers in Port Elizabeth in the Eastern Cape, an early volunteer for the Defiance Campaign, and one of the defendants in the 1956 Treason Trial. In 1963, he was arrested again, for alleged sabotage, and after a drawn-out trial in Port Alfred, far from his home, during which his defence attorney was forbidden to leave Durban, he and his co-accused were sentenced to death. Researcher V. S. Reddy recorded Mini's impact:

> Through all his arrests and victimisation, Mini reacted with that great gift which heartened all who heard him—his singing. His own compositions, which he sang in a magnificent bass in meetings, in prison and during the mass trials, were militant at times:
>
> *Verwoerd pasopa*
> *Naants'indod' emnyama*
> ('Look out, Verwoerd [sic], the Black people are coming');

and at times, nostalgic, especially the song composed during the long and wearying Treason Trial, which expressed the yearning of the accused to return home:

> *Thath' umthwalo Buti sigoduke*
> *balindile oomama noo bab' ekhaya*
> ('Take up your things Brother and let's go, They are waiting,
> our mothers and fathers, at home') . . .

Mini, however, also loved classical music. He sang in various choirs, including the Port Elizabeth Male Voice Choir. Some of the choirs . . . included whites who were not connected with the struggle for freedom. He joked about this afterwards, saying he had carried the 'gospel of Congress' further by way of song. This allusion to the gospel refers to a song Mini had composed during the Defiance Campaign:

> *Mayihambe le vangeli*
> *Mayigqib ilizwe lonke*
> ('Let this gospel spread and be known through the world').[35]

Mini and his two co-accused went to the gallows in 1964 singing 'Naants'indoda', and, according to the accounts of contemporaries who were in Pretoria Central Prison at the time, most of their fellow prisoners joined in.

In any event, the warning to Vervoerd was fulfilled two years later, when the prime minister was stabbed to death by parliamentary messenger Dmitri Tsafendas, a Greek-Mozambican of mixed race but passing for white, driven to insanity by the issues—political and personal—around his identity. Meanwhile, the big money-makers for the white Johannesburg theatres in 1966 were *The Merry Minstrel Show*, *The Black-and-White Minstrel Show*, and the box-office record-breaking *Minstrel Scandals*.

In Johannesburg, it was now only Dorkay House that continued to provide a meeting place for choral, classical, and jazz musicians. Photographer Basil Breakey remembered it as 'a place where artists used to meet—not only musicians but also all those in the creative arts. It was such a wonderful place . . . like a haven, an oasis in Johannesburg at that time, because you could be free there in a sense . . . extraordinary music. The most extraordinary music you wouldn't believe'.[36] Khabi Mngoma was teaching eighteen students a week at Dorkay on a choral adjudication course, as well as an assortment of other music students. Trumpeter Johnny Mekoa was one of them:

> People think that Boet [Brother] Khabi was only a classical musician—no ways! He was a great teacher and a great lover of jazz also. . . . In the early '60s we used to go to Dorkay House. Gideon Nxumalo also used to

teach music there, and we used to get theory lessons from him and from Professor Mngoma.'[37]

Mngoma struggled to keep up with the demand for lessons, turning himself into a multi-instrumentalist in the process, as his daughter Sibongile Khumalo remembers:

There were youngsters who came, actually wanting to learn a violin. This started at the Jubilee Centre, even before Dorkay House. So he was now like: what am I going to do? He was providing training in piano and voice, but now these kids were interested in something else. So the Centre itself found him a violin and a cello; he would strap the cello to his back, put the violin between his legs, get on his Vespa scooter, take a ride to the [white] suburbs, be given violin and cello lessons, and ride back in the evening the same way to teach what he had just learned.[38]

Particularly important until the mid-1960s was Dorkay's informal music exchange. 'There at Dorkay House, there used to be a jam session once a fortnight. Free admission; mixed audience. You really blew! You could play with anyone you wanted to. Musicians with opera singers. Someone would just say: let's play. You exchanged ideas; bands exchanged players. It was quite exciting and I learned a lot', remembers pianist Pat Matshikiza.[39] This mixing of races and musical genres had made Dorkay House the natural successor to the intense, modern jazz forcing-house of Sophiatown's Odin Cinema, so it is not surprising that Dorkay House was the musical home to the members of the most iconoclastic jazz group of the early 1960s: the Jazz Epistles.

The Epistles had grown out of the group that had recorded *Jazz in Africa* with John Mehegan in the late 1950s, toured as part of the Shantytown Sextet, and participated in the *King Kong* house band, Mackay Davashe's Jazz Dazzlers. Reedman Kippie Moeketsi, trumpeter Hugh Masekela, and trombonist Jonas Gwangwa, however, hankered after a more adventurous small group. In an unnamed combo, they worked with Johannesburg-based bassist Mongezi Velelo and drummer Early Mabuza, but decided they preferred some players they had encountered on tour in Cape Town, as Gwangwa recounts:

How we got to form that band, the Jazz Epistles? We were supposed to go to Switzerland to a festival out there, and Kippie, Hugh and I left and went to Cape Town, because Kippie was talking about this pianist he had met on a tour with the Manhattan Brothers and it was Dollar [Brand—Abdullah Ibrahim]. And Dollar came in with Johnny Gertze who was our bassist and we went to ask for Makhaya Ntshoko from his parents. Because Makhaya was a boxer who was drumming, a champion, and he was going for professionals. When we asked that he join the band, you know, we said, '. . . and he'll continue his boxing when we get abroad'. He joined the band and that was the end of boxing! [I]t was a collection like you saw in *The Magnificent Seven*—you know, going around the country and picking the best musicians. And we really put the shoulder to the wheel; it was all original material. We did a whole lot of hard work; we rehearsed for months and months, and of course we didn't make it abroad—the Sharpeville thing came in and state of emergency, all sorts of things. . . . But from that time on, of the Jazz Epistles, that's when one attempted to compose, you know? I was in Cape Town and we were rehearsing there with the Epistles and the guys left me alone—I don't know why, but I woke up and they weren't there! I sat at the piano that whole day, messing around until I came up with this tune . . . 'Carol's Drive'. Then my composing thing was starting out . . . and a style was being formulated, of course, only I was not aware of this. The only thing was, I was striving to compose, and I was thinking that I could improvise, but why can't I compose? I mean, improvisation is spontaneous composition. . . .[40]

Only one recording of the Jazz Epistles survives: *Jazz Epistles, Verse 1*. Its language is recognisably bebop, its idiom unmistakably South African—although precisely what that means, even a skilled jazz musician and teacher like guitarist Selaelo Selota finds hard to define:

I collected albums like *Jazz Epistles Verse 1*. . . . I could hear from Kippie Moeketsi's playing that there were elements of American influence; he did listen to Charlie Parker. . . . I can even isolate a certain melodic fragment [and say] that this is what Charlie Parker played in 1939—and this is what Kippie is doing with it. He's extended it and incorporated the nuances we have in South Africa in our playing. Some people believe that South Africans—or Africans in general—play jazz differently: slightly 'out of tune'. But take it as the South African style. Pushing the notes is the way we sing . . . the pioneers of South African jazz incorporated those styles without having to—it was just so smooth, man![41]

On *Jazz Epistles*, Masekela and Gwangwa are still young men with a lot to say, but in the eighteen months since *Jazz in Africa*, their capacity to say it has grown enormously. The music is mostly hard and fast, angry and assertive; the solos, risky and note-packed. The pace is broken by a ballad of broad, sea-swept chords from Dollar Brand and by the pain-wracked song of mourning, 'I Remember Billy', from Moeketsi. The key track is probably Moeketsi's 'Scullery Department'—for how else could a band describe itself that was good enough to play for white patrons, but only permitted to take its meals in the back kitchen?

Moeketsi said that the Epistles was 'the most exciting band I ever played with'. That was high praise from the best—and most controversial—reed player of his generation. Many retrospectives have focused on the dark and difficult side of Kippie's personality. He was considered, in General Duze's words, 'our young Bird here',[42] and as well as the label, he seems also to share with Charlie Parker the media fascination with the more sensational aspects of his lifestyle, rather than his music. It is certainly true that he was argumentative—particularly with what he saw as exploitative white management or spineless colleagues. He had a brilliant, mordant wit that not all those on the receiving end appreciated: 'His sense of humour got him into trouble', recalled saxophonist Peter Mokono-tela.[43] He suffered increasingly as the years went on from the effects of alcoholism. But most importantly, he was exercising his creativity in an environment beside which Bird's philistine America looks almost benign.

Born in 1924, Kippie Morolong Moeketsi originally derived his middle name from his family's origin among the BaRolong people. It stayed with him as a nickname because it carries another, wonderfully appropriate, resonance: in Se-Tswana, *morolong* means 'swallow' or 'songbird' (or Bird). His elder brothers, Bles, Jacob, and Sampi, were formally trained musicians, and pianist Jacob helped Kippie learn his first instrument, the clarinet, when the family lived in George Goch (Johannesburg's Eastern Native Township). Kippie worked in some of the incarnations of the *Zonk* show, in Bob Twala's Band in Blue, in the Harlem Swingsters, and in Mackay Davashe's Shantytown Sextet, where he met and took under his wing the young pianist Dollar Brand. By the late 1950s, he was being heard in progressive jazz jam sessions, first at the Odin and then at Dorkay House, as well as with the Dazzlers in the *King Kong* pit. After the Jazz Epistles album, he took the trip to England with *King Kong*, where he argued furiously with the management and was eventually committed to a mental hospital. His extreme behaviour may have been the result of a head injury sustained in a family argument just before he left South Africa. He told colleagues the rows were about wages and conditions, and this seems to be supported by a comment from General Duze—a mild-mannered and distinctly nonconfrontational personality—who noted: 'I didn't go to England with the *King Kong* cast. I had disagreements with the management—the same kind Kippie also had'.[44] Kippie was given electroconvulsive therapy before being discharged and sent home to South Africa. He called it all 'a trip to the world of make-believe'.

Back in South Africa, he worked again with the Dazzlers, with young white pianist Chris McGregor, and in a range of other progressive small groups and larger supporting bands. In the late 1960s, he lost, in swift succession, his saxophone (confiscated at a customs post after an African tour) and his daily labour pass, withdrawn by the authorities because he no longer had the tools of his trade. He did not pick up an instrument again for six years. There was insufficient work to justify the cost of a new sax, and Kippie had had a bellyful of wrangling with the authorities for documents.

Some of the musicians I interviewed mentioned that Kippie could be alarming when angry and irritating when drunk. None treated this as anything more than an aside. All stressed that the reality of Kippie lay in his fierce nationalism, his creative originality, his musical erudition, and particularly, again and again, his helpfulness as a teacher. The comments below form a sample from that testimony.

Victor Ntoni:

Bra Kippie? I got to know him when I first heard his sound from the musical *King Kong*. And then he had the reputation to be very daring. He defied all the rules of the then government by moving wherever he wanted, because he was a son of the soil and no-one can tell him where to go. . . . Kippie was like *the* giant, you know? [Eventually, much later] I got the opportunity of staying with him in Alexandra, all bunched together in one room [getting a band started]. It was not only his music. He was a very studious man. Used to check things like intervals. Used to relate things to local ethnic sounds and be modern at the same time. Then, one day everyone was gone, it was just me and Bra Kippie in that room, very lousy and blue because we didn't have money to buy a beer. So he said: Pick up your bass. And he taught me this composition of his. It's a very horn-like melody, it was difficult for me. Something swinging, like an Art Blakey kind of mood; difficult, bebop style. But I tried, and I hobbled along till I got it. He was so proud of me. He said: 'My boy, you go tell them what I showed you'. . . . We used to meet sparsely after that and he'd always ask: did you still remember that tune I taught you?

Jonas Gwangwa:

Actually, how Kippie Moeketsi and Mackay Davashe got interested in both Hugh [Masekela] and I was because we were attempting all those Charlie Parker things, and Kippie said, 'Oh, so you like this music? Come here, let me teach you this'.

Barney Rachabane:

He was my hero. I looked up to him as a live saxophonist—he was the nearest thing to me of everything I used to listen to on record. I always thought: I want to be like that man. . . . You remember that show *Township Jazz*? In the late '50s, right, City, Selborne Hall. I would be in on all those shows playing pennywhistle, and that's where I would listen to Kippie's beautiful playing behind the curtain.

Vusi Khumalo:

The memory that I have about Bra Kippie, is when I was eleven years, sitting at my house—because he was living diagonally opposite at my house in Eastern Township. I used to hear a beautiful melody coming out of his window. . . . And I know that my father, who was also a musician, actually respected Kippie a lot; he always used to talk about Bra Kippie. And I couldn't fully understand why until I grew up and started getting my shot as a musician. . . . [H]e was different, you know . . . he had the Charlie Parker influence.

Sophie Mngcina:

Kippie, he was one of the most wonderful musicians—very talented. He wasn't called the Bird for nothing. He was Charlie Parker, but he was himself. I say we have one up on our white counterparts and the Americans: we have our own languages, our own music, *mbaqanga* . . . and then we still play their music. But now, the [theatrical] agents here didn't even know we existed, didn't even know Kippie—yet he was worshipped. Wherever he played, he was a wonder to listen to. I worked with him, and I know what I'm talking about.

Thandi Klaasen:

Kippie? *Die was my bra!* [That was my brother.] He taught me. . . . We used to meet at the BMSC and he'd say, 'I would like you to sing this song, like maybe "Stella by Starlight". And he'd say, 'O bina ka E flat ['Sing it in E flat']. E flat? I didn't know what that was! Then he'd say, 'Hey man, Thandi! E flat!' and he'd go to the piano and sound a note—ting! Then he sings [the lyrics]. He taught me all those keys! . . . He knew I was a good jazz singer, and he'd also say to other people 'Teach Thandi this tune' or 'Listen to how Thandi's singing this tune'. And, with respect, he was not one of those who would say: come to me at lunchtime and I will make you a star, because they want to have sex with you. . . . There's some of the white people—and some of the brothers here—who'd want to use you for that. But he was just really concerned for me to do my best.

Pat Matshikiza:

When I first met Kippie at Dorkay House, here was this chap with kind of Japanese eyes and bubbling with excitement and jokes. And he just looked at me. Our eyes met, and he asked me who I was and where I was from. I said, 'Queenstown,' and he said, 'Are you a Matshikiza? Todd se bro'?' ['Todd's brother?'] I said: 'No, it's my uncle'. He said, 'No! You lie! Hey, gents, it's Todd se bro', this one. You Matshikizas, you want rule us—but we don't need you, you Queenstown *skappies* [rascals]!' Then he just laughed, and I thought—hey, this is somebody exciting! And to play with him, hey—another story. A perfectionist! One time, we weren't playing so good and he stopped us: 'What was that middle phrase, what chord did you play?' I said in a little voice: 'Er, I'm not quite sure . . .' And he said, 'Watch out—jy spiel off [*if you play off*], you're out of a job!' So you had to learn, at a high level, working with him.

Dennis Mpale:

He was influenced by 'Bird' and by bebop—we all were. You couldn't help it. . . . But Kippie was an original, with his own voice. He was a composer who created some of our best standards. And when you heard him wood-shedding, he was adventurous—closer to Eric Dolphy.

Pops Mohamed:

Apart from the fact that people said he was the South African Charlie Parker, to me he's Kippie. I don't see him as the South African Charlie Parker. I see him as a South African, and the only Kippie Moeketsi that we had. He had a sound that was kind of a calling sound. . . . When he played on Abdullah [Ibrahim]'s albums as well, there was something unique about Kippie that strikes you. You could feel this pulse, and your hair rising, you know? Like, why did this guy go? Why is he not still with us? And I can't compare him with Charlie Parker—to me he was much better. In his own way he was much, much better—he was original, man. He listened to Charlie Parker, the jazz guys—he's taken a lot of their technique and made it his own. He applied his own South African *mba-qanga*, *kwela*, whatever you may call it—he added his own particular feel to it, which made him so unique.[45]

It was not accidental that Kippie scouted fresh talent for the Epistles from Cape Town. The city was growing as a centre for jazz. And while the combination of removals and the rapid implementation of segregation was ripping the guts out of jazz in Johannesburg, the process took longer in the Cape. The clearance of District 6 did not begin until 1966, and the segregation laws, while enforced, were applied much more patchily. White musicians like Chris McGregor, who wanted to collaborate with black colleagues, found Cape Town far freer than Johannesburg from the pressures of both the state and more separatist white players. Many jazz musicians—Banzi Bangani, Lennie Lee, Dennis Mpale—

stopped off for long periods when their tours took them to Cape Town. Singer Dolly Rathebe was another:

Things were so bad with us musicians when they said no more blacks in Johannesburg city and the halls. We were banned. So most of the musicians went down the drain. Many stopped playing and got poor. They said we were taking jobs from white musicians—even if the whites preferred us to their own musicians—I tell you, we were the favourites! It was so bad that when we did perform we'd be hurried in from the back and *manje-manje* [quick-quick] out the back door again. Even our food was served in the kitchen. I saw my musical *broers* [brothers] starting to look into the bottle, so I left. I ended up in Cape Town, where I had friends who smuggled things; selling wine and things. They said: well, you are here, so why don't you join in? That was how I got the money to build my house: I was a smuggler. How else could I do it? I heard about this place [Mabopane, outside Pretoria] and slowly I paid off the cost of a plot. Then I came back to live here, and took Kippie Moeketsi to live here with me.[46]

German photographer Hardy Stockman had settled in Johannesburg, but he was not finding enough music that satisfied his 'craving for jazz. . . . Neither was I happy with the ever more restricted and segregated conditions under which . . . popular artists had to perform'.[47] Stockman moved to Cape Town in 1959 in search of a pianist he had heard about in Johannesburg, Dollar Brand. He found Brand—and the rest of the musicians who were to form the Jazz Epistles—performing at one of Cape Town's jazz spots: the Ambassador 'nonwhite' ballroom dancing school in the suburb of Woodstock.

The place was over-crowded. The band and audience were composed of black and white and anything in-between, mingling freely like nowhere else in the land. This was all the more surprising as there was no dancing and neither food nor drink was available. You either played or you listened. There was nothing else. I felt great; finally, I had arrived 'home'.[48]

The Ambassador was only one of Cape Town's vibrant jazz venues. There were concerts at the Rondebosch and Woodstock Town Halls, as well as occasionally at the University of Cape Town and City Hall. Live jazz featured at, among others, the Vortex coffee bar in the city's Long Street, the Naaz nightclub in Salt River, and the Zambezi Indian restaurant in District 6. Tolerance, however, only stretched so far. When the Mermaid seafood restaurant in the up-market white coastal resort of Sea Point began featuring McGregor's mixed group in sessions and workshops, the authorities took only ten days to close the place down.

It was this scene that had shaped Dollar Brand, born in Cape Town's Kensington suburb in 1934. Learning music in his family home; getting ideas from sources as diverse as radio, cinema, the jingles of ice-cream vans, Xhosa music, AME church hymns, and the *bilal* (call to prayer) and choral music of the Muslim community, Brand made his first records with the Tuxedo Slickers big band in 1954—one of them being an instrumental version of Solomon Linda's 'Mbube'. But his interest was in new music. His nickname, 'Dollar', was a contraction of his given name, Adolphus, but it stuck because he was always, in his own words, 'looking for cash to buy new records from the American sailors at the docks'.[49] By his late twenties, he was already a legendary figure: mercurial, moody, and a breathtaking player. Another pianist, Hotep Galeta (then Cecil Barnard and around ten years his junior), heard of him and went to seek him out:

I heard about this pianist who was doing something new, so of course I wanted to hear him. I went to a few of the places where he played, and eventually, there was this guy. So tall and skinny, dressed all in black with big army boots on his feet. Very silent. He just looked right through everybody; wouldn't talk. Just walked straight to the piano and sat down to play. And when he played—that was it.[50]

Hardy Stockman heard Dollar Brand draw an audience response worthy of a pop star at his farewell concert in December 1961:

[A] lengthy solo performance on the conga drum by Dollar pitched up such an emotional frenzy that members of the audience went crazy and started screaming. A young lady a couple of rows behind me fainted outright. It was tremendous. Incredible that a single musician with a simple drum could create such an emotional storm. But then that single artist with this simple drum was no ordinary musician—it was Dollar Brand.[51]

By this time, Brand's musical and personal partner was a schoolteacher who sang in her spare time, Beattie (later Sathima Bea) Benjamin, a student of pianist Henry February. Benjamin's family were of Saint Helenan descent, and saw themselves as somewhat elite. The headmaster at her school told her firmly that her after-hours activities were inappropriate for a teacher. But Benjamin was hooked on the music:

I was 19 and I would go to these night-clubs—we didn't have jazz clubs yet, we had night-clubs, and the people, white folks, you know, were dancing and dining. We would be on the bandstand and we would be working on this music . . . and I was always the only girl with all the guys.

But they knew I was in it for the music, so . . . I think it was that we were quite rebellious spirits, and we were also very aware of things that were not right, and jazz music itself is a liberating music. It liberates you, because you can take something and do what you want. OK, so it was not a business—the guys would earn a couple of bucks, love the music, go back next week, but we got a chance to be ourselves—so there were just certain people who did that and once I made that decision . . . because you choose this music now called jazz—after a while you get tested and you get chosen; you'll know when you're chosen and you can't do anything else. . . . In the '50s when we were so active and we were doing well, that was apartheid time—nobody cared. I was kicked out of the house; my mother said I went crazy; she said I was running around with Africans—what is she doing? . . . I just had to be brave and say I don't see all these compartments; I never did, and the music had no compartments. After we would be working in the night-clubs, then either Henry's [Henry February] house or somebody else's, we would go after hours; now we go play Billie Holiday, Charlie Parker—I mean, I heard all of those things; 'cos they just took me. And those guys, they drink, they used to smoke pot—not Henry, the other guys!—and I will tell you, not one of them ever said, 'Hey, Sathima, take this; it's nice for you'. Who knows if they did, if I wouldn't have said yes and got hooked on something? But they respected me and knew I was there to learn.[52]

By 1965, this slightly more open environment was being closed up, although other forms of Cape Town musical activity were damaged more rapidly than jazz. The Eoan Group had been founded in 1933 by white philanthropists, a social and educational centre with a heavy emphasis on music training for the city's mixed-race community, somewhat on the model of Johannesburg's BMSC. Eoan trained one opera singer, Joseph Gabriel, who went on to sing at La Scala and the New York Met. But, like the BMSC, the ban on mixed audiences drastically cut its earning potential as a venue. Then, Eoan allowed itself to be almost fatally compromised, according to historian Dennis Constant-Martin: 'In the 1960s, the Eoan Group received a small subsidy from the government and, in order to keep it, accepted to have separate shows for whites and for coloureds. Many of its supporters stopped attending the group's concerts . . . many . . . teachers, singers or dancers, left'.[53]

The Coon troupes suffered most from the Group Areas Act. District 6 was declared 'white' in 1966, and the last of around 60,000 or more of its residents had been shifted to the Cape Flats and other areas by 1982. As well as the ubiquitous 'matchbox' houses, blocks of tenement flats with fire escape–style external staircases were built for the poorest residents, imposing class as well as race segregation. American music journalist Marty Hughley, driving through the coloured areas in 2003, recognised the architectural style instantly: 'You don't have to tell me what those are—they're projects'.[54] During the late 1960s and 1970s, Coon activity was massively constrained by these removals and by laws against public gatherings ('Riotous Assemblies'). Old troupes were broken up as members were moved to different locations, and it took time for new ones to form. Often, a communal rehearsal hall was no longer within walking distance. Stadiums were now strictly segregated, and the city centre was out of bounds.

Some new troupes obeyed the regulations, performed under restricted and segregated conditions, and even staged carnival events during periods of mourning or boycott organised by the liberation movements. Some fell under the control of the gangsterism and racketeering that rapidly pervaded the Cape Flats. But many found ways of expressing covert and even open resistance. This had begun as early as the late 1940s, when the troupes ceased to wear 'Privates' (eighteenth-century colonial) costume. Dennis Constant-Martin calls this a symbolic 'expulsion of European history from the Carnival'.[55] The use of brass instruments and jazz tunes (there were a number of *Zonk* troupes) signalled a continuing refusal to be isolated from other urban and international (especially African-American) culture. Variations on popular songs sung by the troupes included 'It's now or never; Vervoerd is gonna die' and the theme from the 1961 film *Exodus*, which, without any need for improvisation, ran: 'This land is mine / God gave this land to me. . . .'[56]

The Group Areas restrictions masked such resistance, shutting it away in designated performance spaces where it would not disturb white eyes. But while the public profile of carnival in the Cape was diminishing, another platform for popular music and jazz—beer festivals—emerged in the Transvaal.

If one side of apartheid's pacification campaign against black resistance was direct repression, the other was the doomed drive to win hearts and minds. The creation of neotraditional music as a substitute for the moral and political dangers of jazz was one aspect of this. Another was the distribution to Africans of a hitherto banned intoxicant: white man's beer. Those Africans with the means had, of course, been drinking commercial beer and spirits for centuries. But the conditions of illegality around its consumption were a major source of discontent: 'Let the People Drink!' *Drum* had headlined a story. The regulations made otherwise law-abiding Africans into law-breakers, and had created a sophisticated network of unsupervised drinking places where, the authorities suspected, politics were discussed and revolution fomented—and no revenue tax was paid on the liquor. All this was pointed out by a government commission of inquiry. So, while restrictions on unlicensed drinking spots remained (and thus so did bootlegging and its associated organised crime), the 1961 Liquor Amendment Act gave Africans limited permission to buy formerly forbidden brews at licensed outlets.

In a bid to win customers, and drawing on the long association between shebeens and jazz, a number of beer brands sponsored competitive jazz festivals—most notably, Castle Lager, with its series of Cold Castle Festivals at the

Moroka-Jababavu Stadium in Soweto. Other manufacturers of consumer goods followed suit. The festivals produced remarkable music. The recording of the 1962 festival features almost the last performances by Chris McGregor before he and his group left the country: a brisk three-number tour through bebop and the blues with traces of the joyous dissolves into textured chaos that were a characteristic of their work in Europe. A prizewinners' band was put together after the festival, and McGregor directed both the band and a subsequent 1963 album: *Jazz, The African Sound*, with original material from himself, Moeketsi, and Dollar Brand (who did not feature as a player). 'I Remember Billy' reappears, with Moeketsi on clarinet ratcheting up the sadness to a point that is almost unbearable. The opening number, 'Switch', is also his: an intricate, travelling structure of chords not anchored to any single key that showcases his risky modernism.

The rest of the *Cold Castle 1962 Festival* album is dominated by beautifully but conventionally played covers, including the smooth-as-silk—but by 1962 slightly archaic—vocal close harmony of the Woody Woodpeckers. There are two exceptions—and both make the audience hold its breath. One is Moeketsi's solo with the Jazz Dazzlers on 'Kentucky Oyster', which starts as a hoarse shout over vamped piano chords and then flies on the chords with one swift, electric excursion into modal playing. The other is the closing track, 'Pondo Blues', of which more later.

The festivals and the drinking did provide something of a safety valve. 'These festivals were wonderful,' recalls vocalist Sophie Mngcina-Davids, 'because we were singing. We were singing about life, death, marriages, celebrating our life'.[57] Yet they were not a substitute for cultural self-awareness; rather, the best of the music served as a further clarion call. Ndikho Xaba describes one such moment, at the 1962 festival:

> When Eric Nomvete, who was from East London, came on stage with his group, it was such an electrifying moment. When he played 'Ndinovalo Ndinomingi' ('Pondo Blues'), [t]here was a silence when he played those rhythms—and then there was a roar and beer bottles started flying all over the place. Because he invokes a spirit that, look, man, this is what we want to do—there's no need for us to be going anywhere else but look into ourselves.[58]

'Ndinovalo Ndinomingi' starts with a spare, discordant, repeated fanfare, played as it might sound on a ram's horn. The audience holds its breath. Then the band voices big, typically Xhosa chords over a syncopated drum. Against these, first the trumpet and then Nomvete's sax reach for modernist phrases: singer and chorus; call and response. Nomvete's solo sounds like no other player on the planet, although Albert Ayler would have understood his language. African audiences had no problems with certain ways of drawing on tradition; but

those ways would be defined by creators and listeners, not by the white authorities, and would speak to a discourse of genuine independence.

It was within this kind of frame that guitarist Phillip Tabane created *malombo*
music, fusing a modern jazz and blues sensibility with the spirit music of the
Venda people, built around the conversations of a family of upright drums. 'It is
spritual music . . . created from my mother's influence [who] was a *sangoma* and
used to hum songs while healing people. I don't really appreciate people calling
me a musician, but I have to accept it anyway'.[59] Tabane's electric guitar pulls
phrases apart above trancelike percussion cycles, welding ancient and modern
into highly individual combinations that have led overseas critics to compare
him to both Ali Farka Toure and James Blood Ulmer. Guitarist Selaelo Selota
describes the music's interlocking elements of modernity and tradition:

I found the link that it was very much Malopo influenced—which is a
traditional way of celebration, a healing process for the North Sotho–
speaking peoples and the Venda-speaking people. But in that, he's using
the chords that come from jazz, that are heard on Wes Montgomery and
so forth.[60]

Tabane's music was hugely popular at the Cold Castle festivals, winning first
prize for three successive years, 1961, 1962, and 1963. Very little of it, however,
was released on record in South Africa until the 1990s. Many of his recordings
were made overseas, where he began touring in 1971, eventually appearing at
events like the Newport Jazz Festival. Tabane wanted no one's labels:

The jazz label—or any other label—has never worked in my case. Once,
I went to play at a competition in Durban and in the end I was given a
special prize because I could not be categorised. To this day, they still
cannot categorise my music![61]

For musicians, festivals extended the public visibility of jazz, during years
when broadcasting and the record industry were reducing its space. They also
provided much-needed work, but not always a real income. 'They used to pay
you', remembered Dennis Mpale, 'with a case of the product. Maybe a few
pounds, sometimes not—but always a case of the product. And now they critic-
ise, and wonder why so many of us have become drinkers'.[62]

This was typical of the poor financial treatment of musicians. Musicians still
sold their music to recording companies outright for a flat fee. Ntemi Piliso
recalls:

I sold my composer's rights unknowingly! And they used to give me five
pounds just to put down my signature, whereas I was selling out my

rights. What I got was called, I think, composer's fee—instead of royal-ties.[63]

Although the start of the decade had seen a number of victories by Union Artists in securing individual recording contracts with an artist's royalties provision, many artists did not know—and were not told—that this was their right. Some lacked the literacy skills to follow up on what they had signed. Until very recently, the major record companies argued that they had wherever possible respected royalty entitlements, despite apartheid. This view was expressed by music archivist Rob Allingham, writing on behalf of his employer, Gallo, in 1992, in response to an article in the South African music press attacking the company's record:

> Musicians were hardly forced to record if the circumstances didn't suit them . . . the flat fee system was not imposed on a racial basis. Most white artists' recording and composition rights were also purchased outright by the companies. . . . To be sure, most black artists were probably paid less, but the principle was the same. In the '50s, when black musicians began to ask for royalties, they were told routinely—and incorrectly—that it was illegal for companies to pay them on that basis. Eventually, a case of competition provided a breakthrough. In 1958, Gallo was desperately trying to woo pennywhistler Spokes Mashiyane away from their arch-rival Troubadour. Thanks to the counsel of Ian Bernhardt and the Union of South African Artists, Mashiyane agreed to switch labels provided he received a royalty contract instead of the usual flat fees. Of course, word of this arrangement quickly circulated amongst all the other musicians and that was the end of the illegality story. Over the next ten-year period, royalty payments became an industry-wide standard. Significantly, the changeover occurred after the departure of most of the exiles who continued to proclaim loudly from overseas that back home record companies were paying only flat fees and that this was yet another example of apartheid in action. . . .[64]

Graeme Gilfillan, a commercial and contract copyright specialist in the entertainment industry, argues that this is a very incomplete account of the situation:

> The record companies' principal weapon was the English language. Artists often did not know what they were signing away, and I have never seen any material from that period explaining it. Today, we would describe the pressure to 'sign, or we won't make you a star' as duress and intimidation in labour law terms—not to mention the added pressure of simply needing to earn a living.

But, more to the point, what Mashiyane and some others received was only an artist's royalty. Returns on this run on a sine curve: they peak, and then the song may stop selling altogether, or sell sparsely as an evergreen. What artists did not get was copyright on their compositions. So it was something of a Pyrrhic victory.

And then, in the mid-'60s, payments for needle time (payment per radio play) were removed. Up to 1963, one of the SABC's largest costs was royalty payments. When they killed the old broadcasting system and introduced Radio Bantu with its multiple African-language stations, they stood to spend even more and make millionaires out of black artists. So at that point, the previous needle-time provisions were removed. The old colonial performing-rights collection societies were cut out of the loop and replaced with the home-grown SAMRO (South African Music Rights Organisation), as part of apartheid's project of displacing English institutions with Afrikaans ones. Gideon Roos, head of the SABC under [Prime Minister Hendrik] Vervoerd, moved across to run SAMRO. Effectively, the political control of copyright had moved across to the Broederbond.[65]

Until the 1990s, SAMRO paid royalties at two different rates. The black rate was lower.

Jazz was a far more slippery target than literature for the censors. Radio Bantu dealt with it by simply creating spaces for which only 'tribal' music qualified, with white experts like Huskisson, Kittermaster, and Tracey to define the slots. As Nomvete's tune 'Pondo Blues' demonstrates, this was not always effective in keeping out dangerous sounds. In addition, the multiple levels of African metaphor in title or tune continued to convey their own message. Often, listeners understood what censors did not.

A case in point is the top-selling jazz recording of 1968, saxophonist Winston Mankunku's 'Yakhal'Inkomo' ('The Bellowing Bull'). Mankunku's current manager, Christian Syren, estimates that the album sold at least 100,000 copies in its first five years. It may be the best-selling South African jazz album of all time. However, Mankunku's contract had no provision for royalties, and the Teal record company asserted that all sales records had been lost in a fire at the Steeldale warehouse in the 1970s. (Ironically, this situation came to light in the 1980s, when the Gallo label, now the 'owner' of the tune, sold it to Castle Lager for a TV commercial commemorating 'The beer that has stood the test of time'.) On the sleeve notes, the tune is described as expressing grief for the death of John Coltrane. A rural image of cattle roaring on their way to slaughter was, in any case, well in tune with the censors' stereotype of appropriate African subject matter. But that was not the message Mankunku was uttering, nor the one his listeners were hearing:

*Yakhal'Inkomo* was an odd tune. Things were tough then—but don't ask
me about all of that, I don't want to discuss it. You had to have a pass;
you got thrown out; the police would stop you, you know? I was about
22. I threw my pass away; wouldn't carry it. We had it tough. I was always
being arrested and a lot of my friends and I thought it was so tough for
black people and put that into the song. So it was *The Bellowing Bull*: for
the black man's pain. And a lot of people would come up to me and say
quietly: Don't worry bra'. We understand what you are playing about.[66]

'Yakhal'Inkomo' is a slow, lyrical melody that builds to a climax and then
resolves in a series of abrupt, stabbing phrases. As the cycle of the tune unrolls,
Mankunku gradually dismantles the theme into abstract fragments and plaintive
phrases. At the point where dissolution is complete, comes the bellow: not ani-
mal, but quintessentially human; a great roar of 'Why?'

Other musicians had used the same techniques to hide messages or satire
over the years. Zacks Nkosi's '10:10 Special' from the 1950s is based on an old
tune, the marabi 'Sponono', used to mock the pass laws through its title's reference to the last 'safe' train out of the city before the *nagpass* bit. Chris Columbus,
now leading a small group called Die Bafanas (the boys), responded to the silencing of the 1960s with a song that an unwary censor might also dismiss as simple
rural mourning: 'Izwe Lifile'—the land is dead.

Meanwhile, black musical theatre, confined to segregated township audiences, was providing another small source of income for musicians. A young
director, Gibson Kente, managed to steer a path between politically cautious
content and innovative and imaginative staging to create work and educate performers about stagecraft. Thandi Klaasen worked with both Kente and singer
Ben 'Satch' Masinga, who crafted the first Zulu-language musical show, *Back in
Your Own Backyard*: 'Most of us are from Gibson Kente. To know what it is to
sing, and you must know what it is you are singing about, and your pronuncia-
tion must be articulate—that is what I have learned from him. . . . [Then] Ben
"Satch" Masinga used to have his own show called *Back in Your Own Backyard*
. . . and we used to do some tap-dancing. And Letta Mbulu played the girlfriend
to Ben and [they would sing the duet from *Porgy and Bess*] and I'm telling you,
it used to bring the house down.[67]

As the 1960s progressed, even these initiatives were watched suspiciously by
the authorities. This was the decade of what British prime minister Harold Macmillan had called the 'Wind of Change' blowing through Africa. Other countries
on the continent were either achieving, or fighting for, independence and black
majority rule. South Africa had strengthened its military capacity through the
foundation of the Armaments Board (later to become ARMSCOR), to build and
buy the weaponry needed for a war against revolutionary neighbours and internal insurrection. In 1967, the Terrorism Act clamped down on all information
about who had been arrested or the conditions of their detention, as well as

removing the last civil rights from those detained under its provisions. The next year, all nonracial political organisations were banned. The secret police became ubiquitous, standing at the backs of halls taking notes and pictures. The ANC's military wing, MK, was fighting alongside Zimbabwean freedom fighters in the Wankie and Sepolilo campaigns. From their comrades in the camps, the South Africans began to learn a rousing, syncopated marching chant that would over the next twenty years find its way back into the songs and on to the streets of home. It was called the *toyi-toyi*.

Black South Africans were well aware of what was going on in the rest of Africa. A courageous young singer/songwriter, Dorothy Masuka, had already taken advantage of the more open climate of Cuthbert Matumba's Troubadour studios (whose quick, efficient pressing and distribution system could get songs out on to the streets before the authorities noticed them) to record lyrics in support of the 1957 Defiance Campaign and critical of Home Affairs Minister D.F. Malan. In 1961, when first Congolese president Patrice Lumumba was assassinated, she wrote and released 'Lumumba'. The authorities seized the record almost immediately, and Masuka, in Bulawayo with her family at the time, began thirty years of exile from South Africa.

She was not the only musician to leave. Already, Todd Matshikiza was gone, first to London and then as a broadcaster to Zambia. Cecil Barnard, Abdullah Ibrahim, Makhaya Ntshoko, Johnny Gertze, and Bea Benjamin left for Europe in the early 1960s, followed by many members of the cast of *King Kong* (including Jonas Gwangwa and Hugh Masekela), who chose simply not to return when the show's London run ended. Miriam Makeba had gone to Venice in 1959 to promote *Come Back Africa* and was now working in New York. Ibrahim and Benjamin returned in 1968, but a swift survey of the country convinced them they could not remain. Benjamin recalls: 'When we saw how things were, with people being killed [this was the year of Mini's execution and of at least three unexplained deaths in detention] and how people felt, and you couldn't hold a concert—we knew we couldn't stay'.[68] The Blue Notes had left for Europe— Chris McGregor's brother, Tony, remembers Chris's despair at what was happening:

> It just became very, very difficult to be a jazz musician; I think one of the things about jazz is that people who play jazz are generally within themselves free people, and they play a free kind of music. And it becomes very difficult to be free in a society where there are all these laws and regulations governing people's lives to the extent that apartheid laws did. So people left South Africa—many, many talented musicians left. . . . [Chris] had it pretty hard, especially in the early '60s. He came to Johannesburg in '62 for the first time to play at the Moroka Jabavu Jazz Festival . . . and most people at that festival thought he was coloured rather than white, and I don't think he would have been very welcome there from

the authorities had they known he was white. Chris said himself that what finally tipped the scales for him, what finally made him realise that he had to leave South Africa was when they were playing, and I think if I can remember properly, it was an open-air festival in Port Elizabeth. The police started—there was a large crowd listening—and the police started beating up some of the spectators, and it became quite a tense scene. And Chris realised that just by being there, just by playing that music, and being a white playing in black areas mostly, he was actually endangering people's lives. That he might get away with it because he was white, but other people might in fact lose their lives from just listening to the music. And that incident I think happened in 1963, and he realised then that he couldn't stay in South Africa.[69]

For Ndikho Xaba in 1962, it was recording at the SABC Studios that was the last straw:

I will never forget my experience with the studio that was run by Mr [Michael] Kittermaster. That day, Kippie Moeketsi was in that session, Wonder Makhubu on piano, others, good musicians, improvisers. Kittermaster listens to what we are doing, goes over to the piano player and says: 'Look, I don't want you going anywhere with that tune. Just stay on that thing: ka-ting ka-ting—that's all I want you to do'. That's when I said to myself: enough is enough. I'm not going to be involved in this degenerative artistry.[70]

Xaba left with the cast of the musical *Sponono* for New York and did not return until the end of apartheid.

Pinocchio Mokaleng, founder of the Odin Cinema modern jazz sessions, was denied a passport to leave. Thandi Klaasen helped smuggle him to Cape Town, to make his escape by a more covert route:

I remember when we went to Cape Town, smuggling Pinocchio to Cape Town. That's when he left South Africa, went to London. And the police came and I sat on him. Pinocchio was small, you know? So when the [police]man came and said 'Where are the car keys?' and all that, I was just sitting, having this blanket wrapped around me and pretending as if I was pregnant. And I [was praying] he mustn't say 'You!' because the pregnancy was so big—because it was Pinocchio![71]

By the mid-1960s, that stream of departures became a flood. Not just creative artists left, but also those sympathisers and friends who had profiled and documented their work, like photographer Jurgen Schadeberg:

[P]eople began to leave the country. The musicians left with the jazz opera *King Kong*; the writers also left. Many of the politicians either left or were imprisoned. For artists, the only other option was to drink yourself to death. Some of them did. Because for most people it became a very frustrating period. I saw it towards the early '60s, towards 1964. There was the Rivonia Trial. I didn't see much hope of staying here. I was harassed by the Special Branch. They made it difficult for me; followed me around, asking questions about where I was going, what I was doing, and intimidated other people not to talk to me. I became isolated. I thought I'd better leave before I also ended up drunk, in prison or whatever. There was no way that anyone could do anything. . . . We were intimidated by the Special Branch. Most of us were, in one way or another. At one point I had problems entering and leaving the country. I was detained. I had to go up to Dar-es-Salaam in 1964. There was a big uprising in Dar-es-Salaam, in Zanzibar. I had problems—because that was my living; I was freelancing at the time. So I went to the Special Branch building and complained to them. I told them I was a professional. They produced a very big file and in it were all my pictures—my very best portfolio! They said they knew every German publication I was published in. I said: Oh my God! They know more about me than I know about myself![72]

Independent-minded Troubadour producer Cuthbert Matumba died in 1965, and the label was absorbed in 1969 by the much larger Gallo, far more concerned with creating products acceptable to the SABC. Yet at the same time, the music did not stop. Small jazz groups still found ways to survive, and there were many of those, as Johnny Mekoa describes:

[The Blue Notes and Chris McGregor] left for France, the Antibes Jazz Festival, and they never came back—they went into exile. . . . It did leave a vacuum, you know? Because after that there was a certain lull in the early '60s, but that was when Molombo came out. Then the '64 Cold Castle [Festival] and the birth of the Early Mabuza Big Five. That's when we moved into the scene. I was playing trumpet in that band with Barney Rachabane, and Early Mabuza was my mentor. A great jazz drummer— how I wish he was alive today, man! You know, there were great people at that time: the late Mackay Davashe, Blythe Mbityana, who is in New York now . . . [t]he late Johnny Tsakane—great jazz singer. And his wife, Jeanette Tsakane . . . 1967, that's when a whole lot of jazz musicians were finally banned. . . . I hung around and founded the Jazz Ministers in Benoni, 'cos you couldn't just stop playing the music—because it was one's life; it was one's journey. With Aubrey Semane, who's in the Eastern Cape—great saxophone player. . . . And the Jazz Ministers took off and

became a household name. We played all the festivals. . . . [But] it was
very difficult for jazz musicians to make a living in South Africa. It's
either you're working during the daytime and playing jazz in the evenings, you know? And playing a lot of festivals in the townships. . . . It
was kinda difficult to make a living as a jazz musician, but because the
music was very strong, we held on.[73]

By the end of the decade, new music was brewing among young people. American influences remained strong in the townships. For modern jazzmen like Winston Mankunku, there were the spiritual explorations of John Coltrane, to which
he paid explicit homage on his second 1968 album, *Spring*:

> *Spring* was my next album, with Chris Schilder. That was more in the
> mood of Trane. Even today, when I want to play, I take him [Trane] and
> I put him inside of me. Inside [gestures to head & heart]. I know you
> think I'm a naughty old man, but most of the time, when I'm playing,
> I'm really praying. I used to dream of Coltrane. And one time in the '60s
> he came to me, did I tell you that? I was practicing, and I felt something
> funny in the room. My senses were prickling. I knew he was there. I got
> scared and put the instrument away. Maybe I shouldn't have told other
> people—they were nervous around me for some time after that! But he
> never came again.[74]

Another player who greatly admired Coltrane was saxophonist Duke Makasi.
In 1969, with a band called the Soul Jazzmen, Makasi recorded *Inhlupeko* (*Mel-
ancholy*), another coded title for the thwarted creativity now being felt by jazz
innovators, as by all conscious black South Africans. *Inhlupeko* is a recording
suffused with sadness. The title track echoes the cyclical call-and-response of
'Yakhal'Inkomo', and the album also includes a fast, graceful, bitter version of
'Love for Sale'. Trumpeter Dennis Mpale remembers the session, where he was
a studio spectator:

> They put my photograph on the album cover, but I wasn't playing on
> the record. That was some shit idea to sell the record, I think. . . . Pretend
> there are more musicians. I wasn't happy about it, because I was there
> with a bottle, not playing. I hated how that showed us—but I suppose
> the mood of the picture was right. *Inhlupeko* was Duke's tune, a great
> tune. It's hard to listen to it and not want to cry. It was a tune for all the
> beautiful things we wanted to do, the beautiful music we wanted to make,
> and the situation that didn't let you and what the situation was doing to
> us as human beings.[75]

Others were attracted to the spirit of the hard bop music that Horace Silver
and Art Blakey had been crafting in the United States in the late 1950s. Silver

has said that he created the more blues-driven hard bop sound because he felt
the intellectualism of later bebop 'had kinda . . . not totally but somewhat . . .
eliminated the blues . . . like it was demeaning to be funky'.[76] Much the same
impulse inspired his South African admirers. The Heshoo Beshoo Band was
formed by reedman Henry Sithole, who had learned his band skills from veteran
Dalton Khanyile and his improvisation technique from pianist Claude Shange,
another graduate of the *Jazz in Africa* project. But Sithole was a younger man,
born in 1941. The rest of the band included young bassist Ernest Motlhe and
drummer Nelson Magwaza. The band's surviving recording, *Armitage Road*, has
all the characteristics—the two-sax front line inherited from R&B, blues and
gospel-inflected flavour, and solid, danceable rhythms—of early hard bop. Yet
both the rhythms and the melodic story they carry are recognisably South African, particularly in the solos of Cyril Magubane, Heshoo Beshoo's soulful, wheel-
chair-bound guitarist.

Soul was becoming a valued quality. Another group, based in Johannesburg,
called itself the Soul Giants. Their album, the 1968 *I Remember Nick*, continues
the tradition of intellectually challenging bebop-styled music begun by the Jazz
Epistles. Tough soloing from Dennis Mpale and Barney Rachabane is built on
the compositions of pianist Shakes Mgudlwa, whose intricate yet easy-flowing
piano style won him enormous respect from his peers. 'I was in Johannesburg
when they made that', remembers Winston Mankunku. 'The crowds used to go
mad for those songs. Shakes . . . was a short, small guy. Short fingers—but he
could stretch over the keys. A very careful, learned guy—played a lot of classical
music too'.[77]

In America, this was the soul era, not only a musical style, but a complex of
interconnected symbols of black self-assertion: the Afro hairstyle, the dashiki,
Motown, Malcolm X, civil rights, and Black Power. For youngsters in Soweto,
this spoke far more powerfully than some mythical, white-constructed rural idyll.
Township life was nothing like Huskisson's secondhand stereotypes of 'the
Bantu.' It was in equal parts bleak and vibrant. While networks of family, solidarity, and resistance were either surviving or being painstakingly reshaped, money
was short, conditions bare, and crime rife. Large numbers of young men who
had graduated from the limited Bantu education system with prospects of neither work nor further training formed the core of a growing number of youth
gangs. Curfews and exclusion forced that gangsterism increasingly to eat its own
flesh. At night and over weekends, the townships were a pressure cooker of murderous frustrations, with the lid nailed down.

By the late 1960s, the townships were developing cultural and consumption
patterns as distinctive as those that had earlier characterised Sophiatown. Among
young people, there were different and competing dress styles (which sometimes,
but by no means always, signified gang membership). The smart-casual Ivy
League look, with its button-down shirts, ankle-skimming pants, and loafers,
described by Jonas Gwangwa in the late 1950s, was now entrenched among the

more affluent and fashion-conscious. Rivals to the Ivies were the pantsulas, a style that has been the most resilient and long-lived among working-class township youth. It is still seen today—both on older people (you are, one song says, 'a pantsula for life') and on the young. Cutting-edge black fashion designers at the start of the twenty-first century now use pantsula style as a source-book: peaked caps on shaven or close-cropped heads, wide trousers (everything—including socks and underwear—from a 'name' label) for the men. Their girlfriends, called *mshoza*, favoured pleated skirts and berets. Pantsulas created their own innovative dance styles, like the 'monkey jive'. High urban literacy and mass media advertising, which by the 1960s were targeting black buyers as a group, meant that—even if tastes contrasted—a shared black culture was being consolidated. Over time, it spread beyond the big cities. David Coplan gives a perfect description of *mshoza* dress among women in the bars of Lesotho in the 1980s: 'fresh, light-coloured blouses, modest skirts falling below the knee, jaunty berets and caps'. He also notes that they called their fast dancing style *jaife* (jive).[78]

By the end of the 1960s, a third style was emerging: the hippies, with bell-bottomed trousers, bright, decorative shirts, and sometimes combed-out Afro hairstyles that were the opposite of both the pantsulas' *kaaskop* (cheese-head/shaven head) and the Ivies' neat (and, in the case of women, frequently straightened) coiffure. This was the style of the soul afficionados. Sipho Mabuse was a senior school student just beginning his forays into music, and was about to join Selby Ntuli and others to found a group called the Beaters, later to be renamed Harari:

Soweto soul music . . . came from the American soul music influence with Booker T and the MG's—that's how this whole music got to be developed along those lines, because we could not relate to *mbaqanga* because we considered ourselves more . . . literate, educated you know—we considered ourselves learned students. . . . So we developed Soweto soul music from that premise: that we listened to [white] Radio 5 and of course soul music was growing in leaps and bounds—all the influence from Wilson Pickett, Otis Redding and so on. And, naturally, we were influenced by that to start a kind of sound that was essentially South African, and that's how Soweto soul music was developed. The Beaters were one of the groups; the All-Rounders, The In-Lawes, The TNT's, The Flaming Souls, The Movers—the list was just endless. The Emeralds! The Minerals! . . . I mean we could not really relate to some of the music that was happening then: *mbaqanga* and *isicathamiya* and so on.[79]

As Mabuse indicates, this was far more than a stance on fashion and music. In 1969, the South African Students' Organisation (SASO) was launched at the 'tribal' University of the North. Black students broke away from the officially multiracial but white-dominated National Union of South African Students (NUSAS). SASO's leader and spokesman was Steve Bantu Biko, and its philosophy was beginning to be explicitly described as Black Consciousness. For young people like Mabuse and the saxophonist who later joined him in the Beaters, Khaya Mahlangu, there were rich points of contact to be explored between Black Consciousness philosophy and South African roots, soul style, and the common feel that seemed to underpin African-American popular music, hard bop, and even John Coltrane:

There was a lot of music at home. My father had a big hi-fi—what we used to call gumba-gumbas, powered by a car battery. He had a great collection of jazz and his buddies would come over to play their collections. . . . I always say there is a link between African people and the diaspora. Because it is black music, one is easily drawn towards it . . . people like Coltrane and Jimmy Smith.[80]

Sipho Mabuse:

[As a band,] we never wore bell-bottoms, but those were the fashions of the day: Afros and bell-bottoms and very colourful clothes . . . and everything was influenced by the events of the time and politically, people were quite clued-up. Because Martin Luther King was happening, the Black Consciousness Movement was happening at the time and [the Beaters] got caught up in that. . . . We didn't write about politics really until '73, '74 . . . [but] consciousness in our music started creeping in.[81]

By the end of the 1960s, then, there was emerging a contemporary canon of socially aware music. Jazzmen were applying the skills of big band and bebop to a local hard bop style that was drawing not only on American blues flavours, but also on indigenous rhythms and voicings. Popular culture was looking towards soul, and students towards black consciousness. Choristers and serious composers as well as political movements were exploring new nationalist songs. A cultural gulf was developing between all these musics and their fans and the neotraditional sounds promoted by the regime and appreciated by many rural people and hostel-dwelling migrant workers—a gulf that was to have a violent impact on township life in the late 1980s and 1990s.

But where to perform? The last years of the 1960s had seen further legal moves against occasions and places where black people might gather in dangerously large numbers, restrictions that caused many venues simply to throw up their hands and close. Even the Cape Town clubs had gone. What happened in township halls was strictly monitored, and popular resistance to even using these apartheid facilities was growing. The illegal shebeens were too small.

Lucky Michaels, meanwhile, had been developing his entrepreneurial skills. He noticed the gap in the market—and in the social fabric: 'By [the early 1970s] there was not one single venue for black artists to perform in. Not one single place'.[82]

# Notes

1. Humphrey Tyler on the Sharpeville massacre, writing for *Drum* magazine in March 1960, but only published—because of censorship—in the London *Observer* in September.
2. Sibongile Khumalo interview for *Ubuyile*, 2000.
3. Dr. Y. Huskisson, *A Survey of Music in the Native Schools of the Transvaal* (master's thesis, University of the Witwatersrand, 1955), 140.
4. Ibid., 218.
5. Ibid.
6. Ibid., 143.
7. Ibid., 238.
8. B. F. Nel, quoted in ibid., 239.
9. Percival Kirby, 'African Music', in *The Handbook on Race Relations in South Africa* (Johannesburg: IRR, 1949), 620, quoted in ibid., 241.
10. Ibid., 242.
11. Quoted in N. Parsons, *A New History of Southern Africa*, 2nd ed. (London: Macmillan, 1993), 294.
12. O. Mtshali, *Sounds of a Cowhide Drum* (New York: Renoster Press, 1971), 24.
13. D. Coplan, *In the Time of the Cannibals* (Johannesburg: Witwatersrand University Press, 1994), 169.
14. Ibid., 155.
15. A. Impey, 'Refashioning Identity in Post-Apartheid South African Music,' in *Culture in the New South Africa*, ed. R. Kriger and A. Zegeye, Vol. 2 (Cape Town: Kwela Books, 2001), 233.
16. A. Sitas, 'The Autobiography of a Movement: Trade Unions in KwaZulu-Natal 1970s–1990s', in Kriger and Zegeye, ibid., 247.
17. A remote rural area of KwaZulu.
18. Sitas, op. cit., 248.
19. Interview for *Ubuyile*, 2000.
20. Ibid.
21. Quoted in P. Tucker, *Just the Ticket* (Johannesburg: Jonathan Ball, 1997), 176.
22. Quoted in ibid., 178.
23. Lars Rasmussen, *Abdullah Ibrahim, a Discography*, 2nd ed. (Copenhagen: The Booktrader, 2000), 33.
24. Interview for *Ubuyile*, 2000.
25. Z. B. Molefe and M. Mzileni, *A Common Hunger to Sing* (Cape Town: Kwela Books, 1997), n.p.
26. The place was Cape Town City Hall at the end of the decade, where Mankunku had to play behind a screen while a white saxophonist mimed his notes.

27. Interview for *Ubuyile*, 2000.
28. Ibid.
29. *Sing Africa Sing*, ABC Ulwazi radio programme 2, 2002.
30. Interview for *Ubuyile*, 2000.
31. All this material from *Sing Africa Sing*, programmes 2–3.
32. *South African Freedom Songs*, CD disc 1, passim.
33. Tucker, op. cit., 133.
34. Y. Huskisson, *The Bantu Composers of South Africa* (Johannesburg: South African Broadcasting Corporation, 1969), 273.
35. V. S. Reddy, 'Vuyisile Mini', *Notes and Documents*, no. 31/74, Durban UND, November 1974.
36. Photographer Basil Breakey, interviewed by Angela Boshoff at www.kush.co.za.
37. Interview for *Ubuyile*, 2000.
38. Ibid.
39. Ibid.
40. Ibid.
41. Ibid.
42. Ibid.
43. Quoted in *Two-Tone*, 1, no. 3, (Johannesburg) *Vrye Weekblad*, 1992, p. 8.
44. Interview for *Ubuyile*, 2000.
45. All ibid. except Denis Mpale, from an interview by the author for the Johannesburg *Mail and Guardian*, June 1997.
46. Interview for *Ubuyile*, 2000.
47. L. Rasmussen, ed., *Cape Town Jazz 1959–63: The Photographs of Hardy Stockman* (Copenhagen: The Booktrader, 2001), 111.
48. Ibid., 112–13.
49. Interview with the author for *The Star Tonight*, 2001.
50. Conversation with the author, Cape Town, March 2003.
51. Rasmussen, *Cape Town Jazz*, op. cit., 115.
52. Composite from interview for *Ubuyile*, 2000 and interview for the Johannesburg *Mail and Guardian*, May 2002.
53. D. Constant-Martin, *Coon Carnival* (Cape Town: David Phillip, 1999), 135.
54. Conversation with the author, March 2003.
55. Constant-Martin, op. cit., 141.
56. Quoted by ibid., 161.
57. Interview for *Ubuyile*, 2000.
58. Ibid.
59. Ibid.
60. Ibid.
61. Conversation with the author, 1997.
62. Interview with Luvuyo Kakaza in the *Mail and Guardian*, 21 October 1999.
63. *Staffrider*, 4, no. 4 1983, p. 38.
64. Rob Allingham, *Two-Tone*, 1, no. 7 (Johannesburg) *Vrye Weekblad*, July 1992, p. 21.
65. Communication with the author, 18 November 2003.
66. Interview with the author, Cape Town, March 2003.

67. Interview for *Ubuyile*, 2000.

68. Interview for Johannesburg *Mail and Guardian*, May 2002.

69. Interview for *Ubuyile*, 2000.

70. Ibid.

71. Ibid.

72. Ibid.

73. Ibid.

74. Interview with the author, Cape Town, March 2000.

75. Conversation with the author, 1997.

76. Interview with the author, 18 June 2003.

77. Horace Silver, quoted by Gene Seymour in 'Hard bop,' in *The Oxford Companion to Jazz*, ed. B. Kirchner (New York: Oxford University Press, 2000), 373.

78. Conversation with the author, June 2003.

79. Coplan, 1995 op. cit., pp. 150/1 passim.

80. Interview for *Ubuyile*, 2000.

81. Ibid.

82. Ibid.

*Chapter Five*

# Underground in Africa

We move to Denver / because there's work in Denver / We move to
Vlakfontein / No more work in Denver / . . . Mama, oh Mama, you
tame the snakes and scorpions and then you are moved again / Mama,
how I remember / We leave our graves behind.

—lyric from the musical *Phiri*[1]

By the start of the 1970s, the myriad of petty regulations that made up
grand apartheid were firmly in place. Black people were no longer citizens
of South Africa, but of arbitrarily mapped tribal homeland states that may
have been less than a distant memory to their grandparents. Urban 'black spots'
and profitable rural areas were cleared of African landholders. In the townships,
streets and wards were assigned to residents on the basis of this assigned tribal
origin, and home ownership and lease-holding outlawed. Black professionals like
doctors and lawyers were to be discouraged from taking office space in the townships and steered to set up in the homelands. Living conditions worsened, as
more work-seekers came to the towns (or evaded eviction from them) and set
up home in their relatives' backyards. Revenues from sources like the municipal
beerhalls were diverted from township maintenance to homeland construction.
Black education curricula were trimmed to the bone. Arrest—particularly for
suspected political activity—occurred on the flimsiest of pretexts, and being 'endorsed out' of the city could happen at any time, on any arbitrary whim or
mistake, with little recourse to appeal. Black cultural life was segregated and
regulated with the clear intention of annihilating autonomy.

But a vibrant, independent social life survived, and in far more than officially
sanctioned forms. Both history and community sustained it, but two factors were
particularly important in the 1970s, providing an infusion of fresh ideas and
inspiration. The first was Africa. The developing politics of black consciousness

looked now not only to an Africa mediated by Africans in America, but also directly to the newly independent states of the surrounding continent—and to traditional roots within South Africa itself. Young radicals began to take a second look at authentic lore formerly scorned by urban sophisticates and synthesized into tame prescriptions by the regime. They saw tradition as a source not of unchanging, passive separation, but of creativity and unity, as poet Maishe Maponya remembers:

> [We wore] kaftans and the traditional cloth that was woven by women in the rural areas. And we used to wrap that around our bodies, and then we performed. And we used a lot of drumming—the drum became part of our performances. . . . [We memorised all our lines, so that the police couldn't seize papers on us] . . . it created a kind of a free flow out of the performance. One poet would be reading and reciting, and another would jut in with lines . . . and then proceed, and then someone else would come in and create choruses, and sounds, and rhythms. And that for me was what was beautiful: that kind of creativity. . . . We used musicians; we had flutes, Moss Manaka played the flute, and my younger brother also played the flute. Moss also played drum and we had a guy playing the guitar. . . . And so in that sense for us, you know, music became the basis.[2]

News of a wider Africa came in from a range of sources, for the ANC also had offices, military training camps, and refugee centres in a number of independent states, and more as the decade progressed, and transmitted struggle news from Radio Freedom in Lusaka. There were also shortwave broadcasts from the BBC and VOA.

The other important factor intensifying cultural activity was repression and the resistance it provoked. Much of what developed in the 1970s developed underground, clandestine because of its radical content—or simply because of the illegality of unlicenced clubs and gatherings. Painter Sydney Selepe, who grew up then, says various forms of resistance came to be a defining cultural characteristic: 'When I was a kid, if it was not political, it was not art'.[3]

The most basic form of cultural resistance was simply finding space to do what was forbidden. The problem of space—physical and political—was worsening. From the 1960s, there had been a range of attempts to sustain autonomous community arts projects of various kinds, all with a strong African consciousness: the Mhloti (Tears) Theatre group in Alexandra; the Mdali (Music, Dance, and Literature) Institute in Soweto; the People's Experimental Theatre in Lenasia. As fast as these intiatives sprang up, the authorities made attempts to hound them out of existence. Visual artist Thami Mnyele, working with Mhloti, remembers: 'Some members of the community who were supporters . . . were not allowing their kids to attend our performances. . . . Soon the problem came into the open: the people had had visits from the Special Branch and were afraid'.[4] The year 1972 had seen the last attempt of original black drama to stay in the city. The Dorkay House Phoenix Players had launched *Phiri*, a musical adaptation of Ben Jonson's seventeenth-century satire *Volpone* to 1970s Johannesburg. Librettists included black consciousness poet Mongane Wally Serote; the music was by Cyril Magubane and Mackay Davashe. Sophie Mngcina was part of the cast:

Let me tell you something: you know there was a play called *Phiri*, an edition of *Volpone*? I was in the play; Felicia Mabuza was in the play, Abigail [Khubeka] was in it—a lot of us, you know, the cream of the time. That LP was recorded and it was banned, because it spoke about apartheid. But what is political if you say [sings]: *'Madam, please before you shout about your broken plate / ask me what my family ate / madam if you say the driver stinks / Come!—take a bath in a Soweto zinc [bathtub]'?* How political can you get?[5]

The play rehearsed at the BMSC; the day after rehearsals finished, it was shut down. *Phiri* played briefly at the Wits University theatre and in some unsuitable township venues without stage facilities, before the cast broke up, unable to sustain such a daring production further. Gusta Mnguni, who also starred, recalls, 'Our people loved the show . . . white authority perceived it as nothing but "black subversive" politics. It had a strong message'.[6] The song 'Madam Please' remains a classic. Dorkay House waned. Black artists saw little value in training and development without the physical or political space to present the results, and, again, artists went underground into township groups, presenting their work as and when a space (often temporarily) opened.

Much as Dorkay House had brought together musicians across genres, this search for expressive freedom brought together musicians across the country. It had happened in earlier decades, but artists' memories of this period particularly share a leitmotif of moving, travelling, and touring; when asked, it is what they first recall. The most adventurous of the country's bands were national, uniting Johannesburg and Cape Town inspirations and more. While the state was busily inventing folklore and tribal nationalities, a different kind of cultural nationalism was consolidating.

For jazz, the main creative spaces were the unlicenced music clubs that developed, particularly in Johannesburg, in the early 1970s in response to this lack of other venues. Many were short-lived, unable to take the blows of constant raids and restrictions, pay the bribes to township police, or hold their stressed audiences together. But the first, finest, and most resilient (it survived until the mid-1980s) was Lucky Michaels's Pelican in Orlando. He tells the story of those early days best:

[In 1972,] I opened a club. Me and two or three other guys, we decided to open a club. Did we really know what was going to happen in the club? Frankly, I think from day one we had no idea! All we said was: here is a club, here are musicians—they haven't got a venue; we've got a venue—let's see if the guys can gig here. And Dennis Mpale, Barney Rachabane, Mankunku Ngozi, Dollar Brand (as he was at the time), those were the guys that used to come around. . . . I did not set out to create the family environment, Soweto created that. It was already there in the various shebeens we used to go to. This was a bigger place than a normal shebeen; it had more lights—that's all. And the musicians needed a venue. There were no Market Theatres, no nightclubs in [smart northern suburbs] for them; you just couldn't do that. It's either they were cutting a movie, like General Duze, or playing a formal concert. . . . There were stadiums, but there was no daily regular venue. That concept had not arisen. . . . Here, the guys were jamming. They were enjoying themselves. They were getting together, not necessarily playing as a band. We did have a standing band, but these guys were playing as a jam—'Hey, let me get in, please'. . . . [The late] Mike Makhalemele was one of the guys who'd walk around to every other musician he knows and say, 'Listen, guys, why don't we meet at the Pelican. Let's go and jam there'. . . . They'd come in with horns, drums, all sorts of instruments and just play. . . . And it was a venue away from the BMSC, where you'd have to travel back to Soweto by train after you'd played, with a curfew permit. No, here, you were home already! Now, if you took that community, and those musicians, you had a melting pot. Cabaret on Sunday evening was our best: singers like Thandi Klaasen, Sophie Mngcina. People learned how to play here—not from me, but from the other musicians they were interacting with. . . . It was a magical thing that was happening. . . . But if Lucky Michaels says, it was my ingenious ideas—no, it was not. It was the time that made the place.

We got hit—what?—three months after we'd opened. We got hit for being a shebeen, because obviously, to them, we were just a shebeen with a load of lights. They piled as many people as they could into *kwela-kwelas* and took them to Orlando Police Station, which at that time was just a wooden and zinc-roofed building. They put all these blacks behind the counter. . . . And the beautiful problem was they arrested the Mala-wian ambassador. . . . At that time, an embassy had been allowed to happen from Kamuzu Banda to South Africa . . . with all kinds of prob-lems, like, where would a [black] ambassador's children go to school? Soweto? . . . When the station commander came in at around midnight, he saw this guy dressing funny—which the Afrikaners did not under-stand—I mean, Christ, here's a guy sitting here in a long dress and a funny hat . . . and the commander realised: hey, wait man, you've just arrested the ambassador from Malawi. The first black ambassador ever to South Africa! . . . Anyway, most of us paid the R10 admission of guilt fine. . . . I needed to come back and start the business up again, because I knew the police wouldn't come back and raid again that weekend. That's the way it went. . . . What kept us going? Insanity! That's what I had. I had insanity and I had defiance. My defiance was: hey, man, if a white man can sell liquor and have a venue like this and entertainment like this, why can't I? That's all it was.[7]

Many other musicians, like Sipho Mabuse and Menyatso Mathole, acknowledge the importance of the Pelican, and its name crops up regularly in the story of the next dozen years:

There was a night-club called the Pelican—this is where the musicians were . . . that place was the real hub of South African musicians. The late Dennis Mpale was there; [Winston] Mankunku, who was a giant we could relate to. And of course for us, as youngsters, to be able to sustain ourselves even within the realms of jazz, we were lucky enough to have interacted with such musicians as [drummer] Early Mabuza, [bassist] Gordon Mfandu—especially in my case as a drummer Nelson Magwaza, and of course Bheki Mseleku was a peer to us. And the only way we could prove that we were good enough to play, was playing jazz. It was the only way we could prove ourselves—even if we had to play pop music. But it was the fact that you were able to play jazz that created a very strong foundation for us to be able to continue in the jazz field. . . . [L]ater there was [the group] Sakhile, Robbie Jansen in Cape Town, Duke Makasi—all the men who had been there [at the Pelican]. Even though we appreciated pop music, there was always a very strong element of jazz in what we were doing.[8]

According to Mathole, 'The Pelican at that time was recognised as a kind of music university for Soweto, where young musicians developed and polished their skills. . . .'[9]

Mabuse makes the important point that the Pelican did not host jazz only. There were also cabaret and pop music acts—even the best of traditional music found a home there, as Lucky Michaels remembers:

Black Mambazo was not yet Ladysmith Black Mambazo. They were performing at a place called St Mary's Hall, with all this 'Mbube, mbube, mbube' stuff of theirs. And we would go and pick up the winners of the *mbube* competitions and say, do you want to play? And they'd also come here and 'A la-la' and all that. If anybody wanted to play, they'd come to the Pelican, because it was the only place.[10]

Other clubs emulated the Pelican's model in the years that followed. Among them was Club Galaxy, founded in 1978 in Rylands on the Cape Flats, the area to which the city's 'coloured' communities had been removed. Like the Pelican, Galaxy covertly sheltered political activity as well as music. It celebrated its twenty-fifty anniversary in December 2003. Although its programming is now dominated by disco rather than live music, Galaxy was, appropriately, the venue for the jazz jam that marked the raising of the tombstone for Chris Columbus Ngcukana.

Alongside the patronage given by the state broadcaster to certain approved forms of tradition, there were still many places where autonomous music-making flourished. Singer Sibongile Khumalo, whose father was an avid collector of such music, and who as a young girl accompanied him to concerts and competitions, remembers:

> You got a situation where traditional music—the real, *real* traditional music—happened in hostels, in backyards—the kitchens, as they were called. And there was a lot of stunning activity going on there. And that in itself is a vindication of the resilience of the people of this country . . . because if there hadn't been that recognition that I'm a Pedi, I'm a Zulu and this is my music, that music would have died. . . . [U]nfortunately, some musical forms, some styles of playing, some instruments . . . are almost extinct.[11]

It was good there were such places as the Pelican. Elsewhere, musicians faced not only the restrictions of apartheid, but the South African symptoms of a world trend: the rise of the pop group. Four players with electric, amplified instruments could create as big a sound as a dance band. If those players were young, malleable—and cheap—so much the better. Ntemi Piliso saw it happening:

> That was a time when the big bands were down, when the pop music started. They were not playing jazz and swing music on air, so we suffered a lot as big bands. People were listening to kwela music, which was composed of a smaller combination; like one saxophone and a few guitars and so forth. You find that a band of five or six can do better than a big band.[12]

His peers remember other aspects of a grim and reduced music scene.

Barney Rachabane:

> It was getting worse here in the country. A lot of people left, and that was the only way to continue playing. But me, I didn't go abroad. No, I just stayed here and accepted the whip. . . . I just stayed here at home, and played and practised.

General Duze:

> Only the night-spots in Hillbrow, coffee bars and places had work. I had a small group . . . and I got my other talent going, acting. Got involved

in TV. I don't know what the other guys did, but that's what kept me going. . . . I didn't make albums. I just didn't get the inspiration to do it. I felt very bad about the royalties. . . .

Tony Schilder:

All we had left was our love of music. Those were the days when every [musician's] house had a piano and all the musicians just used to get together in somebody's house.

Winston Mankunku Ngozi:

In the '70s, work was scarce. We had to travel to Port Elizabeth, Jo'burg; we were touring all the time. Jo'burg was nice . . . it gave you the chance to meet a lot of other musicians and listen to their music, and I was also listening to a lot of classical music. But it was still terrible. At times we'd just laugh at these people and get drunk—just to make ourselves strong. . . . You just got through the day. If you had just got through the day and nothing too terrible had happened, that was the time to joke, to celebrate, and that was what the music was for. . . . But we never stopped playing. Never! Never went way from the music. We'd be at home. Some work, practicing, listening. It's just we weren't seen.[13]

The coffee bars to which Duze refers were places like the Cul de Sac and Nitebeat, established in the 1960s. These were the forerunners of folk clubs such as Johannesburg's Troubadour. Their clientele was predominantly white and young, and, together with events such as the Wits University Free People's Concerts, they were influencing the cultural tastes and political ideas of progressive young people. In jazz, some players already worked across colour lines whenever they could. By the end of the 1980s, a more explicitly experimental and political white pop music would come into the public eye from these roots.

For trumpeter Banzi Bangani, the pressures and the uncertain lifestyle they imposed were too much. His cousin Elijah Nkwanyana had died in 1969, a young man of only forty. Bangani decided to devote the rest of his life and talent to religion, teaching and playing with church choirs and bands. But even there, apartheid reached:

We lived in fear, man. We were not free even like before. It was worse. . . . As church people, we were with old ladies and so forth . . . and the [police] will start making funny remarks: 'Look at this one with the big __' and so on. . . . Sometimes even in churches. Whites would come to our churches and preach, but you would never see a black man go into a white church and get into the pulpit. Apartheid was right even in the churches. . . . It was terrible. Well, as children of God, we never cared

much, because we knew that one day God is going to answer. . . . There's
a part in the Bible where it says: And the Lord says, at the end of time I
will return Kush back to his city—and He did, truly speaking.[14]

Bangani expresses well the growing liberation politics of many churches,
black and white. Steve Biko undertook much of his early research, writing, and
publishing under the auspices of a church-funded group. When apartheid bore
down more harshly on basic human dignity and security, many people who
had not formerly involved themselves in politics were radicalised. As Sibongile
Khumalo describes, creativity was on the rise in church and choral music:

> The *Messiah* had become an annual tradition in Soweto . . . and there
> was a lot of that kind of music-making happening at [the] community
> level. . . . But also church choirs were a foundation for a lot of people
> who wanted to participate in some kind of ensemble singing. . . . In the
> late '60s, a Mr Nakeni was in charge of the African Teachers' Association
> of South Africa, [which was] the mother body of choral competitions.
> He used to encourage composers to bring in new music . . . and he would
> bring in a panel of musically literate people as adjudicators [who could]
> sit with the composer, sing through the music and decide which is best
> . . . so much new music was generated for choir competitions.[15]

Because such activity was under the auspices of a teachers' union, however, it
could not escape official attention. As well as student activism, the early years of
the 1970s had seen a rise in black labour militancy, both organised and spontaneous, that worried the apartheid state. Some of the strikes involved huge numbers
of workers and were repressed brutally: gold miners at Carletonville, west of
Johannesburg, were driven back to work in 1973 by the shooting of twelve of
their comrades. The productivity of the gold and diamond mines was becoming
vital for the survival of a South African economy wounded by the oil-price infla-
tion that was driving an international recession. While government and companies strove to keep black wages down, the recession and the country's
dependence on certain high-priced exports were giving black workers bargaining
muscle that—despite the continuing illegality of black trade unions—they began
to marshall and exert.

    The authorities responded with their customary combination of hypocrisy
and brute force. A commission into the mine riots recommended a slight easing
of the hostel system to buy off 'key workers', although it also pointed out that
'Southern Bantu tribes [have an] inclination to be violent' and advised tougher
mine policing.[16] The homelands were gradually granted 'self-governed' status as
a prelude to paper independence; their formal parliamentary structures were a
flimsy front for puppet politicians taking orders from Pretoria. Undeceived by

this talk of self-determination, the United Nations withdrew South Africa's accreditation and awarded the ANC and the PAC observer status.

The need for skilled black labour grew as world recession intensified. But the government faced lower revenues and was making ambitious military spending plans to meet the perceived 'communist threat' of radicalism at home and independent black neighbours on the borders. Already spending only one-fifteenth of the white figure on each black pupil, further cost-cutting was instituted. A year was trimmed from black primary schooling, so that huge numbers of less qualified students flooded already inadequate secondary schools, almost paralysing the system.

Indignant students organised through the African Students Movement (ASM), established to protest poor education and youth facilities in 1968. In 1972, the ASM had linked to the SASO and changed its name to the South African Students' Movement (SASM). Through newsletters, leaflets, and often clandestine meetings (some under the camouflage of church youth groups and choirs, or sports and martial arts clubs), the ideas of black consciousness and the critiques of Bantu education and apartheid were disseminated widely. School inspectors, the police, and more conservative head teachers tried to clamp down, and gangs continued their harassment, often with police encouragement.

For everyone—organised workers, township residents, artists and musicians, and students—the early years of the decade saw a heightened awareness of African identity and a flowering of cultural creativity that expressed it. In 1973, Dollar Brand had recorded an album called *Underground in Africa*, the only one to appear on the Mandla label of an independent Johannesburg producer, Rashid Vally. Vally's main output previously had been dance and hard bop music for his Soultown label. His family owned the Kohinoor Store in downtown Johannesburg, selling general supplies like stoves and blankets as well as records and radios, to customers from the townships and to migrant workers on their way to catch a train to the reserves. According to discographer Lars Rasmussen, 'The record contained several political statements: the title referred to the armed underground struggle; the name Mandla was a slight variation (for security reasons) of the word Amandla, which means power, and the logo was made up of African tribal weapons'.[17]

The album, like a number of independent releases during the period, showcased new black art as well as music. Its cover was designed by Hargreaves Ntukwana, a graduate of the Polly Street Art Centre, who had also been a pit musician for the South African run of *King Kong*. On the track 'Ornette's Cornet', the saxes of Robbie Jansen, Basil Coetzee, and Arthur Jacobs exchange spiky phrases that reflect the impression free jazz was making on musicians, while 'All Day and All Night' is South African hard bop, its soulful groove given a *goema* flavour by drummer Nazier Kapdi, who learned his skill in Cape Town carnival bands.

Vally's role in recording challenging, original music was vital, as Barney Rachabane—who featured with Brand on another album of the period, *Black Light-*

*ning*—remembers. Like the clubs, the Sun label was another space for creativity
to operate without restrictions. And, with performances curtailed, artists had a
lot of time to develop their ideas. 'Rashid recorded most of that music: Sun label.
Not the white record companies', Rachabane says. 'We did a lot of sessions, we
were in there all the time. . . . That music was so original, you know: the *mbaqanga* from the '60s, but developed, different chord changes. It was beautiful
music—and a lot of it is still unreleased'.[18]

Without Brand, the band assembled for the *Underground in Africa* session
stayed together as Oswietie (*Ons wietie*: 'We know') and spent nine months touring Angola; the concluding months of the independence war. The experience
made a deep impact on all of them, especially Jansen and Coetzee. They spent
much of the time holed up in hotels under various kinds of military curfews and
began shaping their own view of music as a voice for struggle, as Robbie Jansen
remembers:

> We were searchers, listening to every kind of music we could lay our
> hands on. We'd practice classical music, we got involved in reading
> music, and the theory of it because we realised we couldn't be busk-
> ers—we had to know our instruments in depth. Seeing all the killing and
> not being involved in it created an urgent need to make our instruments
> effective and expressive voices.[19]

In 1975, Dennis Mpale and Kippie Moeketsi made an album called *Our Boys
Are Doing It*, with Pat Matshikiza on piano, and, from the Beaters, the young
Sipho Mabuse on drums and Alec Khaoli on bass. Hugh Masekela had recently
issued *The Boy's Doing It* in America, and, to the record label, this was simply
the recycling of a successful title. The musicians did have that in mind, but
more, too.

Dennis Mpale:

> Yes, it did relate to Hugh's record in a way—we were saying, there are
> also South Africans making good music inside the country. . . . That
> wasn't the big part of it, but it was what we talked about when they
> [the record company] discussed the title with us. But every person in the
> township knew who 'our boys' were—MK: our boys fighting in Zimba-
> bwe and Angola. Like now we say Bafana-Bafana and everybody knows
> it's the football team. Well, in that time, 'our boys' were the struggle
> outside the country, because, hey, there were *impimpis* [informers]
> around to hear you say MK or ANC.[20]

*Our Boys* is *mbaqanga*: three fast-paced tracks led by Matshikiza's piano.
Moeketsi is inventive and audacious; Mpale displays the speed-merchant fingering for which he became famous; Matshikiza shouts exhortations to keep the

improvisation flowing. But it is not the attentuated, pigeonholed *mbaqanga* the state wanted. It is joyous, a defiant show-off of skill and an international jazz vocabulary over chords patterned on marabi: music to keep the listeners strong.

Jazz players were finding a way to import the inventiveness of 1950s African jazz into modern small-group music that the public and the record companies would buy. Ntemi Piliso, by the 1970s a wise old bird observing the music scene through nearly forty years of experience, pinpoints the moment when it happened:

> [I]n 1975, Basil [Coetzee] and Abdullah [Ibrahim] came out with that *Manenberg* thing. Then we thought, no, that big sound is coming back now. It's got all the ingredients to form a big-band sound again . . . even though *Manenberg* was not played by a big band . . . but the style reminded people of the big-band sound. . . . That was the start of the coming-back of big-band.[21]

It is probably stretching the definition to call *Manenberg* a jive tune—even though I have seen dancers jiving to it many times. Rashid Vally now had a new label: As-Shams (The Sun), given its name by Abdullah Ibrahim, and *Manenberg (is Where it's Happening)* was the fourth album Ibrahim recorded for As-Shams. (The other three remain unissued, and two of them untitled.) The album features a quintet: Ibrahim on piano, Basil Coetzee on tenor, Robbie Jansen on alto, Paul Michaels on bass, and Monty Weber on drums, with a second alto, the young white player Morris Goldberg, taking the final solo on the title track. And the title track is all many South African listeners remember of the album, for it has become the most iconic of all South African jazz tunes. Capetonians call it 'our unofficial national anthem', and Coetzee thereafter bore its title (that of a Cape Town 'coloured' settlement to which many District 6 residents were removed) as his professional name until his death. Writer Mandla Langa says, 'The tune became a popular metaphor for all the townships where trouble brewed'.[22] Then a young boy, pianist Moses Molelekoa, remembered how the tune was loved and listened to:

> I remember when I used to visit my grandparents in Alexandra, my grandfather had a few albums, one of which was *Manenberg* by Abdullah Ibrahim . . . and it was a dance song, a party song [like] most of the jazz that was coming out at that period. . . . It was quite heavy, though, because I remember we also had Miriam Makeba and Hugh Masekela but we didn't have much access to those because they were banned [and] you always have to look out if you were listening to such an album. . . .[23]

Abdullah Ibrahim was seeking an indigenous approach to jazz. Robbie Jansen remembers: 'It was very difficult to play African music in South Africa then. I

# DID YOU TELL YOUR MOTHER

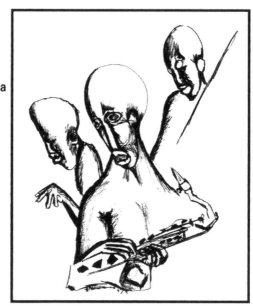

Tete Mbambisa

Basil Coetzee

Zulu Bidi

Monty Weber

**As-Shams/The Sun label album cover with artwork by Hargreaves Ntukwana.** *Credit: As-Shams*

was learning to read music and Abdullah said, "Take that book away; you don't want to learn to be American, you want to play like yourself".'[24] The approach worked, with Jansen playing straight from the heart—something he has continued to do since. Yet subtract the adventurousness of the solos, and what remains is a precise, stately rhythm, along with a cyclical theme that carries hypnotic musical invention for nearly twenty-eight minutes. It is not hard to hear why Ntemi Piliso hailed it as the return of the big-band approach.

The formula travelled further out with the As-Shams album *Plum and Cherry*. In company with pianist Lionel Pillay, who had added so much to *Yakhal' Inkomo*, the album has only two long tracks, Pillay's 'Plum' and Ibrahim's 'Cherry'. You could dance marabi to the organ chords and rhythm of 'Cherry', but Coetzee's tenor uses each improvisation to explore a new flavour: shouts, cries, ideas that could become new tunes or fragments of very old ones with the

inflected wail of South Asian song. Far more formulaic—at least initially—
'Plum' begins with the jangling sound of a 1930s parlour piano, overlaid by
bluesy organ in the style of Jimmy Smith. Then, quite suddenly, the mix pulls
drums and percussion to the front and asserts Africa in the layers of rhythm,
with Jimmy Smith wholly displaced by Osibisa, and Pillay's piano a dazzling,
edgy, staccato percussion instrument in its own right.

'Plum' starts out bump jive and ends up taking risks, pillaging Afro-rock
and prefiguring fusion. Musicians like Pillay, Coetzee, Jansen from the Cape,
Johannesburg saxophonist Duke Makasi, and new young Durban bassist Sipho
Gumede were all also working in other, more experimental combos that offered
greater scope for risk-taking. Many of these groups began around the mid-'70s
but became more prominent in the last years of the decade, when a change in
the mood of audiences and players demanded something more challenging.

These bands and recordings spanned the period leading up to the independence
of Mozambique and Angola in 1975 and 1976. Both won independence and
installed socialist governments, following the collapse of the colonising power,
Portugal, after a coup at home. In Angola, the final victory took longer. South
Africa sent in troops to fight the new government, whose army only finally de-
feated South African forces at the battle of Cuito Canavale in 1988. In South
Africa, Black People's Convention (BPC) and SASO student leaders, who had
led celebrations for these new states across the country, were arrested, and nine
were put on trial. Despite attempts in the state media to downplay these events,
the victories mattered to South Africans, who could access news of them via the
ANC's clandestine Radio Freedom.

Sipho Mabuse believes that the widespread celebrations of Mozambican and
Angolan independence were one of the bridges between wider popular consciousness and the ideas of the students, politicians, and intellectuals. Many people remember the new African nations being toasted in the shebeens, even by
apparently timid and conservative residents. Lucky Michaels describes the political spectrum as he saw it:

> Basically . . . there were two streams of people. You had the social stream
> and the political stream. And the social stream basically believed: no, baas
> [the master] is baas; there's nothing we can do about this; these guys are
> going to shoot us. These guys who went from work to a shebeen and
> then to bed and then to work and so on. The political stream believed,
> no, no no! We've got to defy this. We've got to get this to an end. I do
> not believe that they knew yet when or how it would end, but they were
> determined to finish it. . . . These two streams of people knew each other
> and lived side-by-side with each other.[25]

Black consciousness was challenging fear and passivity, and successful independence wars so close to home underlined the message that struggle could succeed, says Mabuse:

[W]e suddenly realised there was [a] need to identify with who we were. . . . And of course the revolution . . . in Mozambique, SASO in South Africa, just changed the whole thing and we overhauled ourselves into dashiki-clad musicians who were black power saluting and adhering to all Steve Biko's influences and so on. Biko was very important. Because that era—whether you played *mbaqanga* or not—the emphasis of the elite was not lost, as long as it was coupled with understanding of the political objectives of the day. And people became proud of who they were: the type of music that we do must relate to the politics of the day; how we dress must relate to the politics of the day; and the lyrics and . . . the music must derive from our environment, and the environment would be able to identify with the drum, the guitar, the flute, the wood-wind instruments and the singing. Because that was what was happening then: Malombo, the dashiki. . . .[26]

Maishe Maponya calls it 'the process of the rediscovery of the self, the re-definition of the self . . . not only in South Africa but on the continent'.[27] Along-side the discovery of self, the new, tougher township administration policies provided a far closer view of the other: the oppressor. The new township admin-istration boards were staffed by officials of the central government, white Afri-kaners who visited the locations in large numbers to collect overdue rents and evict illegal residents alongside the already omnipresent white policemen super-vising raids for liquor, political activity, or passes.

On the SABC, the dominance of segregated, white-defined neotribal music was weakening. Yvonne Huskisson, so vehement in the 1950s and 1960s in de-nouncing the evils of jazz, was, by 1969, praising her employer, the SABC, for its role in fostering the very same music:

With Dollar Brand in the lead, these Bantu JAZZ men are coming into their own. . . . Radio Bantu has given this JAZZ development every en-couragement. During their lean formative years, while Bantu audiences were being initiated into the intricacies of the JAZZ form and the JAZZ disc-market was slowly finding its feet, Radio Bantu continuously pro-vided these JAZZ combos with recording facilities and featured them in regular JAZZ programmes. . . . Radio Bantu has virtually become the focal point around which much of Bantu music revolves [author's caps].[28]

Huskisson's version of history was the new official line: jazz had no African roots, but was imitative, fostered under and dependent upon the patronage of a white institution. In a sense, she was bowing to the inevitable. Of the over 300 composers listed in her 1969 survey, *The Bantu Composers of South Africa*, a quarter are named as specialising in 'Bantu Jazz', and a further third in the catch-all category 'composing in a light-music vein', which seems to cover some South African jazz as well as pop music. In Soweto, former musician Ray Nkwe had founded the Johannesburg Jazz Appreciation Society. To stay in touch with the music, jazz *stokvels* were formed in the townships. Members contributed to a savings pool, and each month one member was given the accumulated cash to make his or her choice of purchases at a city centre record store (for there were no record shops in the townships). The music was played and dissected at the club's next social gathering—although after 1976, meetings were often curtailed by a district in flames, or under military occupation, or members 'banned' and forbidden to gather in company.

The SABC's aural segregation policies were not working. Particularly in Johannesburg, where a number of different radio stations could be received, black listeners were simply not tuning in to what the authorities intended, as these memories demonstrate.

Pops Mohamed:

Growing up as a kid in SA was quite different because in those days, as a young boy, we didn't have so much radio. As a matter of fact, there was no TV, and the only music we could listen to was [Mozambique-based] LM Radio, [white, commercial] Springbok Radio, and I got attracted to the sounds of Cliff Richards [*sic*] and the Shadows! That's not really what turned me on to music, but my only form of entertainment was listening to the LM hit parade on Sunday nights.

Sibongile Khumalo:

I listened to a lot of Springbok Radio—Creedence Clearwater Revival, Crosby, Stills, Nash and Young—"Carry on, Love is coming to us . . ."—that kind of pop thing; Janis Joplin, the early Carlos Santana, Jimi Hendrix. I listened to all that kind of stuff.

Dennis Mpale:

In Johannesburg it wasn't like in Durban. There, they got Zulu music only. You could tune to most of the stations from Soweto. So if you liked jazz, you knew the hour for the various jazz programmes and it didn't matter what language—because we all spoke all the languages. You'd just surf to find the music you liked. The same with gospel music, choral, everything. And a lot of people listened to the white stations, especially the young guys who were getting into rock music.

Vusi Khumalo, drummer:

There was a time, you know, there was a craze about underground music, . . . rock. There is a band I used to play with Masike Mohapi from Harari—it was called Muddy Bridge. It was strange enough that there was a rock band in Soweto at that time. . . . This was in the '70s, I think, just before '76.[29]

Soweto soul was still booming, and, on the model of pop groups in Europe and America, drawing in many ambitious young men. The Beaters (whose name was, deliberately, only two insignificant letters away from Beatles) were only the first.

Sipho Mabuse:

I'd always liked playing music, but I never really imagined myself being a professional musician . . . it was just coincidental for us because our headmaster asked if there would be any students who would enter a performance. And I had played drums in a cadet band. . . . [W]e suddenly found ourselves volunteering a performance to raise funds for the students who were going to university. And that's how we got the band together: the Beaters. For us it was just an ordinary high school students' performance—little did we realise there would be such a demand for us to do matric [high school graduation] dances and Sunday performances, and the money just started rolling in. I mean, at the age of 15, 16 you're all impressionable and here's all this money that you've never seen before. And we decided, well, we're going to become a serious band from there. [The vocalist] Arthur left the band, Selby [Ntuli], myself, Alec [Khaoli] and the others continued. And there was demand for recordings now—we recorded our first song, called 'Mamsy's Hips'. We had this woman who used to come around and dance and watch our shows—a very popular woman and the guys loved her. So we dedicated a song to her; it was a huge hit.

Khaya Mahlangu:

Well, my mum's family were Salvation Army people, so whenever we were at church there was a lot of brass music, so I guess that's where I got my love for wind instruments. When I was at higher primary, I joined the Boy Scouts and played the bugle. And then when I got to high school, I switched over to trumpet, but my first love has always been the saxophone. So fortunately, around '72, an uncle of mine realised that I really loved saxophone, and he gave one to me. And then my parents wanted to take me away from that group, because they feared I might be what I am today! So they took me to a boarding school out at Ohlange at Durban, that was in 1972. I was still playing the trumpet then, so I teamed up with Brian Thusi, and we started a high school band. . . . S. D. Ngcobo, the late principal, encouraged music, he was a musician himself—he played piano. The vice-principal was a saxophonist, so music was highly, highly encouraged at the school, from choral music to anything. [By 1975,] I was just beginning to be a professional, but I was still learning the instrument so . . . I learned on the job as it were. . . . It was tough. There weren't many gigs around. I remember we used to earn something like 2.5 Rands (today, 60c)—a gig! And sometimes you might be stopped for a pass and stuff, but somehow we managed to get round that, you know. [We played] township halls, as they were called. We would book the hall, or a promoter would book the hall and pay the band. We used to play four-hour gigs! After that I also played with the Beaters, who eventually became Harari.[30]

'Mamsy's Hips' has not survived on record, but the sounds of Harari, the 1981 renaming of the Beaters, are still available. They provide a clear picture of what young musicians saw as 'African' musical characteristics: interlocked layers of percussion with cowbells and shakers prominent; stretched drum breaks and chantlike chorus singing. One track links the music backward and forward, inward and out to the African continent: 'Marabi is the music / Harari is the magic'.

On the model of those first hit-makers, younger players like Pops Mohamed also got hooked on the sound:

The fact that it's from America, the fact that on most of the music that came from abroad, the guys were black—SA guys identified with that. They also identified with the struggles of the black Americans. Maybe a bit of 'anything that comes from America has got to be good', I'm not sure. But I think the guys strongly identified—they had something to cling to. Those days, it was really, really hard for South African musicians . . . and 'Oh wow, this guy's black and he's playing on the radio!' People aspired to own a gramophone, only so that they could buy American music and identify, get closer to this person: I want to play like him. . . . Because it was even hard for us to go to music schools—we couldn't afford it and there were no proper music schools for black South Africans. . . . We sounded like Americans, but it was still very African. I'll give you an example—if you listen to a band called The Movers, in the '70s, they tried to sound like Booker T and the MGs, [who] were big in SA—then we had this sound called the Soul of Soweto. It came from bands who wanted to sound like Booker T and the MGs. The form there was to have organ, guitar, drums and bass. But we didn't quite get it right. We tried to sound like these people, but because of the African in us, the sound turned into something else. Hence, the sound actually became a hit in Soweto and other parts of South Africa. We had bands like the Hurricanes, the Cannibals, the Emeralds—and it was only instrumen-

tals. . . . People tried to sound like Americans, but because we didn't have
the same facilities, studios, instruments; we played with pennywhistles
and tea box bass, even hand-made tin guitars . . . we came up with this
unique sound.[31]

Soweto soul was primarily an urban sound, as Sipho Mabuse discovered
when the Beaters went on tour:

[O]ne thing led to the other and we toured Botswana, Swaziland, Lesotho. But what was funny, when we went to these countries, people didn't
even know our music. I remember we had a show in Botswana and people were standing outside—because Mahlatini [Simon Nkabinde] and
Bra Sello were the most popular musicians of the day. And people would
not come into the hall when we performed. But fortunately, one of our
guys, Monty, knew the songs by Mahlatini and that was the only way we
could survive—I think we had about two people in the hall!—eventually
we played this song and you should have seen how people were just
flocking in. And *mbaqanga* was very, very big then. . . . Bra Sello—he's
an alto sax player—was king. . . . Only then did we realise that the appreciation of our type of music was localised—to Johannesburg, which
was an urban area. People in the urban areas could relate to it—they
were hearing it all the time.[32]

As Mabuse indicates, *mbaqanga* also flourished. A number of reed players
who had been pennywhistlers in the late 1950s and 1960s had matured, realising
that their audience was tiring of the formula and seeking a bigger sound palette.
And so sax jive developed: the old marabi three-chord formula, brayed out
loudly now over the drums, but still in that repetitive, looping form, with each
repeat shifting slightly from the last, depending on the improvising ability of the
soloist.

The dance of the day was the 'bump jive': fancy footwork and pairs of dancers bumping one another with hips or buttocks at the points where polyrhythm
demanded an extra beat. Everyone did it, including pantsulas, who ornamented
the chordal skeleton with ferociously complex competitive dancing: cap tipped
over eyes; wide trousers lifted to display the delicate athleticism—and name-
brand shoes and socks—of feet and ankles.

But the music to which bump jive was danced bridged a broad musical spectrum. Down at the pop end were players like Bra Sello, so loved when the Beaters
visited Botswana. Underpinned by organ chords and relentless, by-the-book,
drumming, Sello pumps out three-minute melodies that—if they are not
'Sponono', or 'Ntebetjane Fana Nem'Femi'—are so close as to be almost indis-
tinguishable from those classics. There is small improvisation, simply enough
ornament on the theme to keep it interesting, played in a warm, capable saxo-

phone voice, sometimes in company with other horns or reeds. Such music had a venerable history: anyone alive on the South African music scene from 1930 would recognise it. For dancing, its groove was, and remains, irresistible. It was a formula: limited, catchy, successfully marketable—and in the hands of an un-imaginative player or a philistine producer, it was enough to make a creative soloist weep.

Precisely because it was a marketable label, however, many players with highly creative imaginations found their work filed in the same convenient cate-gory, as was the case with *Plum and Cherry*. Guitarist Menyatso Mathole believes that this more commercial format let jazzmen express their 'African' ideas to a wider public:

> [The African element] became stronger because of the resistance of the youth in the '70s—we wanted to express ourselves musically, as artists in general. . . . The system [recording companies] also—they wanted to be seen within the struggle, so they let a few of us in the studios to . . . try and express ourselves at that time. . . . [T]his was also a money spinner for them—because the records were selling, our action towards the sys-tem created a market, and another chance for them to make money. Whereas before it was like, no, you can't play that—that won't sell, we can't market that. . . . Before, you'd just take your music and force it into [a foreign model] or take just the rhythm tracks from a certain track from overseas and put Zulu or Afrikaans lyrics and call it a local produc-tion. Because one has to live and maintain your instrument, you take the job [and] go home and feel depressed about it—but you've done it.[33]

The Sithole brothers, who had brought a hard-bop sensibility to marabi in the 1960s, were now working in a new band, the Drive, founded in 1971. Guitar-ist Cyril Magubane had been replaced by Barney Madlandona Luthuli, and a younger saxophonist, Ratau Mike Makhalemele, was filling out the horn sound. Bheki Mseleku, the young grandson of vaudevillian Wilfred Mseleku, sat at the piano. Their track 'Way Back Fifties' happily and explicitly acknowledges its roots in marabi and African jazz. The solos, however, pull in musical ideas from modern jazz and from Africa: the honking and wailing of rhythm 'n' blues, Col-trane's way of playing on the scales rather than the chords, and the vamping piano left hand of boogie-woogie. Polyphonic horns call-and-respond like an African choir. While fitting neatly into the formula, the tune also subverts it, and transcends it.

This climate also created an interest in jazz groups experimenting with more challenging sounds. Spirits Rejoice was formed in 1974 by drummer Gilbert Mat-thews and Duke Makasi, after Matthews' return from an uninspiring stretch on the hotel circuit in Swaziland. It was named after a composition of American free player Albert Ayler. Trumpeters George Tyefumani and Thabo Mashishi joined, as did Tony Schilder's bassist brother Phillip, guitarist Doc Mnthalane, and Bheki Mseleku—and, slightly later, Khaya Mahlangu and Sipho Gumede. According to Mahlungu,

> Spirits Rejoice was a great band—it had a lot of good musicians and composers, like Duke Makasi. He didn't write much, but he was the ears of the band. . . . He was very musical, in a very deep way . . . with Spirits we were mainly doing the American style. We used to do a lot of covers, but there was also a lot of material being composed by the band. But me and Sipho [Gumede] felt . . . we needed to change directions. Unfortunately, we couldn't do it within Spirits Rejoice. Once you have this concept everyone must be attuned to it . . . we wanted to do stuff like Spirits Rejoice—but in an African context . . . sitting back, I think we did achieve something. . . . But we felt that nothing much was being done to elevate the status of African music to a level that can be compared to any other music worldwide.[34]

No recordings of Spirits Rejoice survive, although a cover of Weather Report's 'Birdland' has been reissued under another band name, reflecting the personnel at a later date, when Capetonian Robbie Jansen had joined. Mahlangu describes the music as

> a bit of free jazz, a bit of jazz-rock—Blood Sweat and Tears, Weather Report—but then you had our original tunes as well as covers. It was consciously trying to do what was new in American jazz and copy that approach. We found it quite challenging, and audiences—the serious jazz fans—liked it. The problem wasn't the material, but Sipho [Gumede] and I were starting to think that it's not what you play that makes African music, but how you play. Getting it right the way the Americans did, it was not what it was about anymore.[35]

After several more personnel changes, Spirits Rejoice became the pit band for a white theatrical project: *Black Mikado*. They later worked on the *Sounds Black* stage show with Malombo, and although the band's name survived through the 1980s, and Makasi continued to inspire it, the concept weakened as many younger members, like Mseleku and guitarist Russell Herman, chose to leave the country.

All these new musical ideas—reaching out to a wider Africa and back to the rural areas for inspiration; taking risks with freeform music; reimagining marabi—had been developing since the late 1960s and early 1970s. What opened listeners' minds to them was the turning point of 1976 and the revolution on the streets led by students.

Black education was in crisis. While the Bantu education provisions reached far more learners than the mission schools had, it gave far less: no science, sports, art, or music facilities; poorly trained teachers; no free textbooks (though white schools provided these); primary school pupil–teacher ratios around 50:1 or worse. In the early 1970s, the government—which had hoped to undertake the main expansion of secondary education in the homelands, rather than the townships—had been forced by employers' demands for more skilled black workers to rapidly increase black secondary school provision in urban areas. Employers aimed to replace more costly white workers with blacks. For black teenagers, the educational change had a huge social impact, particularly in Soweto. According to Bonner and Segal,

> Previously, only a small minority of Soweto's youth had progressed beyond primary school, and the interval between leaving primary school and securing a job was often spent with youth gangs . . . [lacking] any clear political consciousness. . . . [Now] a broader and more politically conscious youth identity began to develop. This was perceived by the gangs as a profound challenge to their identity and in the early 1970s there were often savage conflicts. . . . Pupils . . . responded with mass resistance and retaliation and this further cemented a sense of pupil solidarity.[36]

The government feared that these united, better-educated young black people in schools and universities were a serious threat to the status quo. It also needed to appease its own Afrikaner conservatives, alarmed that the proposed introduction of television in 1976, with likely much imported programming, would weaken the Afrikaans language. So the education ministry decreed that Afrikaans would replace English as the medium of instruction in certain key subjects for black schools from the final year of primary school upwards. Many students—and teachers—knew only a few words of the language, and it would clearly cut off any possible access to international education at higher levels, and to the alternative international culture that township residents liked to consume.

Requests by school authorities and students' organisations alike for meetings with the authorities to discuss the Afrikaans issue were met instead by visits from the Special Branch and the arrest of 'agitators'. Students burned consignments of the new Afrikaans textbooks. New freedom songs began to gain currency: 'Senzenina' ('What have we done? Our only sin is to be black') and songs against informers and sellouts ('You are a black dog / On your master's leash'). An updated version of an old Eastern Cape stick-fighting song was heard, 'Lento Andiqondi uVorster': 'The thing I don't understand, Vorster / is fighting with an axe / What cowards!' The traditions of stick-fighting forbade introducing heavier weapons; Prime Minister B. J. Vorster disgraced himself by using guns against unarmed students. Reggae and the beliefs of Ras Tafari had arrived in the townships as another dimension of black nationalism. Songs by Jimmy Cliff and Bob Marley were among the first to be banned in the aftermath of the riots.

On 16 June 1976, 10,000 students from all over Soweto gathered in Orlando for what was planned as a peaceful march. Students would sing 'Nkosi Sikelele I'Afrika', hear some speeches, and disperse. The police ordered them to disperse immediately, and the students replied that they would do so only after the meeting had been completed. The police set dogs on them and fired tear gas. Then they fired live ammunition into the crowd, one of the first shots killing a thirteen-year-old boy, Hector Peterson. More schoolchildren fell.

In the rage following the unprovoked killings, students and their parents alike fought back with stones, bottles, and arson. News of the killings spread to other townships across the country, and so did the fighting. A particular target for township youth were the beerhalls, which the students saw as responsible for their fathers' passivity. The uprising did not stop; it was the start of the struggle that became an integral part of township life into the 1980s. There are still no precise casualty figures. The first official announcement put the death toll at seventeen, but one newspaper collated death figures from police, hospitals, funeral parlours, and families over the first two weeks and came up with a total for Soweto of more than 600 names. 'A later enquiry revealed that most of the deaths and injuries were caused by police bullets, often fired into the back of the victim'.[37]

The day before the uprising, 15 June 1976, Thami Mnyele and two other Soweto artists, Ben Arnold and Fikile Magadlela, had opened an exhibition of original works in the township, called 'A New Day':

[That] exhibition was the most interesting of my life. In my opinion, it was also the most important one because it happened at a crucial time, when we had to take a stand and say: were we involved in the struggle and life around us or were we merely producing 'pictures'? . . . We had people standing at the door and there were more than a thousand people crammed into the place and more waiting outside . . . at the end the students took over and there was almost a riot in the hall. We the artists were very excited because it meant we communicated, you know, something clicked.[38]

The struggle took place on a number of levels. As well as mass actions against police posts and beerhalls, with the assailants swiftly melting back into the community, there were recognisable guerrilla military engagements, such as the shoot-out between the police and MK fighters Solomon Mahlangu and Monde Motloung, which took place in Goch Street, in the middle of downtown Johannesburg, on 15 June 1977.

The uprising against Afrikaans had been a cultural action, and what followed in terms of both resistance and repression had powerful cultural dimensions. Musicians, painters, and poets were moving towards a new role of activism. Eastern Cape bandleader Tete Mbambisa released an album, *Tete's Big Sound*. One track, 'Unity', wordlessly calls on people to move forward together. Another, 'Black Heroes', is, in the words of its original liner notes,

> a musicians' song of lamentation, delivered by sad artists at the graveside, blowing a hymn. This is Tete's infectious dedication to all our great musicians who have left us. A sad piece, a funereal note with a distant drum chanting and calling on the Black Gods to bless their sons and daughters with soul. [Guitarist Doc] Mnthalene and Mbambisa lyrically give this piece their interpretations in between the theme verses—sad rhythm in times of anxiety, hope and faith.[39]

(Note the usual nod to the censors that this is simply a song about musicians—which it was, but, at that time and in that context, it was also about other dead sons and daughters.)

Saxophonist Khaya Mahlangu experienced the riots, and in the early 1980s his band, Sakhile, created the song 'Isililo (Soweto Blues)' to recapture the event and the emotions it inspired:

> In 'Isililo', we tried to capture what happened on that fateful Wednesday. I remember, on that very day I was rehearsing at the Pelican night-club in Orlando, and somebody just came in and said, 'Hey, there's trouble outside there, so will you stop playing music. . . .' I went home—I was still living with my parents then, and it was not far from the school where Hector Peterson was shot. So the township was burning—I remember seeing bodies lying down, I had to take a cousin of mine to Naledi; we got shot at, and at Crossroads in White City. It was terrible. I almost died there—me and my father and my cousin. . . . [It] was terrible, seeing burning cars, bodies lying in the streets. So that image never left my mind. [W]hen we got together finally with Sipho [Gumede], we were experimenting with a whole lot of things, and he wrote the song, and we shaped it up, in terms of arranging it. . . . [B]asically, we felt that these are things that have to be highlighted—we cannot sit back and say we are not part of this society that suffered that injustice. . . .[40]

The Pelican, too, was drawn into the response. According to Lucky Michaels:

> When the Pelican opened, it did not specifically open to become an ANC stronghold. It was not specifically structured to be a political meeting place. It was just a social venue for the black man in the street and an

outlet for musicians . . . [w]hich social venue in hindsight proved itself to be able to support the political wing. Immediately after social consciousness in the black community rose, with '76 having gone, there were many, many political meetings inside the Pelican during the week. It became a venue for them.[41]

The Soweto uprising spread as far as Tony Schilder in Cape Town:

The '70s was a very trying time, especially for the schools. [My son] Hylton was in Standard 8 at the time . . . and in sympathy with the Soweto schools, they all protested. And they were baton-charged, shot at. . . . In '76 during the riots people had these big Afros, and [the police] used to grab them by the Afros and pull them along and throw them in the van. Now, that was very heartbreaking for me. . . . I used to be beaten up by the cops because I took part in demonstrations. I demonstrated whenever there was a demonstration—and it was illegal. You were not allowed to do that. I was never banned, but I was thrown in the back of a police van, taken to a police station, thrown in a cell, and the next morning they'd let you go with a warning: don't you ever do that again. But, you know, you can't stop things like that—it was all part of the struggle. I mean, I paid taxes for thirty years, but I couldn't vote. It's unbelievable—if you can't vote for somebody, how can he take your taxes? . . . But you see, the thing is, I had to be very careful not to be under house arrest, because I had to make a living, and my late wife was a teacher, so if I was banned . . . she's not allowed to go out: the whole family's not allowed to go out. But then again, there were so many people doing these things. I mean, they'd pick up a guy because he'd sprayed water on the smoke canisters: tear gas. So he throws water on it. And for that he's arrested. But he threw water on it because his grandmother inside was suffering from asthma. . . .[42]

After 16 June, censorship tightened again, with the emphasis not so much on building synthetic tribalism as on eliminating anything that might possibly have a hidden subversive meaning. The basis had been provided by consolidating legislation, the Publications Act No. 42 of 1974, which added detail on publications to the very explicit provisions on performances of the 1963 Act. Records were considered publications under the act. The duty of the Publications Control Board, to uphold 'a Christian way of life', was underlined. Board members—nominated by the Minister of Home Affairs or the State President—were required to respond to all complaints; it took only one phone call to bring something before them. There were three main categories of control. The publication, production, import, or display of a specific publication could be completely banned. But a publication could also retrospectively be deemed 'undesirable for possession' even if it had been legal at the time its owner acquired it. The board could also ban all publications from a particular source, or all publications on a particular topic. In the decade between 1976 and 1986, 60 percent of all material considered by the board was banned. And penalties were harsh. In 1980, two members of the reggae band Splash were given five years in jail for covering the Steel Pulse song 'Tribute to the Martyrs', which mentions Nelson Mandela. In 1983, one Jacob Mashigo received the same sentence for possessing a homemade compilation cassette containing one track from the Miriam Makeba/Harry Belafonte duo album.[43]

The SABC had its own censorship procedures and boards, which were often tougher and even more arbitrary than the state. A middle-aged puritanism reinforced by the strictures of the official Dutch Reformed Church worked against local white rock bands trying to sound louche and defiant. All Stevie Wonder's music was banned after he dedicated his Grammy award to Nelson Mandela. Even naive would-be pop musicians, as Pops Mohamed was at the time, fell under suspicion. In 1975, he had made an album called *Black Disco*, modelled loosely on American dance tracks, and using the beat key labelled 'disco' on the synthesizer he had just acquired:

We had a hard time getting this music played on the radio stations, even on black radio stations. Black radio stations were controlled by white guys in those days, and if they found something that didn't quite fit into a category, they won't touch it. [T]hen they look at the titles as well, and if one title sounded politically inclined, they won't play it: we've got to ban this record or censor it completely, you know what I mean? So we had a hard time having our albums played on the radio stations. We called the radio station once and said we've given you three of our albums, why aren't you playing it? And the one guy said to me, it sounds like Chinese music! . . . It was hard to promote the music in clubs as well—we could play in shebeens and venues in the townships, but we needed to play to a bigger audience: we wanted the white people to listen to what we were doing. And then again it was hard to play in the white clubs; you had to have a special permit to perform. The owner of the club had to register; go to the nearest police station and say we're having these four guys coming to play. Even so, it was very risky—they could have lost their licence. Sometimes I used to play in white bands and not show my face to the audience. Play behind the curtain [w]hile some guy's faking my music on stage—all the girls would go for this guy, but he's just miming to *my* music! Damn! It was hard: we couldn't tell our friends or our parents because it wasn't cool: 'You are being oppressed by these people—how dare you still go and play in their clubs!'[44]

Mohamed's follow-up was to be called 'Black Discovery', a title the censor found far too political, so the song became 'Night Express'.

Many pop artists bowed to the censorship, or resorted to self-censorship. For those who did not, the SABC's artificial categories narrowed their potential sales as well as cramping their creativity. Blind *mbaqanga* singer Babsy Mlangeni was born in Orlando Township, and although his family language was IsiZulu, he composed and recorded fluently in several South African languages, including English, with his group, the All-Rounders. He liked his stage shows to reflect variety, too. Jazzmen Dennis Mpale and Winston Mankunku both toured with him in the 1970s, and Mankunku remembers 'that was fun. I did the arrangements and [Mlangeni] encouraged us to write all kinds of stuff in.'[45] Mlangeni's recording sessions reflected the same variety. But his music was released on separate, segregated compilations keyed to the SABC slots: *Babsy Mlangeni Sings Sotho Vocal* and *Babsy Mlangeni Sings Zulu Jive*. Another artist who suffered in this way was singer/guitarist Ray Phiri:

> If I am not mistaken, . . . in 1972 I was five years into my recording career. A song called 'Highland Drifter' was banned and then the record company said: 'We told you to stop writing in English. You've got to do more Zulu' . . . so they were censoring me not to write in a much larger medium whereby I would be able to reach the four communities . . . Indian, coloured, black and white.[46]

Record companies' power to manipulate releases in this way was increased in 1978, when the two industry giants, Gallo and EMI, joined together to launch the low-budget label Music for Pleasure. In 1979, the impossibility of maintaining strict divisions even at the SABC was demonstrated by the song 'Paradise Road'. Sung by Joy, a group developed over three years at the Pelican, comprising Anneline Malebu, Faith Kekana, and Thoko Ndlozi, the track garnered prizes in every category of the SABC annual music awards: best album, best produced single, best producer and best songwriter. Joy were the first musicians of colour to break that particular barrier. The song is a soaring, gospel-styled message '[talking] to people, giving them hope that one day they will be walking through "Paradise Road"', recalls Ndlozi.[47] The song promises: 'Better days before us / And a burning bridge behind us . . . Paradise is almost closing down'.[48]

Kippie Moeketsi remained a teacher and guide. He worked with Sipho Mabuse on some Beaters recordings, and drew Mabuse and bassist Alec Khaoli into other projects from *Our Boys Are Doing It* onwards. Mabuse says the Beaters were amazed—but immensely encouraged—by Moeketsi's interest. That came, Mabuse believes, because they were already casting around for African inspirations:

> A lot of people, even in America, could not relate to how Charlie Parker played. Charlie Parker was seen to be way ahead—I mean, when people talk of jazz, for instance, they will always refer to swing, because it's easy-

listening music. But with Charlie Parker, he went beyond that, and that's exactly what Bra Kippie used to do. How he could play the things he was playing, at that time was just difficult to comprehend. . . . The Beaters was one of those bands that even today people still talk about. The music we did . . . we recorded an album called *Rufaro*. . . . Already, we were exploring Basotho music, we were exploring what people are talking of today, Princess Magogo's [Zulu] music: all that music. And we invited Bra Kippie to come and play. . . . Just after we recorded this album, Abdullah Ibrahim had just won a *Downbeat* Poll award. He came into South Africa—that was the last time that he came. He walked into the studio—he heard this music, he just couldn't believe that at that age we were suddenly playing this music and Bra Kippie was doing things that were just incredible. And Kippie went to Abdullah and said '*Ja, my laaitie—jy's klaar groot nou*'. ('Yes, son, you're all grown up now'.) But we couldn't understand how Bra Kippie could relate to Abdullah as a *laaitie* [kid], you know . . . Because Abdullah had just won that award and there was Bra Kippie with us in the recording studios. . . . But then we didn't even understand him. Little did we know that the emotion that came from his saxophone was saying: I am here, I am alive. Listen to me, because when I'm gone, you'll still be talking'.[49]

The regime, meanwhile, was shaping its 'total strategy': concessions to those elements in black society they believed could be bought off, combined with a strengthening of the police and the army and the closing up of any legislative loopholes in repression. Many of the bribes came in the form of positions in the homeland administrations, as these fake states attained full—but empty—'independence': Transkei in 1976 and Bophuthatswana (a collection of separate tiny, geographical fragments, each situated over a platinum mine) in 1977. Steve Biko was beaten to death in police custody in the same year. SASO, *The World* newspaper, and many other smaller organisations and publications were banned.

The murder of Biko and the authorities' role in the cover-up that followed received wide international publicity and clearly exposed the nature of the South African state. The pressure on overseas artists and sportsmen with any conscience not to visit the country grew. But the lure of high pay still attracted some, especially those whose careers in their home countries were waning. Most made no secret of their reasons for visiting:

[Percy Sledge,] although black, was totally unconcerned about coming here: 'I'm here to make money and let my fans see me, nothing more' he said. . . . [In 1979,] Wilson Pickett was another major drawcard. . . . [T]he Colosseum's manager, Brian Thomas, eventually elicited the information that Wilson was very unhappy with the new Datsun provided for him, as he really wanted a white Mercedes Benz. . . . [T]he next morning, courtesy of Cargo Motors, a gleaming white Mercedes was presented to the star.[50]

Black visiting stars, playing to segregated black audiences, had black South African support acts, such as Thandi Klaasen and her band:

I did shows with Brook Benton and Percy Sledge. . . . I had a good band, and we were saying to ourselves: the Americans are not going to beat us. What have they got that we don't have? . . . [T]hey must respect our talent. And I'm telling you, when I stood on that stage at the [Eyethu Cinema,] whoo! You should have heard that band! I told myself: Brook Benton's gonna hear from me tonight. And the cinema was packed. . . . When I bowed, I had to repeat my last song twice, because we didn't have a fourth song. So Brook Benton says: 'I'd like to talk to that lady who sings—what's her name?' No, man! It's Thandi! 'So call Tandy: I wanna see her'. But in the end he came to my dressing room. I wouldn't go to his. He may be Brook Benton, but I am also Thandi Klaasen! But now when we had the meeting, he cut one song from my show. I must sing only two songs—but even with those two songs, I showed them, I'm telling you![51]

However, not all visiting artists shared this attitude. For some, like Victor Ntoni, overseas visitors provided help and support:

Actually, it was a stroke of pure luck. . . . I had just come back in 1974 from doing the musical production *Meropa*, where we had just done a Royal Command performance, and then I met Maurice Jarre, he's a Frenchman. He recommended the *Meropa* cast for a piece of music that was badly recorded on location in South Africa; they were doing [the movie] *Shout at the Devil*, with Lee Marvin and all those kinds of actors, and then he wanted a real South African sound and invited us. . . . [H]e came backstage and offered me a gig to come and help him out with two or three tracks of the original music from the movie. . . . So we did it, and he was very impressed with that and he came to watch the show, and he said, 'Man, where did you study music?' and I said, 'No, I've never studied music.' And he says, 'I've got a friend by the name of Robert Scher', and I said, 'What's he got to do with me?' He says, 'No, he's an administrator at Berklee School of Music', and that's how it all got off the ground. As I came back, coincidentally, [Dave] Brubeck was coming into South Africa for the first time with his sons Darius Brubeck and Chris and Danny—this is 1976. And with the uprising and everything, we had the social apartheid thing, and Dave had a black American bass player by the name of Eugene Wright. . . . So the South African government wouldn't let Eugene come into the country because he was black and Dave insisted on having at least a local black bass player, and that's how I got [the] gig, which coincided with my arrival from my first twelve weeks of summer courses at Berklee and on composition and arranging. Dave Brubeck happened to be one of the board of trustee members of Berklee School of Music who said also, 'Man, I think you should go back and study some more, and I'll try find a way for you'; and he really tried and . . . I went back to Berklee in 1978 to pick up my studies again.[52]

Others chose not to visit South Africa at all, but to offer help from just across the border. Once more, independent Africa was playing a role. The U.S. State Department facilitated a visit by the Rutgers College music faculty to Maseru, in the tiny independent kingdom of Lesotho, in 1977. Frank Foster, Dizzy Gillespie, and bassist Larry Ridley held a series of workshops, which South African jazzmen, including trumpeter Johnny Mekoa, attended. Before that, Mekoa's band, the Jazz Ministers, led by Victor Ndlazilwane, had become the first black combo to be invited direct from South Africa to the Newport Jazz Festival, as prizewinners in a festival competition.

Both the liberation movement and the government had Africa strategies. Apartheid was trying to build alliances (as it had with Kamuzu Banda's Malawi), support conservative coups (as it did in Swaziland, assisting the autocratic King Sobhuza to thwart parliamentary democracy in 1973), or launch invasions (as it had unsuccessfully done to shore up Angola in 1976). The liberation movement now had refugee camps in sympathetic states like Botswana and Tanzania, military training bases in Angola, and diplomatic representation across the continent. After June 1976, the number of young South Africans clandestinely leaving the country to join the ANC or the PAC rose dramatically. MK established a 'June 16 Brigade'. The liberation movement continued to cooperate with the pro-independence forces in Rhodesia who, by 1979, had pushed the colonial regime into multiracial elections, leading to the Lancaster House negotiations and Zimbabwe independence in April 1980.

But many musicians were now choosing to stay in South Africa and wage their cultural battles there. Their reasons ranged from simple homesickness to an understanding that freedom is not a geographical location.

Abigail Khubeka:

I suppose I could have made it abroad, but don't forget I was young. I mean, I was seventeen. . . . I couldn't stay behind—I missed my mum, I missed my cat, I missed just everything.

Pat Matshikiza:

At the end of the '60s we won first prize at a festival, sponsored, I think, by Lion Matches and some newspaper. Anyway, I was not too keen on the conditions of the prize. A fax came to Dorkay House from Hugh Masekela that we should come over to the States. And I said I would go if the others would, but [guitarist] Allen Kwela said: 'I ain't going because I want to play jazz, not mbaqanga. I know they're calling us to play mbaqanga. That's America. Jazz has got its own clubs there. I want to go and play modern jazz: I can't be playing those other tunes'. So I went home again to PE [Port Elizabeth].

Tony Schilder:

I got opportunities to go overseas, but I wouldn't take it because, first of all, it was difficult for me to get a visa, and if they do give you a visa, it's got to be an exit visa. You couldn't come back again. I love this country. Why must I leave it and go away?

Sophie Mngcina:

Funnily enough, when we arrived in England, we also all thought we were free. We were free from the South African apartheid. But when we got there, I discovered that I wasn't free, I was very uncomfortable, because I could not think in Xhosa or Zulu; we were speaking English all the time, and on the trains was written: Keep Britain White. I was very, very uncomfortable . . . when the contract ended I came back to South Africa. Back to curfews, back to separate development—but it was home. I had to come back; I had a little girl that I'd left, and a mother, who was working as a domestic servant. I needed to go home.[53]

Harsh and violent as the struggle was, new spaces were opening up within the country for performers. Out of a church initiative of the late 1960s, the Study Project on Christianity in Apartheid Society, which undertook community printing tasks on the side, developed the SACHED independent education project and then independent publishing house Ravan Press. From 1978, Ravan published the arts magazine *Staffrider*, publishing poetry, graphics and photography, essays, and interviews. It appeared intermittently because of the pressures of both funding and censorship, but from its pages, with their contributions from community groups across the country, emerges a picture of a rich new independent network of art, literature, and music. Rural 'homelands' are represented as well as urban arts groups; white writers' work appears alongside contributions from black writers—in English, Zulu, the Afrikaans of the Cape's coloured community, and other languages. In pictures and in words, Africa is as important a theme as apartheid.

A dramatic illustration of the breadth of new creative ideas Africa could offer was the pan-African arts festival, FESTAC, held in Nigeria in 1977. Very few home-based South Africans were able to attend; those who did reconnected with South Africans now exiled, such as Jazz Afrika, the band run by Malombo graduates Julian Bahula and Lucky Ranku in London. But the news of the festival came home and made a major intellectual impact, as poet Maishe Maponya remembers:

We were influenced by various other writers and other people involved in the world of the arts; music influenced us a lot. . . . [T]he artists that we actually looked at in terms of jazz music and even other forms of music were black. I can cite for myself musicians like John Coltrane . . . that, for us created a base for us to begin to have something to hold onto. I didn't go to FESTAC, but a lot of people did; it was the biggest festival on the continent, that brought all Africans, all black people together, and it had an objective of actually raising the consciousness of African people. It was in '77 . . . we had just come out of '76, the uprisings, and also the influence of black consciousness in America was very, very strong. . . . Most of the countries were beginning to get independence . . . Mozambique, Angola. . . . FESTAC became the convergence of all those minds saying we would want to do it for ourselves . . . the biggest kind of get-together of black creative minds that would revolutionise our involvement in the arts—and politics also.[54]

Following FESTAC, the ANC in Angola founded a theatre and music group, Amandla, with the assistance of exiled trombonist Jonas Gwangwa. He says that from the accounts of that festival he began to see how South African indigenous music culture—urban and rural—could be presented to world audiences.

Within South Africa, a number of players were experimenting with elements from jazz, reggae, and African tradition. Uhuru was formed in Lesotho but played successfully in South Africa until the state apparently took offence at the lyrics for 'Afrika Shall Unite' (or perhaps their name: Swahili for 'freedom') and deported them in 1978. Reborn as Sankomota (a legendary Lesotho freedom-fighter) some years later, they immortalised the incident in a song, 'Madhouse'. But the group that particularly symbolised the search for an African sound and image was the Durban-based Malopoets. Initially they were a loose collective of student poets and performers, including Eugene Skeef:

Afrika
You are the horizon
To which I turn
To see the sun rise
. . .
You are the river

**The Malopoets.** *Credit: Malopoets publicity release*

That flows with vigour
Carrying the taunting tale
Our forefathers died to tell
Afrika
You are my peace with life.[55]

The group was formed on 17 July 1978, the anniversary of the death of John
Coltrane. 'Coltrane is the godfather of the group. We get much of our inspiration
from his records, although he played jazz and our sound is closer to African
traditional music',[56] said Pat Sefolosha, the group's leader by 1980. Malopoets'
five- or six-piece lineup included drums and percussion, saxophones, and gui-

tars, flutes, and marimba. Three members, including Sefolosha, had previously worked with another Malombo offshoot, flautist Abbey Cindi's Afrika. Playing occasional festivals and student shows, the group had nevertheless become widely enough known in two years to secure a run in Johannesburg and make a first abortive attempt at recording. Gallo gave them no explanation of why their first recording disappeared without trace, though the group suspected that both politics and their traditional, but not classifiably tribal, sounds were the cause.

Pat Sefolosha:

In South Africa you can never do as you want to. We will have to make our arrangements more commercial, otherwise [the record companies] won't take it. If you want music to be on record, it can never be as you desire it to be. Many groups end up playing the producer's music, not their own . . . artists should come together—if we could form a big musicians' union that could accommodate all musicians. . . .[57]

By 1981, however, the Malopoets had released *Sound of the People*. The nine original songs are in IsiZulu, with breaks for shouts and whooping ululation where, in live performance, the performers would have danced or staged extended percussion duels. Guitarists pull popcorn riffs out of Central Africa and sawing chords from traditional *maskandi* music. On the title track, however, the style is big-city: a loud, insistent saxophone riff, *mbaqanga* piano, rock guitar, and a chorus that says it all: 'This is the sound of the people / This is Africa'.

It was less risky than it had been a few years earlier for Sefolosha to talk to *Staffrider* in 1980 about musicians' unions. In 1979, the Wiehann Commission recommended that job reservation be abolished, and that the de facto existence of black trade unions—which had functioned clandestinely as 'worker assistance groups' for at least six years—be recognized. These measures would help ease the continuing crippling shortage of skilled labour, as well as meeting some of the demands and aspirations of the workforce. As black trade unions were established, a new genre entered the South African choral canon. *Mzabalazo* (workers' songs) performed by trade union and factory choirs would be a prominent feature of struggle activities in the next decade.

White South Africa needed concessions, too, particularly the English-speakers not wholly convinced by Afrikaner isolationism. English speakers tended towards political liberalism, and they had not been seduced by the new television service with its combination of government propaganda, Afrikaans drama, and imported—and censored—crime series and soaps. One demand of the English-speaking establishment had been the desegregation of theatres and cinemas. The 1970s had seen a number of moves towards this, often followed by swift retreats. In a particularly absurd ruling, mixed-race usherettes were allowed in white cinemas—so long as they did not watch the film. This led one newspaper cartoonist to portray a blindfolded usherette asking, 'May I feel your tickets, please?'

In March 1978, all theatres operated by registered members of the official theatre management association (many of which were also used as music venues) were opened to mixed audiences. Mixed theatrical companies were permitted the following year. This was not quite as liberal as it sounded. Community halls were not part of the structure. Moreover, the censors could still place restrictions on how a performance could be presented. Many new, experimental, or politically challenging plays were licensed for small art theatres only, and there were none of those in the townships.

The ruling was, however, good news for the Market Theatre, established in 1976, which pioneered new drama, workshopped productions, and the work of new black writers reflecting contemporary debates. For its final workshopped production of the decade, the Market company created *Cincinatti* [*sic*]—*Scenes from City Life*: a tribute to the jazz clubs of the 1970s.

Yet although many of those clubs had been closed down, the Pelican survived. And across the country, the next generation of jazz musicians was growing to maturity. In Port Elizabeth in the Eastern Cape, a reed player named Zim Ngqawana and a drummer, Lulu Gontsana, were being initiated into the mysteries of their craft:

Zim Ngqawana:

In PE you had to deal with politics—so much of that black consciousness thing, Steve Biko. They were loyal to it. It was actually what we call a black experience or African experience—all African people: the diaspora. . . . It was just coming out of the '76 uprising, so my blood was still warm. And there were people who had gone through worse things; all this, they talk about to you, what they had experienced. So it was just there for us to absorb. The music articulated this. You know, if you are playing without consciousness, you can hear it from your sound. One note, and you can say: he has no roots. . . . They had a very significant way of teaching young people history—they would give you a nickname. If you played alto and your sound is from this school, then you are 'Ornette Coleman' or 'Cannonball'. [Adderley]. What that means is you have to literally go out and check who these people are. They've already put you in school. When I first met the oldsters, they said, 'Who's that kid who sounds like Ornette?' I didn't know who Ornette was. So I said, let me go out and find out who he is and listen to him. It took me two years to understand what Ornette was doing. This was in the late '70s. . . . They'll provide the conducive environment for you to do all that and play all kinds of styles for you to be exposed to.[58]

Lulu Gontsana:

Where I grew up was a very rich scene. There was a club, Monde's Place. The main cats were Peter Jackson and his brother, Duke Makasi, Bra'

Dennis Mpale, Early Mabuza, Chris McGregor—the only mlungu [white person] around and speaking fluent Xhosa. He was a very unique cat. Everybody was at Monde's Place; it was like a university. . . . We learned not just about music, but about people, culture, politics. Those old bandleaders insisted we must listen to everything, practice, and develop hip chops. . . . [There was a lot of drinking, but] those guys had reasons for how they behaved. The system stopped them expressing themselves freely. It was a very ugly world they were trying to make beautiful music in. Every single one of them said to us young cats: 'Don't be like us; don't drink'.[59]

Ngqawana was to become one of the most influential jazz players of the 1990s and beyond. Another—though he died tragically young—was pianist Moses Molelekwa. His father, Monk, had been one of the Sophiatown jazz generation, and Molelekwa grew up in Alexandra surrounded by records and intense discussions of music and culture:

Once I got into it, once I started listening more closely and understanding it and feeling it more, I realised that it was a very powerful music created by black people. . . . [D]uring that period of segregation, of all the injustices that came with that period, one needed to look at black people's achievements in general to be inspired. And so the music itself, and the fact that it was created by black people living in America, and also hearing a relationship between the traditional music that I would hear in my township and the jazz I was hearing at home, you know, I could hear a connection there—I could hear a connection in every music that was created by native people. My impressions of jazz basically was that—a music that really touched my soul and was created by black people and inspired me to want to achieve. [There was music about which] I had no choice: I had to listen to records which came with my father. But I'd say the most influential artist/pianist in my life is Herbie Hancock. . . . I started following him then—even when he formed his own band, and the changes that he went through musically as well from just being a traditional jazz musician to . . . coming into the electronic kind of music, I really respected that. That offended a lot of jazz appreciators—I mean, the traditional ones. So I guess he's the most influential, because I know as an artist also how free I'd like to be, and he's the one of the people who also broke barriers, so that jazz can go beyond this . . . it's a constantly evolving art form.[60]

## Notes

1. Quoted in interview with Sophie Mngcina-Davids for *Ubuyile*, 2000.
2. Interview for *Ubuyile*, 2000.

3. Interview with Judy Seidman, 2001.

4. Thami Mnyele, unpublished autobiographical notes prepared in Gaborone, Botswana, 1982.

5. Interview for *Ubuyile*, 2000.

6. In Z. B. Molefe and M. Mzileni, *A Common Hunger to Sing* (Cape Town: Kwela Books, 1997), n.p.

7. Interview for *Ubuyile*, 2000.

8. Ibid.

9. M. Mathole, sleeve notes for *Menyatso Mathole Trio*, self-published album (Johannesburg, 1998).

10. Interview for *Ubuyile*, 2000.

11. Ibid.

12. Ibid.

13. All quotes from interviews for *Ubuyile*, 2000. The Hillbrow to which Duze refers was, in the '70s, a bohemian city apartment area, occupied by whites, among whom were artists and writers, many of them with nonconformist if not outright antiapartheid views. Bar owners there were often supported by their clientele if they broke the segregation rules, but police tolerance was fickle (and often dependent on bribes), and such work was unreliable.

14. Interviews 29 March 2003 and 18 June 2003.

15. Interview for *Ubuyile*, 2000.

16. Gauteng Tourism Web site: Mining.

17. L. Rasmussen, *Abdullah Ibrahim: A discography*, 2nd ed. (Copenhagen: The Booktrader, 2001).

18. Interview for *Ubuyile*, 2000.

19. *Two-tone*, 1, no. 9, p. 5.

20. Conversation with the author, 1997. The national football team nickname, Bafana-Bafana, translates as 'the boys, the boys'.

21. Interview for *Ubuyile*, 2000.

22. M. Jaggi, 'The Sound of Freedom', *Guardian*; available at www.guardian.co.uk/print/0.3858.4315342-13418.00html.

23. Interview for *Ubuyile*.

24. Quoted in Jaggi, op. cit.

25. Interview for *Ubuyile*, 2000.

26. Ibid.

27. Ibid.

28. Y. Huskisson, *The Bantu Composers of Southern Africa* (Johannesburg: South African Broadcasting Corporation, 1969), xi.

29. All from interviews for *Ubuyile*, 2000 except Dennis Mpale, from conversation with the author, 1997.

30. Interview for *Ubuyile*, 2000. As Mahlangu demonstrates, the historic Ohlange Institute was sustaining its support for black music.

31. Ibid.

32. Ibid.

33. Ibid.

34. Ibid.

35. Interview with the author for *Star Tonight*.

36. P. Bonner and L. Segal, *Soweto: A History* (Cape Town: Maskew Miller Longman, 1978), 79.

37. Ibid., 89.

38. Thami Mnyele, in *Staffrider*, September/October 1980, p. 42.

39. Vusi Khumalo, jazz critic for *The World* newspaper, original liner notes reprinted for the 1999 CD reissue (As-Shams/EMI CDSRKS (WL) 12).

40. Interview for *Ubuyile*, 2000.

41. Ibid.

42. Ibid.

43. I. Kerkof, 'Music and Censorship in South Africa', in Rixaka, 2 (1986), Lusaka, African National Congress Department of Arts and Culture, pp. 27–31 passim.

44. Interview for *Ubuyile*.

45. Interview with the author, March 2003.

46. First World Conference on Music and Censorship.

47. Quoted in Molefe and Mzileni, op. cit., n.p.

48. A very young Brenda Fassie, later to become the biggest South African pop star of the three following decades before her death in 2004, regularly deputised as a member of Joy.

49. Interview for *Ubuyile*, 2000.

50. P. Tucker, *Just the Ticket* (Johannesburg: Jonathan Ball, 1997), 271, 371.

51. Interview for *Ubuyile*, 2000.

52. Ibid.

53. Ibid.

54. Ibid.

55. *Staffrider*, March 1979, p. 44.

56. *Staffrider*, September/October 1980, p. 38.

57. Ibid., 39.

58. Interview for *Ubuyile*, 2000.

59. Interview with the author for *Good Weekend*, 1999.

60. Interview for *Ubuyile*, 2000.

*Chapter Six*

# Jazz for the Struggle, and the Struggle for Jazz

> . . . music from the townships / a man expresses / through a horn / songs of people / who have suffered / far too long / music painfully expelled / at a burial / and joyfully noted / in children's laughter / . . . / a man's horn / whose music is / from poisoned wells.
>
> —J. Matthews, 'Poem for Basil Coetzee'[1]

The pictures have changed. Gangsters no longer wear sharp white suits and fedoras. Their faces are hidden by balaclavas and kerchiefs, and their hands hold traditional sticks or police-issue R4 rifles. They no longer cruise the domestic clutter of the streets of Sophiatown, but scurry down the back alleys between tiny township houses and shacks, hurling petrol bombs or firing into bedroom windows. The smoke-blackened tatters of burned-out buildings look on, as soldiers from armoured cars helter-skelter into homes and out again, clubbing those they have grabbed into submission before they exit between rolls of razor wire. Teenagers *toyi-toyi* down the same streets, armed and simmering in their search for retaliatory justice. Everything smells of tear gas. And the nightclub stage has become a wooden platform, the audience of a few hundred grown to a crowd of tens of thousands, the jazz players silhouetted before a banner calling for justice and change.

It was described as mere 'unrest' by the heavily censored mainstream media. But by 1980, a campaign of resistance to every aspect of apartheid was being waged throughout South Africa. Its forms ranged from dramatic hit-and-run attacks on state installations by the guerrillas of Umkhonto we Sizwe, through mass strikes, demonstrations, and boycotts, to simple, individual refusals to conform. Slogans on walls and T-shirts now openly called for action and change.

Some of the thousands of young people who had left the country after 1976 began returning secretly as trained organisers and soldiers. 'The first time I saw people called "cadres" . . . I was expecting to see a clumsy person from the bush who is hungry, but I met gentlemen who were on duty', said Pheteni Khumalo, a Soweto resident.[2] In the first few years of the decade, quasi-legal reform and solidarity groups gelled into what was explicitly a mass movement to make apartheid ungovernable, broadly aligned with the fighters and with the ANC. The state responded with increased viciousness, establishing the military occupation of many townships from 1984 and using those troops as well as *askaris* (turncoats), mercenary thugs, and disguised soldiers ('the Third Force') in a war of destabilisation against not only the activists but the entire fabric of black communities.

In such a climate of 'total strategy', culture moved to centre stage, nationally and internationally. For musicians, the period was characterised not by any single stylistic development (though development was happening) but by an intense focus on communication—how best to reflect what was going on or influence the debates—that blurred the lines between jazz, pop, and the songs of strike and struggle. For the state, the banning of music escalated into physical attacks on musicians and cultural structures and further clumsy attempts to create a reactionary mass counterculture.

Internationally, this was the period when the cultural boycott by the United Nations against apartheid consolidated and could be enforced most effectively. For twenty years, since the British Musicians' Union ban in 1961, the campaign had gathered worldwide momentum, and in 1981 the world's largest performers' body, Associated Actors and Artists of America—an umbrella organisation of all major performers' unions in the United States, with close to 250,000 members—unanimously voted that its members should not perform in South Africa. The focus of the boycott was also broadening. The early bans and boycotts had been against performing before segregated audiences. Now, they were about ending apartheid. In cities in Europe and America, artists' organisations large and small took part in demonstrations like that of the Toronto chapter of the Black Music Association, who mobilised over three hundred members to chant 'Apartheid is wrong, wrong, wrong!' outside the South African consulate in 1986. At the same time, managements overseas were becoming increasingly reluctant to book South African performers, after the *Ipi Tombi* debacle of 1978, when demonstrations in New York had forced the closure of a white-authored South African musical portraying happy, highly rhythmical tribal life. Given the penchant of the state for covert funding, it was hard for managements to know which shows were propaganda creations. There was clearly a need for credible bodies in or closely linked to South Africa that could provide accurate information on the credentials of shows and artists.

Some South Africans saw the restriction of overseas work opportunities that the cultural boycott represented as unfair. Yet this viewpoint—vociferously raised by opponents of the boycott at the time—does not fully or fairly reflect what most of the musicians interviewed for the *Ubuyile* project say they felt. Rather, most of them expressed the view that the boycott had been key—and largely positive—in influencing musical development within South Africa during the 1980s and early 1990s, and, in particular, in creating a national popular sound. What follows is a sample of those views.

Dennis Mpale:

You see, we didn't get the gigs anyway, unless it was something the *boere* wanted to promote overseas, like *Ipi Tombi*. Or we did get the invitations, but if they didn't like you or the project, they wouldn't give you a passport. Or only an exit visa: one-way. So I never saw what the noise was these liberals were making about the boycott cutting opportunities for us. I never heard them before—where were they when Dan Poho didn't get his passport for *King Kong*?[3]

Victor Ntoni:

[Pop singer ]Brenda [Fassie] was the thing—*Weekend Special*—Ray Phiri was coming up with [the band] Stimela . . . Sipho Mabuse had just done *Burnout* and people were really focusing on popular local music, which was great. Because you know at that time the cultural boycott was there and local artists couldn't have access to a lot of things until the ANC started putting up this barrier. We were having big dollops of, like, Kool and the Gang—you know 'Celebrate good times, come on!' We predictably knew every December we were going to have Kool and the Gang at our local artists' expense. So the ANC helped a lot in the sense of putting down that cultural boycott and of course local artists started having [work and] the means of buying cars and homes; living like decent people.

Sipho Mabuse:

The cultural boycott in South Africa was two-pronged in that it obviously enabled South African music to grow within its own means, but at the same time it also deprived us of growth outside—the appreciation of the international community. . . . We were able to create an industry that was vibrant, that was explosive. Suddenly, there were all sorts of musicians coming up: bands like Stimela, Brenda Fassie, Yvonne Chaka-Chaka, Chicco, the Sakhiles, the Bayetes, and there was so much happening.

Khaya Mahlangu:

It was OK and not OK. Not OK, in terms of not being able to travel extensively, because I felt if there was any cultural boycott, why should it be against the people who are the victims of apartheid? And it left a bitter taste. But on the positive side we were able to get more into ourselves. People were able to appreciate that, hey, we have music here—music that we can call South African and be proud of. . . . I felt people got a chance to get into themselves, to understand and know who and what we are.

Ray Phiri:

It helped us hone our creativity . . . helped us focus more on local content.

Sibongile Khumalo:

Culture is a weapon. It is. It was used. We had the cultural boycott and all those things . . . and it made us look inside, at what we have here, and develop it to a higher level.

Cecile Pracher, SABC librarian, 1980–1990:

The cultural boycott was obviously very successful; it was part of other boycotts against South Africans and the ruling government. [If] it [were] not for the outcry worldwide—and part of that being the cultural boycott—it might have taken longer to free [Nelson] Mandela and for him to become president. . . . I am sorry, though, for all the artists who because of that could not fulfill what they wanted to do out there.

Paul Hanmer:

[It didn't affect me because] I had never thought to want to go overseas. I never felt a lack of things from overseas, or a lack of communication, because my whole rediscovery was about who I am, in this country. And what I saw was that, particularly coming to Johannesburg in the 1980s I met people from all over SA and found that a lot of them wanted to do what I wanted to do, which was to play music that's at home and put their heart and soul, belief and strength behind that music. It was wonderful to come into such a community. . . . For the first time, in the late '80s, I had to really look at what I was writing and where it comes from. . . . In terms of isolation, I only felt isolated in terms of my own country. . . . I'm from Cape Town; from a certain neighbourhood. There are things

about that neighbourhood that are very frightening, but there are also
things that are very precious. . . . Out of my community comes music
from the Coon carnivals, from the mosque, from the church, from guys
selling *snoek* [fish] and vegetables. It took me thirty years to want to
realise that this is my community and that part of my sound comes from
it, too. So that's the kind of isolation I'm talking about. I'm also talking
about within the musical brotherhood/sisterhood, there are people [who]
have looked at me and said: you are a bit paler than us, you wear glasses
and you can read music—it means you can't play. . . . [N]ot only did
apartheid succeed in dividing people in terms of socio-economic class
and colour . . . they divided our hearts from our minds, they divided our
work from our play, they divided us from our truths. They divided our
eyes from what we see before us. So those are the kinds of barriers I'm
talking about.[4]

Hanmer was not the only performer rediscovering his roots. The commodified sounds promoted by the record companies and the SABC had never been
the whole story of traditional music, and black consciousness and nationalist
politics had given fresh impetus to the search for authenticity across the country.
By the early 1980s, real performance opportunities for the groups that developed—such as solidarity events for newly legalised unions and other groups—
were opening up.

In the international music market, something called world music was growing
as a marketing category. South African record companies, hamstrung by feeding
the SABC's narrow categories, had not yet grasped its potential, but many of the
ensembles that developed embraced a hybrid musical character with a distinct
pop sensibility. Their reasons, however, were not wholly commercial. They
wanted to reach out, past the backward-looking introspection of apartheid cultural policies, and they sought to rediscover the vibrancy of a living, growing
South African tradition freed from the definitions of Afrikaner ideologues.
Amampondo was a marimba band formed in Cape Town's Langa Township in
1979 with church support. Through Andrew Tracey (the son of ethnomusicologist Hugh Tracey), they augmented their donated instruments with *kudu* horns
and *akadinda* and Chopi xylophones and began creating a complex, layered, fast-
tempo polyrhythmic style, in equal parts pan-African and Xhosa. Their first
high-profile performance was a solidarity concert for striking Cape Town meat
workers in 1980.

Another Cape Town group, the Genuines, formed in 1986 combining jazz
musicians like Tony Schilder's pianist son Hylton (equally interested in jazz and
his Khoisan heritage) and *goema* players like veteran guitarist Mac McKenzie,
rooted in Malay and carnival music. Their first album was called, simply, *Goema*,

after the beat of Cape Carnival music. With his own early background in rock, Ian Herman was their drummer:

> We were talking about and expressing what was going on around us. We were breaking free from our chains, and we were filled with anger. We wanted to turn a negative situation into a positive situation; sometimes we could do it with love, sometimes with hate. The thing that people couldn't take was the ugly side. A lot of the band's energy and what we had to say was ugly, because we were living in ugly times. . . . Other times we would look at the situation and try to show a beautiful, a more sensitive side of how we were feeling. We had those kinds of gigs, too. We even had some ballads, we were influenced by Kippie Moeketsi and Abdullah Ibrahim and that was in our music—that was the soul of our music. At the same time, there was all that anger shouting out. We played electric instruments, and you know Mac used to blow our amplifier every time we played. He was playing with so much feeling he would go overboard. That was the Genuines![5]

In Johannesburg, Sakhile (We Have Built) was formed in 1981, from graduates of the Beaters, Harari, and Spirits Rejoice, and including a dazzling percussion virtuoso, Mabi Thobejane, who had previously provided the cross-rhythms for Malombo. According to Khaya Mahlangu:

> [The Beaters' had been] a beautiful learning experience in terms of what can be done with African music to contemporise it. . . . In Sakhile we used some American harmonies, but I remember we also used to haggle about it—'Hey, but the major 7th doesn't sound African', you know? And we said, no, we can break it, arpeggiate it—you know, hide it instead of just playing it, and I guess we used harmony and some of the rhythms [from American jazz,] but we tried to have the rhythms and melodies of Africa to be prominent, so that whatever we incorporate from other music, the features don't overwhelm the overall sound that we decided on. . . . We were listening to Weather Report, Chick Corea, a whole lot of guys—too many to mention . . . at least at some point Weather Report were dabbling with the African elements of music, so we felt very much attracted to that style of playing. . . . Sakhile came at a time when a lot of bands were looking to the US for their identity. We proved that our music could be developed from its folk roots—if you like—to an American level of sophistication, but still retain our identity and incorporate our politics. That's a hell of a legacy to be proud of.[6]

For Johnny Mekoa, 'Sakhile was a hell of a group—a unique group because their sound was so unified and so African. Musically, there was a lot of jazz phrasing entwined there'.[7]

Sakhile was probably the most sophisticated of the groups seeking to craft a modern indigenous sound. Their melodies were built around call-and-response from a chorus of the players, often a chant, with the same phrase repeated over another conversation: between Sipho Gumede's bass and Khaya Mahlangu's horn. They were able to communicate with a popular audience through music that had space for both the jazz conventions of Mahlangu's sax solos and extended and intricate traditional drum solos from Mabi Thobejane—the percussion break on 'Beautiful Feeling' lasts a few seconds on their first album; it could last ten minutes live. Audiences loved the formula so fiercely it became a straitjacket for band members (and one of the forces leading to Sakhile's first breakup in 1983), as Mahlangu remembers: 'When I was with Sakhile, people would ask, why don't you play more jazz? We want to hear you playing outside! But when I played outside, they'd say, hey, what's this you're doing now? Everything I did was seen in terms of the Sakhile sound'.[8]

Tananas, formed in 1984, was a trio of drummer Ian Herman, guitar virtuoso Steve Newman, and bass player Gito Baloi. Often classified by record buyers as a jazz group, the members did not see themselves like that.

> Tananas is a different animal, because with Tananas I wouldn't even begin to call it jazz. Tananas is hard to categorise because the whole concept of Tananas—well, it is a concept: it is openness. There are all our influences and we are quite different from each other. Three individuals, you know. Steve comes from a very different background, musically and geographically, and so does Gito and so do I. We're completely different stylistically, but when you put us together, there's a chemistry that gels—we play together musically much better than we can talk![9]

*Tananas*, their first eponymous album comprises short, simple tunes with the quality of folk songs, including tunes based on the old marabi chords. They are given texture by singing—again, male voice chants such as Sakhile used, or smoother, more lyrical sambas where Baloi draws on the Latin music heritage of his birthplace, Mozambique. Newman is a guitar virtuoso; even on a simple theme he creates tension, weaving space and densely packed notes. Herman, though, is no folk drummer; he lays down edgy rim shots, rock back beats, and again the fast, shuffling *goema* rhythm. In South Africa, Tananas' members were classified in three different race groups, so the music in live performance made a powerful wordless point about communication across barriers—and their very performances defied segregation laws.

So too did Savuka (later Juluka), a band formed around anthropologist/guitarist Johnny Clegg and traditional Zulu musician Sipho Mchunu. Clegg's fascination with Zulu style and music long predated his university period; as a schoolboy, he used to search out musicians in servants' quarters to listen and learn from them. Drawing from both rock and Zulu music, Savuka produced songs that were descriptive, questioning, and metaphorical, rather than rallying cries, but they made their impact, particularly on university audiences already on their feet to the compelling jive of the group's Zulu-styled guitars.

Bayete made its points with lyrics. Founded in 1983, it was an eight-piece band, using jazz horns and a jazz pianist (Themba Mkhize of Sakhile) alongside a drummer/vocalist, Jabu Khanyile, whose family music background was the Zulu *isicathamiya* of the hostels, and who had polished his skills in hit *mbaqanga* and soul groups like the Editions and the Movers. A repertoire built up over four years found its way on to record in 1987, and included songs like 'Hypocrite'—an allusion to the 'Hippo' police armoured vehicles that terrorised the townships. Khanyile explains the title track, 'Mbombela': 'We took Miriam Makeba's "Mbombela" and wanted to show that the very same steam train was taking people away from their families to seek work in towns. And many fathers never made enough money to ever return home'.[10]

What these groups—and many others, smaller and less well known, across the country—had in common, was their combination of social themes and a musical language drawing on both urban pop and rural tradition, and often jazz, too. It was in many ways an alternative kind of neotraditionalism, crafted—unlike the state's version—from the bottom up. Ironically, it was through migrant labour—the very instrument the state was manipulating to shore up apartheid—that these fresh infusions of tradition were arriving.

Conditions in the homeland puppet states were deteriorating. Corrupt, over-farmed, and underfunded (except for the military and the bureaucracy), these states forced their impoverished and desperate residents into migrant labour, as was the design. Workers moved back and forth to commercial plantations, mines, and big city factories, and to the industrial estates packed with low-wage assembly plants on the homeland borders. What had not been in the state's design was that the trains full of workers also carried authentic tradition (with its histories of anticolonial resistance) into the towns, to challenge ersatz *mbaqanga* culture—and carried news of the political struggle and advancing concepts of organisation back into the homelands.

There was not a huge difference in sound between the real and the ersatz. Zulu traditional *maskanda* music, for example, still relied on the guitar-picking style, *ukupika,* developed by musician John Bhengu (and disseminated by Troubadour) in the 1930s. Songs still opened with an ornamented guitar fanfare and made space for spoken praises for the artist, his clan, or his patron. What had changed were the conditions under which these authentic musical elements were expressed and combined. The studio replaced lived experience: Zulu 'wedding songs' now marked no wedding, but were instead defined by a collection of frozen phrases considered characteristic of real wedding singing. Instead of a communal occasion inspiring music, a set of musical clichés defined the fictional occasion. The studio process made the music a branded product, and this constrained the creativity of performers. In particular, they were limited by their producers' ideas about what would sell, and (closely linked) the apartheid censors' ideas about what was authentic and permissible—which syncretic borrowings from other styles and sources were not. Back in the village, musicians were not ruled by the same considerations. Poet Kelwyn Sole sees the role of migrant workers as, once more, cultural brokers, but in a new context:

> The 1980s . . . made these cultural forms much more available outside of their immediate contexts. Groups such as Savuka and Abafana Bomoya . . . spread Zulu migrant music to a white and international audience: short stories, autobiographies and poems by black workers . . . have been published . . . and no longer are *mbaqanga* musicians, *isishameni* dance troupes, *isicathamiya* choirs and the like treated with the scorn they once were. In this revival, the culture of migrant and contract workers has been particularly forceful. These are the 'people between' who found, historically, little meaningful entertainment or means of expressing themselves in the cities and compounds. Consequently . . . they have created a culture which uses traditional and rural forms as a basis and expands and changes these forms to fulfil new needs. They are uniquely situated to mould traditional and modern, rural and urban, ethnic and class identities into exciting new forms.[11]

The experience of guitarist Selaelo Selota illustrates how this worked in terms of music. Selota was forced out of education and into the mines by family poverty, following the tradition of his uncles. He never had a chance to study music until the late 1980s, and while his chosen genre was jazz, he brought to it a vocabulary that drew from many roots:

> Before I even played music there was a tradition I grew up with: singing with boys at home, singing in the family when there are weddings, or if I would go to church my family would sing hymns and so forth. That part of my youth was very much effective because it taught me the essence of melody, harmony, rhythm [w]hich I didn't know I was going to be taught later, at [college]. . . . I only started learning guitar in 1989. . . . [B]ecause we don't have music in our schools, I had to finish high school before I could start music. . . . [T]he area that I come from, the Northern Province, uses very simple kinds of melodies which are so catchy that even a small child can sing the song. And when I started listening to [traditional] things like *diphela* and *dinaka* [traditional songs and dances], I found that there's just one scale to concentrate on, sometimes enhanced by the voice to add other notes, which is pretty much pentatonic oriented. But the harmonic structure is so complex, because you might be *between* a major and a minor chord . . . [all] that was a part of my growing up. And

then there was an element from my uncles who are [miners] working around Johannesburg, and they would bring home *mbaqanga* records and records from Mozambique and Zimbabwe. Those people were playing guitars in a way that was carrying the whole song—the *maskanda* kind of style from KwaZulu Natal. That captured me, so if I'm playing guitar, I'm carrying everything; I'm not blocking. . . . I think that was enhanced by the fact that I also worked in the mines, staying in the compound, and every Sunday I would watch traditional dancers from Swaziland, Botswana. . . . I started embracing the cultures around me.[12]

The state could manipulate the paper nationality of workers like Selota. It could not change—indeed, it depended on—their identity as workers. The major flowering of the 1980s was that of a shared workers' culture: plays, poems, and music.

In 1983, the United Democratic Front (UDF) was established, a broad alliance of grassroots anti-apartheid organisations, structured at national, regional, and local levels in a way that looked like the first mass political party since 1960, although the law still forbade 'political interference' between race groups. The UDF explicitly called not just for struggle, but for a 'culture of resistance', and from its foundation used graphics and music as key aspects of its activities. A band was brought together for its launch: the African Jazz Pioneers, reuniting as many veteran jazz players as survived. Its manager in those early years was Queeneth Ndaba, herself a saxophonist and now administrator of what survived of the Dorkay House structures. Ntemi Piliso led the band: 'In 1982, when we formed the [African Jazz Pioneers,] I brought back all of those marabi sounds. I re-recorded some of the stuff I had been doing with the Alexandra All-Stars, but put in some new rhythms, like Abdullah [Ibrahim] had done with the rhythms when he recorded *Manenberg*'.[13]

The activists who founded the UDF did not just link their launch with marabi out of nostalgia. The music had a cross-generational appeal, and it recalled the struggles for rights of suburbs like Sophiatown. And it was a national music, says Jasper Cook, who played trombone for the Pioneers: 'It's the only readily identifiable national style: marabi/mbaqanga. If you want to fasten yourself to an identity and call yourself South African, it had to be something like marabi or mbaqanga—that was our identity'.[14]

One of the band's soloists for its first year was Kippie Moeketsi, but he died in 1983. His funeral, with a huge cavalcade of cars and a parade of musicians, was a massive demonstration of the loyalty that not only he, but the music, commanded. As Victor Ntoni remembers:

[T]he saddest moment I experienced was when—here I am in my house in Spruitview—I'm watching this documentary on Bra Kippie—he was sitting under this tree and the last words he said, he was praising the local

**Jasper Cook (trombone) and Sam Tshabangu (trumpet) of the African Jazz Pioneers.**

music and particularly the local jazz. He said, 'But please, people, just help us get this message through to the world. *Nthuse ngwaethu* [Teach the people]. And that was the end of the programme—I felt so sad.[15]

Growing numbers of trade unions were being registered, united, by 1981 in two big federations, the Federation of South African Trade Unions (FOSATU) and the Confederated Unions of South Africa (CUSA). By 1982, a black musicians' union, the South African Musicians Alliance (SAMA), had been founded. In 1985, the two union federations united as Congress of South African Trade Unions (COSATU), linked to the UDF:

> Between October 1984 and about August 1987 . . . taking its name from the ANC call to 'Render South Africa ungovernable' . . . pupils boycotted classes; householders refused to pay rent to township councils; workers stayed away from work on days of mourning. Civics [Community Residents' Associations]—organised down to the level of street committees— even began to take over the functions of local government such as street cleaning. Protests spread to all provinces and were particularly wide- spread in the Eastern Cape, where police shot nineteen people dead in

the Langa township of Uitenhage on Sharpeville Day 1985. Youthful supporters of the civics, known as 'comrades', with MK support, began to punish and sometimes assassinate councillors and some businessmen seen as collaborators with apartheid.[16]

As part of this broad spectrum of campaigning, trade unions and the UDF established 'cultural desks' responsible for policy and strategy, while individual union branches set up 'cultural locals' to organise cultural activities and support members who wanted to develop their skills of writing and performance. The cultural locals were popular initiatives; the desks emerged from discussion with the ANC in exile, which had, in 1982, set up its own Department of Arts and Culture and which felt the need for information and policy feedback from home. The first was the Durban Cultural Workers' Local (DCWL), established in 1984 after the successful national tour of a play written and performed by workers at a Dunlop tyre factory. As well as plays and poems, these cultural locals provided a support base for *mzabalazo*, struggle songs sung by worker choirs. Building on the existing community tradition of choral music, a new genre and canon of songs was being created.

I have sung in choirs ever since I was at school. Then I sang in a church choir. The choir was very strict with training. We sang classical music and there was never any dancing. The Braitex Choir is very different. We sing for workers; we tell them about unions. . . . We try to bring new songs to the workers. We try not to sing old songs, people just get bored. Or the workers will join in—and a large meeting of workers will sing more powerfully than the choirs anyway. Workers have taken some of our songs and now they sing these songs in meetings. We have to work hard looking for and writing new songs:

> Hlangelani basebenzi nibe munye
> Ukuze sinqobe abaqashi ngengeni
> *Come together workers and be one*
> *So we can defeat the bosses with our numbers*[17]

The Sizanani Lucky Stars, one of the most popular groups from the Transport and General Workers' Union, were an *isicathamiya* group—photographs show them in the raven-tail coats and sparkling white gloves inherited from the vaudeville tradition. So were the Clover (dairy product workers) Choir. Both had started in *mbube* concerts and competitions, where they had won many prizes. But they dropped out of the competition environment to sing for their unions, composing new songs in the *mbube* style, reflecting new concerns:

> Anoyibhasoba lempimpi
> Yizo ezokutha izindaba

**Workers' choir.** *Credit: Learn and Teach magazine.*

> Yizo ezokuthela umqashi izindaba
> *Beware of the informer*
> *He's the one who's carrying the news*
> *He's carrying the news to the boss*[18]

On the East Rand, the most successful choir was the K-Team, from the Kelloggs cereal factory. Their main composer, Chris Dlamini, told their story:

> During the uprisings of 1984, many students, workers and activists in Springs and the surrounding areas were detained and killed by the state and its agents. . . . I was also detained during this time and fellow workers at Kelloggs, like Agrippa Xaba, came together and formed a choir. They composed a song which referred to my detention and that of others, as a way of reminding people of our fate. This ensured that no-one in detention from our factory was forgotten despite the clampdown on information by the state. . . . The diverse membership of the group . . . has enriched the content of our music and ensured that it has a wide appeal. All our music is composed by taking into account the prevailing social and political situation and it aims to unify and mobilise the people into action.[19]

Cultural and political networks overlapped and intertwined, sharing information and ideas, engaging in intense critique of works and building the foundations of structures that, by the end of the decade, could provide reasonably accurate and full information on cultural initiatives to organisers overseas. Their networking and impact were facilitated most powerfully by the Culture and Resistance arts festival and symposium, held in Gaborone, Botswana, in 1982. Culture and Resistance attracted 5,000 delegates, the majority from inside South Africa: for a weekend, they took over the then small town of Gaborone with exhibitions, performances, or seminars in every hall, church, and nightclub. The event was organised, with the assistance of international funding, by Medu, a Botswana-based arts group that united South African refugee artists and Batswana artists (see Chapter 7). Performers and discutants included Abdullah Ibrahim, Jonas Gwangwa, and veteran bandleaders Kingforce Silgee and Ntemi Piliso. The theme that emerged from paper after paper was that that culture was an integral part—a site and a weapon—of the struggle:

'There is a point at which "artistic neutrality" becomes a tool of the status quo by virtue of its silence in the face of injustice', asserted writer Dikobe wa Mogale.[20] 'Recently, at Wits [University]', recounted poet Keorapetse Kgositsile, 'there was a benefit concert in aid of detainees and their families. Popular groups like Juluka, Sakhile and Malopoets performed . . . they performed a task that could best be handled by artists in the community. . . . This is part of the struggle for national liberation and in it there is no such creature as a revolutionary soloist. We are all involved'.[21] 'The writer', asserted Cape Town novelist Richard Rive, 'does not only create literature but creates literature in a particular climate. If that climate is not conducive to his realisation of himself as a human being, then he must, through his art, try to change that society'.[22]

Two years later, on 14 June 1985, the South African Defence Force (SADF) attacked Gaborone, targeting in particular the homes of artists and cultural activists, including many Medu members, such as Hugh Masekela and Jonas Gwangwa. Among the fifteen people killed (the victims also included children, Batswana domestic workers, and an eighty-three-year-old refugee) were George Phahle, who organised shows and transport for Masekela; top university science student and war resister Mike Hamlyn, who was Medu treasurer; and the painter Thami Mnyele. Mnyele's works were stolen by the SADF, displayed in an SABC propaganda broadcast by agent Craig Williamson as 'proof of revolutionary intentions', and have never been recovered. Kgositsile, in a poem written following the raid, took issue both with liberal critics who objected to defining culture as a weapon of struggle and narrow-minded commissars who ruled love an inappropriate emotion. For Kgositsile, a revolutionary war nurtured its own definitions of love:

> Need I remind
>         Anyone again that
> Armed struggle
>         Is an act of love

. . .
So who are they who say
No more love poems

I want to sing a song of love
For the woman who blasted the boers
Out of that yard across the border
And lived long enough to tell it
I want to sing a song of love
For that woman who jumped fences
And gave birth to a healthy child . . .[23]

State-controlled media in South Africa and others of the government's apologists claimed that the Gaborone raid had been against MK military bases, and that cultural organisations and activities had existed merely as camouflage for these. Yet while one of MK's several infiltration routes into South Africa was via Botswana, the SADF raid failed to hit this clandestine activity. Its 'total strategy' sights were also fixed on culture and information and on known and vulnerable refugees. Culture and Resistance had sent thousands of South African artists home with a shared vision and direction that made them more prominent and effective in the struggle, and had garnered considerable antiapartheid publicity overseas. One of the purposes of the raid was to ensure such a powerful cultural coup could not happen again.

Many worker singers and poets had participated in Culture and Resistance. In a traditional culture in which orature, song, and dance are not rigidly separated, there was a thin line between lyrics like 'Hlangelani Basebenzi' and the poetry of social commentary declaimed at meetings. Trade union poets and orators at the ubiquitous funerals of people shot by the police sometimes used a style that was literary, allusive, and rich in metaphors drawn from tradition or the Bible. On other occasions they aimed for a simpler, more kinetic form that could pull a crowd together through movement and chorus—and turn into song, as people in the crowd exchanged call-and-response and new, improvised vocal lines with the poet.

The *toyi-toyi*, the high-stepping syncopated march developed decades earlier alongside Zimbabwe freedom-fighters, began to be seen widely at funerals and meetings, and on marches, accompanied by freedom songs and chanted poems:

Toyi-toyi happened everywhere. . . . It kept the morale very high. It brought us hope and joy. When we raised our knees, they came as high as our chests. Then we realised that we are tomorrow's leaders. There was this song which we used to sing which says *Siyaya ePitoli*, meaning that we are going to Pretoria. That was the most famous and loved song. It meant that we were going to occupy the Union Building and remove whoever was in that building.[24]

Some of the new poems and songs were constructed around *toyi-toyi* lyrical or rhythmic patterns. Sipho Mabuse did this with his banned 1989 hit 'Chant of the Marching' (recorded in London), which opens with the sampled sound of marchers *toyi-toying*, and the shouts of crowds, and segues into a song over the same rhythm.

[O]f course, bands like Juluka were around, Roger Lucey. . . . The mood was then very volatile politically and we could feel there were changes in the air, a lot was happening. And of course we wanted to make a contribution as artists. We managed to write albums and lyrics which were banned [like my] 'Chant of the Marching':

> I remember the day / when I heard the sound of marching feet from a distance
> rising all the way / from the sound of stamping feet to the sound of resistance.
> Bullets and pellets from every direction
> sirens and silence and a lot of action
> Someday, when it's part of our history / our children will learn from the past.
> Human rights sacrificed / security fortified
> someone is dead / with a hole in his head
> a mother is crying / another is trying
> to explain / why children will always die.
> Someday, when it's part of our history / children will learn from that past.[25]

All these appropriations and improvisations were firmly in the South African tradition—political and musical—singer Sibongile Khumalo believes:

Choral music has various dimensions. . . . You find, for instance, in struggle music of the '80s, if you wanted to slap a label on it you could easily call it jazz, precisely because of the way it grows. Because people take a church hymn and change the words to it, and the rhythm might change here and there. . . . [T]he issue is about the communal element of music-making in Africa. That's why it's so difficult for Africans to sing in unison. Each person hears the music in different ways, and yet when they communicate musically with other people, it fits in with what they heard the first time. . . . That is also, if I may digress, how our decision-making happens, traditionally. . . . [African people] take what they hear, and own it, and it develops an identity of its own.[26]

The themes of these songs and poems found their way back into the churches, many of which had become centres of resistance where new hymns reflecting struggle and nationalism were being composed and sung. Some historians have suggested that Christianity was a 'useful screen'[27] for struggle, but those working in religious music say that they were drawing on the inherent commitment to social justice in the Gospel, and on a long history of militant church music, including the American heritage of civil rights gospel singing. Mokale Koapeng was in the chorale of the conservative Seventh Day Adventist Church in the late 1980s:

> Our church liturgy was drawn from Western hymns, and there was controversy when some of us began exploring African music and languages; composing new hymns and translating and adapting old ones, bringing in traditional approaches to a tune. But as believers, our beliefs did not let us stand apart from what was going on, and although our church did not encourage political activism on the streets, creating indigenous hymns was a conscious contribution.[28]

Other choral composers felt similar nationalism. Mzilikazi Khūmalo finally completed his monumental oratorio *uShaka*. 'The time has come', he declared, 'for a black view of Shaka'.[29]

Outside the unions and the churches, formal choral activity had almost ground to a halt during the years immediately following 1976. Riots and boycotts made it hard for choristers to travel after work to rehearse for competitions, and the police routinely harassed or banned any large gatherings of black people. In 1978, with sponsorship from Ford Motor Company, the National Ford Choir Competition had been launched, and this shaped choral activity in the 1980s. With monetary incentives (the first year's prize was a bus, won by the Soweto Teachers' Choir), the choir movement grew again. Communities still valued singing in all contexts, Ford organiser Peter Morake says his car was unobtrusively marked by the comrades so that he could travel in the townships unmolested during the turbulent 1980s.[30] For the company, the competition was a valuable marketing tool for its products, and the social conscience it paraded was good camouflage for doing business with apartheid. 'But from those early days of the big competition', says Mokale Koapeng, 'you saw the start of a negative trend where repertoire gets limited to the competition set work and a performance approach designed to appeal to the judges'.[31]

This was very different from the exciting, volatile world of worker choirs, with their intense community involvement and the constant creative stimulus of devising new themes and songs. Many worker choir members had formerly belonged to formal secular choirs and quit; the combination of more active involvement in both struggle and repertoire was irresistible. It was *mzabalazo* songs and poetry that fed into the development of poet/composer Mzwakhe Mbuli, whose recordings of poems with jazz/*mbaqanga* instrumental backing— banned almost as soon as they were released—were among the clandestine hits of the decade. Fellow musician Johnny Clegg also credits censorship with a role in shaping Mzwakhe's form:

> Mzwakhe's . . . was an educative poetry. He taught people to think that what they were experiencing was valid . . . 'this is the mouth of hell and

we have to walk through it. We have to keep going.' I think it was [in 1986] that Mzwakhe first put his lyrics into a kind of musical backing, a development that was linked to the government's banning of political speeches. The government would say, OK, you can have a funeral—one of the few ways that blacks could come together in public—but you cannot have any inflammatory symbolic communication. So the speech-makers would hire a band and would say their political speeches to music, usually just a riff being played over and over in the background. . . . Mzwakhe . . . also had this musical backing because of the possibility of the police coming in. . . . Eventually, he recorded an album of poetry set to music, called *Change Is Pain*, which was instantly banned.[32]

*Change Is Pain* puts dub poetry over traditional drums, over marimbas, and sometimes (in the poem 'Many Years Ago') over marabi. The fat horn line of big-band swing was playing a new role.

By the mid-1980s, as the struggle intensified, censorship had been stepped up even from the severe restrictions of the 1970s and woven more tightly into the structures of the police state. In 1982, the Internal Security Act was tightened, instituting what was called the National Security Management System across the whole country. Army numbers were increased by extending conscription, and white students now subject to the draft formed the End Conscription Campaign to resist, and assist conscientious objectors. In 1983, with the accession of P. W. Botha to the presidency, the powers of the president were increased and the state further militarised. In an attempt to shore up the apartheid divisions, sham democratic elections to a new 'tricameral parliament' (with Indian and coloured houses of parliament in permanent minority to the white house, and Africans completely excluded) were announced. Most voters of colour stayed away. There was a full-scale uprising in the Vaal Triangle, and, in the following year, the UDF led the biggest worker stayaway since the 1950s. Curfews virtually closed down the townships. Protesters were summarily shot in the Cape, and the murderous activities of the Third Force stepped up. A national state of emergency was declared in 1985, the year of the Gaborone raid.

In the same year, a Zulu cultural organisation, the Inkatha Freedom Party, began to take on a far more active role as a political party. Inkatha yeNkululeko ye Sizwe had been formed as a royalist cultural group in the 1920s, and revived in 1974 to shore up the credentials of the KwaZulu homeland. Its leader, former ANC Youth League member Chief Mangosuthu Buthelezi, had broken with both the black consciousness movement and the ANC by 1980. Initially most influential in its home province, the decade saw Inkatha becoming more active in the workers' hostels of Vaal, harassing Zulu-speaking workers who held antiapartheid views, and launching attacks on township political gatherings. The messages of Zulu music began to be redefined, through Inkatha patronage, so that 'authenticity' ruled out antiapartheid sentiments. *Maskandi* musicians involved in the struggle, such as Phusekhemisi, received death threats and beatings.

At the same time, the government offered lavish payments to musicians to join the 'Info Song' recording project: a pop song extolling the virtues of the status quo. *Mbaqanga* players who took the money, such as blind singer Steve Kekana, also received death threats, and many township residents boycotted their concerts and records.

The record companies focused on what came to be called 'bubblegum' music for the black market: lightweight disco. Hugh Masekela—by no means averse to drawing in popular and modern elements to his own music—saw what was going on from Lesotho:

I love you, baby. We'll boogie all night. Shake your moneymaker. Do it to me tonight. Do it to me three times. Now we are trapped, man. Disco is a social tranquilizer; you don't recognise other things. We can't boogie for the whole year.[33]

Cecile Pracher was a music librarian at the state broadcaster, the SABC, during these years:

The lyrics of each and every pop item had to be checked on grounds stemming from the Publications Board. . . . Our rules were more defined than those of the government. Things like, for example, swear words were unacceptable. Unacceptable sexual references . . . bad taste . . . occult elements . . . the usage of drugs, blasphemy, glorification of the Devil, unfair promotion of a political party . . . between the 1980s and the 1990s it was the time of PW Botha and apartheid was in full swing and the State of Emergency was declared and everything became tighter and tighter. Things that would have been allowed five years earlier were frowned upon; therefore it was a very unnatural society to live in. . . . We did not have open airwaves in the sense that there were only two independent broadcasters [commercial channels] and they belonged to the SABC. This committee consisted of all heads of departments, and lyrics were scrutinised beforehand by the manager in the record library. . . . [They] would be passed on to a meeting once a week. . . . My impression was that in those days virtually anything that was perceived as damaging to the state to the SABC or to the National Party was regarded as not acceptable and we would ban it.

Interpretations were broad. Pracher cites Tracy Chapman's songs 'Freedom Now' and 'Material World' from the *Crossroads* album, banned for being 'likely to offend certain sections of the population'.[34] And it was not only broadcast music that was censored. Guitarist Ray Chikapa Phiri led the band Stimela, which used pop music conventions—guitar-led dance rhythms—as the vehicle for thoughtful lyrics about society and politics. (Stimela members, including Phiri, had formerly worked with Mpharanya [Jacob Radebe], whose soul band, The Cannibals, had, in the words of South African soul historian and filmmaker Steve Kwena Mokwena, 'played a critical role in nurturing a spirit of self-pride and defiance.')[35] Performers at public concerts had to submit the lyrics of their songs, too, and Phiri hit trouble with Stimela's big hit of the mid-'80s, 'Whisper in the Deep' / 'Phinda Mzala'. The isiZulu title, literally translated, means 'Dance, old man'—but its implication is much broader, as Phiri explains:

> [T]he concert was in aid for kids who were detained. . . . But before we could perform the police just moved in and tear-gassed everybody . . . we realised that peoples' lives were in danger, we had to go and negotiate with them. That was when one of the top security guys said: 'As long as you're not going to play that Pindamsala'. He did not know the title of the song was 'Don't Whisper in the Deep'. It was more like a national anthem; we were trying to bring awareness to people that they must stand up and speak their mind, stand up, don't be afraid, wake up. At the time it was the height of the struggle and most of us were ready to call a spade a spade. We were doing a lot of protest songs because we believed in calling a spade a spade. . . . [So we negotiated and they agreed to let each band perform for ten minutes each] as long as we didn't sing that 'pindamsala'. When I started singing the song, I sang 'Don't Whisper in the Deep'—which is the same song. And I didn't use that 'pindamsala'— the audience did. So I thought, if they sing then they have to arrest everyone. . . . Everybody sang along and that was the end of the show. They started shooting tear gas and stuff like that. We asked the people not to panic, not to throw any stones or things of that kind. The power of the music prevailed because they listened. . . . They all walked out of the stadium and the police got mad because the people didn't retaliate. The police started shooting innocent people with tear gas . . . but on that day music won.[36]

Disguising meaning in another language, in street slang, or through metaphors, was only one of the ways artists learned, in Sipho Mabuse's words, to 'communicate. We would write songs in such a way that officials could not detect what we meant in our songs. . . . I remember writing a song called "Set Me Free". The intention of this song was obvious but the contents meant something else and of course people in the townships understood exactly where we were because of the political state of the time.'[37] Another instance was the hit song 'We Miss You Manello', by pop star Chicco. Chicco solemnly told the media that the song was about an absent personal friend of his—but every time he performed the song live, the crowd roared: 'We miss you, Mandela'. The music

acquired another dimension of meaning through the process of popular participation. What the censors barred, the people created.

Attempts to muzzle the music were not limited to censorship. Phiri, Afrikaans rock star Anton Goosen, and others have spoken of spies in their bands,
reporting on their meetings and activities to the Special Branch. Jasper Cook, a
white player with a black jazz band, received regular death threats:

> My experiences of hate were all similar. . . . Some flinty-eyed white man
> would approach me, and say that 'people' didn't like what I was doing
> and one day a little red spot would appear on my forehead. And I'd say:
> don't talk about it, just do it and meantime I'll just carry on playing
> trombone.[38]

White protest singer Roger Lucey was the object of a particular campaign of
hate, steered by policeman Paul Erasmus, who tells the story in his draft autobiography:

> A set of Roger's music (from the banned *The Road Is Much Longer*) and
> him airing his views about the SA political scene had been monitored
> during transmission to the Voice of America and I was accordingly as-
> signed to identify him and 'see what could be done about stopping the
> filth'.[39]

Erasmus shadowed Lucey, scared the singer's distributor off with false information that he was a prime terrorism suspect facing arrest, confiscated albums
and cassettes from record shops, and closed live shows by pouring tear gas into
the air-conditioning and making threatening phone calls to club owners. But
while transcribing Lucey's moving lyrics for his reports, Erasmus 'began to feel
bad about the whole thing. What a waste of talent. I really believe that he would
have gone on to great heights in the music scene. But, well, he was just another
"red" that had to be stopped by whatever means possible'.[40] (Erasmus turned
against apartheid in the late 1980s and was granted amnesty by South Africa's
Truth and Reconciliation Commission. He and Lucey have since met and recon-
ciled.) 'I hold no grudge', Lucey says. 'After all, he was also a victim. He was a
young guy that got, like so many of my friends as well, just talked into that whole
story: "The communists are going to come and take over the country. They're
going to rape our daughters and kill our wives'. Those stories were huge in young
people's lives. And they were . . . terrifying. People forget that'.[41]

These 'dirty tricks' certainly created a climate of suspicion among some musicians. Selaelo Selota, a young newcomer to the Johannesburg music scene,
without the links of family or history that could vouch for him, found it 'very
difficult to find proper unity and encouragement from some brothers . . . because
they were coming from a period where other people were either police informers

or . . . you hear stories like there's been a raid on Botswana and artists' houses were raided. . . . [T]he isolation years, we now know was an island, a very marshy, distorted island, artistically and musically. . . . The pieces are so much scattered because that's when the jazz musicians got scattered up and exiled'.[42]

Yet young musicians did find help and support. Selota was offered bar and doorman jobs that helped him gather funds for his studies. Young players found a proving ground at the SABC, after 1983, with two black TV stations as well as the radio bouquet, which eventually ranged over thirteen black stations. They had to contend with censorship and institutionalised racism, but there was also work and training. This was largely, says trumpeter Johnny Mekoa, through the efforts of one man:

That was the great era of Victor Ntoni. His contribution to the music of this country has been enormous. You remember when apartheid was real down on us, but there were some whites who worked for the SABC who felt that, no really, this has to be captured. The powers that be stream-lined it as a separate development issue, because that time they were pushing separate development—but that is how some of the great music was saved. I mean, some of those big band series that Victor Ntoni wrote for. . . . a hell of a series. . . . And this is how you see the contribution that he made, because out [of the] big band era came young players like pianists Themba Mkhize and Arthur Tshabalala; the Bayete guy [Jabu Khanyile] was a drummer, no, a percussionist in the big band. Trumpet-ers like George Tyefumani and Brian Thusi out of Durban . . . and a lot of other players came out of that.[43]

Bassist and arranger Ntoni himself says it was an uphill struggle. Bud-gets and facilities were limited, and Yvonne Huskisson was still imposing a restricted view of black jazz:

The SABC was purely on a job basis. I was struggling, having arrived [back]. . . . It was difficult to find a place for yourself, although there were the grey areas, things starting and so on. . . . So I left Benoni and went knocking on every door in Johannesburg. . . . There was a show, the Astoria Awards, done by the SABC for the highest achievers in black productions. And they needed a music director, and someone had whis-pered to them that there's this guy—local guy—who's back from America: why don't you try him out? And that's how I got my first gig with the SABC. . . . Then I had this haphazard ensemble of a big band—can you imagine writing one trumpet against one trombone and one tenor saxophone against one flute? It was crazy. And then I went and complained. I said, listen, I'd better have the real thing. They said, what do you mean? I said, I want a 7 on 5 with a proper rhythm section, and

From left to right: Sipho Gumede, Khaya Mahlangu, Menyatso Mathole, and Mabi Thobejane: Sakhile. *Credit: Cedric Nunn*

that's the first time I actually got a decent ensemble emanating from the SABC.

[They sent me on a music producers' course, but] . . . what actually helped me to have good productions was that I am a musician. I could actually get the rhythms down, and when the camera should be focusing in on what—not focusing on the vocalist when it should be a drummer's foot on the screen. And, you know, the miming involved was so bad . . . but I slowly started putting things together. . . . [But exposing good modern music was difficult, because] there was the protocol—this thing of dominance. Unfortunately, things have to point back to apartheid, which I hate doing. . . . There was this lady who was the top . . . I don't know exactly what was her title. But she was the one dealing with music. She was very arrogant, thought she knew it all, and other guys, subordinates of hers, who just wanted to please her. They all happened to be the so-called white people. And I just thought this was bad. I mean, how can I be told of something that I know of and somebody tells me how to do it? Not that I'm being arrogant, but I know what is happening in Dube, Langa. I've got the vibe. I grew up there. It's like asking me to be intimate about Bach. I couldn't do that, because I never lived the man's life. . . . And then, of course, there were the budgetary problems—I mean, imagine having only a thousand rands to produce a man like Mankunku. What can you say to that man? How am I gonna reimburse [him] as far as fees are concerned . . . ? I battled and battled and thought: I'm gonna go crazy; I'm ready for the nut-house now! So I left the SABC.[44]

White music producer Ecckie Eckhardt (now retired), who describes himself as 'completely apolitical' but who nevertheless developed, through his own youthful playing experiences with the mixed band Afrozania from 1979, an enthusiasm for black jazz, found the racism extended to him by association:

Working in a band and meeting lots of really, really great musicians . . . was very inspirational to me in terms of now wanting to keep the music alive. I joined the SABC and got involved in the music department, this was in the late 1980s. The brief was 60% Afrikaans music and 40% English, including all others. . . . [But] eventually I got a budget to record more jazz programmes for the English service . . . and that meant [going to] all the clubs where there was live music, like Rumours and Kippie's . . . artists like Bayete, Barney Rachabane, Pat Matshikiza, Bheki Khoza and all sorts . . . in a place like Rumours there was no prejudice. Good music was welcomed regardless of who played it. . . . At the SABC, the first time I took a man of colour, Lionel Pillay—a brilliant pianist, absolutely brilliant—to the canteen (which for me was absolutely quite normal, to say, come, let's have a cup of coffee) a security guy comes to me and says no, black people aren't allowed in this canteen. . . . I made a complaint, and it was all sort of brushed under the carpet . . . but I became a bit of a joke among white colleagues. When they'd see me with a black person, they'd say 'Hier kom Eckkie se pekkies' [Here come Eckkie's tar-babies]. . . . Obviously, it's insulting [and] I've had quite a few conservative Afrikaans okes coming speaking to me, trying to get me to come to church or reform my ways , 'cos they just couldn't believe that anyone could integrate music, you know.[45]

Television had other impacts, too. With two black TV channels, there were now regular programmes featuring traditional and neotraditional music. *Isicathamiya* historian Angela Impey calls this 'the real moment of emergence' for the music, when 'the visualisation of isicathamiya' was facilitated.[46] However, as it showcased, television also changed the music. David Coplan notes that, for traditional Sotho singers like Puseletso Seema, 'the studio process has affected her performances, forcing her to shorten solos to fit arrangements for popular singles. Perhaps as a result, each of her songs on record focuses on a different aspect of her experience, rather than building experiences in into a resonant concatenation as is usually the case with extended shebeen performances'.[47]

African music programmes were usually low-budget affairs, with a set dressed like a tawdry 'native' village scene for tourists or a mine performance arena, and artists miming to their albums. Pianist Henry February, however, had a chance to experience the other side of the picture. His skills were in demand for continuity music, and, as an Afrikaans-speaker, he saw how money was lavished on 'white' music:

> This was now in the '80s, '88, something like that. I can show you how they wasted money on their own. We did Afrikaans tunes for the Afrikaans service . . . something like 3, 3-minute slots, interval music, continuity when the programme is a few minutes short. . . . And just for that they flew us there [from Cape Town to Johannesburg] on an Airbus, put us up in a hotel for which they had to pay, and fetch us there and back to Auckland Park. . . . Anyway, I was the only black one, the other two were white, but I picked them because I liked the way they played. They wanted to get other people, some other bloody drummer, but I said no, I'll pick my own trio![48]

Money was no object for the state in creating an acceptable cultural image. To this end, millions were poured into the 'homeland' of Bophuthatswana to provide infrastructure for the luxury private hotel, casino, and golf course complex of Sun City. Built in a hyperbolic fantasy style by hotel magnate Sol Kerzner (even the palm trees were imported because the local variety was insufficiently 'African-looking'), Sun City had opened in 1979, a massive secure edifice of marble, fountains, and gilding in the middle of a bare, parched, poverty-stricken land with one of the highest infant mortality rates anywhere in South Africa. 'In Bophuthatswana I talked about democratic and social rights', Mzwakhe Mbuli had declaimed. 'Sun City was the answer. Ma-Afrika—I have troubles!' At the Sun City Superbowl, visiting artists could perform to mixed audiences, blithely assured that they were 'not really in' South Africa.

Some overseas performers, despite the well-publicised boycott, did not understand the nature of homeland 'independence'. One who did, was rock guitarist and Bruce Springsteen band alumnus Steven Van Zandt. His campaigning interest in America was on the plight of Native Americans, and the parallels between homelands and reservations did not escape him.

Working with antiapartheid American journalist Danny Schechter and forty-four other performers who shared his views—including Miles Davis, Bruce Springsteen, Bob Dylan, Peter Gabriel, Nona Hendryx, and Run-DMC—in 1985, Van Zandt created a big, rough collaboration song, weaving strands of rap and rock music around lyrics that left no margin for misunderstanding the nature and role of Sun City—or what artists should do about it. It was called, 'Ain't Gonna Play Sun City'.

> Relocation to phoney homelands
> Separation of families I can't understand

> 23 million can't vote 'cos they're black
> We're stabbing our brothers and sisters in the back
> I ain't gonna play Sun City
>
> Our government tells us we're doing all we can
> Constructive engagement is Ronald Reagan's plan
> Meanwhile people are dying and giving up hope
> This quiet diplomacy is nothing but a joke
> I ain't gonna play Sun City.

'I loved it" wrote Danny Schechter. 'It was journalism you could jive to'.[49] The song was banned in South Africa. At Christmas 1985, according to ticket impresario (and opponent of the boycott) Percy Tucker: 'Sun City was pretty much in the doldrums . . . significantly, the Superbowl stood empty over the 1985 holiday season. Indeed, the Superbowl had suffered a sudden and severe decline from light entertainment mecca to sporadic attraction'.[50]

It was not just a song that was squeezing Sun City—although the song had certainly alerted many potential visiting artists to the moral implications of performing there and 'the supply of overseas artists to South Africa steadily diminished'.[51] Tastes and the national and international music market were also changing. Sun City had provided work for many acts who appealed to rich but aging members of white society. Unrest was now so pervasive it could not be ignored, and, after 1985, the economic crisis dampened their enthusiasm for showbiz junketing. Even the black acts who broke the boycott by touring South Africa itself for impressarios like the Quibell brothers were mostly long past their sell-by date in the United States. New trends like world music—and, above all, youth culture—were barely represented.

Yet within South Africa, youth culture was asserting itself. In the townships, it was the 'Young Lions' who had been leading the protests on the streets since 1976. That is why the conscious pop of artists like Mabuse and Phiri forms a major part of the story of black music in the decade. For many white youth, too, it was singers with a message like Roger Lucey and Johnny Clegg and groups like Juluka, Hotline, and Mango Groove, crafting dance music that drew flavours from Africa, that appealed.

Particularly vibrant was the alternative protest music developing among Afrikaans-speaking youth in the second half of the decade. Singers with satirical stage names like Johannes Kerkorrel (Church-organ), Koos Kombuis (Bake-oven), and Bernoldus Niemand (Nobody) sang 'boerepunk', an stringent combination of original tunes (sometimes drawing on Afrikaans traditional folk melodies), cynical, angry lyrics, and the loud, clashing guitar chords—or discords—of heavy metal rock or punk. One band was called the Gereformeerde Blues Band, after the Gereformeerde ('reformed') Kerk, the dominant, rigid Calvinist form of Christianity that found biblical justification for racial separation. In 1983, Niemand recorded 'Hou My Vas Koporal', an anticonscription anthem, credited as the song that launched the movement—and, of course, scratched by the SABC censor.

Conscious black pop music and alternative white rock could not rely on the state broadcaster, established venues, or the big record labels to get their music out. Alternative venues and channels were found or created. Homeland stations like Bophuthatswana's Radio Bop had courageous DJs who would play more challenging music, though this was dependent on the erratic tolerance of their own mini police states. The clandestine broadcasts of the ANC's Radio Freedom station, based in Lusaka, broadcast music as well as analysis and the news of street battles and acts of sabotage the SABC suppressed. Its broadcast began with a jingle punctuated by gunshots:

> Sometimes you hear the gunshots, *khwa-khwa*, over the radio. And then you'd hear a voice coming in, a poetic voice. . . . Somebody speaks about Africa, how it was colonised and how it must be freed. We heard a lot of liberation songs. We used to sit around the radio. My mother used to get annoyed. She said: 'I'm telling you, you will get into trouble and don't call me. . . '.[52]

The enthusiastic collusion of the big record companies with SABC policies was widely recognised. SABC librarian Cecile Pracher saw how, in practice, '[the record companies] were in it for the business—that's very clear—and they were protecting their rights. They knew that most often if a song is not given airtime it doesn't have the same chance of being popular as the next one. So they forced a kind of censorship on their artists'.[53] Johnny Clegg feels that even production styles and the music's sound was harmed by the pressures: 'Textually, censors forced us to develop a symbolic language which the audience would quickly understand . . . but if censorship in that way stimulated linguistic development, it smothered us musically. . . . I remember endless discussions when we were mixing the music. If I wanted more powerful drums or guitar it was always quieted down. Music was meant to "heal" . . . [and] became more toothless'.[54]

Sharp entrepreneurs—some, politically committed; some, simply more aware than the big monopolies of how the international music scene was developing—established small independent labels to record the new sounds. One producer with purely commercial motives, frustrated by the industry's lack of awareness, told journalist Muff Andersson in the late 1970s: 'Sooner or later somebody (and I certainly believe it'll be me) is going to turn in a massive success and then all of a sudden these people are gonna scratch their heads: "Jesus Christ, we may really see monster money start to roll in". Then everyone is going to scramble over their bloody feet to do the same thing'.[55]

Others had a genuine musical mission. Rashid Vally's As-Shams/The Sun continued to give a voice to modern jazz. In Cape Town in 1980, Paddy Lee

Thorpe set up Mountain Records. He had previously been manager of Pacific Express, the city's most adventurous fusion band; their first album, in tune with the times, had been called *Black Truth*. Members of that band, such as Robbie Jansen and Basil Coetzee, put out their first albums with the label, as did Amampondo and the gently satirical Afrikaans folk singer Edi Niederlander. The 1987 album *Sabenza* (a corruption of the Xhosa word for 'work') bears twin dedications, to tenor saxophonist Basil Coetzee's mentor, Abdullah Ibrahim, and 'to the people for the inspiration . . . to the struggle'. Coetzee said the genesis of the music was in the unrest period of 1985. The two saxophones of Coetzee and Jansen have the swooping jazz attack typical of Cape players; they soar, shout, and sometimes—as in Jansen's soprano solo on 'Coventry Road'—braid the scales into the modes of Malay music. Yet, often, it is also music communities could dance *langaarm* to, underpinned by the precision of drummer Jack Momple's strict tempo.

In Johannesburg, Lloyd Ross established the Shifty Studios, so named because the company's base after 1983 was eight-track recording equipment in a caravan that could go anywhere in the country —or to record exiled or banned musicians in neighbouring states like Botswana and Lesotho. 'Shifty was formed in response to the serious lack of interest paid by the existing music industry to original music that either had any kind of social message or was aesthetically different from the mainstream. . . . [T]he local new wave/punk bands . . . were producing music that was far from anything that had been played here before; the music raw and immediate and the lyrics reflecting the kind of anger and confusion that I was feeling growing up in apartheid South Africa', wrote Ross.[56]

Shifty's first project was the Lesotho band Sankomota, banned from South Africa in the 1970s. The fate of their music made Ross see the necessity of running Shifty as a full-scale label, not just a production facility:

All the companies that I took the masters to rejected them out of hand. Those that had the courtesy of responding said that it did not fit the format selling at that time. Consequently I raised the money to get the record pressed and found a company that would distribute it for me. Trying to find radio play for the record was no less frustrating. No SABC station would play it because the band crossed cultural boundaries, i.e. they mixed their language and this did not fit the broadcasters' purity rules. But you can't keep a good record down. It started receiving airplay on a few stations like Radio Bop and Radio Lesotho and the record started selling in small but steady numbers, eventually becoming an evergreen seller on the Shifty catalogue.[57]

Samkomota didn't just mix languages. They mocked their own earlier expulsion from South Africa ('Too much music bad for mad case') urged consciousness ('Sons and daughters of Africa . . . unity is the password'), and warned against fake revolutionaries. The music had generous reggae spicing; not surpris-

Niell Ettridge (drums), Carlo Mombelli (bass), Jo Runde (guitar), Duke Makasi (sax), and Johnny Fourie (guitar): Abstractions. *Credit: Mombelli family album*

ing, since one of the band's inspirations was veteran Lesotho rastafarian and radical nationalist 'Black Jesus'. Simple melodic lines drawn from Sotho tradition and allusions to folktales and metaphors talked about fighting various kinds of demons, including colonialism. All this over a big band with a five-piece horn line whose personnel ranged from Huddleston Band alumnus trumpeter Stompie Monana (who took some neat solos firmly in the African jazz tradition) to young avant-garde white sax player Rick van Heerden. Founder Frank Leepa's musical vision was 'to create the ultimate southern African band of all time. Something like Earth Wind and Fire—but from here, and playing our music'.[58]

For the next ten years Shifty was releasing about six new albums every year, from Boerepunk to poetry to jazz. Among their artists were the Genuines, Tananas, and a brilliant improvising *maskandi* violinist, Noise Khanyile, who resolutely refused to record to prescription as well as various boerepunk artists. 'The biggest single album that Shifty released was *Change Is Pain* by the poet Mzwakhe [Mbuli]. It surpassed gold status without a single note from the album being played over the radio'.[59]

Small groups, such as Carlo Mombelli's Abstractions, were grateful for companies like Shifty.

Carlo Mombelli:

There was only one record label that was interested to bring out anything, and that was Shifty Records, Lloyd Ross; he used to record all the crazy guys like us.[60]

New recording opportunities also brought together artists across communities and music genres. For drummer Vusi Khumalo and his bassist, cousin Bakithi Khumalo, it was a maneuvre to evade police harrassment that resulted in two Afro-fusion players providing the rhythm for white country-and-western bands:

> When Spirit Rejoice broke up, we formed the band Theta. I was from Requero with Bakithi [Khumalo], so we decided to recruit Lawrence [Matshiza, guitarist] and Bushy [Seatlholo, pianist]. And then we went on with Makhaya Mahlangu, the percussion player from Drive. . . . Theta was a very good band at that time . . . and Sakhile—those were the bands of that era which were very prominent. . . . Sakhile was into more Afro-jazz music—and we were into Afro, but at the same time it was contemporary . . . everybody was listening to their favourites. . . . I liked Billy Cobham, and Bakithi was into Jaco Pastorius, Weather Report and Bushy was into Chick Corea—everybody liked different things. We all came up with this influence in the band and we created our own sound. . . . It was tough. I was doing sessions at that time, just before we formed Theta. What was happening was that there was a studio in Bree Street—it was called MC Studios—and I was playing with Roger Lucey and the Zub Zub Marauders. . . . [A]t that time, Roger Lucey wanted me to stay in town and there were heavy pass laws—I couldn't move freely. But then they managed to squeeze me in, and I hanged with them in town. [But] every time when I had to go to town, I had to think 'Oh, by the way—pass book'. I came up with a good idea for me and Bakithi. I said, 'You know, if we go to town early in the morning, like six o'clock or half past six, those guys [police] are not there. We go to the studio, we can hang in there and rehearse and practice'. And that is how we started practicing; because we had no choice—otherwise, if you go outside, you're gonna be arrested. So the best thing to do is to practice, in the studio. And, of course, in that studio there were a lot of [white] country bands that hung around there. And they would ask; they want some session musicians. And this guy would say, 'No; I've got guys here'. And it was kinda strange to these guys that these people were going to play with them! But, I mean, at that time, we were advanced because we were listening to a lot of music . . . there were very few guys who were actually recording with white musicians—in fact, it was not possible. But with help from [producer] Dave Marks—he actually introduced us to that kind of situation—everything just developed slowly.[61]

Alongside the new labels were new venues, and in the city centres, the second half of the decade saw a range of clubs offering a home to the new pop and jazz and—through a range of legal dodges or outright law-breaking—to mixed bands and audiences. In Durban, in 1982, Ben Pretorius and Billy Mthembu founded the Rainbow:

[Ben and Billy] started the Rainbow with R7,000 each and opened their first Sunday afternoon gig with Malombo. There were a few discordant noises: they were forced to consult all shop-owners within a 200 metre radius on whether they had any problems with blacks and whites sitting down and enjoying food, drink and music together. The orthodox Muslim owner of the complex objected to liquor being sold on the premises, so they moved. I still remember the pictures of . . . musicians playing their instruments while walking through the streets of Pinetown behind a banner that read 'Jazz for the Struggle: the Struggle for Jazz'. Then there were the hassles with the security police—usually introduced to the audience with a heavy dose of irony as 'our uninvited friends'. The [Nelson] Mandela birthday concert in 1988 was banned at the University of Durban-Westville so it pitched up at the Rainbow. . . .[62]

In Johannesburg, there were numerous clubs in the city centre and in bohemian suburbs like Yeoville, all of them with room for a range of musics.

Jasper Cook:

There were also, I think, defined little venues that had places for us—places where mixed bands could play. One was . . . the Roxy Rhythm Bar, which had about 130 African musicians going through every week. It was still technically illegal, but we loved that. The owners just took a decision, sometimes moral or political, sometimes business—because good new music brought in the audiences.

Carlo Mombelli:

I had been in a band competition with my band, and Johnny Fourie's band and another three bands were chosen. One of them was . . . called Vukani, from Cape Town, and that was where I met a great bass player from Cape Town, called Spencer Mbadu. . . . I was already starting to get into free music, and Johnny was doing the funk thing—and needless to say, the smoothest of the bands won the recording contract, so already in the beginning of the '80s, the record companies were into that sort of thing. . . . Anyway, having heard me play, Johnny called me for this gig, six nights a week for six months, playing jazz at some disco place. . . . We can go back to the Yeoville time . . . as a centre of what was happening. . . . I had a band with Johnny Fourie called Abstractions and those times in Yeoville, Rumours was open, where they had a real piano and jam sessions on Sunday nights where you all used to get together and jam, and there was also Jamesons, also with a real piano. . . . I was playing at a little club called the Black Sun in Hillbrow on Friday nights at midnight,

a solo gig directly after the Genuines. So there were a lot of diverse things
happening. The Johannesburg Hotel also had jazz every Sunday night.
And the Oxford Hotel. And at the end, Kippie's. . . . Jamesons used to
have these all-day festivals, from jazz to the Genuines, to Bright Blue. . . .
All mixed up. And people trying things. It was a hell of an interesting
time for me. . . .

Johnny Fourie:

The '80s was the search for a broader spectrum of music. . . . So I think
I stopped playing standards for eleven years or so. . . . I formed a band
here with my son Sean and the children of Johnny Boschoff and Hennie
Bekker, who was a bass player and drummer, [a] little band called the
Johnny Fourie Band. . . . [W]e played fusion—a very nice little fusion
band, probably ahead of its time. We managed to keep that going for two,
three years . . . and then of course I got involved with Carlo Mombelli . . .
[and] finished up playing in Abstractions. We did that for about two
years, playing various gigs, but the venue that brought us to the attention
of the other part of our population was Jamesons. At that time it was a
strange kind of place because the name of it harked back to the Paul
Kruger days! Jamesons was a melting pot of all sorts of emotions, a very
vital place of the time. . . .[63]

Jamesons was a particularly important venue, and it had been a particular
target of Paul Erasmus' harassment of Roger Lucey. It was not only its name and
premises that harked back to the an earlier era. The club functioned because it
possessed a 'Kruger' liquor license, issued in the previous century by the president of the Transvaal Republic, and thus was able to bypass more modern laws
about liquor sales and segregation. But, as Andrew Donaldson writes, 'Outside
the bar, . . . on Commissioner Street, the real South Africa was there—and in the
songs James Phillips wrote: 'The Branch', 'Detainees', 'Warsong', 'Shot Down',
'Barbed Wire'.[64]
  For other clubs, particularly in the Johannesburg townships, what critic Sean
de Waal called those 'delirious evenings'[65] were impossible. Clubs faced attacks
not only from the authorities but from thugs and the township comrades, the
Young Lions. The police armed gangsters like the Makabasas in Orlando, and
conservative hostel dwellers, to target venues sympathetic to the struggle, as well
as the homes of activists. Some musicians, however, although open in their support of the struggle, did not reveal how far their involvement was moving. One
was Sipho Mabuse:

When I signed with Virgin Records, I was asked to go to the USA and
. . . I was asked to talk about some of my experiences as a black South

African making music . . . that is how I started getting to know some of
the people within the ANC and the PAC. You know, I learned so much
from that, because there wasn't enough information coming in to South
Africa. But that experience for me suddenly said—Hey! You are sleeping
through a revolution. There is more that you can do as a musician, you
can also influence some of your peers at home so that there is clarity on
what the armed struggle and the political struggle is all about. And then
I had meetings with Pallo Jordan [of the ANC] to explain certain things
that some of us at home were very naive about and when I came home I
was able to interact with the UDF and talk to people—and fortunately
the Special Branch had not yet called on me. . . . Most of the people that
I interacted with, especially on the political front, were people that I had
grown up with. Although I remained an artist, I had an affinity with what
they were doing in terms of the liberation struggle and the armed struggle. I was involved in the movement of information. . . . I worked mainly
underground with people I would get information for, and bring back
into the country . . . one had to be very, very careful about who you're
seen with. . . . So for us, as musicians, it was a better front because we
were able to go out and perform, but we were also able to go out and
bring back information from some of the liberation movements for back
home.[66]

In the decade following 1976, youth had been radicalised by the brutality of
police attacks. Schoolchildren were beaten for leaving their classrooms to go to
the toilet. Groups of children talking on a corner were clubbed for no reason.
Sicelo Dhlomo, age fifteen, was tortured the first time he was detained: 'They
said I must understand I'm in an electric chair and if I don't tell the truth they're
going to torture me and kill me and leave me there to die. Suddenly, I felt the
most terrible pain in my body as they electrocuted me. I lost consciousness'.[67]
Such experiences made young people harder and swifter to act in anger. Meanwhile, detentions and killings were depriving the township movement of a whole
generation of more mature and trained leaders.

Clubs became a target. Sometimes, they were owned by the hated township
councillors or other kinds of collaborators. Restrictions on township trading
were gradually eased as part of apartheid's effort to create a loyal black middle
class in the 1980s, and such people were often among the first to be granted
trading licenses for enterprises such as liquor stores. Many young people also
directly accused alcohol and entertainment of distracting their parents from the
struggle. Lucky Michaels felt it was not the time to be maintaining a nightclub
like the Pelican:

When I saw what was happening in that era, I said to myself I was going
to end up having people killed here. And that was the main reason I

closed it. . . . After '76 up to '86 it worked. When I closed, it was at a high. Business was not suffering. But there was a responsibility that I had to look at. . . . Do you just pay a few rand towards the funeral of some child that was killed at your place, or do you just forget it and go into some other business—which is better? And the better for me at that stage was: *Eina!* I'm not going to bury anybody's child![68]

Some older musicians retreated from an insecure work environment to contract work playing in hotel lounges. Most, like pianist Pat Matshikiza, found it a demoralising experience:

So there was a man who'd seen me playing. . . . He said, I work for Sun Hotels, do you want a job playing piano in a restaurant. I said, yes! He sent me to Venda—I didn't even know where that is!—and [later] to Amatola Sun, which is in Bisho. I was very, very depressed, and I was rebellious. . . . What I didn't like about the job was I couldn't play anything but cocktail music, no jazz, and the people were a little unfriendly. When they walked in, they always told the waitress: don't put us near the piano; we don't want that noise. And that hurt me a lot. And sometimes, people were rowdy, walking in, talking at the top of their voices, talking about their own business, shouting 'Ha-ha-ha!' It's difficult to work like that. At times, I used to get so frustrated that I'd tell the manager I'm going to take a break; this is getting out of hand. . . . Funny enough, after a couple of weeks, some of these people changed. They'd say, 'We've come to listen to you. How are you?' I'd say, huh! You're only coming to make noise, but they'd say 'No, no, we're listening to you. We're enjoying the music'. . . . Twenty years playing in hotels, and all that time I was either a prisoner or a pet.[69]

Another jazz player who retired for a time to hotel work was pianist Ebrahim Khalil Shihab (formerly Chris Schilder; he had converted to Islam in 1979). In 1980, in Cape Town, he, saxophonist Robbie Jansen and drummer Kader Khan had formed Estudio, a trio dedicated to carrying forward the experimentation that had characterised Oswietie and Spirits Rejoice. Later members included Cape Town pianist Tony Cedras and white Johannesburg bassist Pete Sklair. 'For me, Estudio was the best band of the time', says Carlo Mombelli. 'They didn't play free music, but a sort of chamber jazz. It was exquisite, so thoughtful, like an ECM kind of thing'.[70] Estudio was recorded—but never released—by Shifty and found few performance opportunities. Jansen says the depression that followed was, for him, a major trigger for the drug addiction against which he is still battling.

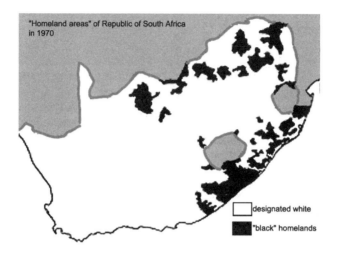

The Homelands under apartheid reflected ideological conceptions of separateness between members of different ethnic groups—as well as economic interests. Each tiny
portion of Bophuthatswana sat over a platinum mine. *Credit: Judy Seidman*

By the middle of the decade, because independent labels and venues had developed and because Johannesburg provided more sophisticated audiences, avant-
gardists like Mombelli's Abstractions were able to function, though they still
struggled. Abstractions was just one band from a major flowering of small groups
across the country, drawing in players from all communities and experimenting
with new music. Almost none of their output has survived.

In the company of Abstractions, modernist pioneer Duke Makasi was able to
advance his own musical journey.

Carlo Mombelli:

We were playing every tune from Zawinul to Charlie Parker, and Johnny
[Fourie] would be telling me: try this; try that; when you improvise,
please try to get this feel. Duke Makasi was also in the band . . . and at
the breaks we all just sat there, asking questions, discussing, learning. It
was like being at Berklee [School of Music] for me. . . . When I started
my band, Duke used to come in. He wasn't a band member, but he'd sit
in, and he recorded some stuff with us. . . . We were playing three nights
a week to small audiences. Jamesons gave us a regular gig, every Thursday
. . . but it got to a point, I don't know, we were in all the arts columns
and everything, but we were still playing to small audiences. . . . I remember one gig, a hotel in Rosebank, where there was one person in the
audience. One person! He had a concert just for himself! . . .

Johnny Fourie:

I played in Carlo's band . . . which was beautiful, because it included Duke Makasi. . . . I loved his music because it was so lyrical and so modern . . . he was very, very sophisticated and had a very advanced harmonic feel.[71]

Younger musicians were drawn to these new ideas. Another aspect of a mass movement seeking to establish structures autonomous from apartheid was the establishment of independent music schools that could provide the necessary skills. There was no formal music education in the black schools that, by now, many teenagers in any case scorned to attend. Unrest in the townships was making the traditional route of apprenticeship to a regularly working neighbourhood band harder. But new music schools were being created around community arts centres, like the Funda Centre in Soweto, with the support of overseas charitable funding. There, youngsters found a curriculum that linked music skills to cultural and social struggles. In Cape Town, Music Action for People's Power (MAPP) was established in 1986. In Durban, the next level of jazz education was created, as Dave Brubeck's son Darius headed up the university's groundbreaking School of Popular Music and Jazz Studies.

In Johannesburg, Selaelo Selota, having finished his first contract as a miner, found his musical opportunities at the Federated Union of Black Artists (FUBA) Academy:

After I had worked in the mines—after those three years underground, that was it! . . . [On a trip to Johannesburg, I saw a sign advertising something called the FUBA Art Gallery]. . . . I've always been interested in paintings, so I went in. When I came upstairs, there was another sign saying: music studies—enrol now. I used the money I'd been planning to spend on clothes to register. . . . I had no money, so I would sneak into an empty storeroom at FUBA to sleep. Those were the days of Bayete, Theta and Tananas at Kippie's—the 1980s. I used to stand at the door trying to listen, until the doorman said one day, do you want a job? . . . [T]hat time, I hadn't made up my mind for guitar, but one night, I heard Johnny Fourie playing a certain chord and asked him how he did it. He showed me, but he said: It may take you a few years to get it right. I went out and bought an acoustic guitar and tried it out all night until I got it right—I thought I'd broken my fingers![72]

Singer Sophie Mngcina was a FUBA teacher, having studied music in at the Central School of Music and Drama in London and then carried her lessons back home:

We can't all be activists and carry guns. Some of us need to educate. Education was not compulsory in this country. If there was an exodus out of this country by musicians—and it wasn't easy: if you keep on saying you want a passport, they give you an exit passport—the ones that remained were keeping the home fires burning and—as if told by God—some of us were teaching: you will give what I gave you. . . . I've got students now who are performing, lecturing. . . . I left my husband, children, so that I could go and learn something. That's my [role in] being an activist. . . . So that's what I did, for more than ten years at FUBA. Sometimes you got paid, sometimes you didn't, because the school was not subsidised by the then government. I used to go to university, take my lessons and then come back to these children. . . . I was teaching 1976 dropouts who thought if they came to school it was going to be easy—smoke a bit of dagga, a few cigarettes. No! It was about education. The blackboard was brought back; they had to write essays. It was a music school that said you had to learn to respect people like Mzwakhe Mbuli, Dr Wally Serote—those people are educated, they are poets, they are black. But it's not just black and proud. It's people who have gone out of the country to bring something back to the country. If you are going to understand Shakespeare, you must understand the ways in which he was also revolutionary, like these guys. They are on a par with Shakespeare. Now, you will learn to read and understand their pain and understand your freedom through black writers. As I say: music is us—you have to write your experiences.[73]

FUBA was close to the Market Theatre, which provided a home for plays and musicals reflecting the new struggles and cultural manifestations—and reflecting back on old ones. In 1986, the theatre staged *Sophiatown*, a play workshopped around the diverse, vibrant character of the demolished suburb. In the same year, the pass laws, the Mixed Marriages Act, and the legislation prohibiting racially mixed political parties were repealed, and in 1987, the country's huge monopoly cinema chain, Ster-Kinekor, fully and finally desegregated all its cinemas.

This social easing did not mean that political repression was lessening. Instead, the focus of state activity over the next few years changed to direct attacks on neighbouring states and an increasing use of both the army and covert forces at home. Lesotho was blockaded and Gaborone attacked again. Mozambican president Samora Machel died in a mysterious air crash probably caused by a South African decoy beacon. A six-day running battle was fought in Alexandra Township. COSATU House was bombed, and proposed legislation reversing many of the gains of the labour movement in 1988 led to a massive general strike. The building was bombed to destroy a newly-installed printing press that would print leaflets and posters. The press was wrecked before it even completed its first run.

Still, in Johannesburg's city centre, more places where music could be exposed were opening. The Market Theatre had established its own Market Music Platform, and, on the basis of the audience this had built up, opened Kippie's Jazz Bar, named after the saxophonist, in 1987. The opening was not without controversy. Many people felt that naming a bar after a man who had died of alcoholism was in poor taste, and the club was housed in a reproduction of a Victorian toilet building that had stood on the site. Moeketsi's family said they had not been consulted. Kippie's was not easily accessible to township jazz fans, who could ill-afford additional transport costs and for whom, as Third Force activity grew worse, travel after dark was very dangerous.

It was, however, the first city centre venue explicitly to declare itself a home for the jazz of the black community. The club was opened by Robbie Jansen, with his new band, Heartthrob, and its seven-day programming rapidly built up a following among those who could afford to attend in safety, black and white.

Deceived by some of the signs of social easing, and unaware of the intensity of repression on the streets, some overseas artists began to seek direct contact with South African players. Vusi Khumalo remembers a studio call from 1986:

And then one day we were still playing with Theta, and there was a guy coming to South Africa who wanted to do a recording. At that time, to us, it was not a strange thing, that we were going to do a recording with a white man. We went to a studio called Satbel Studios, in Marshall Street. And when we got there everything was set up and the next thing they introduce us to this guy: here is a guy, he's from the States and his name is Paul Simon. At that time, to be honest, I didn't know about him. And we started doing some things in the studio, started recording. But it was very strange, because he wanted local music, you know, traditional music, and he wanted to fuse that with American music. And to me, it didn't make sense. And of course, we had this guy from Lesotho, from [Sotho traditional band] Tau ea Matsheka, he was playing accordion. And you know those guys—when they go to a studio they normally just do an album in a day. But with Paul Simon it was different, because we had to do one song for the whole day—and the guy got pissed off. What happened was Paul wanted a bridge in the song 'The Boy in the Bubble'. He felt that the song was boring, because it was straight. I mean, it helped having a bridge, you know? And now Bra Koloi [Lebona, producer] had to explain this to the Sotho guy 'Hey, man, we need a bridge. This song, it's OK, it's nice, but we need a bridge'. And this guy—they don't know anything about a bridge—he was like, 'What bridge? What are you talking about?' And we kept on explaining to him—the guy was really pissed off. And then at the end—'cos he had a *kierie* [stick] next to him—I remember him saying: 'I'm tired of this white man. We've been playing this song for the whole day, and now he wants a bridge from me—I'm gonna hit him!' I'm telling you, we had to cool him down![74]

The project, of course, was *Graceland*, which also drew in jazzman Barney Rachabane and *isicathamiya* singers Ladysmith Black Mambazo. Simon's probably well-intentioned but certainly premature breach of the cultural boycott led to massive controversy and discussions with the ANC at an international level. In his case, a plan was developed for a trust fund for South African causes from the profits of the recording and associated concerts. More broadly, as a news event, *Graceland* led to more publicity and debate about conditions in South Africa. In music terms, the country was now on the world music menu. Bassist Bakithi Khumalo found a home in New York, and Ladysmith Black Mambazo found an international following. It was a two-way traffic. Khumalo, playing with his cousin Vusi in Theta before the *Graceland* experience, was playing the groove-led, percussion-heavy 'African' sound that Harari had begun to shape. On his own album, *Bakithi Khumalo and Friends*, issued in 1988 but featuring an almost identical lineup, he borrowed street-corner dialogues (complete with American accent) from rap, but also, on the track 'Talago', created a spicy South/Central African mix that layered Manu Dibangu's 'Soul Makossa' with segues into and back out of *mbaqanga*. The project of musical reconnection with the rest of the continent had moved into the commercial arena.

While the debate on the boycott between commerce and activism rumbled on, resistance to and reaction from the apartheid regime reached a crisis point. The bantustan structure that had given birth to Sun City was crumbling, with coups in both Transkei and (unsuccessfully) Bophuthatswana. Beaten at Cuito Canavale and in the air by Angola, South Africa entered agreements that saw its troops withdrawn from Angola while Cuban troops also left, and a road map for the independence of neighbouring Namibia was agreed upon. Though the UDF was a restricted organisation, the unions and other antiapartheid groups had organised themselves anew into the Mass Democratic Movement, which launched a New Defiance Campaign in 1989. The presidency of P. W. Botha had been unable to survive the military defeat. In October 1989, his successor, F. W. de Klerk, announced the unbanning of the ANC, the South African Communist Party, and other organisations, and the release of political prisoners, including eight prominent ANC leaders held on Robben Island. Among them was the world's most famous political prisoner, Nelson Mandela.

# Notes

1. J. Matthews, 'Poem for Basil Coetzee', sleeve notes for *Sebenza* (Mountain Records, 1987).
2. Pheteni Khumalo, quoted in P. Bonner and L. Segal, *Soweto: A History* (Cape Town: Maskew Miller Longman, 1998), 109.
3. Conversation with the author, 1997.

4. All extracts from interviews for *Ubuyile,* 2000, except Ray Phiri from First World Conference on Censorship.

5. Ibid.

6. Ibid.

7. Ibid.

8. Ibid.

9. Ibid.

10. Quoted on www.music.org.za (biography of Jabu Khanyile).

11. Kelwyn Soe, in *Staffrider,* 8, no. 3–4, 204–205.

12. Interview for *Ubuyile,* 2000.

13. Ibid.

14. Ibid.

15. Ibid.

16. N. Parsons, *A New History of Southern Africa,* 2nd. ed. (London: Macmillan, 1993).

17. *Learn and Teach,* no. 4, 1985, pp. 16–19.

18. Ibid.

19. *Staffrider,* 8, nos. 3 and 4, 1989, p. 48.

20. Culture and Resistance papers, 5–9 July 1982, Medu, Gaborone, Botswana.

21. Ibid.

22. Interview for *Ubuyile,* 2000.

23. K. Kgositsile, 'Red Song', from *If I Could Sing: Selected Poems* (Cape Town: Snail Press/Kwela, 2002), 62–63. The poem was written after 14 June 1985 and first published in 1990.

24. Interview for *Ubuyile,* 2000.

25. Ibid.

26. Ibid.

27. David Coplan, *Sing Africa Sing* radio programme produced by ABC Ulmazi, Johannesburg, 2002.

28. Interview for *Mail and Guardian.*

29. Coplan, *Let the People Sing,* op. cit.

30. Ibid.

31. Interview for *Mail and Guardian.*

32. Biography of Mzwakhe Mbuli on Third Ear Music Web site.

33. Interview in *Staffrider,* April/May 1981, p. 33.

34. Proceedings of First World Conference on Music and Censorship, op. cit.

35. *This Day,* Johannesburg, 12 March 2004.

36. Ibid.

37. Ibid.

38. Interview for *Ubiyile,* 2000.

39. Excerpt from *Foot Soldier for Apartheid,* Third Ear Music Web site.

40. Ibid.

41. Proceedings of Second World Conference on Music and Censorship.

42. Interview for *Ubuyile,* 2000.

43. Ibid.

44. Ibid.

45. A. Impey, 'Refashioning identity in post-apartheid South Africa music: a case for isicathimiya music in Kwazulu, Natal', in *Culture in the New South* Africa, vol. 2, ed. R. Kriger and A. Zegeye (Cape Town: Kweln Books, 2001), 234–235.

46. Coplan, 1985, 197.

47. Interview for *Ubuyile,* 2000.

48. Ibid.

49. D. Schechter, *The More You Watch, the Less You Know* (New York: Seven Stories Press, Quoted on the Steven Van Zandt homepage.

50. P. Tucker, *Just the Ticket* (Johannesburg: Jonathan Ball, 1997), 445.

51. Ibid., 418.

52. Soweto resident Jon-Jon Mkhonza, quoted in P. Bonner and L. Segal, *Sonets: A History* (Cape Town: MaskewMiller Longman, 1998), 109.

53. First World Conference on Music and Censorship, op. cit.

54. In O. Reitov, 'Inside censorship,' *Djembe,* 26, October 1998, on *Djembe* Web site.

55. M. Andersson, *Music in the Mix* (Johannesburg Ravan Press, 1981), 76.

56. L. Ross, 'Shifty's Track Record,' at *www.sheer.co.za.*

57. Ibid.

58. Interview with Frank Leepa for *Two Tone,* July/August 1992, 14.

59. Ross, op. cit.

60. Interview for *Ubuyile,* 2001.

61. Ibid.

62. Rafs Mayet, in *Two-tone,* 1, no. 2, 1992, p. 13.

63. All from interviews for *Ubuyile,* 2000 and 2001.

64. Andrew Donaldson, *Sunday Times* Web site obituary for James Phillips.

65. S. De Waal, liner notes for *The Cherry-Faced Lurchers Live at Jamesons.*

66. Conversation with the author, 26 January 2004.

67. Quoted in Bonner and Segal, op. cit., 119.

68. Interview for *Ubuyile,* 2000.

69. Conversation with the author, 26 January 2004.

70. Interview with the author for *Star Tonight.*

71. Interviews for *Ubuyile,* 2000 and 2001.

72. Interview for *Star Tonight,* 14 January 2000.

73. Interview for *Ubuyile,* 2000.

74. Interview for *Ubuyile,* 2000.

*Chapter Seven*

# Home Is Where the Music Is:
# South African Jazz Abroad

Exile is a fucker.

—Blue Notes drummer Louis Moholo

There was another South Africa outside South Africa. It was composed of memories and dreams—sometimes prophetic visions—as much as realities. It was more effectively pan-African in vision and action than the geographical South Africa is, even today, after a decade of liberation. The huge diaspora of exiles, in America, Europe, and, very importantly, the rest of the African continent, was braided together by links of friendship and family and by the cultural structures and policies of the liberation movement. And it was to this South Africa that most of the musicians who left—consciously and explicitly—belonged. Too often, South African music abroad is analysed only in terms of its 'success' in the various music industry metropoles where it landed, or in terms of the life stories of individual players. While both these approaches are building up a store of valuable documentation,[1] to be complete they need their frame: the South Africa that preoccupied the hearts and the music of the players.

The earliest South African jazz exile was probably painter Gerard Sekoto, who left South Africa in 1947 and financed his oils and canvases partly by playing piano in various Paris jazz bars—very well, by all accounts. ('The owner of L'Echelle de Jacob asked me if I played the piano, and I told him that I did. . . . [He] gave me a job straight away.'[2]) But the first big exodus took place in 1961, with the departure of the cast of *King Kong* for London, where impresario Jack Hylton had secured a run for the show at the Victoria Theatre. Jonas Gwangwa says the musicians were not originally going to be taken—some had even discussed the dream of financing their own trips—'but fortunately, because of the

221

music style, they [said] "We have to have some people who are going to influence the musicians in London"'. . . .[3]

The experience was an exciting—and nerve-wracking—one for a largely young cast who had in many cases never traveled farther than Cape Town. After forty years, the freshness of Jonas Gwangwa's memories is still dazzling:

> I had always said: the day I fly, I'll be flying out of this country. . . . We flew from Joburg, stopped in Salisbury at the time—Harare—and from there to Livingstone and across to Brazzaville, where we got for the first time a black pilot, which was very exciting. . . . It was a dry plane; they didn't allow any booze, but of course the professionals like Bra Gwigwi [Mwrebi] had a bottle. Thank God that we did because when we flew . . . over the Channel, I was terrified! It always looks like a little river, you know, which is nothing that wide . . . but now every time I looked down and saw the water, I said 'Bra Gwigwi—the bottle!' . . . We went to the Bayswater Hotel and started rehearsals at the Victoria Theatre.
>
> And we were warned, 'Don't take a taxi—take the train!' [But one day I was late] and thought I'll take a taxi. Hmpf! It was like going all over town except where you were going! It goes round and round! . . .
>
> You can take the cold—but it was every day, and London was so grey! When we got to London some of the guys didn't have overcoats, so they used some of the costumes, the Sotho blankets, which came out beautifully on British TV, which was covering the arrival. Of course, we all bought these heavy overcoats. You know South Africans, they've always been buying imported things, [so] people were getting to all the corners, looking for such-and-such labels . . . and when we'd get to the shows, [instead of going straight to the dressing room,] we were profiling in front of the theatre, mixing with the audience, all decked out!
>
> There was a complaint in the paper: 'The Bayswater trains are so noisy since the *King Kong* cast arrived'. . . . We were a rowdy lot—and it was worse when a Scottish football team came to stay in the same hotel—oh boy! You must know that when we left South Africa there was prohibition for blacks. And when we got there, I remember the guys saying, £5 a man! Now, £5 a man is a lot of money for more than thirty guys, and the booze came in a truck. And the hotel manager said, 'I didn't order anything', and the driver said, 'Nah! It's [all] paid for, mate'. . . . And we had a binge on Sunday, Monday night, which were our off nights—but by the time we got to the show on Tuesday, some of the guys had broken ribs. Partying, South African style!—and the booze was so much there was enough for the next two weekends. . . . When we were in the restaurant, those English waitresses would say, 'What do you want, love?' and the guys would say, 'Man, did you hear that? She fancies me!

She called me love!' And then you hear the girl saying the same to the next guy—'No, man, these ones! They love everybody!'[4]

Waitresses, hangovers, and wily taxi drivers notwithstanding, the younger members of the cast enjoyed their time in London. Veterans like Kippie Moeketsi fared less well. He arrived with concussion after a fight with his father-in-law, simmering at what he considered the poor financial deal the cast was receiving and at musically unsound changes in the score to which bandleader Mackay Davashe had aquiesced. Gwangwa says the reedman was prescribed tablets for the headaches and dizziness he suffered, and ignored instructions not to combine these with alcohol. All these factors combined to trigger what Moeketsi himself described as a breakdown. He was briefly committed to a mental hospital, given electroconvulsive therapy, and sent home; he attributed his subsequent occa-sional paralysing bouts of composer's block to the lingering effects of the therapy.[5]

Gwangwa, like Moeketsi, also felt that a slow erosion was indeed destroying the character of the music:

But of course Jack Hylton got one of his arrangers to come in and say: 'It's not quite English; there are some things that we have to put in'. Which I objected to but, well, who was I? But I said: you're spoiling the music. [They changed] some orchestrations where we had the trombones going high, in *Kwela Kong*, and they always wanted to have the ends of songs going higher and much louder than we had them, so it felt like [an English musical comedy]. But, well, we still had the flavour.[6]

It is unlikely most members of the London audience would have noticed this weakening. *King Kong* was received within the customary patronising frame of stereotyped, sexualised, 'African' exoticism by, for example, the *Times* critic:

The naivety [*sic*], the rhythm and the vitality have a characteristic colour and manner of their own. They seem to be conditioned by a particular locality to which the characters belong; and it is perfectly easy to take what appear to us as stage clumsinesses in our stride and yield ourselves up to the rhythm and the vitality. . . .

Mostly the dances are frankly erotic, with the dancers using their hips and legs, or they are war dances, with the gangsters seeking to strike terror with their foot movements. The songs are always strongly, if sel-dom melodiously, sung . . . there is also a wildly uninhibited gangster dance culminating in a murder and an enchanting wedding hymn warmly lit and beautifully dressed, which also culminates in a murder.[7]

However, there was considerable interest in the music from the few West
Indian musicians who, from time to time, occupied chairs in the orchestra pit,
says Gwangwa:

I particularly remember Paul Peterson, who was a trumpeter in *King
Kong*. . . . And we used to try and exchange ideas with them . . . they
were kind of interested, always asking Mackay [Davashe], what's happening now in the music and why this and how this?[8]

Some British jazzmen, too, were concerned to make the players feel welcome.
Several former cast members mentioned bandleader John Dankworth with affection.

Jonas Gwangwa:

SA jazz was recognised, because there was that SA community, even in
the '60s, that had all kinds of records, and we used to go and have jam
sessions at the Tally Ho Club. And people were buying the *King Kong*
record. . . . In '61 I used to play with Johnny Dankworth. He used to call
me to sessions at the Marquee Club, and sometimes I'd just be in the
audience and he'd call me up: 'Did you bring your horn?' and me and
him and the rhythm section would play bebop—ooh! I think those trombone players of his must have hated me!

Thandi Klaasen:

I was encouraged by Johnny Dankworth when I was in London with *King
Kong*. I went to go and see their shows at the Marquee Club. The band
was playing—such a big band! Pinocchio [Mokaleng was by then living
in London, and he] had taken us . . . and I jumped up, me and him, and
we were dancing. I was wearing a skirt to fly out, to show off my panties,
and everybody was clapping. . . . And he'd call us sometimes to the stage
to sing with them. . . .[9]

Dankworth had toured South Africa in 1954, but he refused all subsequent
invitations once he had seen conditions there. He was an early supporter of the
antiapartheid movement and played in one of the earliest London benefits for
the cause, the Treason Trial Defence Fund concert of 1957. London was, by 1960,
the centre of considerable political awareness about colonialism, race, and war.
In 1958, the Campaign for Nuclear Disarmament had been founded. In the same
year, antiracism protests in the English Midlands city of Nottingham were followed by race riots against West Indian immigration in London's Notting Hill,
led by various British Fascist groups and youth gangs of 'Teddy Boys' (the street
fashion was for Edwardian-style, velvet-collared long jackets). In response came

antiracist solidarity activities from trade union, Labour Party, and Communist Party groups (which eventually resulted in the rather half-hearted passage of a Race Relations Act in 1965). In June 1959, a movement was begun to boycott all South African imports, followed by the first of many protest vigils outside South Africa House ('[T]hose people would be there all night, in the rain, sleet and snow', remembers Gwangwa.[10])

In March 1960—named by the British Labour Party as 'Africa Year'—8,000 people attended a solidarity meeting in Trafalgar Square, and, shortly after Sharpeville, the boycott movement, after discussions with ANC diplomat Tennison Makiwane, transformed itself into the Anti-Apartheid Movement. In 1961, with charitable funding from the Catholic Church, the Africa Centre was set up in Covent Garden to provide a meeting place and support centre for African students in London and education about Africa for the British public. Through the 1960s and 1970s, the centre was to become 'more and more a platform for the liberation movements [as] exiles began to swell the African population of London'.[11] Spaces were opening up in London where African music could find an audience who located it in the context—albeit sometimes broadly and fuzzily understood—of politics back home.

*King Kong* closed in December 1961, having failed to secure the hoped-for Broadway run. Within a few months, Gwangwa had chosen not to return to South Africa, but rather to take up a scholarship at the Manhattan School of Music. Masekela had preceded him; he had taken up a scholarship at the Guildhall School of Music almost as soon as he arrived in London, and then moved on to Manhattan. One of their patrons was John Mehegan, with whom they had played in Johannesburg on the 1959 *Jazz in Africa* albums. Another was singer and civil rights activist Harry Belafonte, who was learning more about the plight of South Africans from the star of a show at New York's Village Vanguard jazz club, the singer Miriam Makeba.

Makeba had not joined the *King Kong* tour, but had rather followed the career path opened up by her appearance in Lionel Rogosin's clandestinely filmed movie *Come Back Africa*. She went to Venice in 1959 to make publicity appearances for the movie, followed by singing engagements. By the end of the year, she had secured her first season at the Village Vanguard. Although Vanguard owner Max Gordon certainly considered her a jazz singer ('[she is] a star as exciting as Billie Holiday in her prime'[12]), the publicity surrounding her performances dwells far more on her identity as a member of the 'Xosa' tribe (publicist's misspelling—and only Makeba's father was Xhosa) and on the 'African folk' elements in her performances. Makeba's choice of repertoire increasingly leaned on traditional songs, and musicologist Lara Allen has noted that her interpretations on record sometimes eliminated the jazz swing she had given those same songs back in South Africa.[13]

Commentators have suggested a number of reasons for this, including the patronage and collaboration of Belafonte, whose own vocal style had a distinctly

226                         GWEN ANSELL

folkloric flavour. But it should not be forgotten that Makeba was also an astute
professional who needed to find an audience niche. Among white progressives,
a folk music revival was in progress (it was in 1952 that Pete Seeger and the
Weavers had recorded 'Wimoweh', his incorrect transcription of Solomon Linda's 'Mbube'), and the interest that the civil rights movement and later black
power had sparked among African Americans in African traditions including
dress and song meant that Xhosa folklore was very marketable. Jonas Gwangwa,
indeed, was impatient with some of these U.S. audience preoccupations: 'You
always had to explain all sorts of things. . . . Because it was those back-to-Africa
days, so you had to explain that it takes more than an Afro and a dashiki to be
an African, you know? You have to think and feel it'.[14]

There was, too—and still is—an Amerocentrism in the mainstream U.S. jazz
market that was reluctant to acknowledge or engage with the jazz traditions of
other countries. Both European and African jazz players encountered this when
trying to break into the scene; a 'folk' identity bypassed the issue. In the country
of its birth, jazz itself was a fiercely defended space. The scene, too, was simply
so big that any new musical flavour received scant attention. Bassist Victor
Ntoni, arriving in the early 1970s, says things had not changed much by then:

[M]usically, there were very few people who really wanted to know South
African things. Because . . . in the early '70s everything had just exploded
in America, you know? The Beatles, John Coltrane, George Benson
[were] also coming out, and John McLaughlin and Herbie Hancock—it
was a whole diverse kind of panorama. . . . Except for the very few, who
suddenly would hear you . . . it was really difficult to dent that iron
armour.[15]

Yet Makeba had not sought a niche audience simply to build her career. She
had always been far shrewder and more aware than the pinup babe her South
African promoters had imaged her as. Almost as soon as she left the country, she
began to talk passionately about what was happening at home. Her articulate
anger intensified after Sharpeville. At the end of 1960, attempting a home visit
for her mother's funeral, she was peremptorily informed that her South African
passport had been withdrawn. In 1963, she addressed the United Nations Special
Committee on Apartheid and was declared a 'banned' person. Hugh Masekela
believes her contribution as a campaigner—made possible by her firm base as a
performer—made an inestimable contribution to the early period of solidarity
campaigning:

I think that there is nobody in Africa who made the world more aware
of what was happening in South Africa than Miriam Makeba. Unwittingly—when she went overseas she just went to sing, but because of the
way she described those songs, and what they were about. . . .

This was around 1959. People realised what she was talking about. The more interviews she did, the more people found out about SA. I think that's the way Miles [Davis], Dizzy [Gillespie], [Harry] Belafonte, [and] Max Roach got to know. When Miriam went to play at the Village Vanguard, before I got there, when you went into the audience there'd be Duke Ellington, Count Basie, Miles, everybody—'cos they saw this miracle that looked like it came out of New Orleans or Chicago, but actually came from SA. I think Belafonte picked up the torch with Miriam because he was at the forefront of civil rights. . . . By the time I got to the States, Miriam had educated, unwittingly, African-American and other artists like Bing Crosby, even Frank Sinatra.

The American government was very upset but couldn't do anything about her fame, [b]ecause they were allies of SA, and the whole western world. The SA government was very uncomfortable with our presence overseas and we were under surveillance by the [Federal Bureau of Investigation, FBI] while we were in the States—and I'm sure we still are! Miriam led that brigade, and then in 1963 addressed the [United Nations] General Assembly and for the first time the world became aware of what was happening in this country . . . at the height of her career. It cost her a lot. From that point the West looked at her as an enemy, at the insistence of the SA government of that time. . . . She bit the bullet at a time when she was at the most lucrative stage in her career and by 1967 she forcibly had to leave the States [b]ecause the government made it difficult. . . . When we arrived in the States, we already had secret files on us, [t]hat we were communists. You know, being communist in the 1960s in America was like having the bubonic plague or the last stages of AIDS, you know what I mean? People were, like: 'Damn! You're a communist?' It's amazing that we made it, given the odds. But I think Miriam carried the torch for this country, and I think she kept the names of the Oliver Tambos, Robert Sobukwes, Nelson Mandelas alive in people's minds all that time. . . .[16]

In 1963, Hugh Masekela acted as music director on Makeba's second album for RCA, *An Evening with Miriam Makeba*. In 1965, the two married, and Masekela produced the Grammy-winning *An Evening with Makeba and Belafonte* (for which Jonas Gwangwa was orchestra director). It was the first Grammy ever awarded to an African.

Masekela's own music was following a similar (and similarly self-aware) trajectory. As well as producing Makeba, he recorded prolifically for Mercury and MGM, his output including the satirically titled *Africanisation of Ooga-Booga*. The albums mixed originals and jazz standards (including the South African standard 'Ntyilo Ntyilo') with covers of contemporary pop—and sometimes with spoken introductions informing audiences about some facet of South Africa.

**Ndikho Xaba plays at CASA.** *Credit: Rixaka*

Masekela says he, too, felt the obligation to 'talk about what was happening here. It was natural for me to say: "Hey, you might be enjoying the music I make, but it's not mine. It comes from the people and the people are getting hell out there!" '17

Ndikho Xaba, who arrived with the musical *Sponono* in 1962, sums up the message he believes these efforts had been conveying, aimed most effectively at the African-American community:

With the Masekela/Makeba ensemble, we were basically exposing the American listener to our art forms and dealing with apartheid issues also. We had an agenda which is common to all of us. One: we are black. Two: we have been colonised. Three: we were enslaved. Four: we were victims of imperialism. We are victims of racism collectively—so how can you divorce yourselves?[18]

Sometimes the learning went both ways. Caiphus Semenya and Letta Mbulu were involved with the making of the groundbreaking television drama series on slavery and African heritage based on Alex Haley's novel *Roots*. 'I consider myself blessed,' says Semenya. 'Because it's not everybody who participates on both sides of the Atlantic in a story that is an African story. . . . I had to learn: I had to read the whole book in order to write the music and I learned what the African people as a people went through. They say it's a Chinese curse: may you live in interesting times—and I reached America in interesting times! At that point there was a revolution . . . of ideas, of young people refusing to participate in a war which they saw as unjust in Vietnam . . . the Civil Rights Movement, Martin Luther King, Malcolm X. '*Roots* was the history', says Mbulu, 'that my grand-mother had related to me'.[19]

This commonality of experience with African Americans was instantly recognisable. 'When I got to New York, it was as though I'd come to a twin town', said bassist Johnny Dyani.[20] There were also politically aware American jazz players listening to African music and becoming involved in solidarity struggles. As early as 1960, Max Roach had recorded the *Freedom Now Suite* with its Sharpeville tribute, 'Tears for Johannesburg'. Some American jazzmen were also urging the exiles to mine their African identity for inspiration. 'Every time I saw [Masekela,] I told him to just keep on doing his own thing rather than trying to play what we were playing over here. After a while I think he started listening to me, because his playing got better', wrote Miles Davis in his autobiography.[21]

Yet there were also other images of Africa around, even among African Americans, as Xaba found:

Our first experience when we came off the plane at Kennedy Airport; it was a wintry day. Snow was almost up to our ankles on the ground. Before we disembarked, we were called upon by management to take off our Western clothes and put on traditional clothes—and unfortunately for me, I was garbed in a Zulu outfit. Now, imagine, there are no shirts or T-shirts, right? And bare-footed. OK, there were about four or five of us garbed in these Zulu outfits. Man, as we came down the stairs of the plane towards the building, our African-American brothers who worked in the airport didn't want anything to do with us. Because to them, here was Tarzan—live! You can imagine, here's this guy coming down the

stairs with his assegaai [spear] and shield, looking as if he is going to stab
you any minute. OK, we went through this photo-call and back into the
bathrooms to change now into our suits. What a surprise! Those same
people who ran away from us are now like: 'Hey, my brother! How ya
doin', man? Good to see you!'[22]

It was not only to African Americans that the South Africans were exotic.
With the naivete of visitors, Xaba and his *Sponono* cast colleagues also wandered
into some other places where they caused a stir:

Unwittingly, we broke apartheid—in an Irish bar. From our hotel to this
Blarney Stone Restaurant Bar was just two minutes, so that was the closest place we could orient ourselves from. We found ourselves in this
crowd of Irish drinkers. I'm telling you, our black brothers never used to
come in there. I remember noticing—hey, wait a bit, you don't have
black people coming in here; it's just us. The black people that I saw were
peeping through the main door, amazed. And the Irish guys were like:
'Who are these guys?' But we were just like: 'Hey, man, gin and tonic and
a steiner—this is freedom now, we're in America!'[23]

In 1968, Masekela had his first major U.S. hit: the funky 'Grazin' in the Grass'
(co-composed by Zulu expatriate in New York Philemon Hou, and number one
in both the pop and R&B charts) from the album *Promise of a Future*. A concert
of the album sold out Carnegie Hall. Makeba also made it into the top twenty
with 'Pata Pata'. In the same year, she and Masekela divorced. She married
Stokely Carmichael, leader of the radical black Student Nonviolent Coordinating
Committee (SNCC). The FBI, which had already earmarked Carmichael as a
dangerous subversive, extended its investigations to her. 'Suddenly and inexpli-
cably, her concert engagements were being cancelled and her record company
dropped plans to make a new album . . . she couldn't get a gig. . . . When [Martin
Luther] King was assassinated . . . the FBI accused Carmichael of inciting the
riots that broke out in Washington. . . . Carmichael and Makeba fled to Guinea-
Conakry'.[24]
    The South Africans' view that the FBI was monitoring musicians was not
paranoia. Throughout the 1960s, there had been surveillance of all the aspects of
Caiphus Semenya's 'interesting times'. There was pressure on record companies
not to advertise in the underground press, and an FBI memo of the times alleged
that 'Columbia Records' financial assistance . . . appears to be giving active aid
and comfort to enemies of the United States'.[25]
    Masekela moved to the West Coast, where he founded his own Chisa record
label. From this point on, mainstream jazz writers became increasingly disen-
chanted with his more and more Afro-funk-flavoured output. As for Makeba,

her departure for Africa was treated as though she had dropped off the edge of
the world.

Such critical comments once more reflect the definition-bound conservatism
of some critics as well as the dominant view of music as centred on America—
which it was, but only in terms of industry financial volumes. With Britain ruling
the 1960s pop scene, Europe hosting the most adventurous free jazz, and world
music on the horizon, there was a growing challenge to its hegemony on repertoire, if not revenue. It is certainly true that Masekela's output thereafter was
increasingly dominated by varieties of fusion music. It is also true—as he himself
now freely says—that through the next two decades his professional judgement
was sometimes adversely affected by a cocaine habit he has only recently de-
feated. But it is equally true that America was, quite consciously, not the centre
of *his* musical universe.

This was the era of funk and of the Afrobeat of Fela Anikulapo Kuti. Conscious hard boppers and avant-gardists, as well as pop players in the United
States, were all, in different ways, preaching the gospel of blues and funk. One
of the most politically challenging tracks of the period, Archie Shepp's 1966
*Mama Too Tight*, is built around a funk riff, which it both affirms and subverts.
Music scholar Brett Pyper quotes Pablo Guzman, who grew up with Masekela's
music of the mid-1960s onward, describing how well it fitted into the zeitgeist:

> For my generation . . . Masekela dovetailed neatly with the excitement,
> fusion and politics of Sly [Stone], [Carlos] Santana, and Malcolm [X].
> Here we were, coming into awareness of the *real* social verities and ready
> to go beyond Motown, Stax [record company] and bop and along comes
> Masekela, blowin' a horn that never sounded bush to us—just filled with
> the languid, mellow African sun. Masekela talked some Zulu shit and
> sounded on apartheid 'here' and 'there' and we said *fuck* them jazz nos-
> talgiacs![26]

The quote reflects the oversimplification of 'Africa' that Jonas Gwangwa
found himself constantly correcting—but also the reality that Masekela was successfully speaking to a particular consciousness, which is what he wanted music
to do.

> I remember once Marvin Gaye said to me—I was touring with him—he
> said, 'Hughskie, man, I wish I could sing all those kinds of songs you're
> singing, because we be just singin' about love'. . . . I said: Marvin, why
> don't you? Eventually [in 1971] he came up with *What's Going On*, which
> was a turnaround for black artists in the States getting into social con-
> sciousness.[27]

Back home in South Africa in the 1970s, black consciousness and the debate
on African identity were key cultural strands, and Masekela was not isolated

from those. The ANC had a diplomatic presence at the UN, and exiles with news from home were constantly arriving.

In 1970, Masekela joined Makeba for an African tour. In Lagos, Nigeria, he met Fela Kuti, whose huge ensemble laid funk-based horn grooves and radical political call-and-response over polyrhythms provided aurally by drums and visually by dancers. He also met Ghanaian progressive highlife band Hedzoleh Sounds, already experimenting with modern jazz and Latin admixtures. Like some modern jazz players in South Africa, Masekela was enchanted by the complex interlocking rhythms, which created new kinds of spaces for soloing, and in 1973, he made an album with the Ghanaians, *Introducing Hedzoleh Sounds*. 'I found a certain vitality in Afrobeat', Masekela says. 'Playing with [Hedzoleh Sounds] was like being on a big fat cloud. You couldn't fall off'.[28]

Masekela visited many African states in the years that followed. These were the years when one African state after another was being granted independence. Many South Africans on their way to exile visited or passed through, and, like these others, he, too, was excited by the heady brew of liberation parties freshly in power and cultural reassertion and rediscovery. As well as hooking Fela Kuti's 'Lady' into his repertoire, Masekela took inspiration from the scenes and styles of these countries for his own compositions, such as 'African Secret Society' (Liberia), 'Angelina', and 'African Marketplace' (Zaire). The African years are vital for understanding what happened to his musical character, which paralleled the reconnection with the rest of the continent going on at home during the same years.

As South African jazzmen at home were taking their periodic fresh look at marabi and *mbaqanga* through this different prism, so, too, was Masekela. In 1970, he went to London to make *Home Is Where the Music Is*, with a big group including Blue Notes saxophonist Ntutuzeli 'Dudu' Pukwana. In 1971, he made *Union of South Africa* in the States with Gwangwa and another *King Kong* escapee, saxophonist and singer Caiphus Semenya. Jonas Gwangwa takes up the story:

> The Union of South Africa—when I was in New York, Caiphus arrived, Hugh had formed his group, I had formed my group, but we got together and said let's do something together. Then the guys left and went to California. . . . [A] few years later, 1970, we said, maybe we can do something together now. Something strong, something South African. We rehearsed for three full months, just doing the singing. I mean something like eighteen to twenty hours a day, seven days a week. . . . arrangements and everything until we were really perfect together. The neighbours— because we were rehearsing at Caiphus' place—I thought we were disturbing the people, but they were so attached to the music. When we went away to gig, they said: 'What happened to the music, man?' . . . [We] got the Crusaders to go on tour with us, a tour of the U.S. Wayne

**Saxophonist Kippie Moeketsi, drawn in homage by exiled artist Thami Mnyele (detail from a music poster produced in Botswana).** *Credit: Medu Arts Ensemble Graphics Unit*

Henderson [came] with us. . . . Wilton Felder . . . Joe Sample. So we had two groups married together. We had a national tour of the U.S.—the music was beautiful.

The Crusaders had been working out there with Caiphus [Semenya] and Hugh [Masekela,] and they had really got the feel of South African music. . . . [A]nd there was a good spirit, a good feel, you know, I mean, just personally, amongst the people . . . the people already had an idea of the music. And the band was tight, both bands—the Crusaders used to open for us. I remember when we got to New York, some of my friends, New Yorkers, my neighbours, said: Jonas that concert was good. But after the Crusaders had played we thought that was the end of the show! Laying bets that this is it—we don't know what Union of South Africa is gonna be doing. And of course, backstage, one was worried . . . we listen to the guys and they're burning, and of course I had stiff competition with Wayne [Henderson] here on trombone, man, and there were a whole lot of South Africans in the audience.[29]

The album stretches through Africa, from South, to West, to America (it opens with a pastiche New Orleans funeral march that gives the horn players lots of space to have fun). But in Jonas Gwangwa's 'Johannesburg Hi-Lite Jive' and

'Shebeen' there is beautifully updated *mbaqanga*, and Caiphus Semenya's 'Caution' is a jagged, galloping little modern jazz tune with plenty of opportunities for soloing. There is also some delicious horn playing—particularly the Masekela/ Gwangwa dialogue on 'Shebeen'. What shines out of the album even thirty years on is Semenya's way with polyphony; the way, on his songs, voices layer, interlock, and call to one another across the tune. The words of one are prophetic:

> . . . We've got to go and be ourselves
> So we can hear this voice within us
> To get ourselves together. . . .

Miriam Makeba did not fall off the musical map when she went to Guinea-Conakry. Instead, she landed in a West Africa where cultural nationalism and generous state patronage for culture were important features of the construction of the new postcolonial states. Indeed, when the apartheid state withdrew her passport, several African states had offered her diplomatic papers. So Makeba was able to tour, to sing—and to write new—political songs, and to communicate about South Africa at the highest level, to the heads of states becoming important in the Non-Aligned Movement.

Her own music flowered as a result. In the reissued *Miriam Makeba: The Guinea Years*, she finds again the range of voices that she sometimes left on the shelf singing African folk with Harry Belafonte. Singing in nine languages, she creates sound as well as song, reaching for fuller, deeper, and hoarser tones. With aplomb she selects the right floating praise verses in the role of traditional *djelimuso*, and gets tight jazz swing from backup players, including the doyen of manding guitar, Sekou 'Diamond Fingers' Diabate. She was, in fact, doing exactly what she had done in South Africa: selecting the best musicians and working with them to shape a new sound from traditional, neotraditional, and jazz raw materials. Quite how influential this was on African female singing styles is only now being acknowledged. Asked to name their early influences, singers as diverse as Angelique Kidjo, Oumou Sangare, Tshala Mwana, and Sally Nyolo have all mentioned records by Makeba as an inspiration.[30] In South Africa, the feminisation of popular music had begun early, with women vaudevillians and the close-harmony quartets of the 1950s. '[It] began later in West and Central Africa, partly inspired by Makeba', notes music historian John Collins.[31]

The experience of another female singer, Beattie Benjamin, in Europe, was rather different. Benjamin had left South Africa in 1962 with her partner, Dollar Brand, and bassist Johnny Gertze and drummer Makhaya Ntshoko. Their first series of 1963 club engagements was at Club Africana in Zurich, a city rapidly developing a reputation as one of the centres of European modern jazz, and simultaneously playing host to concerts by Duke Ellington. The two had long considered Ellington 'something like a wise old man of our community in absentia',[32] so Benjamin talked her way backstage and, at her urging, Ellington came to see them:

> Mr Ellington kept his coat buttoned, but he listened to us intently. He asked me, what do you do? Are you their manager? I told him: no, but I sing sometimes. 'Then you must sing', he said. 'Go, sing!' . . . When we went to his hotel the next day, he made an appointment for a recording session in Paris. That was it. No talk about money, no contracts. We weren't even sure what kind of a recording session he meant. But Duke Ellington said that's what we must do—so that's what we did! . . . At the session, he came in with a lady friend on one side and his arranger, Billy Strayhorn, on the other. He asked me, 'What shall we do, darling?' I said 'Solitude' and he said, 'Marvellous! Let's go!'[33]

(Only six tracks from this session were initially released, as *Duke Ellington Presents . . . The Dollar Brand Trio*. The rest of the session was only rediscovered, remastered, and released in 1996.)

The story of Dollar Brand from that point on is well known. Using Zurich as a base, he and Benjamin (who was renamed Sathima by another exile, Johnny Dyani) commuted to the United States and other European venues, returning briefly to South Africa for the birth of each of their two children, whom they wanted born on African soil. In 1977, they set up a permanent base and later a small recording studio and label, Ekapa, in New York.

Ellington's patronage had been instrumental in securing Brand gigs at the Antibes/Juan-les-Pins, and Palermo festivals in 1963, and in getting him to Newport in 1965. Increasingly, though, his own distinctive style spoke for itself and found him willing playing partners on the New York free jazz scene, including Don Cherry and Ornette Coleman, as well as more mainstream gigs with Elvin Jones and a continuing run of festival and club work on both continents.

Brand's route to reconnection with African music was his conversion to Islam (when he took the name Abdullah Ibrahim) in 1968. At that point, in critic Ian Carr's words, he changed 'from a very good musician to a great one':

> In his music of the 1970s and 1980s, composition and structure are as important as improvisation . . . having rediscovered his own identity, his art gains immensely in its power and projection, incorporating African chants, carnival music, rural laments and the sonorities of church hymns—the inner-voicing of chords and the moving (and emotive) bass lines.[34]

Sathima performed and recorded far less frequently. Ellington's question had been prophetic, because she spent much of the 1970s bringing up children and looking after business: the Ekapa label was her project. However, she has told many interviewers that she links bearing her children with the flowering of her talent as a composer and lyricist. And, for her as for Ibrahim, it was the reconnection with Africa that was most influential in what she created. Like many exiled musicians before and since, she began to long for home (and to reshape home in her dreams) almost as soon as she left. This gave her one half of her repertoire in the form of glowing reimaginings of the romantic ballads she had heard at her grandmother's house in the 1950s and sung herself in the 1960s. It provided the other half in the form of new songs, starting with the 1974 'Africa':

> I've been gone so long
> . . .
> I've come home
> To smell your earth
> To laugh with your children
> To feel your sun shining down on me.

Benjamin's biographer, Carol Anne Muller, notes that when Benjamin sang the song in Cape Town in the 1970s, some South Africans did not know what Africa she was talking about, but that people in New York 'understood'—in Muller's words '[this] speaks to a complex interface between the identification of place and cultural and individual memory and imagination'.[35] That weaving of the real, the remembered, and the hoped for was what almost every musical exile tried to express in his or her music, and it is a theme picked up by content, by titles, and by lyrics again and again. For Benjamin, the narrative was overlaid by a running debate (inside and outside South Africa, and within the community itself) on the identity and 'Africanness' of members of the so-called coloured community.

Her relatively rare appearances nevertheless won her enthusiastic fans in New York for what was becoming an increasingly personal and distinctive style. Her own American heroes included other song stylists like Betty Carter, and she was far more interested in shaping a song to reflect the inner resonances it held for her, than in being a crooner or an ingenue: 'I pick songs for what they say *to* me and what I can say *with* them. The music has to follow that'.[36] *Downbeat*, picking up the Eastern inflections of the Cape jazz heritage, described her voice as 'strong as pyramids and creamy as kefir', while the *New York Times* noted 'she could make a word cry out with just a flicker of vibrato'.[37]

Benjamin and Ibrahim returned to Africa in 1982, spending two weeks touring Mozambique and in cultural debates with Mozambican cultural workers. In the same year, their joint project, the *Kalahari Liberation Opera*, combining drama, music, and dance to tell the story of a victorious South African liberation struggle, toured Europe to considerable critical praise. Sathima also composed a three-song cycle, *Liberation Suite*, for her 1983 album *Memories and Dreams*, its song 'Nations in Me' engaging directly with the African character of an ethically mixed heritage. 'Because I'm from South Africa', she said, 'I feel very deeply about the struggle of my people . . . [but] I really don't like to stand up there and make speeches. . . . [In Mozambique] there was something that just touched us so deeply . . . you can see the joy that they feel in just having their country back, even though there's a lot of work to be done. And I got a lot of inspiration from there.'[38]

Ibrahim and Benjamin were able to make a home in America, but the pianist still spent much of each year touring Europe. Europe was, quite simply, less stereotyped in its 'ownership' of jazz and more open to new or experimental voices. It was not only South African players who found it so—avant-garde trumpeter Don Cherry, who settled in Sweden (and who was a regular collaborator with Johnny Dyani), is one of many American examples. As British critics Richard Cook and Brian Morton (in a comment not itself entirely free of stereotypes) put it:

In the 1960s, radical American improvisers (with separatist agenda firmly in mind) renewed their interest in African percussion. What was quickly evident was that traditional African musics frequently anticipated the methodologies of free jazz and that the sometimes anarchic energies of contemporary African jazz were already more abstract than the prevailing American models. In Europe, for a variety of reasons, this was perceived much more readily and there was a quicker and less ideological trade-off between African jazz and popular music on the one hand, and free music.[39]

This did not mean there was a lot of work, or money, an open-arms welcome from all European players, or huge numbers of audience backsides on seats (pianist Chris McGregor told Melody Maker in 1967 that he had actually overestimated the open-mindedness of the British scene), but there was some of all of these. It was the musicians of McGregor's Blue Notes (the pianist himself, saxophonist Dudu Pukwana, trumpeter Mongezi Feza, bassist Johnny Dyani, and drummer Louis Tebogo Moholo) who probably made the largest and most long-lasting collective impact on the European improvised music scene, as well as laying a foundation for the South African players who followed.

The Blue Notes left South Africa in 1964, after a successful national tour. (Saxophonist Nikele Moyake had also been part of the group, but the ill health that presaged his early death from a brain tumour led him to cut short his tour and return home.) They had an engagement at the Antibes/Juan-les-Pins festival that attracted favourable reviews, but after that the band briefly broke up as members followed European work offers, some of which turned out to be illusory. Gradually, through 1965, the band reunited in London, landing in a jazz scene restless for change, where the New Orleans revival music of the 'trad' movement was going nowhere except to debutantes' balls. The Blue Notes 'literally upturned the London jazz scene, helping create an exciting climate in which other young players could develop their own ideas about musical freedom. . . . There were times when rooms more accustomed to the anodyne, four-in-a-bar jocularity of [trad bandleader] Acker Bilk took on the gritty character of a Soweto shebeen. . . .'[40]

*Shebeen* and *kwela* are words that recur (not always accurately) in the comments of even the best-informed British critics (perhaps an indication of what *King Kong* had left behind). For someone who grew up with Chris McGregor, his brother Tony, the sounds of the Blue Notes' first album evoke something rather different:

> [I]n '67, with the group he went over with, called the Blue Notes, they released a first album called *Very Urgent* on the Polydor label. I'll never forget my experience of listening to that album for the first time, and being struck by how African—and not just African, but how Transkeian—it sounded. Here was this group of musicians playing in London, and recreating for me the sounds of the Transkei. . . . [T]here's a particular sound that that haunts me. . . . When I listen and think about it, the sound in the evening, as the sun goes down behind the hills, and all the women have made fires with cow dung, and there's that particular smell of the burning cow dung and smoke, and the sun going through the smoke. . . . [a]nd the young boys herding the cattle back, and they're whistling and shouting. . . . When I hear that album, I can hear the sound of the dogs barking and the herd-boys whistling and shouting to each other. The cattle lowing and mooing. . . . I can almost smell the cow dung burning.[41]

Among the young British musicians who were drawn into this new sound was pianist Keith Tippett, recently arrived in London from the rural West Country:

> One night I went into Ronnie Scott's Old Place on Gerard Street and the Blue Notes were playing. I'd heard John Coltrane, Albert Ayler, Charles Mingus—but I was bowled over by these guys. There was an inherent freedom and flexibility in the playing, coupled with impressive technique and a robust muscularity that I'd never heard live before. To a young Englishman like me, they sounded very African.[42]

In 1967, on the basis of the Blue Notes, Chris McGregor drew together the first incarnation of his big band: the Brotherhood of Breath, a much larger ensemble involving British and later European players and reflecting much of his own philosophy. McGregor was not unaware of the contradictions of being a white player in a black band—although Dennis Mpale, who lived and worked with him in South Africa, said: 'Chris wasn't white—he was just a musician'.[43] Idealistically, McGregor wanted to create a musical 'village' that 'transcended outdated concepts of national identity and the nation-state', and reflected not 'that highly organised compositional aspect of big-band music; I go more for moods, feelings and textures and most of my things are very sketchy—that way the guys themselves can contribute more'. At Brotherhood's birth, *Melody Maker* hailed it as 'the most urgent, explosive and powerfully swinging new big band to have appeared in years'. Brotherhood went through a dozen more incarnations (the next one not until 1970, with help from a British Arts Council grant) before McGregor's death in 1990, and was hailed by Dutch critic Frits Langerwerff as 'the best free jazz big band in the world'.[44]

During those thirteen years, at least three generations of South African exiles were represented in its ranks. Bassist Harry Miller replaced Johnny Dyani, who by then was living in Denmark; white saxophonist Ronnie Beer came in for a while. By the early 1980s, drummer Brian Abrahams, bassist Ernest Motlhe, and trumpeter Peter Segona were in the lineup; by the late 1980s young trumpeter Claude Deppa had joined the group. Playing with the band was an education, as Ernest Motlhe remembers:

> Mongezi [Feza] was an amazing person. I learned a lot from him—things that Weather Report were doing *after* we used to do them with Mongs. . . . [But] the university was when I worked with Chris McGregor. That's when I graduated. I learned to arrange. But he was a different kind of person. He'd show me things without me being aware he was teaching me. . . . [H]e'd write a tune and say, here are the chords, now arrange a rhythm, write a bass line for that. . . .[45]

The Blue Notes and Brotherhood of Breath did not have the uninterrupted smooth ride this part of the narrative might suggest. Some British musicians and critics ignored them; some were baffled by their diverse and unfamiliar sound-world. London itself was not a prejudice-free city. Ernest Motlhe, who arrived in 1972, remembers, 'It was still those Keep Britain White days. . . . I could write a book about finding a place to stay, walking from place to place. One time I ended up sleeping in my car for a while . . . they were very careful not to say [you're black], but you could feel that this guy—oh yeah!'[46]

There were other, subtler or simply thoughtless racisms, as singer Sophie Mngcina, studying in London, also found:

> When I was studying at the Central School of Speech and Drama in London, they had accent teachers—you study the physiology of the voice; we were taught accents. . . . This lady was using [the] wrong tapes. On these tapes was an Afrikaans-accented voice speaking, and she was saying, 'That's how the whites speak', and then she played a tape that she had

recorded of our Bishop [Desmond] Tutu, and was saying this was how we sound. 'Blacks' sound like that. . . . It was so much pain. I was sitting in the class, and she was teaching this pain. I stopped her, and said, 'You can't teach my accent, because the material you are using is wrong. . . . Do I sound like the people you just played?' And she said, no. When she teaches other accents like Welsh or Australian, she talks about their history, about the countries. . . . Why, then, teach mine in this manner? I was so furious that at one stage I wanted to beat her, and then I thought no, no, that'll be spoiling it for other blacks. Then to relieve this anger, I wrote an essay called *Hear Us Speak*, which says, do not caricature my language, because I, the black people, have plenty, plenty languages: my own language, my friends' languages, English and Afrikaans—I'm overloaded with languages and accents—so a little bit of respect, please.[47]

The pressures of this white, cold country and the stresses of exile told on the musicians. The stories of their friends and colleagues talk of restlessness, erratic behaviour, and the inevitable alcohol. Even Chris McGregor, who felt the pain of racism only secondhand, moved around a lot, finally relocating to France, where the logistics of sustaining a pan-national big band were easier to manage. Johnny Dyani settled in Copenhagen. Louis Moholo has spoken of sudden bursts of anger at anything that seemed to impinge on his freedom, even having to 'come in on four' in an arrangement. Apart from Moholo, all the Blue Notes died before they could see a liberated South Africa. Mongezi Feza was the first, of viral pneumonia in a London psychiatric hospital in 1975, where he lay in a bare room all night before his body was noticed. Yet the South Africans in London taught and supported their friends, who remember them with respect.

Keith Tippett:

We really became friends with the South Africans. There was a lot of cross-fertilisation on the scene and we played with everybody, but the Blue Notes—sometimes more than British musicians—enfolded us and encouraged us. Socially, too. They were the people we hung out with.[48]

Music organiser and commentator Robert Abel:

[Pianist] Django [Bates] . . . related how much he had learned from Dudu [Pukwana], of how to *use* one's energy, how to play the same tunes every night and make them *fresh* and of how, when he was with Zila [Dudu's London band], they would tape every performance, and the following morning review the tape. 'Dudu would put the tape on— immediately—so you'd play all night, then you'd get up in the day and listen to what you'd played—it was sometimes hard to handle *that* amount of music!'[49]

Even sympathetic friends brought problems. Many musicians hated being patronised, something Pops Mohamed—in London in the 1990s—summed up as 'you sometimes wonder if they're only listening to your music because— shame! you're a poor, oppressed South African'.[50] In addition, musicians in- volved in solidarity activities were aware that the long arm of the South African Special Branch was still fingering them, and their families at home might be at risk. Ernest Motlhe had his own way of dealing with the first issue. The second just kept him on his toes:

> I used to feel bad when people are feeling sorry for me, so when people ask where are you from, I'll say I'm from 'the southern part of Africa', and while they're still scratching their heads—I'm gone! And I learned really fast not to answer politically because I realised that each and every one of us had the South African Special Branch looking after him. . . . [Once, some band members had document problems returning from Belgium,] and there was this guy just standing there, watching what was happening, and Julian [Bahula] said, please can you help explain to these people, and the guy said—in Afrikaans!—'Tell them yourself; you guys think you're so clever!' . . . We looked at one another, like: what have we done now? But that kind of thing, it sharpens you up.[51]

A number of factors still made London a hospitable base, including the im- portance of the city in antiapartheid activities, its increasingly cosmopolitan de- mographics, the existence of venues like the Africa Centre, and other sources of support, including Arts Council grants and social security payments to musicians without work. (Dudu Pukwana was later the first African composer to receive an Arts Council grant, to work on the soundtrack for Professor Ali Mazrui's television series, *The Africans*.) There was a UK university performance circuit for which both the band's politics and the fact that they played innovative jazz you could actually dance to were very well suited.

The Africa Centre was a mixed blessing: both Gwangwa and Ernest Motlhe have commented on its sometimes haphazard organisational style, with Motlhe remarking wryly, '[It] always struck me as a homeland kind of place—everything was always delayed: I mean, even if you only wanted to buy a beer you'll queue for a long time. . . . 100 Club was better—another home—because you had this vibe of South Africans'.[52] Yet the centre was vitally important as a source of information and cultural contact with home and with the rest of the African continent.

Like their counterparts in South Africa, the Blue Notes dropped the Trane- style dark suits and ties that in South Africa had asserted African modernity against Afrikaner reaction and retribalisation, and began wearing dashikis and Nyerere jackets in solidarity with independent Africa. Pukwana took his own band, Spear, to Festac in Nigeria in 1977. On a personal visit to Botswana in the 1980s, he told me how amused he was that he had ended up giving away almost all his lavishly decorated West African shirts to South African and Botswana musicians who admired them—'And these are things I got in England, and you can't get them here!'[53] Pukwana and his Swiss wife, Barbara, had held their wedding at the Africa Centre. Several South African players in England told me how much they valued the briefings on South African and African politics the centre hosted. But it was for collaboration with the rest of musical Africa that they all remember the place most affectionately. Guitarist Louis Mhlanga (whose family was part South African, but who had grown up in Zimbabwe and Botswana) arrived in London in the late 1970s. His parents believed he was studying refrigeration engineering—and he did, for a few semesters:

> I used to travel and do gigs in other places, Liverpool, Birmingham, working with poetry groups . . . we had all kinds of poets: from Kenya, Jamaica, Ghana and some who were from Britain too. . . . I met a lot of guys from Osibisa, Teddy Osei, Spartacus. . . . But reggae was the most dominant thing at that time, so whatever you do, you always put a little bit of reggae in it. . . . [S]ome of the Jamaicans, when they saw us as Africans, they'd say ah, no, we can't associate with Africans, you can't trust them, and it was always some story about Nigerians, or something . . . so you have to find a place where you can belong and be accepted. . . . I didn't compromise; I couldn't have cared less. I said: OK, if that's how you want it, I will just push to you through the music. And that worked. . . . There was this place called the Africa Centre and it . . . helped to put a lot of people together . . . not just African people, but British people too. Eventually, through that, I just had to go to West Africa: I said, let me just go there and find out for myself, and I went to Nigeria and worked with King Sunny Ade.[54]

London was also part of a small but vibrant network of modern European jazz innovation that critic Charles Fox, in his 1972 book *The Jazz Scene*, dubbed 'Common Market Jazz'. Many of the South African arrivals gravitated towards this kind of experimental playing.

Ernest Motlhe:

> There was quite a culture shock, but I was lucky to meet up with people like Julian Bahula [from home, who introduced me to] Pete Sabatin, Jim Dvorak, Derek Bailey—it was an experience to be working with those guys. . . . Keith Tippett's Centipede; Elton Dean's Ninesense; Trevor

Watts' Moire Music . . . there was a new style of music that was very strong around then, contemporary, playing modal, and that attracted me very much.[55]

Percussionist Thebe Leyere:

Initially, I thought the Europeans had a completely different attitude to free music. I found it a bit hilarious. Here were all these musicians talking and theorising and making a big intellectual deal of this music, whereas in Africa it was a common, everyday thing. We didn't need to talk about it, it was just there. I was really bamboozled by some of the ideas, but eventually I realised we were all alike. . . . It was quite daunting to find it was such a minority music and it frustrated me because I was the only African playing it. When I went to Vienna with Company and met George Lewis, that was important. I thought okay, so there are other black people involved over here. But I'm still the only African. . . . In Africa, we live with art all around us . . . poets, actors and musicians are all available for each other. . . . When I first met Bill Evans, he was working in a group called Coherents. They had all these things going on: slides, visual art, poetry. It felt like being back in Africa for me.[56]

Lepere, however, also felt the constraints of being put in an ill-understood category of 'African' musician, even on the free scene:

At first when I started playing over here, people saw a contradiction with me using traditional African rhythms in free music. I try to get around that by making sure that whatever rhythm I chose fitted what was happening in the music. Gradually, I'm beginning to leave that and try new things, inventing new rhythms, creating new textures and combinations of instruments. I can't be trapped by playing in just one style, my concepts and ideas would just shrivel. I play free music because it's honest. It either happens, or it falls flat on its face.[57]

Out of all these collaborations came the real, long-lasting impact of South African music on the British and European jazz scenes. It happened in three main areas. The big-band style of Chris McGregor seeded British big bands of a new type: joyously eclectic, slightly anarchic, and often employing the call-and-response patterns of African music. One such was the early Mike Westbrook Concert Band, also developed at Ronnie Scott's Old Place. Its 1967 debut, *Release*, has even fooled a few South Africans into guessing it a South African band.[58] Some of that impression is created by South African Harry Miller's bass lines, but there are also the joyous dissolves into free jazz that had characterised Brotherhood's sound: the way the solos bounce around between the horns; Dave

Holdsworth and Bernie Livings sounding, on the second reprise of 'The Few', astoundingly like Mongs [Mongezi Feza] and Dudu [Pukwana]; and the fact it's all done over strict-tempo dance-band drumming from Alan Jackson. The benevolent wings beating over the music are those of Glenn Miller and Gene Krupa: a shared heritage.

The innovative big bands lived into the 1980s and 1990s. They often had South Africans or musicians who had played with them on board. Both pianist Django Bates and flautist Eddie Parker who had played with Pukwana were leading lights of the '80s free collective Loose Tubes, while the younger South African trumpeter Claude Deppa played in the Jazz Warriors, with black Britons Courtney Pine, Steve Williamson, and Julian Arguelles, all of whom had worked in Brotherhood. The Jazz Warriors in particular helped shape the next new wave of British jazz, one whose tide Ernest Motlhe was detecting just before he left the UK in 1990: 'The biggest change was when the West Indian kids started to play jazz. . . . [E]ven I ended up playing with Courtney Pine. It was something that was growing slowly. People were learning to appreciate and stretching out. . . .'[59]

The contribution to improvised music was huge and continuing. Whether Thebe Lepere with George Lewis in Vienna, Johnny Dyani with Don Cherry or Okay Temiz in Copenhagen (or with Abdullah Ibrahim—Dyani was one musician with whom Ibrahim continued to love playing free), Louis Moholo in dialogue with Irene Schweizer in Switzerland, or Dudu Pukwana duetting with John Stevens in London, the albums have become legends. Those players who still live, like Moholo, and the younger generation, like Deppa, Sean Bergin based in Holland, and percussionist Thomas Dyani, the bassist's son, still attract critical acclaim. So, too, do the haunting recitals of pianist Bheki Mseleku, although his story belongs more to the 1990s, when what guitarist Selaelo Selota called the musical 'fragments' began to be gathered back together.

Many UK sessions were released on the Ogun label, founded by South African bassist Harry Miller and his wife, Hazel, in 1974. Their first release was by the Brotherhood of Breath, followed by work from Chris McGregor, the Blue Notes, Keith Tippett, and Miller himself. Hazel Miller's twenty-fifth anniversary reminiscences of the label indicate the breadth of the London free jazz scene, and the way the label related to a general political conscience in jazz circles:

Ogun promotions were responsible for organising concerts, tours for the groups, even a nine-week series of Jazz Riverboat specials on the Thames, with Derek Bailey, the Harry Miller Four, with Willem Brueker and Trevor Watts, Mike Westbrook, Lol Coxhill and the Mike Osborne Quintet, etc. Great fun! It was such a busy and productive time, especially running Lambeth New Music Society, formed by Stan and Jackie Tracey, John and Janet Surman, Mike and Louise Osborne, Harry and I. Organising a weekly jazz club, Grass Roots in Stockwell, South London, a jazz summer school, promoting various concerts at Lambeth, Islington Town

Halls, and the final event, three concerts in the garden of the V & A Museum. During this period, Jackie Tracey and I organised The Musicians Action Group and spent a couple of days in the MU [Musicians' Union] offices, addressing envelopes to all the musicians to pressure the Union to back their claims that the media, radio and TV were not supporting this music. Forming Ogun was all part of these activities and convictions.[60]

Their quality and the intensity of the musical communication at this time can be judged from the CD re-releases of that material that are now reappearing. The 1970 *Outback* teams Chris McGregor, Harry Miller, and Louis Moholo with Barbadian flugelhorn player Harry Beckett and the fiercest and most searching British altoist of the period, Mike Osborne. Two twenty-minute tracks explode starbursts of phrases from Beckett over rumbling, clattering, helter-skelter percussive piano from McGregor, while Osborne reaches out to touch the edges of a song.

In Scandinavia, similarly intense communication was happening between bassist Johnny Dyani and a range of other players, including American exiles Don Cherry and John Tchicai. On the 1978 *Song for Biko*, with Cherry, Dudu Pukwana, and drummer Makhaya Ntshoko, there is bluesy sadness, elation, and lyricism, in the opening abstract ballad, 'Wish You Love', which Dyani dedicated to 'my people'.

South Africans played across the musical spectrum, even sessioning on the pop scene, with Dudu Pukwana getting airplay (and then radio banning) for a mildly risqué pop cover, 'Telephone Girl', and guitarist Lucky Ranku clandestinely invading the indie charts with a cracker of a solo on Jimmy the Hoover's 'Kill Me Quick'. Their third major contribution was the creation in the UK of a market for a genre that might justifiably be dubbed 'London Township'. Bands like Julian Bahula's *malombo*-styled Jabula and Jazz Afrika, Pukwana's Spear and Zila, and the ensembles of later arrivals like drummer Brian Abrahams' District 6 pianist Mervyn Africa and guitarist Russell Herman, all grew an enthusiastic British audience for the more dance-oriented side of South African jazz, particularly through regular sessions at London's 100 Club. That legacy remains, in bands like Township Express, steered by Ranku and singer Pinise Saul.

The music found an audience because it was infectious and skillfully played, but its development also coincided with increasing overseas interest in South Africa, through the antiapartheid activities of the 1970s and 1980s. If Sharpeville was the first major atrocity to wake up some European media, the 1976 uprising—and one iconic picture, of a dead child, Hector Peterson, being carried from the slaughter by two other weeping school students, one his gym-slipped sister—was on front pages around the world. Solidarity organisations grew everywhere: in Europe, most prominently in Britain, the Netherlands, and Scandinavia.

The commercial music industry was slower to catch on. Johnny Clegg recalls taking his music overseas to try and secure recording contracts:

> I personally took [*Litany* and *Universal Man*] to EMI in Germany, and they said, 'Look, that's incredible but we don't care about the Zulu wars or these funny little issues in South Africa, please don't bother us with them. If you have an experience which is universal, then write about it, but don't lay us a heavy about Africa, we're not in Africa; we're in Germany'.[61]

If one component of South Africa's exiled diaspora was the informal networking of players, the other was the framework provided for that by the international cultural activities of the African National Congress.

Jonas Gwangwa believes that South African music before the 1980s did not make the impact it should have, because '[people said,] "Oh, interesting . . ." but it was just our style [as individual players]. It was not really seen as South African music, not getting the attention that people gave to highlife or bossa nova, say, because at that time there was nothing overall coming in from South Africa to back it up. . . .'[62] There was a government, and it was backing musical exports—like *Ipi Tombi*—but both had all the credibility of a seven-pound note. The ANC's diplomatic and cultural offensive from the late 1970s provided a way to create credible relations with South Africans that bypassed a pariah regime, through the ANC's Department of Arts and Culture, whose most high-profile activity was the touring theatre show of the Amandla Cultural Ensemble.

Gwangwa followed his studies with a varied career in the United States:

> I got into writing music for movies, I've done plays and all of that was just a daunting challenge until you get past it. . . . The fact that I had worked on this album for Harry Belafonte and [Miriam] Makeba—*An Evening with Makeba and Belafonte*, which was a Grammy award winner, opened doors a little bit for me. . . . I had a group of my own, I travelled, and did some concerts in colleges and a few gigs here and there. . . . But I figured that before I became an Americanised African, I have to go back home and try to regroup and grab a little kryptonite![63]

It was Africa—home—that would provide the strength and power to keep Gwangwa's music flying:

> I started doing work for the ANC. I was called to come and help with music, because there was a group of young musicians and singers who were in Angola—they were MK cadres, and I was supposed to help with their music, but when I got there, I just got into doing a play of sorts.

Wrote some scripts, got a little bit more acting and everything, and came out with this show called *Amandla!*, the cultural arm of the ANC. Travelling the world, telling the international community about apartheid and exposing the indigenous culture of South Africa . . . mobilising support— spiritual, financial, material. . . . They were doing all the traditional dances of all the ethnic groups. . . . I knew I could create a show that would have universal appeal: the musical structure is very simple, the rhythm will get you, the dances are attractive—we even had one of the girls playing saxophone, which surprised some people. . . . And that was my main job, of course. [In the mid-1980s,] we hit London with *Amandla!* after flattening out Britain—starting in Aberdeen and going all the way to Brighton, crisscrossing the whole country.[64]

The cast of *Amandla!* came from the ANC military training camps in Angola, augmented by a number of older, more experienced South African musicians, including Gwangwa, trumpeter Dennis Mpale, and later saxophonist Steve Dyer. The post-'76 exodus of young people had included many talented writers and performers, and both the ANC and the international authorities looking after refugees had, from the earliest days, tried to foster self-made entertainment and provide cultural as well as general education. Exiled South African academic Jack Simons, who was in the Nova Catengue camp in Angola in 1978–1979 running political economy classes, recorded in his diary an account of the kinds of entertainments that were developing as a result:

At night, a cultural evening . . . followed by [a] concert (highlight a drama, centred as usual around a shebeen—the most vividly remembered social aspect of Soweto life—coupled with crime. Bantustan removals and resistance—the political element a relatively new note in shebeen acts).[65]

*Amandla!* as it developed under the direction of Gwangwa and the tutelage of other professionals, however, was far more sophisticated than these early agit-prop skits. Gwangwa had learned in the United States about the necessity for slick, disciplined stagecraft and variety in programming. Over its long run, *Amandla!* also took on board ideas about acting and dance from clandestine contacts with a flowering new theatre scene in Johannesburg and Cape Town. So scenes telling political stories did so through rapid-fire, witty dialogue from well-costumed actors making carefully orchestrated stage moves. Music interludes sandwiched the drama: struggle songs sung by marching workers, rural dances from traditionally garbed villagers, elegiac ballads, and jazz numbers that allowed established and aspiring instrumentalists solid space to solo. The show stayed in touch with contemporary South African music fashions: when the neotraditional hit parade at home was dominated by the *mqashiyo* sounds of Mahlatini and the Mahotella Queens (a male 'goat-voiced' singer with an energetic female chorus),

*Amandla!* used *mqashiyo* style to sing about Umkhonto we Sizwe. Gwangwa employed the same technique in the script:

[In Britain,] they knew about SA—but whether they knew the actual facts, that's a different story, and that's what we were doing with *Amandla!* . . . People always used to come and say: this story you're doing, is it a story or is it true? And everything was true. Because I always added or changed something to the script to tally with whatever's happening inside the country. Even mid-stream . . . we were in Moscow at the International Youth Festival, and they bombed the Kouberg power station, and I said: man, we're putting that in the show tonight! The cast were backstage, and I just wrote something. I had these two fantastic actors, Papa and Dikeledi, and they'd just shut themselves in the toilet, go through it, come out and chew them up on stage! . . . [T]he audience always thought we had a tape behind, like *Ipi Tombi*. . . . [T]hey kept quiet, listened, which disturbed us at first—and then the applause: so many ovations![66]

If *Amandla!* was the most public face of ANC cultural activities, it was underpinned by a range of others at organisational and diplomatic levels: clandestine work with performers based in South Africa; meetings with various governments on aspects of the cultural boycott; arts education for refugees; seminars and publications (from 1985, the ANC Department of Arts and Culture published its own discussion journal, *Rixaka*). Policy—the cultural boycott abroad; culture as a weapon of struggle at home—was vigorously debated.

But as *Amandla!* signalled, these activities were as practical as theoretical. Just as in South Africa jazz players were revisiting traditional roots with the pan-African awareness of the 1970s and 1980s, equally interesting musical bridge-building was going on in Botswana, though the Medu Arts Ensemble.

Botswana had long been home to a large community of South African exiles. Medu was founded in Gaborone in 1978, with the aim of providing an organisation for refugee writers, artists, and performers and point of contact for those still living just across the border in South Africa. There had been some tensions between early refugees and local people, so another aim was to build a platform for collaboration with local counterparts, and in southern Africa more broadly. Medu ran art classes in schools and prisons, staged plays, concerts, and exhibitions, held discussions, and published a regular newsletter containing graphics, poems, stories, reviews, and debates. By the 1980s, both Jonas Gwangwa (who was a founding member of Medu) and Hugh Masekela had homes in Gaborone, and the Medu music unit found itself the home for two bands: Kalahari (led by Masekela) and Shakawe (led by Gwangwa). Both combined South African and Botswana musicians.

Medu was the organising force behind the 1982 Culture and Resistance Festival. That brought together overseas exiles like Abdullah Ibrahim, home-based players like Kingforce Silgee, and Botswana-based musicians. Those still living in South Africa who attended saw performances by people who had been away so long their names and achievements had become (often censored) legends. Those who came from afar were affirmed by the demonstration of vibrant, militant activity at home.

When, on 14 June 1985, the SADF launched its murderous raid on Gaborone, the Medu structure was a prime target. Artists and organisers were among those killed (see Chapter 6), and homes owned by or rented to players were destroyed. In the days that followed, unmarked cars cruised the Gaborone streets by night, looking for those they had missed. Gwangwa tells the story of a terrifying twilight chase. As he turned from the main road to smaller and dustier lanes, his suspicion that a car might be hunting him became certainty; it relentlessly followed his every unlikely detour. He was saved by local people: when he reached a suburb of more crowded traditional housing and recounted his plight, they let him move on foot through their homes into alleys too narrow for a car to follow. 'And then I had to run with my family', Gwangwa recalled. 'I had to take those same roads again: London, the U.S. Again'.[67]

Refugee artists were on the move again, trying to get partners and families to safer homes elsewhere. Medu ceased to exist overnight; its formal activities relocated to London and Lusaka. Informal infrastructure—particularly the network of personal relationships—however, survived. The music did not stop, although artists like Gwangwa and Masekela now became occasional visiting guests rather than regular performers.

Kalahari toured and recorded with Masekela, who brought a twenty-eight-track mobile studio into the country to make his 1992-released album *Beatin' Around de Bush*. Kalahari lead guitarist John Selolwane ended up touring with Paul Simon. Bassist Aubrey Oaki now fills the bass chair in Lucky Ranku's Township Express in London.

But it was Shakawe—which never toured outside or recorded—that best realised the Medu vision of working collaboratively with local players and creating a sound that drew on SeTswana tradition alongside Johannesburg and New York modernity. The band included Jonas Gwangwa, Dennis Mpale, and Steve Dyer, plus keyboardist Tony Cedras (whose occasional alternate was piano-playing Motswana journalist Rampholo Molefhe). Cedras had worked with Oswietie, Estudio, and Pacific Express before leaving South Africa. The rest of the band were Batswana: a bassist and occasional additional horn players came from the ranks of the Botswana Defence Force, the guitarists Bonjo Kedepile and Whyte Kgopo and the drummers Tsholofelo Giddie and Jaapie Phiri.

Much of Gwangwa's current repertoire was developed during his time leading this band. Some of it draws explicitly on folklore—'Ledimo' ('The Giant') and the hunters' song 'Batsumi'—but it was in performance that the dynamism of the collaboration most strongly emerged. Kedepile's guitar was heavily influenced by veteran traditional players like Ratsie Setlhako and George Swabi, and he brought their style of extended guitar narrative into his solos. The exiles, in turn, were feeding in new ideas about music and presentation, giving spare traditional songs marabi, *mbaqanga*, and modern jazz arrangements. Gwangwa's trombone voice did not always speak with the bluesy swing of America; he also used it to carry simple pentatonic melodies: soft, delicate, breathy.

The collaboration worked well because Gaborone's relative prosperity, as the capital of a diamond economy, provided bustling performance venues every weekend: most notably, for South African jazz, the Blue Note, and the Woodpecker. The city was just 15 kilometers from the South African border; the Woodpecker fronted a river that was the border—musicians used to joke that they were providing entertainment for the South African border post troops. Bands like Sakhile, Bayete, Malombo, and many more visited these venues, feeding into the dialogue with Botswanan musicians. On the dance floor, another electric mix of styles was happening, as South African visitors demonstrated the latest Soweto steps alongside the older styles of local people who had been migrant miners—or were farmers just visiting town from remote rural areas. At the same time, ideas and information were travelling in and out of South Africa: some of it struggle-related, as Sipho Mabuse described in Chapter 6; some of it the personal news of family and friends that was one component of Gwangwa's 'kryptonite'.

Around Medu and these venues a community thrived. Drummer Tsholofelo Giddie summed it up: 'Working with these people, and meeting people from South Africa just shows: as musicians, we all sit under the same tree'.[67]

The tree had huge branches. By the late 1980s, cultural solidarity was an international enterprise. In December 1987, the ANC Department of Arts and Culture, the Dutch Anti-Apartheid Movement, and the CASA Foundation hosted the Culture in Another South Africa conference in Amsterdam. They had set it up in close, clandestine collaboration with union and UDF cultural desks inside the country. Culture and Resistance was the model for the combination of performance and debate, and many of the same delegates managed to make their way overseas to attend. For Jasper Cook of the African Jazz Pioneers, it was an eye-opener:

> It was just announced: you are going to Amsterdam. Because it was couched like that, I understood it was a secret thing. When we got there, it was the most wonderful experience for me. More particularly because I was white, I was completely a victim of the information shadow, if you like. I had no idea that the ANC had so successfully focused on the incarceration of Nelson Mandela and that they had become so big, and so respected. When I got to Amsterdam and found that our 102 from South Africa were joined by over 200 exiled musicians and all of them with a commonality of purpose—well, it just blew my socks off![68]

**The Genuines.** *Credit: Lloyd Ross/Staffrider*

For Ian Herman, with the Genuines, the emotions were overwhelming. The band let rip as never before:

I remember, there was something called the CASA conference. A whole bunch of artists went over to Amsterdam. They had this big gala evening and [the Genuines] were on stage playing before thousands of people in an opera house. It wasn't the right venue for us, because when we came on, people said we played so loud: we played jazz, we played rock, we played *goema*—sometimes all at the same time. We didn't play one ballad. We just looked at one another and played. Some people—even South Africans—were furious with us: 'What are you guys doing?' They thought we had a fuck-you attitude. But that's not what it was. We were just expressing ourselves, just trying to play the music.[69]

Writer Mandla Langa remembers:

In the nightclub called The Milky Way, Basil Manenberg Coetzee and his group Sebenza were to perform. Standing in the wings were Jonas Gwangwa and Dudu Pukwana . . . the hardest moment was the moment of parting. Here were South Africans from all over the world, including

Basil Coetzee plays at CASA. *Credit: Rixaka*

South Africa itself, who for seven days had discussed, argued, resolved issues, moved, using the same step, laughing, singing and sometimes crying. The moment of parting was laden with a mixture of sadness and hope: sadness that we would be separated by all these boundaries; hope because we all felt that the event had become another rock against the edifice of apartheid.[70]

By the late 1980s, too, solidarity against apartheid was attracting the kind of major profile—and the kind of commercial and marketing interests—that had previously told Johnny Clegg to forget his 'funny little issues in South Africa'. It had begun with a shift among Western governments, which Hugh Masekela asserts was linked to the impact antiapartheid music was making on the young.

> Because the international music community became our friends, they went to find out more about SA, and by the 1980s it was the rule rather than the exception to put political songs into your repertoire. . . . [E]veryone was getting educated about what was going on in their countries by the artists. And by then the Western governments had to turn around, because the populations of their countries said: 'According to our musicians, we shouldn't be friends with that government'. And that's what really turned the country around because America, France, Germany had to say to [F. W.] de Klerk . . . that if [he] wanted to stay in office, things would have to change, because 'our musicians have contaminated our people's minds'.[71]

Music was only one factor among many others, including economics and geopolitics, but it was certainly a major presence in the campaigns. There were movies, too, including the 1987 *Cry Freedom*, for which Jonas Gwangwa co-composed an Oscar-nominated score, and internationally touring theatrical productions, many of which had begun their life at the Market Theatre.

By 1988, the example of *We Are The World* and the power of cultural and political campaigns led to the staging of a massive Nelson Mandela birthday tribute at Wembley Stadium with TV rights syndicated worldwide. The idea came from Jerry Dammers of British radical Ska band the Specials (one of the founders of Artists Against Apartheid in London) who had previously staged antiapartheid concerts at big outdoor venues like Clapham Common; the production was subcontracted to Tony Hollingsworth of commercial concert promoters Elephant House Productions. A crowd of 72,000 attended, and although there was some controversy about the lineup and staging, 'in areas where local political movements were able to use the Mandela Tribute to advantage, it served as an important buttress to local organising and education'.[72] (Most of the righteous messages did not make it into the U.S. transmission by conservative channel Fox-TV, which Steven Van Zandt described as 'neutered'.[73])

It felt a little different for the South African musicians. Jonas Gwangwa, who played at both the birthday tribute and the 1990 Wembley concert to celebrate Mandela's release, describes how, as South Africa began to become an international brand, there were ominous signs that the ownership of the music was again contested terrain:

> Such problems! . . . [T]his guy who is supposed to be in charge, producing—Tony Hollingsworth. We had such a fight with him because he said: this is not a political show; we don't want any political music. And we are saying, but we are South Africans, for us this thing has been going on for a long time and we can't just be singing love songs . . . we're talking about a freedom show. But that guy didn't want anything of that. . . . [And that was the second time that happened] because at the eightieth birthday concert, where I was supposed to play the national anthem, they said, 'A trombone can't play that . . . we're going to get some little small instrument to do that solo' and [ANC cultural representative in London] Wally Serote said, 'Well, *this* time a trombone is going to do it. If you've never heard a trombone leading the national anthem, you'll hear it now!' [But it was a moving thing] because we got the Manhattan Brothers to perform, who were about the same age [as Nelson] Mandela and that was almost the last time they performed together; and the crowd—they accepted us and, well, it *was* a celebration. . . .[74]

Factors were falling into place to create more opportunities for South African artists to work and study overseas. Big public events, films, and commercial projects like *Graceland* drew attention to some musicians. So did the solidarity network with its concerts, while the cultural structures of the ANC could and did facilitate contact between musicians in South Africa and, particularly educational, opportunities overseas.

As the apartheid regime came under increasing international pressure (and was, in fact beginning covert talks with the liberation movement), it became slightly easier to obtain travel documents, although the process was still arbitrary and secretive—and many people known to be involved in the struggle continued to be denied permits.

In 1986, a British producer, Mike Perry, took Winston Mankunku to London to record his first album in more than a decade, *Jika*, on which both Bheki Mseleku and Russell Herman guested. In 1989, South African producer Koloi Lebona was able to take a larger group to London. Among them were Chris Columbus's saxophonist son, Ezra Ngcukana, whose resulting album was called *You Think You Know Me (But You'll Never Know Me)*. The title song had been written by Mongezi Feza. The album is full of soaring, defiant, straightahead solos, applied to tunes from the canon—like Chris Columbus's 'Izwe Lifile'—and new compositions such as the restless modern jazz of 'We Will Win', with its chanted chorus of 'We will win—solidarity!' At the other end of the age scale was a much younger saxophonist, McCoy Mrubata, whose album was called *Firebird*. The title track was composed by pianist Jabu Nkosi, who had worked with Sakhile and whose father had been Zacks Nkosi, one of the giants of the early township big bands. The number starts as a gently coasting fusion groove, which then miraculously segues back and forth between America and *mbaqanga* without losing either the potential for dancing or the cues for fluent, attacking solos from the young reedman. Like the phoenix of the album title, South African jazz at home was rising from the ashes of the 1980s.

Other players, such as drummer Vusi Khumalo and his bassist cousin Bakithi, found that the *Graceland* record was creating the opportunity for overseas touring:

> [A]fter a month or two or so I got a call—I was still staying in Soweto at the time and I didn't have a phone in my house—I got a call from a neighbour and when I went there I heard this funny accent: 'Hey, are you Khumalo?' I said yes, I'm Khumalo. 'We want you to take your passport to an office in town; we need you guys to come to the States on such and such a date'. I was like, 'Wow! Man!' This was a dream to us, you know; we always talked about these kinds of things, listening to all these guys from overseas. And in a week's time, everything was arranged and we went to the States. When we got there, there were limousines—it was like in the movies! . . . [J]ust imagine, from South Africa where you always pick up your own drums, I mean we had technicians there; I didn't even have to pick up my sticks at some stages; I'd leave my sticks there and when I got to my room everything is there; whenever I want to go somewhere, there is a car to pick me up. . . .[75]

A few white musicians, not under passport restriction, had made that kind of journey much earlier. One was guitarist Johnny Fourie, who worked in London at Ronnie Scott's Club and in the Ray Ellington Orchestra, then returned to South Africa to work on new ideas:

> One night, a guy walked in with the *Downbeat* magazine . . . showed me that I had managed to poll eight votes in the category Talent Deserving of Wider Recognition. Which made me think a little bit, 'cos now I was back here in South Africa. . . . I stayed here for two years, changing my style—got involved with Miles Davis' *Bitches Brew* stuff, and then I felt, right, now is the time for America. So I went to New York. . . . I just jumped on a plane and went, not thinking about all the ramifications of legality and things like that.
>
> I stayed in the States for two and a half years. It wasn't so awesome, because I had the English experience, which is pretty big, you know. Dur-

ing the London days I had been to the Catskills [mountains in New York state] with Ray Ellington, so I knew what the place looked like. Even though it's such a huge place, it still just an island—so within the first two or three weeks I was getting phone calls—people knew I was there. Everything was going very nicely there; I was playing quite good, I was getting calls and I was doing things. In fact, I think I had been there for about two weeks when I recorded an album with Charles Earland, which included some very famous guys—Billy Cobham, Hubert Laws, Jon Faddis—it was also the last recording of the trumpet player Lee Morgan. That happened inside two weeks and it looked all on track. But I could just not get the green card right, no matter what I did. That eventually culminated in me coming back home in the middle '70s, and [I] immersed myself in the studying of music on a more formal scale than I had ever done—and I've been here ever since. . . .'[76]

Fourie's colleague in Abstractions, Carlo Mombelli, went to Munich just over a decade later. His reaction on arrival demonstrates how South Africans from all communities remained wide-eyed about the overseas scene:

Me, being young and naive, I think I'm going to walk down the street and I'll say, 'Oh, there's Keith Jarrett over there having a coffee—Hi, Keith!' . . . Second day in Munich I walk into the ECM offices, say, 'Hi, I'm Carlo Mombelli, I'm from South Africa, I'd love to make a record with you guys. I want Jack de Johnette on drums, Nana Vasconcelos on percussion and on guitar I want John Abercrombie. Here's my cassette, here's my number'. . . . [T]hey must have looked at me and thought, who *is* this guy?[77]

Others, too, felt that rather scornful response from a scene awash with jazz players.

Barney Rachabane:

It looks a very tough place to be, New York. Maybe I was lucky to be there playing with Paul [Simon]. I could never in my mind imagine hustling in that place. Arrgh! Very tough. And almost everybody's a musician there. You'll see a guy sleeping in the park and he's got his saxophone. Street sweepers are jazz players. People working in offices. . . . It's so different. People are also a bit cold.

Ian Herman:

Americans are very puritanical generally, you know. . . . [P]eople think that America's the world. So it's hard for outside music to really break in here, but in New York, San Francisco and [Los Angeles], where people are more open-minded, it's easier. But as for the rest of America, whoo! It's tough. They aren't ready for the world.[78]

Yet there was some interest in what South Africa had to offer, particularly from other musicians. Ian Herman believes the late 1980s was the right time to arrive in America, with U.S. jazz riven by the debates over neoclassicism and smooth jazz and a search for styles that were neither:

Jazz education was lacking for my generation in South Africa, so our interpretation of it . . . was a long bridge for us to cross, because it was a foreign thing. . . . [G]uys started from a fusion standpoint. Which is OK, but you're jumping in the middle of the pool before you can swim. . . . For me, going to New York was like crossing that bridge, [t]o see the land and the people and have a feeling for the music. Tony Cedras was there, the Khumalos were there, who'd been playing with Paul Simon. Ray Phiri was also there . . . so I was able to stay there through my connections with the guys from back home; nurturing and looking after each other like brothers. . . . [American jazz players] were interested in me because I was from South Africa. They wanted to know what I could bring to the table.

Barney Rachabane:

[Saxophonist] Michael Brecker used to say this is unique, man. He never hears anybody in the world play the way we play. Even if you try to play the American tunes written by Americans, you still have our flavour. We're born with it. A mixture of African and American sounds—it's just different.[79]

Yet by 1990, it was not America but home that was the focus for musicians. With the freeing of Nelson Mandela and the expected liberation of society and culture that must follow, where would the music fit? The 1990 Zabalaza Festival in London—in some ways, a follow-up to CASA—intensified the debate within the ANC (now clearly, a government in waiting) about the future options for cultural policy. As well as the usual concerts, exhibitions, and platform debates, more than 400 delegates also workshopped on possible postliberation strategies for education and training in the arts, and on options for government policies and structures.

For young saxophonist Zim Ngqawana, overseas on a short-term International Association of Jazz Educators (IAJE) study scholarship in 1991, it was Max Roach who helped him to crystallise the questions and the tasks:

When I heard Archie Shepp on record, I knew it was for me—the sound! the emotion! He had a class called 'Revolutionary Concepts in Black Music.' I know some students, especially white students, would walk out of that class. They couldn't handle the content. . . . But he taught a lot of things about the saxophone itself, the technique and the philosophy behind it, the whole society-political-economics around it. . . . My master, Max Roach, taught me a lot of things inside and outside the music. When I was leaving the U.S., at the airport, he embraced me; he reminded me our responsibility is to maintain and preserve our cultures. My goodness! I didn't know anything about his culture and I realised, standing there at JFK [Airport], that I didn't know nothing about so-called African culture either! . . .[80]

# Notes

1. See, for example George McKay, *Circular Breathing* (Duke University Press, TK).

2. G. Sekoto, *My Life and Work* (Johannesburg: Viva Books, 1995), 77. Sekoto encountered an almost automatic assumption that as a black African he must be musical; fortunately, he was able to live up to these expectations and even published his compositions in Paris. But his biographer, Barbara Lindop, notes that his African compositions often adopted an exotic 'Zulu' image, despite his origins among South Africa's Pedi people. 'It was another aspect of the alienation that distressed him so much,' says Lindop (conversation with the author, 19 February 2004).

3. Interview for *Ubuyile*, 2001.

4. Ibid.

5. Keorapetse Kgositsile, conversation with the author, Botswana, 1984.

6. Interview for *Ubuyile*, 2001.

7. (London) *Times*, 24 February 1961, p. 17, quoted in B. Lindfors, ed., *Africans on Stage: Studies in Ethnological Show Business* (Bloomington: Indiana University Press, 1999), 78.

8. Interview for *Ubuyile*, 2000 and 2001.

9. Ibid.

10. Ibid.

11. History of the Africa Centre, Africa Centre Web site at http://www.africacentre .org.uk.

12. From Beril Becker Associates press release, November 1959, quoted in B. Pyper 'Draft working paper on South African Jazz in New York' (New York, 2003), 12. I am indebted to this source for many stimulating ideas related to the experience of Miriam Makeba and Hugh Masekela in New York that have contributed to this chapter.

13. Paper delivered at the University of the Witwatersrand, WISER symposium, August 2003.

14. Interview for *Ubuyile*, 2000.

15. Ibid.

16. Ibid. (In fact, though Makeba's first trip to Guinea was in 1967, she did not permanently leave the United States until 1968.)

17. Ibid.

18. Interview for ABC Ulwazi series on exile and return, 1999.

19. Quoted in the liner notes to Dyanyi's 1978 Quartet album, *Song for Biko*, Steeplechase (SCCD311109, 1987).

20. Interview for *Ubuyile*, 2000.

21. M. Davis and Q. Troupe, *Miles: The Autobiography* (London: Picador, 1990).

22. Interview for *Ubuyile*, 2000.

23. Interview for *Ubuyile*, 2000.

24. K. Braun, liner notes to CD *Miriam Makeba: The Guinea Years* (Stern's Music, 2001).

25. Quoted in R. Jacobs, *The Way the Wind Blew: A History of the Weather Underground* (London: Verso Books, 1997), 107.

26. P. Guzman, 'Masekela No Lose It', *Village Voice*, 11 September 1984, quoted in Pyper, op. cit., 9.

27. Interview for *Ubuyile*, 2000. *What's Goin' On* was released in 1971.

28. Interview.

29. Interview for *Ubuyile*, 2000.

30. Various newspaper articles; Kidjo in an interview with the author, 1995; and, to the author subsequently, the entire lineup of backup singers for both Manu Dibangu and Femi Kuti.

31. J. Collins, 'Some Anti-hegemonic Aspects of African Popular Music', in *Rock the Boat: Mass Music and Mass Movements*, ed. R. Garofalo. (Boston: South End Press, 1992), 193.

32. I. Carr, D. Fairweather, and B. Priestley, *Jazz: The Essential Companion* (London Paladin, 1988), 246.

33. Sleeve notes to *One Morning in Paris: Duke Ellington Presents . . . The Dollar Brand Trio* (Enja, 1997).

34. Ian Carr, in Carr et al., op. cit.

35. C. Muller, 'Sathima Beattie Benjamin Finds Cape Jazz to Be Her Home Within', in *Sathima Bea Benjamin—Embracing Jazz*, ed. L. Rasmussen (Copenhagen: The Booktrader, 2000), 34.

36. Conversation with the author, 2001.

37. Quoted by Muller, op. cit., 33.

38. Interview for the Swiss magazine *Jazz* with Sally Placksin, quoted in Rasmussen, op. cit., 18.

39. R. Cook and B. Morton, *The Penguin Guide to Jazz on CD, LP and Cassette* (London: Penguin Books, 1994), 909.

40. Valerie Wilmer, quoted in T. McGregor, 'Prophets Without Honour', *Two-Tone*, September/October 1992, p. 11.

41. Interview for *Ubuyile*, 2000.

42. Interview for *Mail and Guardian*, 19–25 April, 1996.

43. Conversation with the author, Botswana, mid-1980s.

44. All quotes from McGregor, op. cit.

45. Interview for *Ubuyile*, 2001.

46. Ibid.

47. Ibid.

48. Interview for *Mail and Guardian*, op. cit.

49. Quoted by Robert Abel in his unpublished article on promoter John Edgecombe and the South African music scene in London, 'Hearing Secret Harmonies'.

50. Interview for *Ubuyile*, 2001.

51. Interview for *Ubuyile*, 2001.

52. Ibid.

53. Conversation with the author, Botswana, mid-1980s.

54. Interview for *Ubuyile*, 2001.

55. *The Wire*, reprinted in *Two-Tone*, July/August 1992, p. 7.

56. Ibid.

57. Ibid.

58. This happened to me when I brought the tape to Botswana in 1983 and played it to a houseful of South African exiles.

59. Interview for *Ubuyile*, 2001.

60. Hazel Miller, '25 Years of Ogun Records', on the Ronnie Scott's Club Web site at http://www.conniescotts.co.uk.

61. Interview in *MEDU Art Ensemble Newsletter*, Gaborone MEDU Art Ensemble, 1984, p. 9.

62. Interview for *Ubuyile*, 2001.

63. Ibid. and interview for *Medu Newsletter*, 1, no. 4, December 1979, p. 32.

64. Material from both *Ubuyile*, 2000 and 2001 interviews.

65. Ed Sparg M. J. Schreiner, and G. Ansell, *Comrade Jack: The Political Lectures and Diary of Jack Simons* (Johannesburg: STE, 2001), 108.

66. Interviews for *Ubuyile*, 2000 and 2001.

67. Conversation with the author, Botswana, early 1980s.

68. Interview for *Ubuyile*, 2000.

69. Ibid.

70. M. Langa, 'Report on the Amsterdam Cultural Conference', *Sechaba*, March 1988, at http://www.anc.org.za/ancdocs/history/solidarity/conferences/casa.html.

71. Interview for *Ubuyile*, 2000.

72. Garofalo, op. cit., 60.

73. Quoted in ibid., 57.

74. Interview for *Ubuyile*, 2001.

75. Interview for *Ubuyile*, 2000.

76. Ibid.

77. Ibid.

78. Both ibid.

79. Both Ibid.

80. Ibid.

## Chapter Eight

# The 1990s and Beyond: Not Yet Uhuru

We have been importing music for so long. Well, fine. Now the world needs to hear how we sound.

—Jonas Gwangwa[1]

The space between the euphoric release of Nelson Mandela in 1990 and the inauguration of democracy four years later was long, fraught with complex political horse-trading, and bloody. In the Gauteng area,[2] 572 people died in train violence alone between 1990 and 1993, and the pattern of violence was repeated across the country. People died in bombings, massacres in townships and settlements, internecine fighting between factions, and especially intensified attacks by the 'Third Force': terror manipulated in a last vicious gesture by the apartheid regime's security forces.

Although the ANC was now legal, by the late 1980s struggle structures in the townships had been weakened through the detention (and, particularly in KwaZulu-Natal, assassination) of many leaders. The persecution of activists did not cease until after a new constitution and a new ANC government were in place. Street gangs who could be bought by the highest bidder—or were simply bent on rape and 'repossession' on their own account—flourished. Guns were easily accessible, as the weapons the South African government had distributed to destabilize independent Mozambique and Angola found their way home. This volatile mix was intensified by political rivalry between largely ANC-supporting settled township families from all ethnic groups and the temporary residents of the all-male migrant hostels. These men were predominantly rural, Zulu-speaking, and under the sway of hostel bosses—'warlords'—determined to spread the influence of the Inkatha Freedom Party. As historian Phil Bonner describes it:

Hundreds of young warriors arrived from Natal and formed a 'military core'. . . . The warlord . . . established a quasi-military regime in the hostel

261

and collected taxes from residents to pay for guns and ammunition. . . .
Rooms in the hostel were turned into weapons stores and arms factories.
. . . The warlord [told] the inmates the ANC wanted to undermine the
Zulu nation, its traditions and practices.[3]

Hostel dwellers who were of the 'wrong' ethnic group or political persuasion
(for by no means all Zulu-speakers supported Inkatha) were chased out and
sometimes also killed. Bands of well-armed hostel dwellers, with police-issue
rifles mysteriously prominent in their arsenals alongside traditional clubs, sticks,
and pangas, launched murderous nighttime attacks on township homes, killing
men, women, and children. Although the ANC had declared in August 1990 that
it was suspending the armed struggle, it nevertheless had to back the creation of
armed township self-defence units: too many people were dying. Many parts of
South Africa were effectively at war. The police, to paraphrase Nelson Mandela,
were fomenting the violence rather than quelling it.

It was not safe for people to walk the township streets, certainly after dark
and often even in daylight. Trains became too dangerous to ride. A township
music scene that had survived liquor raids, pass laws, and worse suffered its
death blow, and even music in the city centres, just beginning to open up again
to black patrons and players, had its audiences diminished. 'It was a big blow,
because there was no neighborhood scene any more. That was where young
players used to work on their chops and polish up their acts. Youngsters were
expected to arrive at the big jazz clubs with everything ready-made, but there
was now no place to do that preparing', recalled Dennis Mpale.[4] In the years
following, many more of the young players coming to national prominence in
jazz came via formal music institutions such as universities. The informal cradles
that had historically nurtured the music no longer functioned—and were not
replaced. And while the dominance of university-trained players today is the
result of a welcome growth of jazz opportunity in higher education, it holds a less
comforting message for youngsters from poor homes, with limited education.

The process of negotiations between the ANC led by Mandela and the last
apartheid government under F. W. de Klerk moved fitfully forward—almost de-
railed, at several points by some particularly vicious action, such as the right-
wing assassination of ANC and Communist Party leader Chris Hani. Grass-roots
campaigners fought for the message of the national peace accord. The date for
the country's first nonracial, all-party, universal suffrage election was set for 27
April 1994. When all the votes were in, the ANC ruled the country, with minority
representation in national government for Inkatha, who controlled KwaZulu-
Natal after a compromise over disputed votes was brokered, and for the former
ruling party, victorious in the Western Cape. At the national level, what were
considered the less strategic ministries went to the minority parties. One of them
was culture, allocated to Inkatha. (After the 2004 election, the Ministry of Culture returned to the ANC.)

This reflected the sea change in the official attitude of the ANC towards culture that had been brewing for some years. As poet Keorapetse Kgositsile points out, it took the ANC nearly seventy years from its foundation to establish a Department of Arts and Culture. But from that foundation, in 1982, grass-roots cultural organisations at home and ANC-backed conferences and events overseas had made the arts an important and high-profile part of the antiapart-heid struggle. In 1989, however, ANC activist and jurist Albie Sachs had presented a paper called *Preparing Ourselves for Freedom*. In it, he had called for a ban henceforth on the term *culture as a weapon of struggle*. The term, he argued, had elbowed out artistic nuance in favour of sloganeering and had led to criticism that evaluated righteousness above quality. Besides, it was time once more to sing love songs.

Sachs's intention was not to attack individuals or their efforts. But many artists, writers, and musicians were devastated. 'It felt like being kicked in the guts', said Dennis Mpale. 'Like no-one valued what we had done. And like there was going to be nothing for us to do in the future. Which is not true, because, politically, we're not there yet. Winning elections is just the start'.[5] In 1992, singer Letta Mbulu made her first South African album. It was titled *Not Yet Uhuru* (*Uhuru* meaning 'liberation'). Other musicians, too, argued then and now, that social tasks remain in which they should play a role.

Sophie Mngcina:

Music is storytelling. It should conscientise and talk about [the things] that are happening in this country. . . . We're not free yet; we've just been liberated.

Pops Mohamed:

For me, South African jazz is about people. It's about their struggles, their everyday lives. . . . Listen to Zim Ngqawana, he plays and expresses himself so that you could almost cry. If you listen to Kippie Moeketsi—the wailing of the saxophone—you know the guy's trying to make a statement. That's what our jazz is about.

Bheki Mseleku:

Jazz has to do with people fighting for their freedom. It's not just an American thing. What helps me to understand [John] Coltrane are the Zulu musics, Xhosa musics, Indian musics I was born among. My music says: I want to be free. [But] those who have marketed jazz were the ones who were oppressing its makers.

Zim Ngqawana:

Music isn't just notes. Every note has a social meaning. I'm singing my
mother's knowledge of the plants that grew around her; my father's religion; the African transformation that we need. . . . We are not scared to
say that the revolution is not over. We still need to work and refine our
music, education, economics, everything. It's in the interest of some people to perpetuate what is already in place . . . to go forward in blindness,
we have to hide in ignorance. Ignorance and arrogance—that's a bad
combination! That's one of the problems with this 'African' nonsense:
African Renaissance—what does it mean? It means nothing. . . . The
system is no longer about South Africa. It's about controlling the whole
world. We are being gobbled up in a global village.

Moses Molelekwa:

I think jazz is quite a spiritual music. . . . [You need] the freedom to
choose a route no matter what anybody says—go ahead and do it and
then you've awakened something. . . . But there's a social responsibility
that comes with that as well, because a lot of artists . . . feel what people
in general feel, and they try to reflect that—or also show maybe another
way, another approach. Besides music being a powerful industry, it is also
a very special way to deliver messages and influence people. . . .[6]

Sachs's statement impacted at the point when the South African arts community needed to start designing new structures and processes to redress the inequalities of the past and simultaneously deal with both a globalised cultural free
market and the drying up of antiapartheid cultural funding from abroad. (Do-
nors believed the government would now take over support for the arts.) Its
effect was to further alienate grass-roots cultural activists from an arts establishment relieved that the 'distractions' of apartheid and struggle were over—and
weaken the ability of activists to participate effectively in the debates. Writing in
1992, Kgositsile noted 'even now, the Department of Arts and Culture (DAC)
remains somewhat like a tolerated, mischievious stepchild of the [ANC] Movement, though in our various indigenous traditions and customs we have no
concept of a stepchild and we have no indigenous language that . . . carries such
a social aberration'.[7]
   (By the end of the 1990s, culture as a weapon of struggle was firmly back on
the agenda, this time in the service of a new cause. According to arts commentator Mike van Graan, 'in the struggle of people living with HIV/AIDS, their families and friends . . . the parallels with the Eighties are astonishing. There are new
freedom songs. There are AIDS exhibitions, AIDS poetry evenings, AIDS plays,
AIDS film festivals. . . . [A]rtists are being called upon to use their influence to

mobilise support for this struggle. . . . And there's . . . Nelson Mandela leading from the front yet again'.[8])

The new government, meanwhile, faced huge tasks. It formed a national Department of Arts, Culture, Science and Technology to replace the eleven racially and ethnically based education departments that had previously handled the arts. The unified ministry created arm's-length structures to allocate funding fairly: the National Arts Council, the National Film and TV Board, and the Pan-South African Languages Board. It restructured libraries, museums, archives, and sites though a unified Heritage Board and ended the SABC monopoly by granting licenses to an additional free-to-air TV channel and many (to date, over one hundred) small, independent community radio stations.

With limited funds available—and arts only one aspect of a huge legacy of unequal development—the government did not increase the overall spending on arts and culture. In the longer term, it envisaged that apartheid's regional Performing Arts Councils (PACs) would privatise themselves and become self-supporting. In the short term, it merely redistributed a small proportion of funds to other bodies. (The PACs are today privatised and reduced in scale, but they still receive a core government grant.) Even this was highly contentious, since any reallocation of funding from 'high' to majority culture was interpreted by some sections of the white community as a racially motivated or philistine gesture against them.

South Africa's 'high' culture had already caught the international malaise of shrinking audiences and rising costs, yet paradoxically it retained its government cushioning. In the period of adjustment, it was the independent and popular small community arts structures that collapsed. Donor support gone, their base communities simply could not afford to pay for the arts or arts education as a commodity at a market-related price, and the government would not pick up the bill.

In a process that took years, newly constituted local and provincial governments (these, too, had to be restructured—a complex process—to eliminate apartheid's duplication and separation) moved in to provide some support for community arts. The first years of democracy, though, were years of discontinuity between the vibrant, radical 1980s and the market-focused late 1990s.

In arts education, too, the same break occurred. Over time, schooling was restructured and desegregated, and parents with the means were able to place their children in what they judged the best state-run schools. State education in South Africa is free, but school bodies are permitted to levy fees to finance 'extras'. Parents have to buy uniforms and often need to finance some educational consumables. Private education is expensive. All private schools, but only very few public schools (largely those in former white areas), have music on their curricula, and music education has historically been financed as an 'extra'. A new universal curriculum, containing various aspects of arts education, including music (although subsumed under the rubric of 'Life Skills'), is still in the

making; it is currently targeted to launch as 'Curriculum 2005'. No specialist
music teachers have yet been trained for it, and no detailed teaching programmes
or textbooks have been published. In areas where donor-supported community
arts educators have lost support and the new curriculum has not yet arrived,
there is less arts education than formerly.

Drummer Lulu Gontsana describes the impact. He teaches at the country's
largest jazz summer school, the weeklong National Youth Jazz Festival at the
Grahamstown National Arts Festival:

> It's a wonderful opportunity, but it's not equal for everybody. Kids who
> go to the good schools can leave here, and go back to find instruments,
> music rooms, teachers, and practice and build on what they get here. So
> the next year, they can apply to come back and they have moved up a
> level. Kids from the township may have nowhere to practice and no-one
> to tutor them, even if they have an instrument. It's hard for them even
> to hold on to what they've learned from year to year. Some do, but I
> think many more fall.[9]

In the last few years, both donor and local government support have slowly
begun to return. Funded by a major bank, the National Youth Jazz initiative has
run classes in centres around the country, as well as during the annual National
Arts Festival in Grahamstown. Donor-supported foundations like the National
Field Bands (for brass instruments) and Buskaid (for string players) offer free
courses with performance groups, where talented students can display their
skills. Other arts festivals offer free short workshops, and the National Arts
Council has given grants to music education initiatives. A number of musicians—for example, Abdullah Ibrahim with the M7 Academy in Cape Town,
and Johnny Mekoa with the Gauteng Music Academy in Daveyton on the East
Rand—have found funding to set up their own jazz schools. Many more teach
privately, often using Robin Hood fees to subsidise their poorer students.

Provision at higher education levels has expanded enormously. Darius Brubeck's pioneering Centre for the Study of Jazz and Popular Music in Durban
now has company, with jazz courses in many university and technikon music
departments, including Pretoria, Cape Town, and Rhodes University at Grahamstown. University fees are high, but there are scholarship opportunities: a
student with very limited means, like guitarist Selaelo Selota, was able to progress
by this route from the community FUBA Academy (one of the institutions
forced to close when donor funding stopped) to the University of Cape Town,
where he further financed his studies by gigging around the city.

The backdrop to all these changes was South Africa's reemergence into the
world. Isolationism, censorship, and the cultural boycott ended. In their place
came the hosting of international sports contests and showbiz events and an
opening of the gates and airwaves to all kinds of global cultural products, includ-

ing those previously banned. South Africa's own cultural expressions swiftly had to become competitive in this market, too—indeed, a dominant theme in government statements on culture was the need to foster 'the cultural industries'.

While this was a sensible, realistic acknowledgment of the need to enhance professionalism and create real jobs in the arts, it also had other implications. The South African 'product' had developed on self-reliant roots during the isolation years. Much had not been documented or publicised, and styles did not always reflect international fashion. Some artists felt they needed to mimic overseas—in music, American—aesthetics in order to succeed, particularly if they had ambitions to work abroad. Some of the big record companies, especially in the early 1990s, stepped up the pressure for an 'international' sound. At the same time, imported television shows were suggesting a wholly different cultural framework.

Hugh Masekela:

Some of my African-American friends come here and say: 'Man, the thing that breaks my heart when I come here is I come to look for Africa, but I find a cheap imitation of myself. I find a wannabe me. You might wonder why we go to look at the animals in Kruger Park instead—it's 'cos we can't find the people!' . . . It's the last generation—the aged—who know our backgrounds, and who we are, and if we don't collect as much of that data as possible, we're gonna end up merely the wannabes that we wannabe! . . . The music and the traditional myths and all that stuff are not in our curriculums, you know? It's there, but we're not experiencing or absorbing it—or celebrating it.

Ernest Motlhe:

I had a trumpet student, very dedicated. I asked him, who do you listen to? And he said: 'I've heard them all, Wadada Leo Smith, everybody—but my main man is Don Cherry'. I asked him, what about Mongezi Feza? 'Who?' . . . [T]hese are the things we have to talk to these kids about.

Sean Fourie:

It despairs me greatly that everybody wants to leave the country and live overseas, where they think it's better. It's not better. This is the most amazing place in the world. . . . Other places have passed their sell-by date, while here, there's such a vibrancy. . . . Africa has been ignored since the New World Order, and here we sit with an undiscovered supply of music and culture [from] the land, and the way we live.

Paul Hanmer:

Americans have got a category for every conceivable type of American music, but for the rest of the world they've got one . . . insulting, lazy category: world music. . . . It's so unfortunate that people here are trying to copy things like gangsta rap, based on a culture that's about two millimetres deep, when we have a culture here that is measurelessly deep.

Pops Mohamed:

Everyone thinks to be an American is cool, but I'm saying it's cool to be African. . . . People today have lost their cultures—it's all about watching TV and 'Oh, I have a good reason to kill somebody: I saw it on TV' [rather than] 'It is against my culture to kill someone for their cellphone'.

Sibongile Khumalo:

This whole thing that we see on television of people walking out on arguments and banging doors—that's very rude. In African culture, you simply do not do that. The point is to reach consensus. . . . Isn't that how democracy works? If you do not agree with somebody, you don't have to walk out and be rude to them or go out and shoot or stab them. . . . The ability to put a burger together very quickly has negatively affected our ability to put a cast-iron pot on the stove and let something brew properly. . . . And in music, too, you can come up with something very quickly: programme it . . . but it doesn't give you that complete sense of satisfaction. It lacks the element of human flaw—the guy that misses a beat or a note—which is what makes music, music—Thank God they haven't managed to replace the human voice yet![10]

Record companies urged young artists to 'go American' because imported products were winning the competition war. Economies of scale meant major international labels could send complete packages for their artists—masters, artwork, promotion and publicity materials—into South Africa for a far lower cost than local companies needed to spend on developing and launching new talent. The returns on much local music were small, partly because of the highly niched marketing that apartheid categories had imposed: records sold into tight language groups with low disposable income, each a fraction of the total market. In another irony, it was the subversive, category-busting music that had brewed underground during apartheid, that was to prove the new success story and modify this situation. The big companies were slow to adjust. It was independent labels that turned the tide.

By the mid-1990s, a young white music marketer, Damon Forbes, was getting restless with the limited vision of his industry.

I sunk my teeth into jazz because it carried a world music message for me; it was truly culturally representative. . . . I just looked at the market and I saw the economics of the people of South Africa changing, due to better access to education. . . . [And] the workplace was going to change; a lot more black people getting into jobs that are of medium and higher income levels. . . . With all that, comes the aspiration to listen to better quality music. [So] the market in the long term is going to increase.[11]

With what he calls 'R1, 500 [just over $200] and a dream', Forbes established his own label, Sheer Sound.

The first artist he approached was singer Busi Mhlongo. Mhlongo had cut her teeth in the 1960s on Dorkay House jazz and on pop music, scoring South African hits both with a cover of Millie Small's blue-beat hit 'My Boy Lollipop' and a starring role in the Gibson Kente musical *Manana the Jazz Prophet*. Impatience with a small—and politically small-minded—South African scene took her to Europe, where she sang regularly with Dudu Pukwana and Louis Moholo at London's 100 Club and became hugely popular in the Netherlands with her own band, Twasa. After twenty years, in 1993, she returned home, her music now honed into a sophisticated blend of jazz and Zulu roots, with a stage show designed to appeal to international world music sensibilities. It was 'that world music flavour', says Forbes, that appealed to him. Sheer Sound took on the distribution of Mhlongo's Belgian-recorded debut album *Babhemu* in 1995 and sold 2,000 copies in the album's first year.

World music was beginning to scratch at South African ears. Shifty Music's Lloyd Ross and Warric Sony were selling albums licensed from labels like Sterns Africa out of cardboard boxes at the Saturday morning flea market that had sprung up in the car park of the Market Theatre. The formerly white SABC stations sometimes aired African or Latin tracks: the erudite Richard Mwamba was engaged to present an hourlong African music show for the main English-language station, SA-FM. On the newly repositioned black, assertively urban SABC Radio Metro, a remarkable DJ called Shado Twala took a maverick attitude to playlists, airing soukous, rai, and samba alongside *mbaqanga* and American jazz on her show. The pioneering Mesh Mapetla also offered a highly individual selection of music to jazz listeners, as he had tried to do even when apartheid controlled the airwaves. *Babhemu* garnered modest airplay, and Mhlongo began appearing on prestige platforms like the 1995 Grahamstown Festival. Encouraged, Forbes signed up more artists, to originate albums in South Africa for his shoestring label, including pianist Paul Hanmer and saxophonist McCoy Mru-

**Paul Hanmer playing in his own orchestral project at the Johannesburg Civic Theatre.**
*Credit: Cedric Nunn*

bata. 'I tried everything', says Mrubata. 'I talked to the big companies, and they
said they loved my style, but then again they wanted me to sound like something
else; use more sequencers, more electronics. I was on the verge of doing it myself.
I'd begun knocking on my bank manager's door to raise the money. Finally,
Sheer Sound came and took all that off my shoulders. They've been a godsend'.[12]
Mrubata titled the album *Tears of Joy*. He has stayed with Sheer, and his original,
often large group recordings, pick up the big-band feel and tradition established
by leaders like Tete Mbambisa and Victor Ndlazilwane in the 1970s.

Meanwhile, another maverick had also entered the scene. UK-based Robert
Trunz was chairman of the B&W speaker company and record label. Earlier in
his career, he had organised and promoted jazz in Switzerland, as he describes
it, 'hanging out with the Miles [Davis] posse'. He came to the newly liberated
South Africa to scout the new voices and seek out commercial opportunities,
and attended the 1993 Guinness Johannesburg Jazz Festival, held in the square
outside the Market Theatre. 'I was walking across that bloody square, when I
heard this piano and I thought: that's not Abdullah Ibrahim—but, hey, it's certainly got something!'[13] The piano player was Moses Molelekwa.

In 1995, with additional sponsorship from *Straight No Chaser* music magazine, Trunz pulled together Molelekwa and an eclectic gathering of more than
fifty other players who had caught his ears at two studios, in Cape Town and
Johannesburg. The team included reedman Zim Ngqawana, guitarists Mxolisi

Mayekana, Baba Mokoena, and Johnny Chonco, Pops Mohamed, former Sakhile members Sipho Gumede and Mabi Thobejane, veteran pianist Tete Mbambisa, Amampondo, vocalist Max Mntambo, and traditional healing singer Susan Hendricks and her percussionists. To the mix, he added some international B&W artists like trumpeter Byron Wallen, drummer Andrew Missingham, and Brazilian multi-instrumentalist Airto Moreira. The result was three CDs under the overall title *South Africa: Outernational Meltdown—Healers' Brew, Free at Last*, and *Jazzin' Universally*. The sessions are big, spontaneous, sometimes chaotic— and as stuffed with new ideas as a Christmas cake with raisins. Here, Ngqawana's 'Migrant Workers' Suite' gets its first airing. Molelekwa jams on tracks that, just months before, he had laid down for B&W on his debut album, *Finding Oneself*. Mohamed blends groove and Khoisan healing chants, as he was later to do with London DJs. Mntambo weaves his modern vocal style around Zulu song, an approach that would later win him a national music award. Club music meets roots meets acid jazz. Rough and cluttered as the CDs sometimes are, they are also an essential archive of the fresh impulses in South African music in the early 1990s. 'I still go back to [that period] for inspiration', says Mntambo. 'What we did was so spontaneous and creative, mixing with a bunch of crazy geniuses'.[14]

Trunz and Forbes were able to pioneer in this way because each had a strategy for bypassing immediate market pressures. For a time, their companies worked together on distribution and marketing. Trunz fed his innovative recording activities on the profits from high-end sound equipment. As the 1990s came to an end, however, changing technology and a changing market made this less viable. Many of the B&W (now MELT 2000) South African recordings had been too audacious to sell in huge volumes (though they attracted loyal specialist collectors).

Sales were hampered, too, by the conservatism of major record-shop chains. There were no record shops in the townships. Even today, ten years later, township dwellers can find locally only pirated cassettes, CDs, and DVDs sold by hawkers at bus stations, or low-priced pop cover albums in the supermarket branches that are beginning to put township small traders out of business. To buy specialty jazz, it is often still necessary to take a trip to a large mall, although mail-order collectors' clubs also function.

Facing these roadblocks, the impetus behind B&W's South African marketing initiative faltered. While the label still has a presence and continues to record local players, often in highly innovative formats, such as the *Sanscapes* blend of San music and club beats, its local profile is much lower than in its pioneering days.

Forbes simply kept costs to a minimum in the early days by doing almost everything himself, with a tiny support staff. Recording was hands-on; launches were phased over time, starting with a live concert where some tickets were sold, rather than a lavish free press junket. With some companies, Forbes says, a 'launch involves going to a boardroom, and everyone gets free alcohol and the record plays while they chat to one another. But for me, the essence is to actually penetrate the listener's heart and give them something that leaves them saying: that was really different, that was great; and feeling inspired'. These strategies allowed him to give artists considerable creative freedom, since he was not projecting for rapid, large-scale sales: 'There's a different definition of a successful album for a small company and a large company . . . where the album is done on a massive budget, the company has to sell massive quantities just to reach break even.[15] . . . A pop album has to make it over seven weeks. I'm sometimes looking at what I think is a jazz classic that might make it over seven years'.[16]

Sheer has grown exponentially on this careful base, with an average year-on-year growth rate of 24 percent to a current yearly turnover of R24 million. In 2003, it racked up its one hundredth album release. It has won twenty South African Music Awards across jazz, dance, and ethnic music categories; in 2003, it was the largest presence in the lists. There are now distribution deals in both the UK and the United States (with the HeadsUp label), and some Sheer albums have achieved impressive sales, even against overseas competition; Zim Ngqawana's *Zimology* has, for example, sold 18,000 units. The label has established a supergroup, the Sheer All-Stars (Sipho Gumede, McCoy Mrubata, Louis Mhlanga, Wessel van Rensburg, and Frank Paco), to showcase its artists overseas. Such outcomes were barely in Forbes's dreams in the mid-1990s, as he and his family sat, on a Sunday afternoon, individually hand-packing the delicate rice-paper inner liner of Paul Hanmer's debut album, *Trains to Taung*.

Yet it was those two early piano releases—Molelekwa's *Finding Oneself* for B&W and Hanmer's *Trains to Taung*—that marked the point when tracks labelled jazz reasserted themselves again as popular music for young people: the crossover moment. *Trains to Taung*, for example, sold only 200 copies in its first month, but over the next year rose to around 1,000 units a month. The album went gold in May 2002 and still sells a couple of hundred copies a month.

Neither album fits neatly into conventional jazz categories like 'mainstream' or 'fusion'. But nor are they broad-brushstroke *mbaqanga*, using limited instrumental jazz technique to paint a formula by numbers. Although 'jazz' through the 1980s had become a more diffuse presence, as it had elsewhere in the world, it remained an important source and reference. And each of these recordings, in its own way, is an explicit attempt to use the jazz process of invention, improvisation, and communication to revisit and re-present aspects of historic South African music.

*Trains to Taung* builds on a series of slow quintet grooves dominated by intense conversations between Hanmer on piano, Louis Mhlanga on guitar, and Jethro Shasha on drums. Some themes unroll sequentially, rather than following the head—middle eight—head recipe: travelling music with the piano percussive as often as it is melodic. The nine tracks of *Finding Oneself* range from stark marabi to complex, modern, multi-instrumental arrangements. Both releases share very similar musical goals.

Zim Ngqawana. *Credit: Cedric Nunn*

Moses Molelekwa:

Initially, you have a lot of African influences [and then] . . . the similarity
is in the phrasing and the rhythm—the swing . . . but there's a whole lot
more to South African jazz than just the swing. . . . I'd like to say [it's]
African jazz, because there are also African musicians in Paris doing
amazing work under the jazz title: using influences from their countries,
especially rhythmic ones, which also inspires me. I used to resist the jazz
label, [but] in Europe I . . . started understanding certain things about
the beginnings of the music and the history of jazz—and to understand
that what I'm trying to do is in the tradition. African jazz would be bringing your African roots, the African elements in raw form, and mixing
them with the existing jazz—that's quite a mouthful! . . . [On the track
'Ntate Moholo'] . . . I wanted to write a tribute to my grandfather, who
was a pianist . . . a song with a South African feel, with influences that
have come through artists like Kippie Moeketsi, Abdullah Ibrahim, Dudu
Pukwana: that feel . . . and also the influences that I got directly from
hearing traditional dancers and singers in the township, in particular,
travelling Pedi musicians and dancers. When I first heard them, I was
knocked out . . . hearing those rhythms gave me a bigger room to compose in. I also wanted to write something that was quite interesting rhythmically. As far as I knew, the only song that wasn't 4/4 or 6/8 that was
popular in South African jazz circles was *Take Five* by Dave Brubeck . . .
so I saw another angle of that rhythm—we could play the same time
signature and make it sound quite different. The rhythm element is a gift
and an important element in all native music, so I incorporated the 5/4
rhythm and the melody is based on a pentatonic scale: one of the oldest
scales . . . most marimbas, kalimbas, flutes were made on that scale. Those
were the elements I used.[17]

Paul Hanmer:

*Trains to Taung* was written soon after the period when I was having
doubts about my music. . . . I wanted to answer the question: where is
Paul Hanmer from? Where are all of us from? One way to do that was to
take very simple, age-old blocks—the I–IV–V, the marabi chords, which
[are] a basic format for so much music that has come out of this country
. . . in the way that, say, twelve-bar blues has become a format for so
much that comes out of America. But I thought that it must be extremely
old, because it relates to a lot of folk music from all over the world. It's
like marabi is the mother of a lot of music. . . . So, I thought, let me write
something that is based on this chord progression, but it's got a few
funny angles, and it's also quite sad, and the 12/8 groove—how slow it

was—reminded me of a train. I thought of a train going back in time, to that place that marks how ancient is the African human heritage: Taung[18] . . . the place where the Khoisan made the ancient elements of music, and the place where marabi came about is probably one and the same . . . it's an imagined space and time.[19]

*Finding Oneself* began an impressive (but tragically short: he died in 2001) career for former FUBA student Molelekwa. He worked in bands like McCoy Mrubata's Brotherhood and Umbongo, dedicated to keeping alive the music of Victor Ndlazilwane. After his meeting with Trunz, he teamed up with Mayekana, Mntambo, and UK drummer Andrew Missingham in the short-lived, high-energy combo Barungwa. He toured with Hugh Masekela in the trumpeter's South African band, Lerapo, toured on his own account to European festivals, and developed a highly creative piano partnership with British player Joanna McGregor, when *Guardian* critic John Fordham described him as 'the inheritor of Abdullah Ibrahim's mantle, a creator of hymn-like harmonies rolling under jubilantly jazzy melody lines, propelled by the leaping vitality of South African township music'.[20] His second album, *Genes and Spirits*, included a dazzling duet with Cuban virtuoso Chucho Valdez. Yet he found the South African scene frustrating:

The culture of jazz in this country is still the stokvel scene. That started off really radical: it was there that people latched on to bebop, Coltrane, other radical things in those days. And you can still see that fresh vision in the way old guys at stokvels dance: they work with old-style swing but they're always creating something new. But today listening is a lot more limited. Very little music from the rest of Africa finds its way there . . . the scene has become conservative.[21]

That conservatism affects other players, too. For many young musicians, the legacy of Sophiatown and township music is felt equally as inspiration and straitjacket.

Singer Gloria Bosman:

If there's one thing that's painful, it's being stuck. . . . We are willing to move from Sophiatown; to move from this year to another year and be doing new things. Jazz is here to stay, but at the end of the day, [music is] just do-re-mi-fa-so-la-ti-do, and that's it. We're tired of sitting in shady places, in corners of smoky bars—as if that's the only place where people can appreciate us!

Zim Ngqawana:

Taking my unit through America has confirmed . . . that our music has
a place in the so-called jazz tradition. We do not have to retreat to the
township thing that has become our comfort zone. . . .[22]

New platforms where musicians ought to be free to experiment have developed: clubs, festivals, a few commissions, and a preparedness from some theatre
managements to stage jazz in a concert setting.

Two landmark stage productions demonstrated the potential of jazz to move
outside a club setting and provided models for several later productions. Mo-
thobi Motloatse's *Nkosi: The Healing Song* at Wits University, with music directed and arranged by trumpeter Prince Lengoasa, explored the history and
meaning of the new national anthem. And at a newly respectable Sun City, Victor
Ntoni was musical director for *One Night's Journey into Jazz*, which offered a big
band made up of the country's top players, young and old, interpreting classics
from the South African canon.

Reformulated and with new sponsors, the South African Music Awards began
to move away from their original narrow ethnic musical categories—although
an artist who is clearly aiming at a 'world' sound, like vocalist Max Mntambo
(whose stage identity is now Shaluza Max), still finds his accolades within 'Best
Zulu Music'. South Africa is a regular finalist in the pan-African Kora Awards.
But few of these contests offer the opportunity to create original music through
commissions. The Standard Bank Young Artist Award at the National Arts Festival offers a platform for a well-resourced performance; only the Daimler-Benz
arts prize—awarded each year to a different creative genre—has made jazz composition possible. The 2003 winner, pianist Themba Mkhize, used the prize to
create an album based on his interest in traditional and popular vocal styles.

In Johannesburg, many 'jazz' clubs opened alongside Kippie's in the mid-
1990s. Some had the life-span of a mayfly, and not all staged jazz under any
interpretation of the term, but two at least did. Sof'town, founded in 1997, was
a huge supper club, managed by Garnett Godden, who had run jazz in exile with
such efficiency and vision at Gaborone's Blue Note in the 1980s. It showcased
established artists like Hugh Masekela, but more notably hosted the city's first
regular, open to all comers, jam session for many years. Out of those Tuesday
nights came a number of today's soloists, such as tenor saxophonist Sydney
Mnisi, today in the front line of a number of the city's most interesting bands.
Sof'town, though, was situated in an inner-city area on the economic way down
and became unviable after just over a year.

In the formerly prim white suburb of Melville, not far from historic Sophiatown, Brad Holmes founded the Bassline, in a shoebox converted shop, in 1994.
For nine years, the Bassline provided music six nights a week, including residen-
cies and a platform even for the most avant-garde. Out of the Bassline came

Voice, with Mnisi, trumpeter Marcus Wyatt, pianist Andile Yenana, bassist Herbie Tsoaeli, and drummers Lulu Gontsana and later Morabo Morajele. Voice functions as the city's most in-demand rhythm section, but it is also the kitchen for the music that most consciously picks up the heritage of the 'modern jazz' of those 1950s Odin Cinema sessions. The music of Voice, and of bands led by its pianist Andile Yenana, revisits South African classics like Moeketsi's Scullery Department in modern arrangements, but it also creates new classics in the same mould: intense, unafraid improvisation whose vibe is such that, in Paul Hanmer's words, 'you can almost smell the smoke and see the suits'.[23] The Bassline closed in late 2003: the one hundred or so covers the place could hold were increasingly failing to pay the musicians or the bills.

Kippie's beside the Market Theatre soldiers on, though now with music staged only at the weekend. Its role was eroded during the late 1990s by a large-scale, long-term redevelopment programme across the Newtown area where it is situated. Demolitions, roadworks, and derelict buildings made the area unattractive to both theatre and club-goers. Kippie's survived by becoming more of an amiable pub with live jazz. Only now, in 2004, with the Newtown redevelopment close to complete, can it seriously work on reconstructing the solidity of its reputation as a jazz club. Yet owner Sipho 'Hotstix' Mabuse says people continue to visit the club explicitly for the jazz experience:

> Jazz in this country has taken a turn for the better. . . . I'm actually amazed when I see who comes to the club—I mean, twenty-two-year olds—and when I ask them why have you come, when some of your peers wouldn't be seen dead here, the answer was: look, we come to listen to jazz, because we grow up, you know, when we listen to jazz.[24]

Other specialist jazz clubs were overtaken by the generation gap. Rumours, run by jazzman Art Kelly, flourished in the early 1990s when the mixed flatland of Yeoville was home to media workers, returned exiles, and students, and the entertainment strip of Rockey Street hosted coffee shops, bookstores, and even a little theatre, the Black Sun. The late-night Saturday jam round the Rumours piano was where players from all the city's other clubs could be found, after their engagements were over. But as the film directors, politicians, and graduates moved up and out to more spacious suburbs, Yeoville became home to many much younger, less well paid South Africans seeking a home close to the city centre, and to many recent immigrants from the rest of Africa. Its surviving clubs—now minus Rumours—shake to hip-hop, ragga, highlife, and soukous.

The dilemma of these Johannesburg venues is reflected in other South African cities and itself reflects an international trend. Jazz worldwide is now a niche music; in South Africa, the niche is quite large but often occupied by people with little disposable income. That pervasive poverty is the other part of the local spin on a problem compounded by the demise of neighbourhood venues in the townships. Uptown, upscale venues need to attract large numbers of high-paying patrons with possibly softer musical tastes. What survives is usually the venue with good food and a hospitable bar, where jazz is a background attraction not encouraged to astound, challenge, or drown out conversation.

The same pressures have also affected jazz festivals. A number of commercial interests, including Guinness, supported festivals in the early 1990s, but much of this sponsorship was short-lived, and by the end of the decade the scene was dominated by two major players. The Joy of Jazz circuit, with extensive support from Standard Bank, has linked a number of the discrete, smaller festivals into an annual circuit, its development activities focused on a weeklong youth jazz programme at the Grahamstown National Arts Festival. Like many similar international events, the circuit's programming is eclectic—its 'jazz' stars are equally likely to play reggae or R&B—and the festivals themselves range from seated concerts to huge (but very affordable) informal picnics on open fields or in stadia. Liquor is often prominent in festival branding. The smaller festivals remaining outside the Joy of Jazz circuit follow a similar formula (though some are far more haphazardly organised). Musicians have mixed feelings.

Sibongile Khumalo:

On the jazz scene, one is seeing a huge regeneration of interest in jazz, the festivals and the clubs. You're seeing some measure of experimentation and original writing coming up, which can only be good for the music. And what I'm liking . . . is that there is much more collaboration happening. Maybe some people would feel more secure if they knew there was a gig coming up and they could reliably call on the same people. But the flipside is that precisely because you do have to call on different people to help you, people bring in different energies and ideas. Take the ending of a song. You'll say, we normally end it this way. And they'll say, well, that's a very difficult way. Can't we try it this way? It keeps you on your toes; keeps the creative juices flowing.

Ernest Motlhe:

[At festivals] because the whole thing is treated like a picnic, the musicians struggle hard to gain people's attention, so they end up resorting to gimmicks, these catchy little things which boil down just to marketing. So I have a problem in that setting of not really knowing what 'jazz' is. My playing is very African; I have that within me—but I don't call myself a jazz musician. I'm an improvising musician. People just use these labels for marketing. Phillip Tabane is not just playing 'African' music. Phillip is a brilliant innovator and those labels have denied him that.

Zim Ngqawana:

The industry, sponsors, financial institutions, liquor companies, record companies have ganged up against serious musicians to turn them into marketing tools for their companies. They have no regard for the musician . . . they are trying to reduce him now to a liquor salesman.

Barney Rachabane:

Now there's an opening, opportunities we didn't get back then. These guys make a lot of records, and it's original music, which is nice. . . . But the history is not written anywhere. There's been albums, and now you don't even know what those albums were. The history of our jazz has been thrown away, so you can't blame [the youngsters] if they don't know about our heritage. And the whole thing, the festivals, is being controlled by the record companies. So you don't know if the guys are playing what they want to, or are being given direction. There's confusion about who or what is a jazz musician.

Jonas Gwangwa:

Too much is still the same. We still have promoters putting up shows with no financial resources, no planning, no written contracts. We still have clubs, which cannot provide a decent sound system and which treat artists in ways that, in the U.S., would have the Musicians Union picketing outside![25]

The other major festival player is the two-day Cape Town North Sea Jazz Festival (NSJF), sister event to that in Den Haag in the Netherlands. Cape Town North Sea, launched in 1999, sets standards in a number of ways. Building on the extensive experience of the Dutch event, it is tightly organised, attempting to maintain a clockwork schedule across multiple stages. Mixing musical genres to increase audience numbers is, it says, an economic imperative, but North Sea maintains one stage exclusively for sounds within the broad jazz church, and audiences for that stage have grown steadily. There was a gentle riot in 2002 when the room proved too small for all those wishing to hear Ahmad Jamal. (The festival has since moved to larger premises.) Unusually, NSJF balances representation, with thirty-plus acts split equally between South Africans and visitors. And it runs an extensive programme of free workshops and lectures supervised by former Hartford teacher Hotep Galeta, with direct, deliberate outreach to Cape Town's townships. NSJF believes it will reach break-even, as projected, in its fifth year: 2004. In 2003, it attracted nearly 15,000 visitors and generated R58.4 million (nearly $8.5 million) in revenue.[26] Unlike a Joy of Jazz picnic, NSJF is an expensive weekend out, particularly for jazz fans from other parts of the country. But I have encountered groups of mature and young people from township jazz *stokvels* who save up to attend, their presence evidence that the music's support base does survive.

But what are they supporting? The economic pressures on the music business, and the measures taken to counter them, have thrown the meaning of the J-word even more into contention.

Gloria Bosman:

You get to a point where you ask yourself what is real jazz at the end of the day—between New Orleans and Sophiatown?

Victor Ntoni:

People have the wrong perception of jazz today. The problem lies with the companies. There's no-one to make a musical analysis of what's actually involved, and you find it's either pure disco or some imitation of traditional music.

Bheki Mseleku:

Can you tell me what jazz means? A word that people can use about John Coltrane and Kenny G simultaneously? It says nothing about what the music is.

Zim Ngqawana:

Today we are hearing so-called jazz musicians—actually, people who surround themselves with jazz musicians, hoping to achieve with that. It doesn't work. If you meet up with people who do not practice the art form as sincerely as you do, [you may both say] 'Ja—this is my passion, my life, I want to marry this jazz music—let's do it', but their intentions are completely different—to rape the music! . . . [Y]ou'll come out of the recording session and feel filthy, like you need to shower and fast for a month! . . . This name jazz. We did not create it, we were given it to corrupt our expression. People are embracing it, adding to it, *kwai-jazz* and all this nonsense, [when] we do not yet understand our music.[27]

Ngqawana's reference is to the recent popular fusions of jazz with *kwaito*, South Africa's version of house music. *Kwaito*'s history is another instance of musical hybridity. Its roots draw from the flimsy pop ephemera of 1980s 'bubblegum' music, from imported house music records, and from the assertive, long-lived culture of the 1970s pantsulas. Pantsula dance and dress styles coexist on the *kwaito* dance floor with moves and modes from American rap and hip-hop. The name comes from the term *kwaai*, whose closest street translation is the Jamaican 'wicked'. One of the *kwaito* pioneers, singer and producer Arthur Mafokate, worked regularly with music video producers from the white (and, even in white musical terms, minority) industrial music scene. The images that made him a star combined gritty urban realism—the apartment roofs and Nigerian music clubs of Hillbrow—with the sinister and the surreal: in the video for his 'Oyi Oyi', giant white rabbits relentlessly pursue studio personnel. In the music, heavy bass lines (in the early days, emphasised by slowing the records on the turntable) support chanted African-language and urban slang vocals, sometimes aggressively sexist (Oscar's 'Isidutla' translates as 'fat bitch'), sometimes sharply socially aware (Mafokate's first controversial hit was '[Don't Call Me] Kaffir')—and often both. In live performance, male singers are stylishly scruffy and loose-limbed; for women, the dress code is skimpy bling with African touches, displayed with a defiant bounce. As a dance music, *kwaito* has enjoyed huge success; in some venues, it dominates over American sounds.

Producer Don Laka had the idea of combining the *kwaito* groove with more stylishly played instrumental solos to invent '*kwaai-jazz*', a catchy formula that energises crowds at festivals, although it does not display Laka's genuine ability as a pianist and composer. Unsurprisingly, many jazz musicians view such developments with a wary eye—some, because they believe it represents an important sacrifice of musical integrity; others because, like the parents of teenage music fans everywhere, they stand on the wrong side of the age divide, that age divide itself felt as culturally alien to African tradition.

McCoy Mrubata, who wants his music to reflect 'the new atmosphere of urbanisation', has punningly declared that he finds this teenage craze 'kwaitall right! Though I think they could make a richer sound if they used live instruments—and sometimes the lyrics are too vulgar and anti-women'.[28] Shortly before his death, Moses Molelekwa began experimenting in a collaboration with *kwaito* group TKZee:

> [C]reating music people can dance to is important, because it's important to win younger listeners for jazz music. . . . Look, kwaito is here to stay. And there are things in it I like very much—like the emphasis on groove and the use of chants and call and response in the vocals. But outside that . . . it uses a musical language that is very western, very American. I'd like to look at that idiom but find an alternative musical language that has more African elements.

Jonas Gwangwa:

> It reminds me of when I got to London in 1961 and rock n' roll was so strong. . . . [W]hen I got back here, kwaito was so strong and there's very

little space for other types of music, jazz included—and here, as soon as you take a solo, they label it jazz. . . . The struggle is still on, though there's a little bit more work happening. The other thing is the audiences. We used to have a listening audience, but now what's happening is a dancing audience, and that's precisely because of the venues. In the stadia it's only young people; people in their fifties and sixties are being starved.

Abigail Khubeka:

I wouldn't say that nothing good has come out, because some people love the kwaito we're listening to today. I admire the kids for being creative . . . but please let's not kill the other kind of music—mbaqanga, isicatham-iya—because that's where everything started from; it's our roots. We are very rich in music to fall back on, but we're inclined to wish we were somebody else.

Sophie Mngcina:

When that rap thing came up, people saw that the kids were into rhythm. But it became rubbishy when they started using swear words. As far as I'm concerned, let the kids make money—but they need to know they should move away from that quagmire.

Pops Mohamed:

There's still a lot of bad things happening, but I think more doors have been opened. We're seeing home studios all around the country, black people owning their own record companies. Young producers on the kwaito and rave scenes; great musicians like Mdu [Masilela], Brenda Fassie, Arthur Mafokate—even some semi-millionaires among our young people. I'm very proud of that—although I'd like to see some of it happening on the jazz scene, too. . . . [Traditional instruments and music are] dying a painful death. We have these new platforms now—drum n' bass, hip-hop, techno, house: all the things kids are listening to now. . . . Kids want to understand, but to listen in their own way. So we have to fuse the sounds with what [they] are doing. . . . Overseas, I've seen younger people going up to the DJ, asking what is playing . . . and when they go back to school—I've seen it happen in Germany—they start doing research. I've seen at least four students coming to Rhodes [University] because of that.[29]

Even within *kwaito* itself, some performers are becoming impatient with both programmed backing and limited melodies. Live instruments are beginning to

**Sophie Mngcina.** *Credit: Cedric Nunn*

appear, and some groups are looking back to the marabi and *mbaqanga* canon for inspiration. Infamously, in 2002, the group Mafikizolo 'borrowed' Sophie Mncgina's composition 'Mangwane' for their hit 'Ndihamba Nawe' without acknowledgment. After a painful newspaper spat, the group acknowledged their debt, and a royalties settlement was reached. But for Mafikizolo, the combination of house beats, marabi, and *mbaqanga* has now become a trademark: their 2003 album was called *Kwela* (with Hugh Masekela featured on the title track), and their videos and publicity shots show the group in sharp suits and Wooldro fedoras, with lead singer Nhlanhla Mafu in a '50s-style tea-dress. Whether this is a fashion-led fad or an illustration of the resilience of South African jazz sounds in township communities is still not clear, but at the time of writing at least three other *kwaito* groups are exploring the same formula. Thandiswa Mazwai, former lead singer with another pop group, Bongo Maffin, released an album in 2004 called *Zabalaza (Rebellion)*. The songs are mixed with clips of traditional Xhosa women's singing, and speak of the death of revolutionaries, the forgetfulness of their children, and the poverty and AIDS which—in a phrase recycled from the repertoire of the traditional praise singer—'should not be happening in my father's house'.[30]

Broadcasters, too, are looking back at the jazz tradition. The SABC has, slowly, begun to make space for the music in documentaries and magazine programmes and in other contexts; its TV channels, however, are going through a process of privatisation; new local programming is increasingly dependent on sponsorship potential. The free-to-air TV broadcaster, e-tv, memorably injected jazz into its youth-oriented soap opera *Backstage*. Set in a nightclub, the programme marked Freedom Day 2002 with a 'guest appearance at the club' by Abdullah Ibrahim.

One result of the opening of the airwaves was the appearance of independent and community radio stations. Many rely heavily on record shows, since they do not have the resources for independent feature production. Some broadcasters have complained about pressures on playlisting from advertisers, who feel that high-spending listeners are more likely to be attracted by a commercial sandwiched by 'international' (meaning American) music. Community stations in rural areas, however, can also provide a refreshing new context for both jazz and traditional music, airing them alongside gospel, pop, and hip-hop in a stimulating mix very different from apartheid radio's tight ethnic boxes.

Some radio stations have quite deliberately set out to follow new formulae. Cape Town–based P4 describes itself as a smooth jazz station, but its definition of smooth includes much South African jazz from all categories. Johannesburg's independent 'adult contemporary' Kaya-FM (whose initial patrons and contributors included Hugh Masekela and Sibongile Khumalo) aims at sophisticated urban tastes: its music features pan-African and jazz sounds in large helpings throughout the day, as well as in specialist jazz slots. Kaya also features the country's currently most popular world music DJ, Nicky Blumenfeld. The most iconoclastic of the newcomers is Y-FM, a youth station that set out from day one to win the youth and scandalise the parents (its launch invitation came in a mocked-up petrol bomb). Its initially tight R&B, hip-hop, and *kwaito* programming has proved flexible, with pan-African dance music and occasionally jazz making an appearance. On local content, Y-FM exceeds proposed legislated targets, with more than 50 percent of its music from South Africa—the top station nationally in this respect.

Y-FM DJ 'Rude Boy' Paul Mnisi has taken a different approach to African jazz. He has used historic tracks like Solomon Linda's 'Mbube' and modern riffs from artists like Zim Ngqawana as the basis for dance mixes: fast, compelling rhythm pulses punctuated by samples that advance and recede, with space over the top for live raps. In Cape Town, which has its own well-established local variant of hip-hop and club music, similar reimaginings are happening, with hip-hop DJ Ready-D and the anguished, edgy modernism of saxman Robbie Jansen a favoured collaboration. Overseas, Pops Mohamed has collaborated with the London Sound Collective, trip-hop musicians, poets, and others to produce innovative dance mixes, like the London club hit 'Fading Light': 'Teaming up with the London Sound Collective . . . [was] purely hardcore drum n' bass, so it was a challenge for me. I've taken samples from my kora playing, samples of Khoisan, Xhosa and other traditional sounds from South Africa and also strong vocal messages—why are black people behaving the way they do today?—and started sampling them onto drum n'bass'.[31]

These intersections between dance, sampled electronica, and jazz point to another development: the rise of a new South African avant-garde. The free jazzers and experimenters of earlier decades—Kippie Moeketsi in his era, then the Blue Notes, Robbie Jansen with Estudio, Carlo Mombelli with Abstractions, and others—had found South Africa deeply inhospitable at both musical and political levels. They left the country, or stopped playing, or switched to more conventional sounds. One of the positive aspects of the tsunami of international contemporary music hitting the country in the 1990s was that it opened a few ears, across all communities, to new aural possibilities.

South African jazz players take musical risks in various ways. Carlo Mombelli, in his group Prisoners of Strange, has used unexpected instrumental combinations that are drum-free, or pair two trumpets in place of a conventional front line, or feature a club dance drummer. There are samples: a child's dreamy voice; legendary operatic soprano Mimi Coertze. Texture, harmonies, and pulse displace catchy melodic riffs, and vocalist/trombonist Siya Makuzeni swoops, shrieks, and declaims as much as she sings. It is not music designed to be mass-marketed, but it has built up a solid following that cuts across age and race divisions.

In Cape Town, the group Tribe has bucked the city's affection for easy-listening dance beats to create improvised original music based on the duelling of Mark Fransman's piano and Kesivan Naidoo's intense, tightly packed drumming. Back in Johannesburg, reedman Zim Ngqawana has achieved the remarkable feat of staying one of the Sheer label's top-selling artists, while encouraging his audience to accept jazz with poetry (with former '80s struggle poet Lefifi Tladi); big, splashy orchestral abstractions in the spirit of Charlie Haden; simple, minimalist traditional themes; and ferociously abstract saxophone improvisation.

Bassist Ernest Motlhe says he is 'surprised to find how much appreciation for avant-garde music there is here. I know someone who runs a record shop in a little township, Silverton, and even there people are buying some of that stuff. But it's not always full appreciation. People are taking part in the music, which is good, but free improvised music is very dodgy, and you need education too. . . . Young musicians have learned something very dangerous: to market themselves and float on top of the music without really getting inside it'.[32]

The role model for much of this searching, exploratory music is Bheki Mseleku. The pianist served his early apprenticeship playing electric organ with R&B groups and then piano with Henry Sithole's Drive. He left South Africa with Hugh Masekela in the mid-1980s and stayed in London, working with fellow exiles like guitarist Russell Herman and as a solo pianist. His debut performance at Ronnie Scott's Club led to collaborations with a number of younger generation UK players, like Courtney Pine and Steve Williamson. His debut album, *Celebration*, set music with Latin and South African accents against the hard-driving rhythm team of Americans Michael Bowie and Marvin 'Smitty' Smith

**Bheki Mseleku.** *Credit: Cedric Nunn*

and was nominated for the Mercury Music Prize. Next, the solo live recording *Meditations* melded his vocal chants in traditional Zulu *izintu* style with helter-skelter keyboard runs and abstract, one-handed tenor saxophone motifs. By his third outing, the 1993 *Timelessness*, he was signed to Verve and working with Pharoah Sanders, Elvin Jones, and Abbey Lincoln. Each subsequent release intensified the connection Mseleku feels with the music of John Coltrane and with Eastern spirituality. But his postreturn album, *Home at Last*, made in 2003 after a long period of searching for the right backup team, was a surprise. Produced by veteran Koloi Lebona, it is a sketchbook of short, simple melodic themes. Like many other South African players, Mseleku is intrigued by the possibilities of simplicity. As another Coltrane admirer, Winston Mankunku points out: 'It's like Trane playing "Nancy". It's simple, but a lot has to go into it and sit behind it. You have to reach a certain place, here and here [he gestures to his head and his heart] before you can do that'.[33]

Some of the interest in new music is building fresh bridges between jazz and concert music. The conservatism of the South African 'classical' music establishment under apartheid was legendary. Black composers were discounted even more than excluded: large-scale black choral works were viewed as craftworks rather than serious compositions, and there were no opportunities for black composers to write for the all-white orchestras with any hope of performance. Even avant-garde composers, at the SABC's symposium on new music in 1983, were, in university music lecturer Mary Rorich's words, 'too white, too blinkered, too needy, too up our own orifices . . . to engage with context and change'.[34] Conservatism towards repertoire was reinforced by the arrival in South Africa of many Eastern European orchestral players, after the collapse of the communist states ended sinecures in national orchestras there. Paul Hanmer describes the situation as it existed in the late 1990s:

> There's a failure of imagination somewhere, a very fundamental one, in venues where mostly white people go to listen to orchestras as they have done for many years. Those halls are mostly empty, but when an orchestra goes to play in Soweto, the hall is jam-packed. The orchestra can be enjoyed by a huge number of people, but it's just plain racism and shortsightedness that the music coming from this rich tradition is not shared with more of the people of our country. And again, the people who would like to write for orchestra, or combine elements of jazz and South African music, get very little chance to do so—unless you are dead, orchestral musicians here don't play your music with any sort of respect. . . . They land here with an attitude that 'I've still got my salary; I speak Bulgarian or whatever, so who gives a shit anyway? I'll work with the orchestra and never go out to belong to the community of South Africa'.[35]

By contrast, choral music is big business. Since the Ford Choir competitions of the 1980s, the mass following of the music in the black community has at-

tracted commercial and media sponsors. Through this sponsorship, and competitions such as the *Sowetan* Nation-Building mass choir festival, choirs,
composers, and conductors are acknowledged and rewarded. Some winning or
well-known choirs have also been called upon to form the chorus for opera
productions.

The rewards, however, are not universal: to get the accolades, a choir must
have access to the event and be prepared to concentrate on the set works. Some
rural choirs lack funds for transport or for the lavish costumes that have become
essential for competition. While these requirements provide a direction, they also
discourage originality. When the Seventh Day Adventists South Africa (SDASA)
Chorale in 1997 collaborated with British a capella singers I Fagiolini on a programme of music ancient and modern, the resulting CD, *Simunye*, suffered from
this narrowing of choral vision. While the Virgin record store in London stacked
the CD high in the window, Gallo in South Africa had no idea how to distribute
it. It fell too far outside the 'normal' choral context, and choral music broadcasts
gave it little airplay.

Radio choral music is dominated by gospel—in particular by songs in the
American-influenced Pentecostal style by superstars like Rebecca Malope and the
Holy Spirits Choir. Malope sells more albums than all South Africa's jazz stars
rolled together. On television, the screens are filled by the costumed competition
choirs. Sibongile Khumalo feels the balance is wrong but is confident the scene
is still evolving:

> After big business recognised the potential of choral music, there was the
> sponsorship and all that. But it was good for the scene, because again one
> sees young composers putting pen to paper; creating new stuff. Some of
> it is almost like choral pop music; there's a lot of dancing and things
> like that—because choral music has various dimensions, and at present
> emphasis tends to be put solely on that kind of song. . . . But things will
> work themselves out, because you're actually seeing people writing again
> from scratch in functional harmonic terms, music that is singable and
> appreciable. . . . That's where choral music has gone, with a whole sense
> of: this is who we are; this is how we define ourselves.[36]

Yet veteran Banzi Bangani has found a place for jazz even within gospel. For
many years, he had abandoned his jazz style, feeling it was inappropriate for his
new identity as a born-again gospel preacher:

> I was released by a white American from the General Conference of our
> church. He heard me playing a gospel song, but playing it straight . . .
> and asked me, 'Bra' Banzi, you have been in jazz. I hear it in your sound:
> you are a jazzman. So why can't you do the things you do for the Lord
> in jazz? Me and you are going to play "Saints Go Marching In" and I

want those jazz notes for the Lord!' So I looked at him, and said: 'All right, Pastor, let's go!' Man, I moved! At the end of that song people didn't know whether to say Amen or start jumping and clapping. Now, up to today, I play my horn freely in church—with those jazz notes.[37]

The situation for concert music, too, is changing. The Soweto String Quartet, which kept the flame of classical string playing alive under apartheid, now tours and records regularly: on their most recent album, the quartet used jazzman Bruce Cassidy as arranger to introduce new repertoire. Younger string players are learning their skills in the Buskaid project. The National Arts Festival now has a New Music Indaba in its programming. Convenor Michael Blake has described its mission as 'to showcase new music—by which we mean not only music that is of the current century, or recently composed, but also music which is likely to be new to listeners outside its community of origin in South Africa. So, in our context, choral music is certainly "new" and so is jazz'.[38] One project of the New Music Indaba is an extended series of commissions under the title the Bow Project. Composers are invited to arrange and reimagine for string quartet and soprano, the traditional mouth bow compositions of legendary Xhosa musician the late Mrs. NoFinishi Dywili. Among composers who have contributed are Carlo Mombelli, Paul Hanmer, and Mokale Koapeng, a former director of the Soweto Youth Jazz Group and member of SDASA, as well as director of the University of Pretoria Chorale.

The Bow Project links jazz not only with concert music, but also with roots. It is part of a broader musical reconnection with Africa that extends through touring, collaboration, and composition, and seeks those roots at home and in the rest of the continent. Pop stars Yvonne Chaka-Chaka and Brenda Fassie now have a large following in continental Africa. They tour regularly, and Chaka-Chaka was chosen in 1990 by Pepsi as the face of their Nigerian marketing campaign. Fassie included a duet with Congolese superstar Papa Wemba on her 1997 album *Now Is the Time*. (Though Congolese music has not overwhelmed local styles in South Africa in the way it has in Kenya, Tanzania, and Zambia, it has made an impact—and not just through the lifestyle of many West African immigrants to the country. Top *mbaqanga* producer and sax jive star West Nkosi was the first to pick up on the groove, in the 1994 track 'Sebenza'—a play on the Nguni word for 'work' and the name of the repeated guitar motif of soukous: the sebene.)

Singers like Ringo Madlingozi and Jabu Khanyile have won Kora Awards for music with elements of both South African tradition and jazz—Madlingozi's vocal hero is bandleader Victor Ndlazilwane; Khanyile leads the current incarnation of Bayete—costumed and packaged for the world music market. Hanmer's *Trains to Taung* drew its distinctive flavour partly from broader African spices: the guitar of Louis Mhlanga, brought up in Zimbabwe and a former collaborator of King Sunny Ade, and the drums and percussion of Zimbabwean Jethro

Shasha. McCoy Mrubata, whose early band was called Cape To Cairo, has written
tunes like *Fela*: a direct tribute to and riff on what he calls Afrobeat pioneer Fela
Anikapulo-Kuti's 'rich raw sound and wonderful harmonies.'[39]
   Two of South Africa's top-selling jazz players are guitarist Jimmy Dludlu and
singer Judith Sephuma. Both work within formats that make their music radio-
friendly and accessible to a broad audience. But both have also incorporated
distinctively African elements into their sound. Dludlu today works with a big
band featuring brassy call-and-response and the honeyed voice of singer Jaco
Maria. Its 'Latin' flavour is in fact the sound of Mozambique, one which Dludlu
grew up very close to, in Swaziland. The guitar solos are shaped deftly within
this framework, with more than a nod to George Benson. The overall effect is
infectiously danceable, a tribute to a root characteristic of African music: its
refusal to draw barriers between the pulse of the music and the footfall of the
dance.
   Sephuma can and often does sing the standards of American jazz, but the
album that won her every local music award in 2002–2003 is based around the
simple melodic lines typical of Pedi music: the music she and her co-composer,
guitarist Selaelo Selota, grew up with. Her music is released on yet another new,
small label: Giant Steps, an offshoot of the giant BMG. With the contraction of
the overseas parent company's BMG Jazz imprint, says label boss Dave Thompson, 'we found ourselves with infrastructure for promoting jazz that was a bit
under-used'. He picked the name nostalgically, to commemorate the days 'when
I worked in retail here and we could sell 100 LPs of *A Love Supreme* in a month'.[40]
   South African pop music, of course, also markets itself as African—very successfully in instances such as Chaka-Chaka's impact on Nigeria, and the impact
of *simanje-manje* collections like the multivolume *Indestructible Beat of Soweto*
on the London world music market. When the major record labels woke up to
the end of musical apartheid, it was this potential that interested them most.
Neotraditional music retains a huge internal market among older and rural record buyers, but that market is now shrinking. In a very recent study, *Sound of
Africa: Making Music Zulu in a South African Studio*, Louise Meintjies describes
how musical 'Zulu-ness', already squeezed by the definitions laid on it under
apartheid, is once more redefined to fit the desired international market:

   [They] are fashioning an image in sound and visual representation of an
   African Other . . . emplaced in South Africa. For the domestic market
   they are carving out a regionally and ethnically specific niche, rather than
   directing their products at black urban youth. . . . The world and domestic regional markets overlap in the way they both nativitize contemporary
   mbaqanga musicians; that is, they highlight their ethnicity and downplay
   their urbanity; the attempts to reach 'overseas' and to regain their heyday
   overlap in the need to reproduce aspects of their old sound.[41]

Real continental reconnection was a path travelled first and most famously by Hugh Masekela and Miriam Makeba. They, like other returnees to the country in the 1990s, were overjoyed by democracy, but not by some of the professional conditions they encountered. Makeba was particularly shocked by the low esteem given to musicians: poor backstage facilities and 'when I have played at State occasions elsewhere, the dignitaries are always keen to meet us, and they are brought backstage, or we go to their boxes. Here, when I played in Cape Town, not one person, even from our own government, even acknowledged our presence although we were playing for them'.[42]

Louis Mhlanga, though never an exile, has worked in several African states. He, too, has noted a tendency to undervalue musicians, while making political use of their music: 'It's a shame that some of our governments here in Africa don't see the importance of music. They only think about music when they want to have their rallies or party meetings—and maybe that's where they have a little glimpse of the light: that music shapes the culture of people, of all races. It's quite sad, really. I wish they could see it more'.[43] Like Mhlanga, others who have spent time overseas draw on their experience to detail the many practical steps still needed to develop the music.

Khaya Mahlangu:

Going into the '90s there was generally optimism, hope. But personally I feel that if musicians cannot make a decent living, then we're still very far from the dream. Check: theatres are closing down, much of the music played on the radio is still foreign music.

Carlo Mombelli:

What can we learn from Europe? Let me start with pianos. Clubs [here] don't have acoustic pianos. People don't realise that's the foundation instrument . . . the acoustic vibrations of that string, it's a spiritual thing for the music and it isn't there in getting a little electric piano to try to sound acoustic. . . . Sound engineers don't seem to listen. . . . [Instead] they play around a lot. In Europe, the engineers let the dynamics come from the musicians. Here, they'll tell you, don't bother [trying to make it get louder or softer], I'll do it in the mix. But it's not [their] decision! . . . Most importantly, what we need to learn is that people who are in charge of the arts, of record companies, booking agents, engineers over there all have a deep knowledge of the music. And they're as passionate about it as the musicians themselves.

McCoy Mrubata:

There is a real jazz renaissance happening . . . but studios are too small and too few. . . . [Many engineers can't handle] the kind of one-take, spontaneous jazz we should be laying down.

Zim Ngqawana:

We need facility, technique, conservatory training—that is very necessary if you are going to develop your own language . . . and there are jazz federations [in overseas countries], clubs have pianos. Good audiences, who come to listen . . . the understanding of the role of the artist, with commissions, grants . . . none of this nepotism and corruption—I haven't met one person sent to this country from overseas who was not deserving of their grant. . . . Our Department of Arts and Culture shouldn't have to make us come running to them with proposals. . . . They have radios in their cars and their homes, they have ears, they should research what needs commissioning.

Wessel van Rensburg:

[Some form of support or grants] is needed. If you want art to advance, you need musicians at the frontier of it. I'm not sure I want to be there— but you need somebody to take the bullet! And you need to support them. Because they open up our consciousness for the ones that are be-hind. They just push us a little bit further. And you can only do that if you have support. . . . I don't know if this country can afford it. Although music is very important, you can live without it in a way you can't live without water and bread. But on the other hand, when I see packages for other projects like two-and-a-half million rands for arms or something [that isn't even about development]. . . .[44]

There is still optimism that the problems can be solved. Sean Fourie, while acknowledging limited movement so far, says nevertheless: 'People in govern-ment are just so much more hip to the music than they ever were before, and that's got to be helpful in some way. . . .'[45]

Damon Forbes:

I think one of the richest things in this country, outside of tourism, is our music, because it reflects our culture and it's [unique] . . . guys can come here and sample our music, but they can never do it from the heart. You can't put a marketing value on the massive role as ambassadors that, for example, Ladysmith Black Mambazo, play. Forget the earnings—the marketing value for the country is phenomenal. If government and the industry could work well together, as they do for example, in Canada, we could see benefits for both the musicians and the country—showcasing our bands outside the country, local content legislation, a world-class attitude to the value of our intellectual property, an effective musicians' union, continuing and improved business sponsorship. . . .

Vusi Khumalo:

Why haven't I settled in the States [like other Graceland players]? Whew! I'm torn between. But I just have this thing that we cannot all go and live there. What about South Africa? . . . This place can work, you know? The music is really going somewhere.[46]

This optimism is partly founded on the crumbling of the old racial barriers. Race no longer keeps black players off stages or out of studios or music schools (though lack of financial resources certainly still does). White players, too, are more free to choose their context. Wessel van Rensburg, currently playing piano with Barney Rachabane, Gloria Bosman, and McCoy Mrubata, sees opportunities for real partnership:

In the '80s and early '90s there was still a lot of that sense of demarcation—you were either a Black musician playing African music or a white musician playing Eurocentric music. But now I see it changing. Like when the late Moses Molelekwa played at the Grahamstown Festival with classical pianist Joanna McGregor, or when Louis Mhlanga collaborates with Eric van der Westen. Because in the end it's only music. And there should be dialogue . . . it's not about the music, it's about the relationship. A relationship with the other musician I'm playing with is, to me, more important than demarcating what I am. The moment you start demarcating, you're showing your own insecurity and inability to speak to other people.[47]

And while Sean Fourie has sometimes found that 'people think that because I'm white I'm un-funky—but I'm one of the funkiest guys I know', he also recognises 'those are the hangovers that will live with us in our lifetime. I can't expect the world to change in this short time'.[48] The two biggest jazz festivals in the country are both controlled by black-owned promotion companies: North Sea by esp Afrika and Joy of Jazz by T-Musicman—and black executives are moving into real positions of power in the record and media industries, and, though not quite so quickly, or in such numbers, into the finance and investment companies behind them. It may be, though, that class is now overdetermining race. As Zim Ngqawana says: 'You don't even have to be exposed to another race these days to experience racism . . . it has gone up to the level of class. Today, we're suffering from the black elite—you'll be amazed how you can be oppressed by your own people!'[49]

Jumping the barriers of gender prejudice seems even harder. While female singers have always played a prominent role in jazz, not since the era of vaudeville have they featured as bandleaders. Female instrumentalists have rarely received recognition—indeed, in 1962, young singer Lynette Leeuw of the Randfontein Dolls was given a saxophone simply as a 'marketing gimmick. They desperately needed a hit. They took me and showed me how to play an alto saxophone. They made me practice the instrument for two hours and the following day a studio was booked for recording'.[50] That debut—*Girls Can Blow*—gave Riviera Studios a hit. But Leeuw confounded her exploiters by later enrolling at FUBA, genuinely mastering her instrument and, from the early 1990s until her death in 1997, leading an all-female group: Basadi—Women of Jazz. Basadi has gone through several personnel changes but still works regularly. Other female instrumentalists, such as saxophonist/singer Franka Insinger (regular sideman for Sankomota) and trombonist Siya Makuzeni, are beginning to assert their right to space. Johnny Mekoa's jazz school has tried to encourage women to take up instruments—'Why shouldn't a sister play a horn?' he demands.[51] Yet most women in jazz remain singers, although behind the scenes female promoters and organisers, female sound engineers like Sheer Sound's Sarah McGregor, and female A&R executives are making their mark.

Gloria Bosman says this situation has to change:

It's mostly men in jazz, and they're controlling it; they're in charge. So you feel like you just have to be a voice, come there, look smart, put on a bit of makeup; smile a lot and say [in a little quiet voice] 'Um, please how should I do this song?' And then everybody's happy. . . . [But ] I feel that if you're a woman and feel jazz is your thing, get in and be in charge. Start your own band if you have to; be part of the whole production process that goes on on-stage. Know what's happening. Ask why are they playing this song instead of that one . . . come up with your own repertoire. When somebody plays a line over your voice and you don't like it, tell them so. Jazz is about the people that do it, so the respect must go both ways: males and females.[52]

Still unresolved are many of the problems relating to payments and royalties. Musicians have learned the importance of contracts. 'In my father's day', recalls Duke Ngcukana, 'it was music, music, music. Today, before you even play a note, you must look after business'.[53] Yet while the big companies are beginning to make restitution for the past—in 2003, both the surviving Manhattan Brothers and the late Solomon Linda's estate received payments from Gallo—artists with limited education still struggle to secure solid deals. Music recorded by the SABC under apartheid is sold for soundtracks and commercials, with its composers often unacknowledged. And while national legislation now links South

Africa to the international intellectual property rights system from which apart-heid severed it, individual artists do not necessarily benefit. The ability to play the system depends on an understanding of the law and fluency and confidence in English. In addition, the militant SAMA (South African Musicians Alliance) union of the 1980s, now MUSA (Musicians' Union of South Africa), has had problems surviving the transition to democracy. While its structures continue, many musicians question its representivity and capacity to deliver, with officials elected these days at sparsely attended meetings. In 2003, musicians including Hugh Masekela, Jonas Gwangwa, and Sibongile Khumalo came together to per-form and record a CD for the annual conference of South Africa's trade union federation, COSATU. At the launch of the CD, *Solidarity Together*, COSATU announced an initiative to help the performing artists' unions improve their effectiveness.

Paul Hanmer argues the biggest change is that it is now worth fighting on all these issues, because the possibility of winning exists:

> The first music that I ever spent money on, in terms of making a demo, was awful. But I took the recording by hand and foot to various compa-nies. . . . I'd phone them from a post office, and then foot it into town and took my cassette and, shame, they listened to it. And [nobody] told me: listen, this is awful. . . . Now I try to go in with a positive attitude and, yes, I do have battles with my record company; battles towards a purpose—my purpose and the company's purpose—and they're impor-tant, because there's so much to be alert to in this country. . . . Musicians have been exploited, terribly, but I'd rather help to change that fact [and] rejoice in what you can become.[54]

At the start of the twenty-first century, then, the problems of South Africa's jazz world are coming increasingly to resemble those of its international counter-parts. The music, though, retains much of its distinctiveness. Radio-friendly, smooth music has taken its place on the stage, but the exploration of apparently simple traditional themes—mentioned and demonstrated by many of the *Ubuy-ile* interviewees—is equally prominent, part of a new, sharper focus on roots. When players describe their sound, the country itself, and narratives of personal reconnection are frequent themes. Music is integral to these, not additional. 'It's not music, not playing. It's living. It's how you say hallo', says Winston Man-kunku.[55]

Zim Ngqawana:

> We have to learn from the masters—Abdullah Ibrahim, Gideon Nxu-malo, Winston Mankunku, Jonas Gwangwa. . . . First, music should be informed by history, have experience in it, but second is the spiritual,

metaphysical side the sound we are finding right now—the music of the ocean and the mountain and how we are connected to it.

Carlo Mombelli:

Whether Picasso comes in and paints one stroke, and then Chagall comes in and paints another—they're not in competition with one another. And that's what I realised: that I've got my voice and that's what I have to stick to. [But] it took time to understand how I could sound as a South African. Before I went away, people asked: why don't you play South African stuff? I said: look, I didn't grow up in a township. So I'm not going to make that kind of music just to sell more records. But when I went to Europe, I became more South African. I started going to record shops looking for South African CDs. Everything from Zim Ngqawana to the Mahotella Queens. We used to order South African food from catalogues. We used to make our own biltong (spiced strips of dried meat)! We never felt European—ever. I become more and more in love with this country . . . and now I'm back, I'm writing new material where that love for this country is going to seep in, because it has to be there.

Pops Mohamed:

The reason I play the kora is it's telling me more about what's happening in myself, not in Africa—more about who I am. . . . I'm sitting here in my futuristic digital recording studio, but I don't forget where I'm coming from.

Wessel van Rensburg:

I couldn't stay longer. I tried, because my wife is Dutch. But I actually wanted to come home. I missed a lot of things. I was dreaming about the veldt. . . . I longed for the South African landscape so much. That's where my compositions about rainfall come from. I love storms: the sound of thunderclaps; that deep grey-blue colour of the sky; the smell of the earth after rain. For me, in the end it was more difficult to play when I was away from my roots.

Bheki Mseleku:

Maybe there's something here I can't find elsewhere. . . . If I'm abroad, and I hear people talking Zulu, it draws me—but then comes the question: what are we going to talk about?[56]

The end of apartheid, though, has transformed the relationship with roots. Apartheid defined ethnic identity as restrictive, closing those who embraced it off from other identities and from the possibility of growth through contact. Many of the most positive recent musical developments have grown from the breaking down of the barriers of genre and ethnicity raised by apartheid. In this new context, it is possible to embrace roots proudly, without closing any doors. Zim Ngqawana at the start of this chapter did not question the concept of 'African Renaissance' because he doubted it, but because it had been so ill-defined:

> I'm getting more interested in new ways of giving the music a Xhosa cadence. I'm trying to phrase it the way my father would have sung a hymn. . . . I try to look at music as a circular thing, because as I look around at indigenous structures, most of it is in circles: our houses are in circles, our gatherings are in circles, our games that we play are in circles—there is a lot of power in circles. . . . We don't have to shift around consciously between [John] Coltrane, [Duke] Ellington and the Blue Notes, so I think we expose South Africa [as a place where] jazz is experienced the way African-American people experienced it. And we inject new things into it—instruments like harmonica, an extended, very free vocabulary of singing and sound like we were using as kids. . . . Not just format blues. In [my composition] 'San Song' we had a very simple, minimalist song at the same time a very complex one. One line—the kind of line that has an answer in itself. It resolves itself, working within a time signature that's not explicitly thought, but controlled naturally by your way of breathing. . . . That comes from a tradition. Old women in the rural areas are singing this kind of melody.

Max Mntambo:

> When you're composing, you can be too clever, and pen the listener in to just one meaning. I prefer the African ceremonial idiom, where the songs are circular: just two or four lines full of hints that people have the freedom to interpret for themselves.

Selaelo Selota:

> On [my song] 'Mma Modiegi', the song you'll find me singing is Pedi—North Sotho—which is so simple and catchy. But if you check on the chorus, what I'm using is parallel guitar chords, moving from one to the one above. Which is very much a foundation of Xhosa music. That element came because I was now based in Cape Town. I found a way of marrying them together, as a South African who grew up with that element of South African-ness all around me.

**Selaelo Selota.** *Credit: BMG*

Gloria Bosman:

You try and find some kind of balance, fuse all that together and keep it young at the same time; trying to stay African and trying to keep it like real jazz. . . . [There may be] a bit of R&B in it without you being aware of it; a bit of pop; a bit from Dorothy Masuka or Dolly Rathebe; [things] that simply represent the way you're feeling at the time.

Guitarist Bheki Khoza:

It's hard to explain, but everything in my music is built on a foundation of Zulu guitar. I learned so early that I can't even pinpoint when, or when I started thinking about myself as a musician. It was just natural. When I started playing pop chords, my grandmother would be there, questioning, telling me: 'That thing doesn't answer. Play it this way'.[57]

Moses Molelekwa:

In my music I try to break barriers. I grew up to a whole lot of music. Growing up in a township you're influenced by everything, everybody. By everybody who takes speakers and pumps out the volume on their stoep [front porch]. Those sounds when you're sleeping and you can't avoid it. So nobody who grew up in the township can say they don't understand reggae or jazz or pop—even rock. I think it's also for the human spirit to break those barriers—to say that this is all music and it expresses a certain emotion or spirit or message. So I incorporate everything that has inspired me. Within jazz especially, I find self-expression through improvisation. I can go wherever I want, really, in that space.[58]

That, for most South African jazz players, is the musical future: breaking barriers and building new musical communities on African foundations.

Johnny Fourie:

There's a lot of tuition going on and a lot of talent coming through, and a lot of pride in trying to find our own voice; that's what's happening. . . . Rhythm is always going to be important, but I'm hoping that the harmonic side will become more evident. . . . Big harmony. I love chords; I like movement, modulation, counterpoint. . . . I think it's going that way. . . . We can definitely show the Americans something fresh.

Pat Matshikiza:

[Because of all the other music they hear,] sometimes our music is too . . . harsh, rough and staccato for people's ears—black or white. So what

I'm aiming for now is music that is originally and recognisably from here—but the exposition is different. The development of how the music unfolds. Not that thump-thump-thump anymore—that's boring now!

Selaelo Selota:

The style is going to develop into something new; it's still in the stages where it's developing . . . we're going to develop a kind of jazz which is jazz in terms of melodic interpretation, mixed with South African nuances and simple, popular or public domain melodies or phrases. . . . But it's going to lose some kind of thing which is American-oriented . . . because it's not swinging in the rhythm—it can swing in the melody, but in the rhythm it's becoming groovy, which is the African element we have been alienated from . . . older musicians would say if it's not swinging, then you're not playing jazz. . . . But you can only dance [to swing] in a certain way; with groove you can see different dances and styles coming up that are from South Africa.[59]

Most players assert their music is still proudly and authentically South African, however infused it now is with flavours of Latin, or fusion, or club electronica. Responding to critics who demand *mbaqanga* or marabi from him all the time, McCoy Mrubata says: 'I am playing it. I make the choices of what mood or groove I add. I'm an African and what I do is true to myself and true to our music'.[60] Ernest Motlhe is more cynical: 'I have a problem with this thing that when you go overseas, they say you must "stick to your music". Yet you know, when overseas artists come here, the first thing they want to do is play our music!'[61]

Part of that South Africanness is that the politics are still there. They are no longer the politics of a party, or of protest against an apartheid law. But songs, or instrumentals with richly allusive titles, about social topics, abound. They talk about drugs, about gender or labour rights, about AIDS, about poverty, about the need to preserve tradition or call politicians to order, about globalisation. They come not only from the elder statesmen of the music, the Masekelas and Gwangwas, but from young players like Mrubata and Ngqawana, too. Indeed, Kgositsile argues that music has retained its vision far more effectively than literature in the new South Africa:

There is a lot of music that explores the social reality, with a bit of laughter here, some social criticism there, and celebration with pride elsewhere. Pick up a random selection of jazz mbaqanga or maskanda released in the past 10 years and listen to what I'm trying to say. But where is the major novel or body of poetry that explores the social fabric of the new South Africa. . . . The nation is still waiting.[62]

Pat Matshikiza. *Credit: Cedric Nunn*

That reality, laughter, and pride in the music wants to cease being challenged for its pass, at home or abroad. As young singer, Gloria Bosman puts it: 'We want to see if this language called music can be understood the way it should be understood. . . . We wanna be out there on those big stages—dancing with the kings and the queens!'[63]

# Notes

1. Interview for *Ubuyile*, 2000.
2. The province including Johannesburg and Pretoria.
3. P. Bonner and L. Segal, *Soweto: A History* (Cape Town: Maskew Miller Longman, 1998), 149.
4. *Red Pepper*, 1, no. 1 (London: Red Pepper Collective).
5. Conversation with the author, 1997.
6. All from interviews for *Ubuyile*, 2000 and 2001.
7. K. Kgositsile, 'Culture as a Site of Struggle', *Staffrider*, 10, no. 4, 1992, p. 48.
8. *Mail and Guardian*, 5–11 December 2003.
9. Interview with the author at Grahamstown, July 2002.
10. All from interviews for *Ubuyile*, 2000 and 2001.
11. Interview for *Ubuyile*, 2000.
12. Interview with the author for the *Mail and Guardian*, 13 June 1997.
13. Interview with the author for *Star Tonight*.
14. Ibid.
15. Interview for *Ubuyile*, 2000.
16. Interview with the author for *Mail and Guardian*, 1997.
17. Interview for *Ubuyile*, 2000.
18. Taung is the site where the skeletal remains of the earliest humans were uncovered.
19. Interview for *Ubuyile*, 2000, and with the author for the *Mail and Guardian*, 14 February 1997.
20. John Fordham, *Guardian* (UK), 13 June 2000.
21. Interview for *Ubuyile*, 2000.
22. Ibid.
23. Interview with the author for *Star Tonight*.
24. Interview for *Ubuyile*, 2000.
25. All ibid. except Jonas Gwangwa, interview with the author, *Star Tonight*, 15 September 1999.
26. Press release issued by Thompson n'team on behalf of NSJF, December 2003.
27. Interviews for *Ubuyile*, 2000, and Bheki Mseleku in an interview for *Star Tonight*, 1999.
28. Interview with the author for *Star Tonight*, 5 June 1999.
29. All interviews for *Ubuyile*, 2000, except Moses Molelekwa in an interview with *Guardian*, 14 February 1997.
30. Thandiswa Mazwai, *Zabalaza* (Gallo, 2004).
31. Interview for *Ubuyile*, 2000.

32. Interview for *Ubuyile*, 2001.

33. Interview with the author, June 2003.

34. *Mail and Guardian*, 18–24 July 2003.

35. Interview for *Ubuyile*, 2000.

36. Ibid.

37. Ibid.

38. Interview with the author, 2002.

39. Interview with the author for *Star Tonight*, 5 June 1999.

40. Interview with the author for *Star Tonight*.

41. L. Meintjies, *Sound of Africa: Making Music Zulu in a South African Studio* (Durham and London: 2003), 161–62. Meintjies' analysis of how Zulu music under studio pressures converts authentic characteristics into what are sometimes elements of parody is far too complex to summarize here, but is a pioneering study of what 'ersatz' traditionalism means.

42. Interview with the author for *Saturday Star*.

43. Interview for *Ubuyile*, 2001.

44. All ibid. except McCoy Mrubata, interview with the author for *Saturday Star*, 5 June 1999.

45. Interview for *Ubuyile*, 2001.

46. Interview for *Ubuyile*, 2000.

47. Interview for *Ubuyile*, 2001.

48. Ibid.

49. Ibid.

50. Z. B. Molefe and M. Mzileni, *A Common Hunger to Sing* (Cape Town: Kwela Books, 1997), n.p.

51. Interview for *Ubuyile*, 2000.

52. Ibid.

53. Ibid.

54. Ibid.

55. Interview with the author, June 2003.

56. Interviews for *Ubuyile*, 2000–2001, except Wessel van Rensburg, interview with the author for *Star Tonight*, 18 January 1999, and Bheki Mseleku, interview with the author for *Star Tonight*, 17 September 1999.

57. Interview with the author for *Mail and Guardian*, February 1997.

58. All interviews for *Ubuyile* 2000–2001 except Max Mntambo, interview for the *Star Tonight*, September 2002.

59. Interviews for *Ubuyile*, 2000–2001.

60. Interview with the author for *Star Tonight*.

61. Interview for *Ubuyile*, 2001.

62. K. Kgositsile, 'In search of the democracy text,' *ThisDay*, 6 February 2004.

63. Interview for *Ubuyile*, 2000.

*Appendix*

# Interviewees and Recordings

*These are brief biographical/discographical sketches of the musicians whose oral testimonies were the basis for this book (particularly those undocumented elsewhere), provided in the hope that readers will be inspired to hunt out their music. Such sketches do scant justice to the richness of either their lives or their music—there are a great many detailed biographies waiting to be written.*

**BANZI JORDAN BANGANI, trumpet, bass**
Born in Springs in 1930, Banzi left Payneville Methodist School early to support his widower father and family. He learned guitar, bass, and drums and worked in the Merrymakers vaudeville band. There he learned trumpet (which he also helped his younger cousin, Elijah Nkwanyana, to learn) and formed his own group, Seeba, which performed instrumental backing for the African Inkspots close-harmony singers. He played in the band for the 1949 film *Jim Comes to Jo'burg* and thereafter worked backing a range of vocal groups and in touring shows until the 1960s. After he married, he took on a factory job to support his own family, and for a time he gave up jazz when he became a devout Christian. Now retired, he plays and teaches music with Christian youth groups. Bangani played with a dazzling range of jazz and mbaqanga groups in the 1950s and 1960s, and can be heard (with the Elite Swingsters) on *Marabi to Disco* (Gallo) and (with the ND Hotshots, King Jury's Band, and the Snqamu Jazz Band) on *African Jazz n'Jive* (Gallo).

**SATHIMA BEA BENJAMIN, vocalist, composer**
For an extensive biography and discography, see various essays by Carol Anne Muller and Lars Rassmussen's *Sathima Bea Benjamin: Embracing Jazz* (Copenhagen: Booktrader, 2000).

**GLORIA BOSMAN, vocalist, composer**
Gloria Bosman was raised in Pimville, Soweto. She began her career singing in a church choir. After a role in a production at the Market Theatre in 1993, she

was awarded a scholarship, enabling her to study opera. She has performed live at numerous clubs and festivals throughout the country, sharing the stage with many other star names. Gloria was a South African Music Award finalist in three categories for her debut album *Tranquility* and won the award for Best Newcomer; she has been a SAMA nominee every year since, and has also been a regular finalist at the pan-African Kora Awards. Besides performing at numerous jazz festivals and concerts, she has been able to cross over successfully into the Afrikaans music scene. Her four albums are all released by Sheer Sound: *Tranquility*, *The Many Faces of Gloria Bosman*, *Stop and Think*, and *Nature Dances*.

**JASPER COOK, trombone, composer, arranger**
Born in 1945 in Pietermaritzburg, Natal, Cook started copying Spokes Mashiyane on pennywhistle at eleven and took up trumpet at twelve. He began earning money with a University of Natal–based band called Swing Inc, in which his brother played clarinet. As a result, he was booked by the Shange Brothers for two gigs in the township of Mkhumbane, the second of which was terminated by a riot around the venue. He continued to play with them, but the police took a dim view of what they were 'doing' with a *wit seun* (white boy). By that point (1961), apartheid had effectively killed all local black music. Cook freelanced in Pietermaritzburg through two and a half years at university. He left, worked a year on the railways as a stoker, then left for England 'to find the Blue Notes', but when he did so 'I was too shy ever to admit to Chris McGregor that I was a player'. He returned after four years and went professional at age twenty-nine in 1974 on the hotel scene. He spent eight years in the army, concurrently in George Hayden's Big Band and various dance bands. He joined the African Jazz Pioneers at the end of 1986. After nine years with them, he spent four years in various small groups led by Dennis Mpale, until the trumpeter's death. Since then, he has freelanced live and in recording sessions. Hear him on various albums by the African Jazz Pioneers and on McCoy Mrubata's *Tears of Joy* (Sheer Sound).

**GENERAL DUZE, guitar**
Born in the mid-1920s to a musical family whose earlier generations included choral and vaudeville composer R. T. Caluza, Duze played in several of the best-known groups of the 1950s and 1960s, including Mackay Davashe's Shantytown Septet, Davashe's Jazz Dazzlers, the Johannesburg *King Kong* orchestra, and the Jazz City Nine. He eventually took a day job as a storeman for the Gallo Record company, but he continued to play—primarily as a session musician— well into the 1970s. When live music gigs got scarce, he started a second career as a TV actor. Duze retired after suffering a stroke in the late 1990s and died in early 2003. Duze was guitar sideman of choice for many early bands and artists; he can currently be heard (with Miriam Makeba and the Skylarks) on *African Jazz n'Jive* (Gallo) and (with the Solven Whistlers and the Jazz Dazzlers) on *Marabi to Disco* (Gallo).

**'ECKKIE' ECKHARDT, saxophone, guitar, vocals**
Founded Afrozania in 1979 with bassist Glen Mafoko, drummer Larry Friedman, and pianist Levy Phahle. He joined the SABC and worked as a music producer until his retirement in the late 1990s, but he still plays for fun in a number of groups.

**HENRY FEBRUARY, piano**
February worked mainly in Cape Town, where he was one of the earliest accompanists of (and influential mentor to) singer Sathima Bea Benjamin in the 1950s. He resisted recording on what he considered unfair terms for much of the apartheid era, but in 1999 he came out of retirement to work with Benjamin on *Cape Town Love* (EKAPA CD001, S.A.).

**JOHNNY FOURIE, guitar**
Fourie was born in the early 1940s in Postmasburg in the Eastern Cape. His professional career began in 1958 in a group with Afrikaans accordionist Nico Carstens. He taught at Dorkay House and did session work for Gallo. In 1961, he moved to London for six years, touring with the Ray Ellington Orchestra and working in the house band at Ronnie Scott's Club. He returned to South Africa and worked in the Hennie Bekker Band, among others. He featured in the *Downbeat* Critics' Poll as TDWR. Johnny spent 1971–1973 in the United States, working with many big names, including Lee Morgan. He returned to Johannesburg and worked with groups including the experimental mid-'80s Abstractions with Carlo Mombelli and Duke Makasi. Since the 1990s he has taught and worked with groups running the gamut from mainstream trios to his son Sean's acid jazz groups with UK saxophonist Dave O'Higgins, to Mombelli's latest avant-garde outfit, Prisoners of Strange. A narrow, commercially oriented South African music scene gave him far fewer recording opportunities as a leader than he merits, but his recent work can be heard on (as leader) *Solo Duet and Trio* (Sheer Sound), (as guest) with Wessel van Rensburg (*q.v.*) *So Fine* (Sheer Sound), and (as guest) with Carlo Mombelli and the Prisoners on *Strange When Serious Babies Dance* (Instinct Africaine).

**SEAN FOURIE, piano, keyboards**
Son of John (*q.v.*), Sean started music early and even featured as a teenage vocalist in the mainstream SABC radio hit parade under the soubriquet Sean Fury in the 1980s. He composes and plays in acid jazz and club music groups including Jaci Dazz and the Short Attention Span Band. Longtime collaborator of UK saxophonist Dave O'Higgins. Hear him (with the Short Attention Span Band) on *Jaci Dazz* and *Fingerprints of the Gods* (Sheer Sound), (with Interzone) *The Man from Interzone* (Sheer Sound), and (with Steve Dyer and others) *Mahube* (Sheer Sound).

## HOTEP IDRIS GALETA, piano

Born Cecil Barnard in Cape Town in 1940, Galeta worked in the Cape Town music scene of the 1950s, admiring the playing of Abdullah Ibrahim and Johnny Gertze, before leaving for New York in 1960. He studied and played extensively, most regularly with Jackie McLean, but also with many South African exiles, including Ibrahim, Chris McGregor, Dudu Pukwana, and Hugh Masekela, as well as U.S. players, including John Handy, Bobby Hutcherson, and Dizzy Gillespie. He became professor of African-American music at the University of Hartford, Connecticut, before returning home to South Africa in 1990. Since his return, he has played and taught extensively and now, among other responsibilities, serves as academic supervisor for the music education programme run by the Cape Town North Sea Jazz Festival. Hear him (with Woody Shaw and Bobby Hutcherson) on *Live at the Montreux Jazz Festival* (Sun, 1990), (with Jackie McLean), on *Hotep Heading Home* (SMG, 1990), and on *Solo Piano* (October Records, 2001) and *Malay Tone Poem* (Sheer Sound, 2003).

## LULU GONTSANA, drums

Born in the Eastern Cape in the 1960s, Gontsana worked with the Soul Jazzmen, Spirits Rejoice, and other bands before enrolling for jazz studies at the University of Natal–Durban Centre for Popular Music and Jazz (run by Darius Brubeck) in 1984. There he was a founding member of the Jazzanians band, whose other members included Johnny Mekoa and Zim Ngqawana (*q.v.*). The Jazzanians played at IAJE Conferences in the United States in 1988 and 1992. Gontsana also played at the 1990 New Orleans Jazz and Heritage Festival with bassist Victor Ntoni (*q.v.*) and pianist Brubeck. He has since revisited the United States several times. Since the late 1990s, Gontsana has increasingly concentrated on teaching, although he remains part of the rhythm section of choice for a number of top South African and many visiting overseas stars, including, most recently, Terence Blanchard. Hear him (with Voice) on *Quintet Legacy Volume 1* (Sheer Sound), (with Zim Ngqawana, *q.v.*) on *Zimology* (Sheer Sound), (with Victor Ntoni, *q.v.*) on *Afro-Cool Concept* (Tusk), and (with Darius Brubeck) on *Still on My Mind* (Sheer Sound).

## SIPHO GUMEDE, electric bass

Born in 1950 in Cato Manor, Durban, Gumede was a self-taught guitarist and pennywhistle player. As his skills grew he worked with Durban's African jazz legends including guitarist Cyril Magubane and bandleader Dick Khoza. In 1971 he travelled to Johannesburg, where he worked at Dorkay House with the Phoenix Players and at The Pelican nightclub in Orlando. He was a member of Spirits Rejoice and a founder of Sakhile as well as a session player in high demand. He toured overseas in the late 1980s, and on his return continued to record prolifically, in addition to playing live, producing, and teaching back in his home-town of Durban. Among others, he collaborated regularly with Pops Mohamed (*q.v.*).

After his 1992 award-winning album *Thank You for Listening*, Gumede was a regular music award nominee and winner, most recently with the album *Blues for My Mother*. He recorded for the Sheer Sound label, which has all his recent output in catalogue, including his 2004 work with the now re-formed Sakhile. Gumede died of lung cancer on 26 July 2004, as this book was going to press.

**JONAS GWANGWA, composer, vocalist, trombone**
Born in Orlando East in 1939, Gwangwa was a founding member of the Huddleston Boys Jazz Band at Saint Peter's School in Rosettenville. He later worked with Peter Rezant, Mackay Davashe, Ntemi Piliso (*q.v.*), the vocal group the Boston Brothers, and many others before joining the house band for *King Kong* in 1958. Out of the modern jazz sessions at the Odin Cinema in Orlando, Gwangwa, (with Hugh Masekela, Abdullah Ibrahim, Johnny Gertze, Kippie Moeketsi, and Makhays Ntshoko, formed the Jazz Epistles, which won first prize at the 1960 Cold Castle Festival. Gwangwa went overseas with *King Kong* and, through scholarships, went on to study at the Manhattan School of Music. Following his studies, he went on to produce, compose for film and theatre, and tour the United States with his own groups, including the Union of South Africa with Masekela and Caiphus Semenya (*q.v.*). In 1978, he began putting together the ANC's Amandla Cultural Ensemble in Angola, which he continued to develop and tour with through the 1980s. He had settled in Botswana, working with the MEDU cultural organisation and the Botswana/South Africa band Shakawe until 1985, when apartheid forces raided Botswana, killing thirteen people, including artists and organisers. Gwangwa and his family left for London. He was commissioned with George Fenton to co-compose the Oscar-nominated soundtrack for the Richard Attenborough film *Cry Freedom*. The score also secured many other nominations and awards, and Gwangwa subsequently received many more composing commissions. He returned to South Africa in 1991, re-formed his own band, and now plays regularly at concerts and festivals, as well as continuing to compose. He is currently in discussions on the formation of a national cultural ensemble. Hear him (with the Jazz Dazzlers) on *Marabi to Disco* (Gallo); (with the Jazz Epistles) on *Jazz Epistles Verse One* (Gallo); (with Masekela and Semenya) on *Union of South Africa* (MoJazz); (as composer) on *Cry Freedom Original Soundtrack Recording*; and (as leader) on *Flowers of the Nation, A Temporary Inconvenience*, and *Sounds from Exile* (all Sony).

**PAUL HANMER, composer, piano**
Born in Cape Town in 1961, Hanmer studied classical piano as a child and education at the University of Cape Town before leaving to follow a full-time music career. His work has ranged from cover, recording session, and dance bands to creative original music with partners like drummer Ian Herman and saxophonist McCoy Mrubata (*q.v.*). He worked with Miriam Makeba on her first shows and recording on her return to South Africa in 1991. His 1996 album *Trains to Taung*

was the first major crossover jazz album after liberation. Hanmer's musical collaborations—especially with Mrubata—have sustained and strengthened; now he is also teaching and composing in the contemporary serious music arena, with scores for string quartet and voice in The Bow Project. Hear him: (with Pete Sklair and Ian Herman in Unofficial Language) on *Primal Steps; Move/ Moves* (Sheer Sound); and (as leader) on *Trains to Taung, Windows to Elsewhere, Playola, Naivasha,* and *Water and Lights* (all Sheer Sound).

### IAN HERMAN, drums, percussion

Born in Cape Town, Herman's early apprenticeship was in rock groups; he also worked for a time with the African Jazz Pioneers as well as holding the drum seat in the Genuines. Tananas was formed after he met bassist Gito Baloi and guitarist Steve Newman at Jameson's club in Johannesburg. He also hooked up with Paul Hanmer (*q.v.*) and Pete Sklair in Unofficial Language. Herman has toured extensively and accompanied many musicians visiting South Africa, including Sting. He is now based in New York, but he returns to South Africa annually for a Tananas reunion gig. Hear him (with Tananas) on *Tananas Orchestra Mundo* (GMP 40476, 1994); *Unamanacua* (BMG); *Seed* (BMG); (and with the Genuines) *Goema* and *Nights with the Cape Gypsies* (Mountain Records).

### ABDULLAH IBRAHIM (Dollar Brand), composer, piano

For a full biography, discography, and essays, see Lars Rassmussen, *Abdullah Ibrahim: A Discography*, 2nd ed. (Copenhagen: The Booktrader, 2000).

### ROBBIE JANSEN, flute, alto and soprano saxophone, vocalist, composer

Born in Cape Town in 1952, Jansen started his career in the teenage pop band the Bismarks and later toured London with the group the Rockets. He then joined the jazz-rock outfit Pacific Express, recorded with Abullah Ibrahim, and toured Angola with Oswietie. He was a member of Duke Makasi's Spirits Rejoice from 1977; in the 1980s, he worked with a range of ensembles, including the short-lived avant-garde Estudio with Phillip Schilder and Tony Cedras, his own Heart-throb and Workforce, and Basil Coetzee's Sabenza. Since the early 1980s, Jansen has courageously battled addiction; that has not prevented him from recording and touring, including a very successful exchange visit to Cuba in 2002, recorded in Jonathan de Vries' award-winning documentary *Casa del Musica*. Hear him (with Abdullah Ibrahim) on *Dollar Brand Underground in Africa; Manenberg* (both As-Shams/The Sun); (with Sabenza) on *Sabenza* (Mountain Records); (as leader) on *Vastrap Island; The Cape Doctor* (Mountain Records); (as guest) on Tananas, *Unamanacua* (Gallo*)*; and on Allou April, *Bringing Joy* (Sheer Sound).

**ABIGAIL KHUBEKA, vocalist**
Khubeka was one of the members of the popular 1950s female close-harmony group the Skylarks, which also included Miriam Makeba. She went to London as part of the *King Kong* cast, but returned to South Africa when the run ended. Khubeka matured into an immensely popular concert and cabaret singer who has toured Europe and Africa. She is also an accomplished stage and TV actress.

**SIBONGILE KHUMALO, vocalist, composer**
The daughter of the late Professor Khabi Mngoma, Khumalo is best known as an award-winning opera and recital singer who has toured internationally. Khumalo has appeared on world music stages in collaboration with Oumou Sangare, and she is also a songwriter. She has taken up popular, traditional, and jazz songs—including compositions by the late Moses Molelekoa (*q.v.*)—as part of her mission to develop an authentic, indigenous South African vocal canon. This side of her repertoire can be heard on recordings such as *Ancient Evenings* and *Immortal Secret* (both Sony).

**VUSI KHUMALO, drummer, composer**
Born in Soweto in the 1960s, Khumalo began playing drums at age twelve and by his late teens was an in-demand session player with a penchant for rock as well as jazz. In 1982, he formed the fusion band Theta with his cousin Bakithi Khumalo, guitarist Lawrence Matshiza, pianist Bushy Seatlholo, and vocalist Wings Segale. He also worked with radical singer-songwriter Roger Lucey in the Zub-Zub Marauders. Khumalo featured on the recording of and in the tour for Paul Simon's *Graceland* album and since then has found regular work overseas, while maintaining his home base in South Africa. He has been the drummer for experimental 1990s band Iconoclast with Hylton Schilder, Victor Ntoni (*q.v.*), and Khaya Mahlangu (*q.v.*) as well as on the jazz mainstream. With bassist Fana Zulu, he forms the core of many rhythm sections, as well as their own group, Dondo. Hear him: (with Theta) on *Dark Streets, Bad Nights* (Teal); (with Moses Molelekoa) on *Finding One's Self* (B&W, 1995); (as leader) on *Follow Your Dreams*; and (with Dondo) on *Changing Times* (Sheer Sound, 2003).

**THANDI KLAASEN, vocalist, songwriter**
Born Thandi Mampambane, Klaasen grew up in Sophiatown and sang with some of the great dance bands of the era before forming her own all-girl group, the Quad Sisters, which predated and influenced other female groups like the Skylarks and which scored a huge hit with the 1952 song 'Carolina Wam'. She worked and toured with Alf Herbert's African Jazz and Varieties and was with the second-run London cast of *King Kong*. Klaasen suffered a tragedy in 1977 when a jealous rival hired thugs to scar her face with acid, but, indomitable, she recovered and forged her career afresh. She is still a hugely popular voice on the

club and cabaret circuit and has worked in Canada with her daughter Lorraine, also an accomplished singer. Hear her on her 1997 album *Together As One*.

## MOKALE KOAPENG, vocalist, composer, piano
Composer and singer Koapeng has championed the creation of indigenous repertoire for concert hall, choral recital, and jazz players. He has taught at the Madimba Institute for African music, led the Soweto Youth Jazz Band, and directed the University of Pretoria Chorale, as well as touring overseas and participating in a number of musical exchange projects. One collaboration was between the Sdasa Chorale of his Seventh Day Adventist Church and the UK a cappella group I Fagiolini; the results of this work were released by Gallo as *Simunye* in 1998. Koapeng has also composed an opera and works for string quartet and voice. His work *Utlwang Lefoko* was selected for performance at the 2003 World Music Days in Prague.

## FRANK LEEPA, guitarist, vocalist
Lesotho-born Leepa worked first with the group Black Uhuru, whose name and risky lyrics led to their expulsion from apartheid South Africa, then with their successor, Sankomota. Sankomota was decimated by a car crash in the mid-1990s, but Leepa re-formed the group and continued to tour with them and as a solo artist until his death at age fifty in November 2003, shortly before he was to receive an award for his work as a songwriter. He also taught, mentored, and produced new-generation Lesotho traditional groups like Buzada. Hear him with Sankomota on *Sankomota, The Writing Is on the Wall; Dreams Do Come True,* and *Frankly Speaking.*

## SIPHO 'HOTSTIX' MABUSE, drums, saxophone, flute, vocalist, composer
Born in Soweto in the 1950s, Mabuse began his career as a drummer, dividing his talents between pop music work with the Beaters and Harari and jazz accompaniments for Kippie Moeketsi and Abdullah Ibrahim. Like many others of his generation, his apprenticeship was at the Pelican Club in Orlando. Socially conscious pop music won out for him; he added reeds to his instrumental palette and scored international hits in the 1980s with the compelling, rhythmic disco tracks *Jive Soweto* and *Burnout*. At the same time, he was active in ANC underground structures. His banned *Chant of the Marching* commemorated the youth activism of the last days of apartheid. While continuing to compose and produce, in the late 1990s, Mabuse took over Kippie's Jazz Club, which he continues to run and where he also sometimes plays.

## KHAYA MAHLANGU, saxophones, composer
Born in Soweto in 1954, Mahlangu learned to play bugle with the Boy Scouts, imitated stars such as Elvis Presley, whom he heard on the radio, and later joined his boarding school band at the Ohlange Institute, switching from trumpet to

saxophone after he heard the Crusaders. He formed his first group with school-mates and appeared on an SABC programme, *Future Stars*. He turned professional in 1975, working with pop groups before joining Harari. He also worked at Soweto's Pelican Club and in Dick Khoza's Big Band before studying music at the University of Zululand. Mahlangu met bassist Sipho Gumede after joining Spirits Rejoice, and their search for a more authentic African sound led to the formation of Sakhile. He toured Germany with the Malopoets and eventually recorded his first solo album in 1982. Since then, he has worked extensively as a soloist and with groups, including various re-formations of Sakhile. He is a regular member of Jonas Gwangwa's (*q.v.*) live band and has worked with Iconoclast, Carlo Mombelli (*q.v.*), and the late Moses Molelekoa (*q.v.*), among others. Hear him (as leader) on *To You My Dear* (Gallo), *Streams* (Sony), and *Best of . . .* ; (with Sakhile) on *Sakhile* and *Phambili* (Teal); (as part of a re-formed Sakhile) on *Togetherness* (Sheer Sound, 2004) and (with Moses Molelekoa) on *Live at the Nantes Jazz Festival* (MELT, 2000).

**HUGH MASEKELA, trumpet, flugelhorn, vocalist, composer**
Masekela was born in Witbank in 1939, but he moved to Alexandra Township with his family ten years later. He attended Saint Peter's College in Rosettenville, where, encouraged by Rev. Trevor Huddleston and inspired by the movie *Young Man with a Horn*, he took up the trumpet chair in the Huddleston Boys' Band and later played a horn donated to the Anglican foundation by Louis Armstrong. He played in a number of other bands before joining the innovative and risky Jazz Epistles, featuring Kippie Moeketsi and Dollar Brand, which made South Africa's first modern jazz LP. Selected for the local cast and then London tour of the musical *King Kong*, he chose not to return to South Africa, winning scholarship support to the Guildhall and then the Manhattan School of Music. In New York, he worked with and later married Miriam Makeba and scored success with his own recordings, most notably 'Grazin' in the Grass'. He set up his own record label, Chisa, and worked and toured in the United States (with his own groups and in the Union of South Africa), Europe, and throughout Africa, from which he drew important inspiration. He settled in Botswana in the early 1980s, establishing a local band there, Kalahari. Forced out of Botswana after a murderous South African raid, he worked again in Europe and the United States and continued to record prolifically. He joined Paul Simon for the *Graceland* project and settled in South Africa again after liberation. Continuing to perform, produce, record, and mentor, Masekela has also become a powerful antidrug campaigner, establishing a foundation to assist artists with rehab. His recordings are too numerous to list comprehensively here, but a sample includes (with the Huddleston Boys Band) *African Jazz n'Jive* (Gallo); (with the Jazz Epistles) *Verse One* (Gallo); (with Jonas Gwangwa and Caiphus Semenya) *Union of South Africa* (MoJazz); and (as leader) *Best of . . .* on Triloka, Tomorrow, Uptownship, Sixty, and Time (all Sony). His autobiography, *Still Grazin'*, was published in June 2004.

**MENYATSO MATHOLE, guitarist, composer**
Born in Bloemfontein in the late 1950s, Mathole moved to Johannesburg at age eighteen and began playing with a range of pickup bands, eventually becoming part of the house band Era at the Pelican Club. He joined the Drive in 1976 and later worked with Chosen Few, the All-Rounders, and others. Between 1981 and 1990, he was lead guitarist for Sakhile; between 1990 and 1995, he studied music at Natal and then Cape Town universities. Since then he has led his own groups as well as undertaking session and stage work. Hear him (with Sakhile) on *Sakhile* and *Phambili* (EMI), (with Letta Mbulu) on *Not Yet Uhuru*, and (as leader) on *Trio Live* (Sheer Sound).

**PAT MATSHIKIZA, pianist, composer**
Born in Queenstown in the 1930s into a highly talented musical family, Matshikiza learned piano and later played organ at boarding school and qualified as a teacher before quitting the Eastern Cape and teaching to seek a musical career in Johannesburg in the 1960s. Highly regarded as a pianist, he worked with Mackay Davashe's Jazz Dazzlers, Kippie Moeketsi, and many others, and ran his own group, the Big Five. Family responsibilities forced him to take long-term work as a hotel restaurant pianist in the 1980s. Now retired, he undertakes rare, impressive club gigs and continues to compose. Hear him (with Kippie Moeketsi) on *Tshona!* and *Sikiza Matshikiza* and (with Moeketsi and Dennis Mpale, q.v.) on *Our Boys Are Doing It* (As-Shams/The Sun).

**LETTA MBULU, vocalist, composer**
Yet another graduate of the Skylarks and *King Kong*, Mbulu also toured with African Jazz and Varieties and starred in the first Zulu-language musical, Ben Masinga's *Back in Your Own Backyard*. In 1964, she joined her husband, Caiphus Semenya (q.v.), in New York. She toured with Cannonball Adderley and toured and recorded with Harry Belafonte. She later worked with Semenya on the TV soundtrack for Alex Haley's *Roots,* for which they jointly won an Emmy. She contributed to the movie soundtrack for *The Color Purple* and—among other collaborations with Quincy Jones— contributed to Michael Jackson's song 'Liberian Girl'. She toured Africa with the musical *Buwa!* and returned to South Africa after a twenty-six-year exile in 1992. Since then, she and Semenya have divided their time between the United States and South Africa. Hear her (as leader) on *In the Music, The Village Never Ends; Streams Today, Rivers Tomorrow;* and *Not Yet Uhuru.*

**JOHNNY MEKOA, trumpet, composer**
Born into a horn-playing family in the East Rand in the early 1950s, Mekoa worked with a number of local big bands and groups, including the Woody Woodpeckers. He got his first formal lessons at Dorkay House before joining Victor Ndlazilwane's Jazz Ministers, the first South African band to play the New

Orleans Jazz and Heritage Festival. Mekoa taught at the FUBA Academy and graduated in jazz studies from the University of Natal (where he played with the Jazzanians) before spending a further two years at Emory University in Atlanta. On his return, he set up the Gauteng Music Academy in Daveyton, taking youngsters with no chance to study music at school and turning them into accomplished big-band instrumentalists. The band has played at the IAJE Annual Conference; several of its graduates are now studying music at university, teaching, or leading their own groups. The school is his main project, but he also plays trumpet in the group of Jonas Gwangwa (*q.v.*). Hear him (with the Jazz Ministers) on *Zandile, Nomvula's Jazz Dance*, and *Mdize Bonono;* (with the Jazzanians) on *We Have Waited Too Long;* and (with Jonas Gwangwa) on *Sounds from Exile.*

### LOUIS MHLANGA, guitarist, vocalist, composer

Mhlanga's family has branches in South Africa, Zimbabwe (where he grew up), Botswana (where he attended school), and Mozambique. He began playing guitar in Harare pop groups, influenced by local teacher and pianist Chris Chabvuka, as well as Jimi Hendrix, among others. He went to London to study refrigeration engineering but was rapidly drawn into the African music scene. He then went to Nigeria and spent time with King Sunny Ade's studio stable. Returning to Zimbabwe, he teamed up with drummer Jethro Shasha and bassist James Indi to form Musik ye Afrika. He also worked as a producer for, among others, Chimurenga music king Thomas Mapfumo and was a lecturer at the Harare College of Ethnomusicology. He then moved to South Africa, where he has built up a career as both a soloist and a session guitarist of choice. He has re-formed Musik ye Afrika and also works with many modern jazzmen, such as Paul Hanmer (*q.v.*). In addition, he has toured the Netherlands and developed a playing partnership with Dutch bassist Eric van der Westen; their instrumental duo *Zvinoshamisa* was chosen by Oxfam for a worldwide child poverty campaign. Hear him (as a leader) on *Mukai* and *Shamwari* (Sheer Sound); (with Musik ye Afrika) on *Musik ye Afrika* and *United We Stand* (Sheer Sound); (with Paul Hanmer) on *Trains to Taung* and *Playola;* (with Eric van der Westen) on *Song for Nomsa;* and with Paul van Kemenade on *Zvinoshamisa.*

### SOPHIE MNGCINA (married name Sophie Mngcina-Davids), vocalist, composer

After winning a Union Artists' talent contest, Mngcina-Davids became a member of the *King Kong* cast; she returned from London when the show's run ended and worked as a vocalist in various productions centred on Dorkay House and from 1966 as a translator of lyrics for the SABC. Her big hit was 'Mangwane', recorded in 1964 (and re-recorded—but never released—with Winston Mankunku in 1974). She played the lead in Mackay Davashe's musical *Phiri* (based on Ben Jonson's *Volpone*) in 1971–1972. Later, she spent five years overseas, studying singing at the Central School of Music and Drama and working in the United States. On her return, she took lead roles in a number of musicals and toured overseas again with the play *Poppy Nongena* in the 1990s. For nearly a decade, beginning in the late 1980s, she was director of music studies at the independent FUBA Academy. Mngcina was vocal arranger for the international film *A Dry White Season*. She still teaches but now performs far more rarely. None of her output is currently available on CD, but fellow professionals hail her as 'a musician's singer' and possibly the finest vocalist of her generation.

### ISMAIL 'POPS' MOHAMED, multi-instrumentalist, composer, producer
Born in the now-demolished vibrant East Rand township of Kalamazoo at the end of the 1950s, Mohamed and his family were removed to bleak Reigert Park outside Benoni. He begged his father for a guitar and lessons in his teens, and studied after school at Dorkay House, later forming his own group, the Valiants, playing kwela and pop covers. His next band, Children's Society, achieved his first hit in the townships: 'I'm a Married Man'. He then teamed up with Abdullah Ibrahim's saxophonist, Basil 'Manenberg' Coetzee, and Sakhile's bassist, Sipho Gumede, landing a record contract that resulted in four albums, including *Black Disco* and *Movement in the City*. After this date, session work and recordings with a range of groups were combined with Mohamed's study of indigenous African instruments and a mission to keep alive the historic sounds of the vanished townships. He plays the *kora*, the *mbira*, the didgeridoo, and the *berimbau*, as well as the African mouth bow. Mohamed produced Moses Molelekwa's (*q.v.*) double award-winning album *Finding Oneself*, which won both the Best Contemporary Jazz Album and Best Traditional Jazz Album in the 1996 FNB music awards. Through the 1990s, Mohamed's solo career as a multi-instrumentalist took off, including international touring and duo collaborations with artists like Barney Rachabane (*q.v.*), ex–Blood, Sweat and Tears trumpeter Bruce Cassidy, British performance poet Zena Edwards, the London Sound Collective, and Andreas Vollenweider. Hear him (with Sipho Gumede and Basil Coetzee) on *Night Express* (Al-Shams/The Sun); (with Bruce Cassidy) on *Timeless* (Sheer Sound); (as leader) on *Kalamazoo, Volumes I, II, III and IV; Society Vibe—New Hope;* and *Yesterday, Today and Tomorrow* (Sheer Sound); and (with Zena Edwards) on *Millennium Experience* (MELT, 2000).

### MOSES MOLELEKWA, pianist, composer
Born in Alexandra, Molelekwa's father, Monk, ran jazz *stokvels* and was an ardent and erudite fan. He helped Moses to attend the FUBA Academy, where his unusual and precocious talent was soon noticed and led to gigs with established bands like Umbongo and the Young Lions with drummer Lulu Gontsana (*q.v.*), and Hugh Masekela's (*q.v.*) Lerapo. A show with Umbongo at the 1993 Guinness Johannesburg Jazz Festival drew him to the attention of then B&W record label boss Robert Trunz, leading to a 1995 album debut and work with Andrew Miss-

ingham and others in Barungwa. International touring and festival and concert work with artists as varied as Cameroonian guitarist Bryce Wassy and UK concert pianist Joanna McGregor followed, as well as a second album as leader and participant in many other projects. Molelekwa died tragically by his own hand in 2001 age twenty-six. Hear him (with Barungwa) on *The Messenger* (B&W) and (as leader) on *Finding Oneself, Genes and Spirits,* and *Live at the Nantes Jazz Festival* (MELT, 2000).

**CARLO MOMBELLI, bass, electric bass, composer**
Born in Pretoria in 1960, Mombelli began playing professionally in the group of Johnny Fourie (*q.v.*) and Duke Makasi in 1984, as well as leading his own group, Abstractions. He left South Africa in 1987, subsequently recording and performing with, among others, Egberto Gismonti, Charlie Mariano, Lee Konitz, and Barbara Dennerlein and in the Brazilian group Raiz de Pedra. From 1997, he was also bass lecturer in the jazz faculty of the Richard Strauss Conservatoire, Munich. He returned to South Africa in 1999 and settled in Johannesburg, working with Bruce Cassidy, Johnny Fourie, Tony Cox, Marcus Wyatt, and Andile Yenana, among others. He also continues to compose and to work overseas occasionally, and leads a new edition of his band Prisoners of Strange. He has written works for ballet and film and lectured at the National Youth Jazz Festival at the Grahamstown National Arts Festival. Mombelli's work *Observations from the Hideout* (written for the Stockholm Saxophone Quartet) was selected as one of four South African works for the ISCM World Music Days in Switzerland 2004. Hear him (with Prisoners of Strange, Germany) on *Bats in the Belfry* (Baobab Art, 2002); (with Prisoners of Strange South Africa) on *When Serious Babies Dance* (2003 Instinct Africaine); (with Marcus Wyatt) on *Gathering* (Sheer Sound, 2002); (with Abstractions + Charlie Mariano and Mick Goodrick) on *Dancing in a Museum* (ITM Pacific, 1992); and (with Attila Zoller and Lee Konitz) on *Open Hearts* (Enja, 1998).

**ERNEST MOTLHE bass, electric bass, composer**
Born in Atteridgeville, Motlhe began his musical career accompanying a vocal quintet, the Dominos. He worked with the Heshoo Beshoo Band, Mackay Davashe, Pat Matshikiza's (*q.v.*) Big Five, and many others, as well as with stage plays such as *Phiri,* before going into exile in 1973. In London, he worked with drummer Louis Moholo, Dudu Pukwana, UK saxophonist Mike Osborne, Jim Dvorak's Joy, Centipede with Keith Tippett, the Jazz Warriors with Courtney Pine, and Chris McGregor's Brotherhood of Breath, as well as with Johnny Dyani's band Witchdoctor's Son in Copenhagen, and with Americans Archie Shepp and John Tchicai. He returned from exile in 1991 and has worked as musical arranger for a number of big concerts, taught at the Mmabana Cultural Centre, and directed a music education programme attached to the State Theatre in Pretoria. Hear him (with Brotherhood of Breath) on *Country Cooking.*

## ZIGQIBO DENNIS MPALE, trumpet, flugelhorn, composer

Mpale was born in 1938 in Queenstown in the Eastern Cape. He grew up in Orlando, Johannesburg, carrying instruments for big-band heroes including Mackay Davashe's trumpeter 'Kleintjie' Rubushe. He took portering work at the Indian Fruit Market to buy his first trumpet at seventeen and taught himself to play, briefly taking over Hugh Masekela's chair in the Huddleston Boys' Band when Masekela (*q.v.*) left. His American trumpet hero was Clifford Brown. Mpale worked across the jazz spectrum, with African Jazz and Varieties, Davashe, Chris McGregor, Abdullah Ibrahim, Pat Matshikiza (*q.v.*), Winston Mankunku Ngozi (*q.v.*), Kippie Moeketsi, and many more, and was a member of the African Jazz Pioneers. He was also active in underground military work for the ANC and in 1983 had to leave South Africa ahead of imminent arrest. He settled in Botswana, working with the local band Shakawe, and also toured internationally with the ANC's *Amandla!* and with the Caiphus Semenya/Jonas Gwangwa musical *Buwa!* He stayed for a time in London, playing at the Mandela release concert and working with Dudu Pukwana's Spear. Mpale returned to South Africa and Orlando in 1991 and began working again with small jazz groups, including those of old playing partner pianist Tete Mbambisa and Zim Ngqawana (*q.v.*) and his own, including saxophonist Sydney Mnisi, trumpeter Marcus Wyatt, pianist Wessel van Rensburg (*q.v.*), and Jasper Cook (*q.v.*). Mpale enjoyed hit parade success with the crossover *Paying My Bills* in 1996 but died in August 1998. Hear him (with Kippie Moeketsi) on *Our Boys Are Doing It*; (with Abdullah Ibrahim) on *Soweto (African Herbs)*; and (as leader) on *Paying My Bills* and *Nothing But the Jam* (Gallo).

## McCOY MRUBATA, saxophones, composer, leader

Born in Cape Town in the 1960s and named after McCoy Tyner, Mrubata spent his early career gigging with a range of bands, from the backup group for South African reggae star Lucky Dube to McCoy and Friends, Umbongo (dedicated to the music of Victor Ndlazilwane), and Brotherhood, with whom he won first prize at the Gilbey's Music Contest. He has accompanied stage shows, being musical director for a dramatised biography of Kippie Moeketsi, and toured overseas. He has played at the North Sea Jazz Festival in The Hague and starred in productions about Bob Marley and John Coltrane for Oslo's Nordic Black Theatre. His first album, *Firebird*, was followed by *Tears of Joy, Phosa Ngasemva, Hoelykit?*, and the 2003 award-winning *Face the Music* (all Sheer Sound). He can be heard on the albums of Paul Hanmer (*q.v.*) and many other younger generation South African jazz artists. Mrubata's joyous attack and big, infectious arrangements have made him a very popular performer, acknowledged as an inheritor of the approach of the bandleaders of the 1970s and 1980s.

## DUKE NGCUKANA, trumpet, flugelhorn, choir director, composer

Ngcukana was taught the horn by his bandleader father, 'Mra' Chris Columbus Ngcukana, and in the Salvation Army. Duke studied science and education at

Fort Hare University, but by the 1970s, he was combining a Cape Town teaching career with work in bands such as Pacific Express and the Soul Jazzmen as well as with choral groups. In 1981, he founded the Langa Adult Choir. In 1989, he became director of the community school Musical Action for People's Power, where he established the combination of choral music and traditional African instruments he christened *chorimba*. Now a headmaster within the state education system, Duke still plays jazz in his spare time, working with brothers Ezra and Fitzroy, and with youth jazz groups whom he mentors.

**WINSTON MANKUNKU NGOZI, alto and soprano saxophone, composer**
Born in 1937 in Retreat in the Cape, Ngozi learned piano at home and later was tutored by trumpeter Banzi Bangazi (*q.v.*) and by veteran saxophonist 'Cups n'Saucers' Nkanuka at the start of his professional career in the 1950s. By the 1960s he was working with Duke Makasi and Dennis Mpale (*q.v.*) in the Soul Jazzmen. In 1968, he recorded *Yakhal'Inkomo*, the top-selling jazz album of its— and later—eras. He refused invitations to work overseas (including one from Herbie Hancock), but in the 1980s, he travelled to London to record *Jika* ('Turn') with a group of British and exiled musicians and establish his own publishing label, Nkomo Records. More albums have followed, most recently *Abantwana Be Afrika*. Since liberation, he has starred in a number of self-led and big-band concerts, in clubs, theatres, and at festivals, including some dazzling collaborations with pianist Bheki Mseleku. Hear him (with Lionel Pillay and others) on *Yakhal'Inkomo*, (with Mike Perry, Bheki Mseleku, Lucky Ranku, Johnny Dyani, and others) on *Jika* (Nkomo), and (with Lulu Gontsana, Andile Yenana, and others) on *Abantwana Be Afrika* (Sheer Sound).

**ZIM NGQAWANA, saxophones, flute, bass clarinet, keyboards, harmonica, composer**
Born in 1959 in New Brighton in the Eastern Cape, Ngqawana only began his music career in his twenties, playing flute for reggae cover band the Black Slaves. Moving towards jazz, he worked in a late version of Pacific Express in Cape Town before taking up music studies at Rhodes, then Durban University. He was one of the first batch of graduates from Darius Brubeck's jazz studies course; the graduates' band, the Jazzanians, played at the 1988 Detroit IAJE Conference. This opened up scholarship opportunities: Ngqawana studied under Yusuf Lateef, Max Roach, and Archie Shepp and played in the Amherst Graduate Band. Back in South Africa, he worked regularly with Abdullah Ibrahim as well as in his own formations. He visited Norway, where a collaboration with Norwegian musicians produced his debut album, *San Song*. Ngqawana's vision of a South African avant-garde jazz voice drawing deeply on traditional Xhosa roots has made him one of the top-selling jazz artists in the country. He has scored ballets and films, and in 2003 he spent six months as a guest lecturer at Tennessee

University. Hear him (as leader) on *San Song, Zimology, Ingoma, Zimphonic Suites,* and *Vadzimu* (all Sheer Sound).

**VICTOR MHLELI NTONI, bass, electric bass, composer**
Born in 1947 in Langa, Ntoni played guitar and sang before gravitating towards the upright bass as his instrument of choice in the band Uptown Sextet. In the 1960s, he collaborated on the musical *Meropa,* which toured overseas. He worked with Dave Brubeck on the pianist's first visit to South Africa; this led to a scholarship to Berklee School of Music. Ntoni worked with Abdullah Ibrahim and Kippie Moeketsi on the album *Dollar Brand + 3* and on other Brand albums. He worked as a producer and arranger for the SABC, as a teacher at the Mmabana Cultural Centre, and as musical director of a number of concerts and festivals, including the late 1980s Carling Circle of Jazz. He toured internationally with Darius Brubeck as part of the Afro-Cool Concept, who played the 1990 New Orleans Jazz and Heritage Festival. Ntoni has worked with Iconoclast and is still in demand as a musical director and arranger, most recently contributing in this capacity to the 2003 Dondo album *Changing Times.* Hear him (with Abdullah Ibrahim and Kippie Moeketsi) on *Dollar Brand + 3 with Kippie Moeketsi* (Shams/The Sun); (with Abdullah Ibrahim) on *Peace*; (as leader) on *Heritage* (Sony, 2004); and (with Darius Brubeck, Lulu Gontsana, and others) on *Afro-Cool Concept Live in New Orleans.*

**NTEMI PILISO, alto saxophone, composer**
Born in Alexandra Township in 1925 into a family of seven, Piliso heard the street music of the Amalaita and American jazz on wax 78 rpm records and attempted to copy the music on a pennywhistle. In the early 1940s, a nonplaying bandleader from Cape Town called Casablanca recruited Piliso to play saxophone and clarinet and arranged music lessons for him. That first band fell apart when Casablanca was arrested and jailed, but Piliso continued to play, often with his trumpeter brother Shadrack, in a number of bands, eventually leading his own Alexandra All-Stars. He was successful and popular as a player, leader, and composer until the decline in the popularity of the big bands in the 1970s. In 1982, he was a founding member and later leader of the African Jazz Pioneers, whose success stretched through the struggle era and beyond liberation. In the 1980s, the *Pioneers* played at solidarity events and the CASA Festival in Amsterdam; in the 1990s they entertained the World Economic Forum at Davos, Switzerland. Piliso continued to live in Alexandra, in the house where he was born, until his death in 2001. He taught many young saxophonists, including one of the current young stars, Moses Khumalo. Hear him on any recording by the African Jazz Pioneers and on many tracks of the Gallo early jazz compilations *African Jazz n'Jive* and *Marabi to Disco.*

**BARNEY RACHABANE, alto and soprano saxophone, flute, composer**
Born in Alexandra in the 1940s, Rachabane followed bandleaders like Zacks
Nkosi and Kippie Moeketsi, earning unofficial lessons in return for carrying in-
struments. He then began to study more formally at Dorkay House, where he
was in the band for the musical *Isintu*. He made an impact playing with the Early
Mabuza Quartet at the 1964 Cold Castle Festival; he later worked with Chris
McGregor, with Shakes Mgudlwa in the Soul Giants, and in Tete Mbambisa's
small group, the Jazz Disciples, and the pianist's Big Sound. Rachabane recorded
and toured with Paul Simon on the *Graceland* project and with the Afro-Cool
Concept. He remains one of Simon's saxophonists of choice, spending much of
each year overseas. In 2003, he was leader of South Africa's National Youth Jazz
Band. Hear him (as leader) on *Blow Barney, Blow* (Gallo) and *Barney's Way*
(Gallo); (with Paul Simon) on *Graceland*, *Born at the Right Time*, and *Live in
Central Park*; and (with Afro-Cool Concept) on *Live in New Orleans* and *Still on
My Mind*.

**DOLLY RATHEBE, vocalist**
Orphaned young, Rathebe grew up in 1930s Sophiatown. In 1949, she won the
lead in the film *Jim Comes to Jo'burg*, the country's first black feature film, which
also featured established stars like the Manhattan Brothers. The hit she made in
the film and the following *Magic Garden* opened doors for her as a recording
artist, *Drum* cover girl, and stage star with African Jazz and Varieties. Rathebe
was a superstar, adored for her beauty and vivacity. She was the first vocalist of
the top band the Elite Swingsters and one of the first performers to make an
impact in black TV drama in the late 1970s. Her career suffered, like all others,
from the intensifying repression of the 1980s, but in the late 1990s, she began to
tour nationally and internationally again. Today, she still sings (with the surviving Elite Swingsters), acts (most recently in the 2003 international film *Hijack
Stories*), and has completed a French TV documentary of her life. Hear her on
the 1990s recordings of the Elite Swingsters.

**TONY SCHILDER, piano, keyboard, composer**
Born in Cape Town in 1937, Schilder got his first piano lessons from his mother,
a major influence on the whole Schilder musical dynasty. He completed technical
studies as a diamond setter, but he soon gave up the profession for music, working with a range of bands in cinemas, clubs, and cafés, and for private parties,
including some stints of work on the hotel circuit. He still plays and composes.
Hear him (as leader) on *The Tony Schilder Trio* (Mountain Records), (as soloist)
on *Solo Piano* (October Records), and (with son Hylton Schilder) on *No Turning
Back* (Sony).

**SELAELO SELOTA, guitar, composer, vocalist, producer**
Born in what is now South Africa's Northern Province, Selota left school and
followed his older male relatives into mine work. Although he had always been

interested in music, apartheid schools offered no opportunity to study it. After one contract, however, he decided that music was his destiny. He enrolled at Johannesburg's FUBA Academy, where he studied alongside Moses Molelekoa (q.v.), working as a barman and theatre usher to support his studies. He went on to study at the University of Cape Town, where he worked in groups with other students and with some of the city's professional musicians. On graduation, he was selected from finalists in a national jazz competition to make his first album, which was instantly successful, leading to a second. He has played at the New Orleans and North Sea jazz festivals. Selota now teaches and composes, as well as performs live, and has mastered both a strongly roots-influenced guitar style and another more oriented towards commercial radio play. Hear him (as leader) on *Painted Faces* and *Enchanted Gardens* (both BMG ) and (with traditional percussionist Sello Galane) on *Free Kiba Live at the Market Theatre.*

### CAIPHUS KATSE SEMENYA, saxophone, vocalist, composer

Born in Alexandra Township in the late 1930s, Semenya's musical family encouraged him to sing, but they ensured he got a good schooling at a Benoni high school far away from urban gangsterism. His first vocal group was formed there: the Katzenjammer Kids. The group won national contests and was recruited for the *King Kong* musical; he later toured overseas again with *Sponono*, and at that point, in 1972, decided to stay in the United States, bringing his wife Letta Mbulu (q.v.) to join him. As well as performing with Hugh Masekela (q.v.) and Jonas Gwangwa (q.v.) in the Union of South Africa, among others, he began to build a career as a composer and arranger, was admired by Quincy Jones, and won an Emmy for the co-composed score for *Roots*, on which he worked with Jones and Mbulu. The same team won more awards for *The Color Purple* score. Live performance moved into the background. Semenya established his own record label, Munjale, and continued to work in the United States and Africa until his return home in 1991, although he still spends some of each year responding to demands for his skills in the U.S. Hear him (with Masekela and Gwangwa) on *Union of South Africa* (MoJazz), (as leader) on *Listen to the Wind* (Munjalo Music), (with Letta Mbulu) on *Not Yet Uhuru*, and (with Quincy Jones) on *Back on the Block.*

### PHILLIP NCHIPI TABANE, guitar, vocalist, composer

Born in Mamelodi in 1945 into a family of guitarists, Tabane began playing informally before he left school. By 1959, he had formed his first band, the Lullaby-Landers. In the 1960s, he became more interested in blending Venda and Pedi traditional musics with modern instruments. He formed Malombo, which won first prize at the Cold Castle Festival in 1964. Malombo went through a number of personnel changes as colleagues such as Julian Bahula and Lucky Ranku went into exile; a constant was percussionist nephew Gabriel Mabi Thobejane. In 1977, Malombo was invited to the Newport Jazz Festival; Tabane toured the United States and also played at Montreux and Northsea. Tabane became well known on the world music circuit overseas; at home, his music was largely ignored: as a fusion of traditions, it was unacceptable to apartheid, and Tabane's uncompromising politics scared commercial promoters. His overseas recordings were largely unobtainable. Only after liberation did his phenomenal technique and inventiveness receive recognition. With a new band, he has played seasons at the Market Theatre and at festivals and has been awarded an honorary doctorate from the University of Venda. Hear him (as leader) on *Cold Castle Festival 1964*, *Malombo* (Atlantic), *The Indigenous Afro-Jazz Sounds of Phillip Tabane* (WEA), and *Pele-Pele* (WEA).

### WESSEL VAN RENSBURG, piano, keyboards, composer

Pretoria-born van Rensburg studied law at Stellenbosch in the Cape, but eventually he decided that his true interest was music. By the early 1990s, he was playing at venues like Kippie's and working with Vusi Khumalo (*q.v.*) and others. He spent a year in London and a further period in Amsterdam, studying at the Sweelinck Conservatoire and playing at the avant-garde Bimhuijs. He returned to South Africa to play, teach, and compose, his main source of income being film and television soundtrack music. He has performed live with Dennis Mpale (*q.v.*) and Barney Rachabane (*q.v.*), and in 1999, he released his first album, *Song for E*. Success, however, came with his second, the largely smooth-oriented *So Fine*. As well as leading his own group, van Rensburg now plays regularly with the Sheer All-Stars and produces for and accompanies artists such as singer Gloria Bosman (*q.v.*). He continues to compose in both a popular vein and more abstract exploratory works. Hear him (as soloist) on *Song for E* (Sheer Sound), (as leader) on *So Fine* (Sheer Sound), and (with the Sheer All-Stars) on *Dance with Me* (Sheer Sound).

### NDIKHO XABA, multi-instrumentalist (including piano, assorted percussion), composer

Born in 1934 in Natal, Xaba is the son of a minister. He completed high school, then left for Queenstown, where he worked with Lex Mona's Tympany Slickers. Already a political activist, he left the Eastern Cape for Johannesburg to evade police scrutiny, and worked with a number of Dorkay House and Soweto-based bands. He left for America with Alan Paton's musical *Sponono* in 1962 and did not return until after liberation. In the United States, he worked with the radical loft scene in Chicago and with various African-American activist groups, as well as collaborating with fellow exiles, including Hugh Masekela (*q.v.*) and Jonas Gwangwa (*q.v.*). He also lectured at the ANC refugee school in Dakawa, Tanzania, establishing a musical instrument-making workshop as well as teaching music theory and practice. He returned to South Africa in 1994 and now lives in Durban. He performs rarely, unenthusiastic about the conservatism and commercialism of the music scene, but continues to teach both music and instrument making. Xaba's best-known composition is *Emavungweni*, recorded by Masekela on the album *Uptownship*.

# Glossary

*abaphakathi*: nineteenth-century IsiZulu term for those who were neither rural tradition-alists nor respectable, white-collar Christian converts. 'Middle people': urbanised Africans who lived on their wits, by manual labour or by entrepreneurship.

*amajoini*: IsiXhosa term for migrant workers who had signed up on contract with the big mine recruitment agencies.

**Amalaita**: young men's gangs on the Ninevite (*q.v.*) model in Natal and the Transvaal. In the Transvaal, Amalaita developed characteristic marching-band pipe music and had fe-male members.

**AmaSkotish**: later term for the marching pipe-and-drum bands of youth gangs derived from their uniform of kilts or tartans.

**apartheid**: draconian system of South African laws after 1948, building on earlier en-trenched white privilege to define and separate the population along neo-Darwinist, os-tensibly ethnic lines, deprive citizens of colour of all democratic rights in what was defined as 'white' South Africa, and create a totalitarian state to ensure compliance.

*baas*: 'boss': how South Africans of colour were expected to address white men; the female equivalent was 'madam'.

**Bantu**: used correctly of the largest group of sub-Saharan African languages, and incor-rectly by the apartheid regime to define the race of most South African blacks.

**beerhalls**: official drinking places constructed by the white local authorities for blacks as an element of social control; bleak, men-only, and rigidly controlled, their profits were intended to finance township facilities and policing.

**bioscope**: cinema: the term still survives as a South African colloquialism

**Boer**: lit. 'farmer': used generally of any white Afrikaans-speaker, and in the plural to refer to the apartheid authorities, police, and army ('die Boere').

*Boesman*: 'bushman': incorrect white apartheid term for southern Africa's First People; often also used broadly and even more incorrectly for people of mixed heritage.

**Broederbond**: A freemason-like secret organisation dedicated to advancing Afrikaner cul-ture to which many high-ranking members of the apartheid regime belonged.

**bubblegum music**: 1980s term for the lightweight pop-music descendant of *mbaqanga* (*q.v.*) favoured by the state broadcaster.

**Ciskei**: one of the colonial/apartheid geographical divisions imposed on the Eastern Cape region.

**coloured**: term used for South Africa's communities of mixed heritage. Apartheid attempted to classify the 'coloureds' as an Afrikaans-speaking 'appendage' to whites; their heritage and languages are in reality far more rich and diverse than this suggests.

**Concert and dance**: all-night performance for black audiences running from 8 P.M. to 4 A.M. to circumvent curfews and pass regulations. The first four 'concert' hours were based on vaudeville (*q.v.*); the second segment saw the chairs cleared away for dancing.

**Coon Carnival**: early and persistent name for the New Year parades of music and dance troupes in Cape Town's mixed-heritage community, derived from the tours of American 'coon' and minstrel shows in the second half of the nineteenth century. Cape Carnival is often now preferred.

*dagga*: colloquial term for marijuana.

*djelimuso*: title given to a female praise-singer in Mali and Guinea.

*dop* **system**: ('tot' system): payment system for vineyard workers in the Western Cape where a portion of already meagre cash wages were replaced by free wine.

**Dutch**: in the eighteenth and nineteenth centuries, South Africans of traceable Netherlands (as distinct from English or French Huguenot) ancestry. By the early twentieth century, the term was used loosely of any white Afrikaans-speaker irrespective of descent.

**Ethiopian churches**: various Christian churches of black South African communities that sought to express nationalism through the incorporation of traditional music and ritual elements. Later in close alliance with the (American) African Methodist Episcopal Church.

*famo*: urban music and dance occasions of Sotho-speaking people, particularly before the 1960s; derived from traditional courting dances and women's songs, but often combined in the city with alcohol and sex to fire up 'Russian' (*q.v.*) gangsters for a fight.

*flaaitaal*: 'clever speech': black urban argot combining elements of various African languages, Afrikaans, and English (especially the slang of American gangster movies) with wordplay to mask meaning.

*goema*: (sometimes *ghoema*) 'drum': a hand drum of the Malay community, the syncopated rhythms produced on it, and by extension the style of instrumental music played over the beat.

**homelands**: The reserves (*q.v.*) were converted into nominally independent, tribally based states, and black South Africans were deprived of their South African citizenship. Whatever their family history, their assigned 'tribal' identity gave them only 'homeland' citizenship.

**hostels**: apartheid-era, single-sex, labour barracks in cities or beside mines or industrial areas, designed to house and discipline black migrant workers (*q.v.*), to prevent them from forming normal social ties or settling, and thus to segregate them from urban life.

*impimpi*: stool-pigeon, informer.

**Induna**: traditional Nguni headman; also used for black hostel dormitory supervisors and others placed in positions of small delegated authority by apartheid.

*ingoma*: 'drum': traditional drum-accompanied Nguni male dance with athletic high kicks.

*ingom' ebusuku*: 'night music': eclectic choral/performance style based on elements of Zulu traditional music, rehearsed and performed after hours in migrant workers' hostels.

*is'cathulo*: 'shoe': a style of dancing originated in Durban by schoolchildren slapping their new school shoes. Forerunner of urban workers' 'gumboot dances'.

*isicathamiya*: 'step lightly': Zulu song and dance form, the direct descendant of *ingom'ebusuku* (*q.v.*).

*itimitin (timitin)*: 'tea meeting': originally, teetotal musical evenings or music contests, designed by missionaries to counter traditional music-based ceremonies. Later, in the cities, the term was sometimes used for events where alcohol was served.

*izingoma zomtshado*: traditional Zulu wedding songs/dances.

*jwejwe*: IsiZulu term for homebrewed liquor.

*kaaskop*: 'cheese-head': township slang for a shaven head.

**kaffir**: originally the Arab/Islamic term for a nonbeliever; used by white colonialists as a derogatory term for people of colour.

**location**: term used for black city settlements; in township slang today it has become *loxion*.

*khalifa*: Sufic-inspired religious dance of the 'Malay' (*q.v.*) community.

**Khoikhoi**: group settled over much of the Western Cape when the first colonisers arrived.

*klevah*: *tsotsitaal* (*q.v.*) term for a hip person or smart operator.

*kwaito*: contemporary township house music.

*kwela*: flageolet and tea-chest bass street music of the 1950s, often played by teenage boys and drawing on diverse sources from marabi to boogie-woogie.

*kwela-kwela*: street term for a police van.

**Langa**: historic black township of Cape Town.

*langaarm*: 'long-arm': characteristic Cape popular dance style for couples, employing elements of folk and ballroom dancing, including swooping turns with extended arms.

*makwaya* **music**: performance-oriented choral singing, often with costumes and choreography, associated in the nineteenth century with mission-trained choir composers and conductors.

**Malays**: blanket term used for Islamic residents of Cape Town assumed to be of South Asian or Indonesian descent; derived from *malayu*, an important language among many—but not all—early slaves and political prisoners of the Dutch East India Company.

*malombo*: Venda spiritual music, played or sung over conversations between a family of upright drums; modernised by guitarist Phillip Tabane with whose name the style is indissolubly associated.

*manyano*: religious sisterhoods of Tswana-speaking communities, often supporting marching brass bands.

**marabi**: syncretic black urban music of the 1920s and 1930s, based on cyclical use of the I–IV–V chord structure and originally a simple (organ/percussion) instrumentation. Also used for the social setting of the music, its performance events, and its dance styles.

*maskanda*: IsiZulu term for (especially itinerant) professional neotraditional musicians and their music (especially guitarists and violinists). Sometimes derogatory—*maskanda* musicians were not considered respectable by church-going Christians; more often simply descriptive.

*mbaqanga*: In the 1950s, the most widely used term for commercial African jazz and for music with strong, recognisable jazz influences, such as improvised instrumental solo breaks. By the 1960s and increasingly in later decades, the term was used for neotraditional (*q.v.*) popular music that employed jazz instruments but fewer and fewer (and increasingly limited and retro) references to the jazz idiom. The term means 'maize bread', but as its musical reference changed, so did its resonance: from 'home-cooking' to 'fast food'. Today, the term is used far more loosely, with implications of approval or disapproval largely discernible from context.

*mbila*: (*timbila*): traditional xylophone played by migrant miners from the Chopi kingdom in Portuguese East Africa (Mozambique), where it was a court instrument.

*mbira*: 'thumb-piano': tuned metal keys on a wooden resonator or in a gourd; played two-handed by migrant workers from Zimbabwe (until 1980 Rhodesia).

*mbube*: originally title of hit song recorded in the *ingom'ebusuku* (*q.v.*) style by Solomon Linda and His Original Evening Birds in 1939, and thereafter used loosely for Zulu singing in this style.

**migrant workers**: men forced to take short-term labour contracts with urban industries or mines in order initially to pay colonial taxes and later simply to finance family survival in impoverished rural areas.

*moegoe*: tsotsitaal (*q.v.*) term for a stupid person or country bumpkin.

**moppies**: up-tempo Malay choir songs.

*mqashiyo*: simanje-manje (*q.v.*) style particularly associated with the Mahotella Queens, whose lead singer, Mahlatini, employed a traditional 'goat-voiced' singing style.

*msakazo*: 'broadcast': a derogatory term used by black critics and serious jazz fans and players in the late 1950s for the steadily dumbed-down *mbaqanga* (*q.v.*) the state broadcaster preferred to air.

*mshoza*: female pantsula (*q.v.*).

*mzabalazo*: style of militant choral music developed by workers' choirs in the 1980s.

*nagpass*: 'night pass': document that a black person must carry to be out in the city after curfew.

*nduduma*: ('mine dumps')—term used by Zulu-speakers for their own urban adaptations of traditional music in the shebeens (*q.v.*) of the 1930s.

**neotraditional music**: music where elements derived from tradition dominate, but played on modern instruments and adapted to (often stylised or cliched) modern performance or recording formats.

**Ninevites**: originally self-protection gangs organised by urban Zulu domestic workers; later sophisticated criminal networks set up on this basis.

**Ntsikana**: Xhosa prince and composer of the Great Hymn; one of the earliest converts to Christianity in 1816.

**pantsulas**: township youth style that began to form in the late 1960s and still survives (there are now pantsulas in their late fifties). The fashion included wide trousers and cropped or shaven heads for men; there were associated eccentricities of slang and dance style.

**Peruvians**: derogatory term for impoverished East European Jewish immigrants to South Africa in the early twentieth century; excluded from white high society, many entered the bootlegging trade.

*phalaphala*: traditional large war horn of the Pedi people.

*ramkie*: a long-necked, hollow-bodied, strummed instrument played in the western and northern Cape and by emigrants from that region to elsewhere in South Africa.

**Rediffusion**: cable broadcasting service into some South African townships by the South African state broadcaster.

**removals**: term for the uprooting and relocation of communities of colour in line with the apartheid classification of the greater part of South Africa, urban and rural, as 'white'.

**reserves**: areas of South Africa classified as 'black'; often barren rural areas with no resources. They were reserves of labour, not land, to which black workers were consigned when industry did not need them (*q.v.* homelands).

*rooi gevaar*: 'red peril': cold war–inspired fear of communist takeover of the independent African states neighbouring South Africa, and of communists fomenting revolution among South Africa's black workers (*q.v. swart gevaar*).

**royalties**: percentage payments supposed to be made to musicians or composers each time a copy of their recording is sold, or the recording is broadcast, under intellectual property provisions. The precise mechanism of royalty payments is specified by a contract and can—and did, in South Africa—vary widely from a steady source of income to a token, short-lived payment, to nothing at all.

**Russians**: self-chosen title for urban gangs of Sotho origin after World War II.

**SABC**: South African Broadcasting Corporation, the South African state broadcaster.

*sangoma*: traditional healer and diviner.

*sebono morao*: 'those who have turned their backsides to their homeland': SeSotho term for those who had left rural tradition for the city and did not intend to return.

**shebeen**: Irish slang, 'little shop': term for an unlicensed black drinking spot usually in a private home.

*simanje-manje*: 'now-now!': Zulu neotraditional music that sets a lead male singer against a bouncy female chorus in fast-paced song-and-dance routines.

*skokiaan*: home-brewed alcoholic drink, sometimes relatively weak traditional grain beer; increasingly, as the twentieth century progressed, dangerous, chemically boosted, highly intoxicating brews. Also known as Barberton, pineapple, kill-me-quick, and by numerous other names.

*Slegs vir Blankes*: 'Whites Only': the sign that was apartheid's most pervasive marker; found on everything from hospital wards to park benches to the main entrances of shops.

**slumyards**: term for overcrowded, multiple-sublet, black urban residential areas in the early twentieth century; often associated particularly with Doornfontein in Johannesburg.

**spends**: Cape Town variant of concert and dance (*q.v.*) performances.

*stokvel*: savings club or other form of mutual benefit organisation designed to cushion the economic hardships of township life through a system of rotating obligations and benefits.

*swart gevaar*: 'black peril': moral panic among the white ruling class about black revolution, black sexual predation, or any one of countless other racist neuroses.

**syncretic**: a cultural form that blends and borrows from many sources, not simply to quote, but to create something new and different from all its antecedents.

*Tickey draai*: 'spin on a threepeny piece': fast-paced, whirling Cape folk dance and music style.

**township**: the title given by white local authorities to the spartan residential areas they constructed for black citizens.

*toyi-toyi*: high-stepping syncopated marching style developed by ZAPU freedom fighter in then Rhodesia (Zimbabwe) but taken on to the South African streets by township youth during the rebellion years of the 1980s and now a regular part of political demonstrations and rallies.

**traditional**: musical or cultural forms so long-established within communities that they are accepted as wholly indigenous and free from external influence.

**Transkei:** one of the colonial/apartheid geographical divisions imposed on the Eastern Cape region.

*tsaba-tsaba*: a popular black dance style of the late 1930s and the music—increasingly with strong swing elements—that accompanied it.

*tsotsi*: gangster or thug, but also used more loosely of any city-slicker wise guy. Allegedly derived from the 'zoot suit', with its wide-legged, narrow-ankled trousers popular in the cities in the immediate post–World War II years. Still used today, its meaning has narrowed back to 'thug'.

*tsotsitaal*: 'thug speech': successor of *flaaitaal* (*q.v.*), the slang of the black cities. Its grandchild—the youth street slang of the 2000s—is called *iScamtho*.

*tula n'divile*: Xhosa urban song of the 1920s with a modern feel, used to attract patrons to drink parties and shebeens (*q.v.*).

**two-band stage:** competitive form of the 'dance' segment of concert and dance (*q.v.*), where two bands competed for audience approval in alternate numbers or sets.

*ukupika*: distinctive guitar-picking style developed by John Bhengu in the 1930s which came to be accepted and disseminated as the typical Zulu style by record companies.

*umfundisi*: (*mfundisi*)—term for a priest or peripatetic preacher.

*umngqolokolo*: overtone singing style of the Eastern Cape.

*umrhube*: traditional mouth bow played in the Eastern Cape.

*vastrap*: 'fast-step': Cape folk dance and music style heavily influenced by Dutch rural music.

**vaudeville:** eclectic touring variety shows, including drama, music, dance, recitation, and comedy; it combined elements from English music hall, African-American minstrelsy, high concert culture, and tradition. (*See also* concert and dance.)

# Bibliography

Abrahams, P. *Tell Freedom.* London: Faber & Faber, 1964.

Alfred, M. *Johannesburg Portraits.* Johannesburg: Jacana Books, 2003.

Anonymous ('A Lady'). *Life at the Cape over a Hundred Years Ago.* Cape Town: Struik, 1998.

Andersson, M. *Music in the Mix.* Johannesburg: Ravan Press, 1981.

Ballantine, C. *Marabi Nights: Early South African Jazz and Vaudeville.* Johannesburg: Ravan Press, 1993.

Barber, K., ed. *African Popular Culture.* Oxford: James Currey, Indiana University Press, 1997.

Bonner, P., and L. Segal. *Soweto: A History.* Cape Town: Maskew Miller Longman, 1998.

Carr, I., B. Priestley, and D. Fairweather. *Jazz: The Essential Companion.* London: Paladin, 1988 (largely republished as *The Rough Guide to Jazz*).

Chapman, M., ed. *The Drum Decade: Stories from the 1950s.* Pietermaritzburg: University of Natal, 1995.

Clingman, S., ed. *Regions and Repertoires: Topics in South African Politics and Culture.* South African Studies, Vol. 7. Johannesburg: Ravan Press, 1991.

Constant-Martin, D. *Coon Carnival.* Cape Town: David Phillip, 1999.

Cook, R., and B. Morton. *The Penguin Guide to Jazz on CD, LP and Cassette.* London: Penguin Books, 1994.

Coplan, D. *In Township Tonight!* Johannesburg: Ravan Press, 1985.

———. *In the Time of the Cannibals.* Johannesburg: Witwatersrand University Press, 1994.

Dargie, D. *Nguwe Lo! A Listener's Guide to a Selection of Xhosa Music.* Munich: self-published, 1994.

Garofalo, R., ed. *Rock the Boat: Mass Music and Mass Movements.* Boston: South End Press, 1992.

Huskisson, Y. *A Survey of Music in the Native Schools of the Transvaal.* Master's thesis, University of the Witwatersrand.

———. *The Bantu Composers of South Africa.* Johannesburg: South African Broadcasting Corp., 1969.

Jacobs, R. *The Way the Wind Blew: A History of the Weather Underground.* London: Verso Books, 1997.

Jeffrey, I. *The Sharpetown Swingsters: Their Will to Survive.* DSG Dissertation Series, no. 6. Johannesburg: University of the Witwatersrand, 1985.

Kirby, P. *The Musical Instruments of the Native Races of South Africa*, 2nd ed. Johannesburg: Witwatersrand University Press 1968.

Kichner, B., ed. *The Oxford Companion to Jazz*. New York: Oxford University Press, 2000.

Kgositsile, K. *If I Could Sing: Selected Poems*. Cape Town: Snail Press/Kwela Books, 2002.

Krige, R. and A. Zegeye, ed. *Culture in the New South Africa*, Vol. 2. Cape Town: Kwela Books, 2001.

La Hausse, P. *Brewers, Beerhalls and Boycotts*. Johannesburg: History Workshop/Ravan Press, 1988.

Lindfors, B. *Africans on Stage: Studies in Ethnological Show Business*. Bloomington: Indiana University Press, 1999.

Lukhele, A. K. *Stokvels in South Africa*. Johannesburg: Amagi Books, 1991.

Matshikiza, T. *Chocolates for My Wife*. Cape Town: David Phillip, 1985.

Matthews, F. *Remembrances*. Cape Town: Mayibuye Books, 1995.

Mbeki, G. *The Peasants' Revolt*. London: IDAF, 1984.

Meintjies, L. *The Sound of Africa: Making Music Zulu in a South African Studio*. Durham and London: Duke University Press, 2003.

Molefe, Z. B., and M. Mzileni. *A Common Hunger to Sing*. Cape Town: Kwela Books, 1997.

Moloi, G. *My Life*, Vols. 1 and 2. Johannesburg: Jonathan Ball, 1991.

Mtshali, O. *Sounds of a Cowhide Drum*. New York: Renoster Press, 1971.

Nauricht, J. *Sport, Cultures and Identities in South Africa*. Cape Town: David Phillip, 1997.

Ngcelwane, N. *Sala Kahle District Six*. Cape Town: Kwela Books, 1998.

Nichol, M. A. *Good-Looking Corpse*. London: Minerva, 1995.

Odendaal, A., A. Grundlich, and B. Spies. *Beyond the Tryline: Rugby and South African Society*. Johannesburg: Ravan Press, 1995.

Parsons, N. *A New History of Southern Africa*, 2nd ed. London: Macmillan, 1993.

Van Heynigen, E., ed. *Studies in the History of Cape Town*, Vol. 7. Cape Town: UCT Press, 1994.

Rasmussen, L., ed. *Abdullah Ibrahim: A Discography*, 2nd ed. Copenhagen: The Booktrader, 2000.

———. *Sathima Bea Benjamin: Embracing Jazz*. Copenhagen: The Booktrader, 2000.

———, ed. *Cape Town Jazz, 1959–63: The Photographs of Hardy Stockman*. Copenhagen: The Booktrader, 2001.

Ricci, D. *Reef of Time: Johannesburg in Writing*. Johannesburg: A. D. Donker, 1986.

Sampson, A. *Drum: A Venture into the New Africa*. London: Collins, 1956.

Schadeberg, J., ed. *The Fifties: People of South Africa*. Johannesburg: Bailey's African Photo Archives, 1987.

Schechter, D. *The More You Watch, the Less You Know*. New York: Seven Stories Press, 1999.

Sparg, M., J. Schreiner, and G. Ansell, eds. *Comrade Jack: The Political Lectures and Diary of Jack Simons*. Johannesburg: STE, 2001.

Thema, D. *Kortboy: A Sophiatown Legend*. Cape Town: Kwela Books, 1998.

Tracey, Hugh. *Dances of the Witwatersrand Gold Mines*. Johannesburg: Johannesburg Music Society, 1952.

Tucker, P. *Just the Ticket*. Johannesburg: Jonathan Ball, 1997.

## Periodical Archives and Documents

*Learn and Teach*
*Mail and Guardian*, Johannesburg

*MEDU Newsletter*, Gaborone, Botswana
*Rixaka*
*Staffrider*
*Star*, Johannesburg
*Vrye Weekblad/Two-tone* Johannesburg
Papers of the Culture and Resistance Conference, Gaborone, Botswana

## Web Sites

The Africa Centre: http://www.africacentre.org.ak
African National Congress: http://www.anc.org.za
Chimurenga: http://www.chimurenga.org.za
First and Second World Conferences on Music and Censorship: http://www.freemuse.org/ sw3541.asp (1st) and http://www.freemuse.org/sw4723.asp (2nd)
*Guardian* Online: http://www.guardian.co.uk
Kush: http://www.kush.co.za
Melt 2000: http://www.MELT2000.com
http://www.music.org.za
Ronnie Scott's Club: http://www.ronniescotts.co.uk
Sheer Sound: http://www.sheer.co.za
Third Ear Music: http://www.thirdearmusic.com

# Index

Homelands, 21, 84, 103, 150, 162, 172, 187, 204, 214, 326, 329
Hoover, Jimmy, The, 245
Hopkinson, Tom, 66
Horne, Lena, 54, 68
hostels, 19, 31, 36, 39, 47, 77, 85, 110, 111, 139, 148, 150, 187, 197, 211, 261, 262, 327
Hou, Philemon, 230
Huddleston, Trevor, 96–97, 100, 208, 309, 313, 318
Hughes, Langston, 48
Hughley, Marty, 126
Huskisson, Yvonne, 109, 110, 113, 116, 131, 137, 156, 201, 333
Hylton, Jack, 221, 223

Ibrahim, Abdullah, *see also* Dollar Brand, 4, 16, 29, 45, 70, 113, 118, 123, 133, 153, 154, 169, 185, 189, 193, 207, 235–37, 244, 248, 266, 270, 274, 275, 284, 295, 308–20 passim
Impey, Angela, 111, 203
ingoma, 117, 327
ingom'ebusuku, 31, 327, 328
Insinger, Franka, 294
is'cathulo, 9, 327
isicathamiya, 31, 85, 111, 138, 187, 188, 191, 203, 218, 282, 327
Islam, 12, 12, 213, 235, 327, 328
itimitin, 9, 31, 56, 327
izingoma zomtshado, 17, 327

Jabavu Township, 76, 133
Jackson, Alan, 244
Jackson, Peter, 176
Jacobs, Arthur, 151
Jacobs Nancy, 79
Jamal, Ahmad, 279
James, Harry, 52
Jansen, Robbie, 147, 151–55, 162, 207, 213, 217, 284, 285, 310
Japanese Express, The, 45

Jarre, Maurice, 170
Jarrett, Keith, 256
Jay, Gideon, 59
Jazz,
 definitions of, 2–24, 29–48
 festivals, 2, 127, 278, 306, 322
 programmes, 47, 87, 88, 157, 203, 278
Jazz Epistles, The, 70, 73, 100, 118–20, 124, 137, 309, 313
*Jazz in Africa*, 98, 118, 119, 137, 225
Jazz Maniacs, The, 44–56 passim, 72
Jeremiah, Ma, 29
*Jim Comes to Jo'burg*, 75, 305, 321
Johannesburg All-Stars, The, 72
Jones, Elvin, 235, 287
Jones, Quincy, 314, 322
Jonson, Ben, 145, 315
Jordan, Louis, 71
Jordan, Dr. Z. Pallo, 116, 212

Kapdi, Nazier, 151
ka Seme, Pixley, 58
Kasrils, Ronnie, 116
Kedepile, Bonjo, 249
Kekana, Faith, 168
Kekana, Steve, 198
Kelly, Art, 277
Kente, Gibson, 132, 269
Kenyatta, Jomo, 58
Kerkorrel, Johannes, 205
Kerzner, Sol, 204
Kgopo, Whyte, 249
Kgositsile, Keorapetse, viii, 92, 193, 263, 264, 300, 334
khalifa, 12, 327
Khan, Kader, 213
Khanyile, Dalton, 31, 45, 49, 137
Khanyile, Jabu, 187, 201, 289
Khanyile, Noise, 208
Khaoli, Alec 'Om', 152, 158, 168
Khoza, Bheki, 203, 299, 308
Khubeka, Abigail, 83, 113, 145, 171, 282, 311